Royal Letters, Charters, and Tracts, Relating to the Colonization of New Scotland, and the Institution of the Order of Knight Baronets of Nova Scotia, 1621-1638

ÆTATIS SUÆ LVII ✳ VERA EFFIGIES GULIELMI COMITIS DE STERLIN·

ROYAL LETTERS,

CHARTERS, AND TRACTS,

RELATING TO

THE COLONIZATION OF NEW SCOTLAND,

AND THE INSTITUTION OF

THE ORDER OF KNIGHT BARONETS OF NOVA SCOTIA.

1621—1638.

EDINBURGH: M.DCCC.LXVII.

PRINTED BY GEORGE ROBB (SUCCESSOR TO JOHN HUGHES) THISTLE STREET, EDINBURGH

THIS VOLUME,

CONTAINING TRACTS REPRINTED

AT THE EXPENSE OF

THE BANNATYNE CLUB.

IS COMPLETED

AND PRESENTED TO THE MEMBERS

BY THE EDITOR.

RIGHT HON SIR WILLIAM GIBSON CRAIG, BART, LORD CLERK REGISTER

THE MARQUESS OF DALHOUSIE, K T —(DECEASED)

THE EARL OF DALHOUSIE, K T

GEORGE HOME DRUMMOND, ESQ

HENRY DRUMMOND, ESQ, M P —(DECEASED)

30 RIGHT HON SIR DAVID DUNDAS.

GEORGE DUNDAS, ESQ

WILLIAM PITT DUNDAS, ESQ

THE EARL OF ELLESMERE, K G —(DECEASED)

JOSEPH WALTER KING EYTON, ESQ

LIEUT.-COL. ROBERT FERGUSON

SIR CHARLES DALRYMPLE FERGUSSON, BART —(DECEASED)

THE COUNT DE FLAHAULT

THE EARL OF GOSFORD, K P —(DECEASED)

WILLIAM GOTT, ESQ —(DECEASED)

40 ROBERT GRAHAM, ESQ —(DECEASED)

THE EARL OF HADDINGTON, K T —(DECEASED)

THE DUKE OF HAMILTON AND BRANDON —(DECEASED)

SIR THOMAS BUCHAN HEPBURN, BART

JAMES MAITLAND HOG, ESQ —(DECEASED)

PROFESSOR COSMO INNES

DAVID IRVING, LL.D —(DECEASED)

JAMES IVORY, ESQ —(DECEASED)

DAVID LAING, ESQ —(SECRETARY)

JOHN BAILEY LANGHORN, ESQ

50 THE EARL OF LAUDERDALE.—(DECEASED)

VERY REV PRINCIPAL JOHN LEE, D D —(DECEASED)

THE LORD LINDSAY

JAMES LOCH, ESQ —(DECEASED)

THE MARQUESS OF LOTHIAN

THE LORD LOVAT

JAMES MACKENZIE, ESQ

JOHN WHITEFOORD MACKENZIE, ESQ

KEITH STEWART MACKENZIE, ESQ.

WILLIAM FORBES MACKENZIE, ESQ —(DECEASED)

60 JAMES MAIDMENT, Esq

SIR WILLIAM MAXWELL, Bart

THE VISCOUNT MELVILLE.—(Deceased.)

THE HON WILLIAM LESLIE MELVILLE —(Deceased)

THE EARL OF MINTO, G C.B —(Deceased)

JAMES MONCREIFF, Esq

JAMES PATRICK MUIRHEAD, Esq

HON SIR JOHN A MURRAY, LORD MURRAY —(Deceased)

ROBERT NASMYTH, Esq

HON. CHARLES NEAVES, LORD NEAVES

70 THE EARL OF NORTHESK

ALEXANDER PRINGLE, Esq —(Deceased)

JOHN RICHARDSON, Esq —(Deceased)

THE DUKE OF ROXBURGHE, K.T

REV HEW SCOTT, D D

JAMES ROBERT HOPE SCOTT, Esq

THE EARL OF SELKIRK

PROFESSOR SIR JAMES YOUNG SIMPSON, Bart , M D

ALEXANDER SINCLAIR, Esq

JAMES SKENE, Esq —(Deceased)

80 WILLIAM SMYTHE, Esq

JOHN SPOTTISWOODE, Esq —(Deceased)

EDWARD STANLEY, Esq

PROFESSOR WILLIAM STEVENSON, D D.

THE HON CHARLES FRANCIS STUART —(Deceased)

THE DUKE OF SUTHERLAND, K G —(Deceased)

ARCHIBALD CAMPBELL SWINTON, Esq

ALEXANDER THOMSON, Esq.

SIR WALTER CALVERLY TREVELYAN, Bart

ADAM URQUHART, Esq —(Deceased)

90 ALEXANDER MACONOCHIE WELWOOD, Esq —(Deceased)

THE BANNATYNE CLUB

LIBRARIES

THE BRITISH MUSEUM

THE SOCIETY OF LINCOLN'S INN, LONDON

THE FACULTY OF ADVOCATES, EDINBURGH.

THE SOCIETY OF ANTIQUARIES OF SCOTLAND

THE SOCIETY OF WRITERS TO H M SIGNET, EDINBURGH

THE UNIVERSITY OF CAMBRIDGE

THE UNIVERSITY OF EDINBURGH

THE UNIVERSITY OF GLASGOW

TRINITY COLLEGE, DUBLIN

100 THE SMITHSONIAN INSTITUTION, WASHINGTON, UNITED STATES

THE ABBOTSFORD LIBRARY

THE ROYAL LIBRARY, BERLIN

CONTENTS.

PREFACE.

THE Tracts contained in the present volume relate to the earliest attempts made in Scotland for the establishment of Colonies in North America. It is several years since they were reprinted for the Bannatyne Club. They were not circulated at the time, as it was proposed that the volume should embrace an extensive series of Original Letters and other documents, not only in connexion with this subject, but more especially with the institution of the Order of Knights Baronets of Nova Scotia. This hereditary dignity, it is well known, had its origin in having been engrafted upon the schemes of colonization which were projected in this kingdom by Sir William Alexander in the year 1621.

After collecting from the public Records, and from Sir William Alexander's Register of Letters while Secretary of State for Scotland, and other sources, the chief materials for this portion of the intended volume, its completion was deferred, partly in the expectation that some important documents might be obtained from originals deposited in H.M. State Paper Office. But when in London in 1853, I was informed that the permission which the Home Secretary had previously granted, and which enabled me, as occasion offered, to examine and transcribe papers relating to Scotland during the sixteenth and seventeenth centuries, did not include such as were classed under the Colonial Department. I had therefore to make a special application to the Foreign Office, but after explaining the

A

object in view, as it was deemed inexpedient, from particular circumstances, to allow these papers to be examined or printed, the application was accordingly withdrawn   Since that time, these early Colonial Papers have been transferred to the Public Record Office, and are
now of easy access for historical purposes, through the liberal arrangements sanctioned by the Master of the Rolls, besides the advantage of
having an elaborate Calendar of them in a printed form.[1]

I afterwards obtained for the Club transcripts of such papers from
this great repository as seemed to be particularly suited for the present
volume.   But my hands being full of other work for the Club when it
was drawing to a termination, this particular volume it was thought might
be reserved for the last of the series, to be completed either in a larger
or in a more restricted form, according to the means that should remain
at the disposal of the Committee.   Latterly, it became sufficiently
evident that there would be no surplus funds to carry out the original
design to its full extent.   Had it even been otherwise, the anxious
desire to bring the affairs of the Club to a speedy close would have kept
me from interposing any protracted delay in completing the volume.
I have, however, along with notices of the authors of the Tracts, given a
very copious selection of all the original letters, and Acts of Privy
Council which appeared to be of importance, without enlarging either
on the subject of Nova Scotia Baronets, or attempting to prepare any
detailed account of this unsuccessful episode of Scottish enterprise.

DAVID LAING.

October 1866.

---

[1] Calendar of State Papers, Colonial Series, 1574–1660, preserved in the State Paper
Department of Her Majesty's Public Record Office   Edited by W Noel Sainsbury
Lond 1860, royal 8vo.

I.—CAPTAIN JOHN MASON.

JOHN CABOTO, a Venetian, resident in Bristol, and his three sons, obtained from Henry the Seventh of England letters patent, dated 5th March 1496, for a voyage of discovery, and they reached the island of Newfoundland, 24th June 1497. A second patent, dated 3d February 1498, specially refers to "the Lande and Isles" late found by the said John,[1] he having reached the continent of North America, sailing from the confines of Labrador to the coast of Virginia, twelve months before Columbus, in his third voyage, by landing on the South American continent, had completed his own great discovery. Nearly a century later Sir Humphrey Gilbert, with a comprehensive patent granted by Queen Elizabeth, took possession of Newfoundland; and various settlements were attempted at subsequent times, among others, by Alderman Guy of Bristol in 1610, by Captain Whitbourne in 1615, by William Vaughan, and by Captain Mason, and others John Guy was governor of the English colony there, and remained with his family for two years. Purchase, in his Pilgrimes, inserts the chief part of a patent granted by King James for New-found-land, together with a letter from Guy, to the Council of the New-found-land Plantation, dated at Cuper's Cove, 16th May 1611.[2]

But the person who was most successful in directing the attention of the people of England to this settlement was Captain Richard Whitbourne of Exmouth. He states that he became an adventurer into foreign countries at fifteen years of age, was captain of a vessel of his own in 1588, and rendered good service at the time of the Spanish invasion. Having been employed more than forty years in making voyages to and from the island, he says, as "for the Newfoundland, it is almost so familiarly known to me as my owne contrey." He was

---

[1] See Biddle's Life of SEBASTIAN CABOT (one of the sons), to whom he assigns the honour of this discovery, compared with Bancroft's Hist of the United States, vol i p 9.

[2] Vol. iv p 1876   Lond 1625, folio

the author of "A Discourse and Discovery of Newfoundland," Lond., 1620, 4to., "A Discourse, containing a loving Invitation," &c., Lond., 1622, 4to., and a republication of both, with alterations and additions, in the same year. In a letter addressed to George Duke of Buckingham, in 1626, Whitbourne states that his "Large Discourse" had been presented to King James, and that his Majesty had ordered it to be printed, and distributed in every parish throughout England, to shew the benefits of settling a plantation in Newfoundland.[1]

CAPTAIN JOHN MASON, on the other hand, addressed himself to his friends in Scotland, and his account of Newfoundland may have largely influenced the proposed schemes for founding colonies on the continent, in Nova Scotia. He seems to have been a native of England, but his name first occurs in the years 1610 and 1611, when engaged on the west coast of Scotland, along with Andrew Knox, Bishop of the Isles,[2] in attempting to curb the restless and predatory disposition of the islanders. In this enterprise Captain Mason was employed for fourteen months, and must have possessed means to have incurred considerable expense, amounting to £2,238 sterling, which still remained due in 1629, as we learn from the subjoined Declaration.[3]

[1] Colonial Papers, Sainsbury's Calendar, p 82

[2] Bishop Knox had received, in 1609, a commission for life as Steward and Justice of all the North and West Isles of Scotland A brief account of his proceedings at this time is given in Donald Gregory's History of the Western Highlands and Isles of Scotland, from A D 1493 to A D 1625 Edinb 1836, 8vo

[3] "To THE KINGES MOST EXCELLENT MA^TIE —The humble Declaracion of Capt JOHN MASON Theasurer for your Mat^s Army, concerning his service ffowerteene Monethes in the Redshankes Islandes

"Humbly sheweth That having in the yeares 1610 and 1611 bin ymployed by the especiall order of his late Matie yor ffather of famous memory, gevin at Thetford, for furnishing and setting forth of Two Shipps of Warr and Two Pynnasses to attend his Mat^y service comoyntly with Mr Andrew Knox, then Bishopp of the Isles, for subduing of the then rebellious Redshankes in the Hebrides Ilandes, and for settling the Lawes of the Realme of Scotland there, which accordingly tooke good effect In which ymployment the said Capt John Mason was engaged personally w^t his said Two shippes and Two pynnases and ffowerscore Marriners, besides certaine Gentlemen volunteers, in warlike manner, furnished by the space of ffowerteene monethes, vppon an Aggreement made by the Earle of Dunbarr then Lord Chancellour and Thesaurer of Scotland in his Mat^ie name, to pay the whole freight, victnalls, and wages, and other charges of the Expedicion But the said Earle dying ere the voyage fynished and noe course by him taken for satisfacion, the said Capt John Mason was enforced to discharge the whole debt,

Being of an active enterprising disposition, Mason, who was for some time governor of Newfoundland, undertook a careful survey of the island. In a letter addressed "To the right worshipfull Mr John Scot of Scottisterbatt, in Scotland, Director to His Majesties Court of Chancery there, at his house on the Cawsy of Edenborough," he promises to send him some account of his discoveries The letter is dated "from the plantacion of Cuper's Cove in Terra Nova. ult. Augusti 1617 "[1] After alluding to the various hindrances to his duty, he expresses the hope that "I shall affoord you a Mapp thereof (Newfoundland), with a particular relacion of their severall parts, natures, and qualities." He then continues,—"I am now a setting my foote into that path where I ended last, to discover to the westward of this land, and for two months absence, I have fitted myselfe with a small new galley of 15 tonnes, and to rowe with fourteen oares (having lost our former). We shall visite the naturalls (natives) of the country, with whom I purpose to trade, and thereafter shall give you a tast of the event, hoping that withall *Terra nova* will produce *Dona nova*, to manifest our gratificacion. Untill which tyme, I rest and shall remayne *tuus dum suus*, JOHN MASON."

The "Brief Discourse" which Mason sent to Sir John Scot was

viz Two Thowsand Two hundred thirty and eight pounds An Accompt whereof particularly drawn vpp, he then offered to your Matie ffather with a certificate allso vnder the handes of the Bishopp of the Isles and other Lords Temporall of his good services done, by many yet justifiable Wherevppon was delivered vnto him, his Ma^{tys} letter to the Earle of Dumfermlin then the Lord Chancellor and to the Lordes of the Councell of Scotland for passing of a grant of the King's Assise Herring due from all the fishing Shipps and Boates on those coastes, to the said Capt John Mason, who forthwith receaved commission therefore, and made collection of some part of the same in anno 1611 But vppon the marriage of the Queene of Bohemia the States Ambassador after congratulacion of the said marriage, and presents delivered, made suit to the King for a Remission of the Payments of the said Assise Herring due by their Nation, which was granted to the disannulling of the said Capt John Mason his whole interest therein, who never since receaved one penny towardes recompence, saving onely a promise of certain Lands in Ireland, which tooke noe effect Your Maties most humble and obedient Servant JHON MASON "

There is annexed "An Accompt for the Interest " due on the principal sum of £2,238, for nineteen years, at the rate of 10 per cent, which, with the accummulations, reached, in 1629. to the large sum of £12,489, 7s sterling , which probably he never received —State Paper Office, Scotland, 1625–1638.

[1] Epistolæ Virorum Doct ad Jo. Scot, &c MS (Advocates Library)

published by the latter at Edinburgh in 1620. The original tract, now reprinted, consists of seven leaves, and is so rare, that only three copies are known to be preserved.

It is not necessary to trace Captain Mason's subsequent history. At a later time he is styled " Vice-President of the Council for and Vice-Admiral of New England." He was alive in 1639. Several grants and papers relating to him among the Colonial Papers are described by Mr Sainsbury in his Calendar. One of these is a protest of Joseph Mason on behalf of Ann, widow of Captain John Mason, with respect to her lands in New England, July 4th, 1651.

In 1628 there appeared a quaint bombastic work, entitled " Quodlibets, lately come over from New Britaniola, Old Newfoundland. Epigrams and other small parcels, both morall and divine. . . . All of them composed and done at Harbor-Grace, in Britaniola, anciently called Newfound-Land. By R. H. (Robert Hayman), sometimes Gouernour of the Plantation there." London, 1628, 4to. One portion the author dedicates " To the far admired, admirably fair, vertuous, and witty Beauties of England." His lines addressed to Captain Mason, and to Sir William Alexander, may be quoted.

THE SECOND BOOKE OF R. HAYMAN'S QUODLIBETS, p 31

79 *The foure Elements in Newfound-land   To the Worshipfull Captaine* John Mason, *who did wisely and worthily governe there divers yeeres.*

> The Aire, in Newfound-Land is wholesome, good,
> The Fire, as sweet as any made of wood ,
> The Waters, very rich, both salt and fresh ;
> The Earth more rich, you know it is no lesse
>   Where all are good, *Fire, Water, Earth,* and *Aire,*
>   What man made of these foure would not live there ?

80 *To all those worthy Women, who have any desire to live in Newfound-Land, specially to the modest and discreet Gentlewoman* Mistress Mason, *wife to Captaine* Mason, *who lived there divers yeeres*

> Sweet Creatures, did you truely understand
> The pleasant life you'd live in Newfound-land,
> You would with *teares* desire to be brought thither
> I wish you, when you goe, faire wind, faire weather ·
>   For if you with the passage can dispence,
>   When you are there, I know you'll ne'er come thence.

95 *To the right Honorable Knight*, Sir William Alexander, *Principall and prime Planter in* New Scotland: *To whom the King hath giuen a Royall gift to defray his great charges in that worthy busines* —P 35

> Great *Alexander* wept, and made sad mone,
> Because there was but one World to be wonne.
> It ioyes my heart, when such wise men as you,
> Conquer new Worlds which that *Youth* neuer knew
> The King of Kings assist, blesse you from Heauen;
> For our King hath you wise assistance giuen.
> Wisely our King did aide on you bestow
> Wise are all Kings who all their gifts giue so
> 'Tis well giuen, that is giuen to such a One,
> For seruice done, or seruice to be done
> By all that know you, 'tis well understood,
> You will dispend it for your Conntries good.
> Old *Scotland* you made happy by your birth,
> *New-Scotland* you will make a happy earth

96 *To the same Wise, Learned, Religious Patriot, most excellent Poet.*

> You are a *Poet*, better ther's not any,
> You have one super-vertue 'mongst your many,
> I wish I were your equall in the one,
> And in the other your Companion
> With one I'd giue you your deserued due,
> And with the other, serue and follow you

Hayman addresses verses to other persons connected with New Foundland, such as:—" To the right worthy, learned, and wise Master William Vaughan, chief Vndertaker for the Plantation in Cambrioll, the Southermost part of Newfound-Land, who with penne, purse, and person hath, and will proue the worthines of that enterprise." Also, " To the same industrious Gentleman, who, in his Golden-Fleece, styles himself Orpheus Junior."

Among the persons who had undertaken to plant large circuits in the southern part of " the island, commonly called the Newfoundland," was this William Vaughan of Tarracod, in the county of Carmarthen, Doctor of the Civil Law. Under the assumed name of Orpheus Junior, he published at London, in 1626, a fantastic work, entitled " The Golden Fleece . . . . Transported from Cambrioll Colchos, out of the southernmost part of the island, commonly called the Newfoundland, by

Orpheus Junior, for the general and perpetuall good of Great Britains" London, 1626, 4to. He mentions in terms of high commendation Captain Mason, Sir William Alexander, and other adventurers, and gives an engraved map of the Island, by Captain Mason (of which an accurate facsimile accompanies this reprint of Mason's Tract, 1620). But it forms no part of the design of the present collection to enlarge on the history of Newfoundland, and its great importance to this country for the fisheries and navigation.[1]

II.—THE KING'S PATEN FOR THE PLANTATION OF NEW SCOTLAND, 10th September 1621.

This Patent or Charter is printed at full length, in a subsequent part of this volume, from the Great Seal Register. The abridged extract, contained in the well known and valuable work Purchase's Pilgrimes,[2] is given on account of the information which is added in regard to the proceedings for the Plantation   It is here accompanied with an extract from a rare tract, published at London in 1622 by the President and Council of New England

[1] Copies of the following early tracts are preserved in the British Museum   For this note, I am indebted to the kindness of W   C   Hazlitt, Esq

1 A Letter written by Captaine Edward Winne, to the Right Honourable, Sir *George Caluert*, Knight, his Maiesties Principall Secretary   From *Feryland* in *Neufoundland*, the 26 of August, 1621   Imprinted MDCXXI   Sm 8vo 12 leaves. . . Includes a 2d Letter not mentioned on the title   Another Letter of the 28 of August, from the said Captaine *Winne*, vnto Master Secretary *Caluert*   This occupies the 11th and 12th leaves

2 A Letter from Captaine *Edward Wynne, Gouernour of the Colony at* Ferryland, *within the Province of* Analon, in Newfound land, vnto the Right Honourable Sir George Calvert Knight, his Maiesties Principall Secretary   Iuly, 1621   4to 9 leaves.   ∴ Includes Letters to Calvert from Capt Dan Powell, and Capt Wynne [17 Aug. 1622] and even from N H a Gentleman living at Ferryland to his friend W P 18 Aug 1622   There is no regular title, but the above headline occurs on Sign A   The last leaf is marked C

3 A Short Discourse of the New-Found-Land   containin[g] Diverse Reasons and induce-ments, for the planting of that *Countrey*   Published for the satisfaction of all such as shall be *willing to be Adventurers in the said Plantatioun*   Dublin, Printed by the Societie of Stationers M.D C xxii 4to 14 leaves   . Dedicated by T C. to "The Right Honovrable Henry Lo Cary, Viscount of Falkland," &c.

[2] Vol iv p. 1871.

III.—SIR WILLIAM ALEXANDER OF MENSTRIE.

SIR WILLIAM ALEXANDER of Menstrie, VISCOUNT and afterwards EARL OF STIRLING, is usually said to have been born in 1580.[1] It is more likely that it was two or three years earlier. Some persons would trace his descent from Alexander or Allister, or Mackallister, whose progenitor was Donald, King of the Isles, son of Reginald, King of Man and the Isles.[2] This has a magniloquent sound, and suits the style of peerage writers, but no proof has or can be adduced to confirm it. Alexander Alschinder (as the name Alexander was frequently written during the sixteenth century) was the son of Andrew Alexander of Menstrie, and Catherine Graham. He, with Elizabeth Douglas, his spouse, and Andrew, their son and apparent heir, had two charters from Colin, Earl of Argyle, of part of the barony of Menstrie, in 1529, confirmed under the Great Seal, 20th April 1530.[3] He died in 1545.

Andrew Alexander, mentioned in these charters, predeceased his father. His wife's name is not recorded; but we may infer from what follows that she was the daughter of Alane Coutis.

Alexander Alschinder of the Mains of Menstrie appears as a witness, along with his grandfather, of the same name, in a seisin dated 19th April 1541. Instead of surviving till 1594, as stated in Douglas' Peerage, his death occurred on the 10th of February 1580-1. His last will was confirmed by the Commissaries of Edinburgh on the 24th of May 1581.[4] Five days before his decease he nominated James Alexander, his father's brother, John Alexander of Pitgogar, and Elizabeth Alexander, relict

---

[1] Marshall's portrait, rarely found in the copies of the Earl's "Recreations with the Muses," Lond, 1637 (see frontispiece to the present volume), represents the Earl of Stirling ætatis suæ lvii , but it is not certain that 1637 was the actual date of the engraving

[2] See Buchanan of Auchmar's Highland Clans, &c.

[3] Regist. Magni Sigilli, Lib. xxiii No 196.

[4] Edinburgh Commiss. Confirmed Instruments, vol ix.

B

of umquhile John Leicheman, burgess of Striveling, his executors ; also his gude Lord and maister Coline, Earl of Argyle, and Alane Coutis, his guidschir (maternal grandfather), as oversmen ; at the same time he constituted the said James Alschinder to be " tutor-testamentar to his bairnes, to wait thairupon for putting of his roomes and gudis to prof feit for the sustentation of his bairnes, and uphald of the hous to thame, and putting of thair geir to proffeit quhill thair perfyt aige," &c. ; or, failing his acceptance of this trust, John Alexander of Pitgogar, who seems to have undertaken it.   In the list of debts awand bo the said Alexander Alschinder of Menstrie there was one to my Lord of Aigyle, maister of the ground, in anno 1580, 24 bolls of wheat, at £4 the boll ; 24 bolls of bear, at £3, 6s. 8d. ; and 24 bolls of meal, at £2, 10s 6d. ; and to Margaret Alschindei, his sister, 100 merkis.   The names of the children are unfortunately not given, and no mention being made of his wife, she had most likely predeceased him.

No particulars are recorded of Sir William's early history and education.   He probably studied at St Andrews, without remaining to take his degree of Master of Arts.   Sir John Scot states, " that he travelled through Italy and France with his Lord superior the Earl of Argyle, where he attained to the French and Italian languages "[1]   This must have been Archibald seventh Earl of Argyle, born in 1576 ; and we may suppose that their visit to the Continent was before the close of that century.   His first appearance as an author was in 1603, having published at Edinburgh " The Tragedie of Darius.   By William Alex ander of Menstrie ;" and, addressing the Reader, he says, " I present to thy favourable viewe and censure the first essay of my rude and unskil full Muse in a Tragicall poem "   It was dedicated " To the most excellent, high, and mightie Prince James the 6 King of Scots, my dreade Soveraigne : "

> Whose Sacred brow a twofolde laurell beares,
> To whom Apollo his owne harpe resignes,
> And everlasting Trophies vertue reares.

In the following year Alexander published, at London, " Auroia, con taining the first fancies of the Author's youth," being a collection of Love

[1] Scot's Staggering State of Scots Statesmen

Sonnets, Sextains, &c., dedicated to the Lady Agnes Dowglas, Countesse of Argyle. At the same time his Darius, somewhat polished in its style, was reprinted, with the dedication "To His Sacred Majestie," amplified from three eight-line stanzas to thirteen stanzas. His tragedy of Crœsus was joined to this republication, along with his "Parænesis to the Prince. In 1607, these and his other tragedies, in rhyme, the Alexandræan, and Julius Cæsar, formed one volume, with a general title, "THE MONARCHICKE TRAGEDIES, &c., Newly enlarged.' In a complimentary sonnet to the author, Sir Robert Aytoun, in reference to this title, says,—

> The worthiest Monarch that the sunne can see,
> Doth grace thy labours with his glorious Name,
> And daignes Protector of thy birth to be
>   Thus all Monarchick, patron, subject, stile
>   Make thee the Monarch-tragick of this Isle.

But leaving his tragedies, and other poetical works, it may be noticed, that like many of his countrymen, Alexander had followed James to London, to seek preferment at Court, and was appointed Gentleman of the Prince's Privy Chamber. Before Prince Henry's untimely death, in November 1612,[1] he appears to have obtained the honour of knighthood; and shortly afterwards the King made him Master of Requests for Scotland.

During his residence at Court, Sir William, who could not be ignorant of the English settlements in Virginia or New England, of the French possessions in Acadie or Canada, and of the great importance of Newfoundland for its fisheries, was led to contemplate the advantages of an intermediate settlement on the same coast. In this, he says, "being much encouraged heereunto by Sir Ferdinando Gorge, and some others of the undertakers for New England, I shew them that my countrymen would never adventure in such an enterprise, unless it were as there was a New France, a New Spaine, and a New England, that they might likewise have a New Scotland." Having thus resolved to embark in colonial adventure, with a due regard to his personal dignity and pecu-

---

[1] The date usually given is 1614. But on the title page of "An Elegie on the death of Prince Henrie," Edinburgh, 1612, 4to, his name occurs signed as "Sr. William Alexander of Menstrie, Gentleman of his Privie Chamber," and, at the end, "S W A"

niary interests, he had no difficulty in obtaining from King James a grant of a large and extensive territory on the mainland, to the East of the river St Croix, and South of the St Lawrence, "lying between our colonies of New England and Newfoundland," as a foreign plantation. On this subject the King addressed the following important letter to the Lord Chancellor and the members of the Privy Council of Scotland, which is here given from the original,[1] and is probably now first printed.

JAMES R

RIGHT trusty and welbeloued Cosens and Counsellours and right trusty and welbeloued Counsellours Wee greete you well. Haueing euer beene ready to embrace anie good occasion whereby the honor or proffete of that our Kingdome might be aduanced, and considering that no kynd of conquest can be more easie and innocent than that which doth proceede from Plantationes specially in a countrey commodious for men to liue in yet remayneing altogither desert or at least onely inhabited by Infidells the conuersion of whom to the Christian fayth (intended by this meanes) might tend much to the glory of God; Since sundry other Kingdomes as likewyse this our Kingdome of late, vertuously aduentring in this kynd haue renued their names, imposeing them thus vpon new lands, considering (praysed to God) how populous that our kingdome is at this present and what necessity there is of some good meanes wherby ydle people might be employed preventing worse courses Wee think there are manie that might be spared who maie be fitt for such a forraine Plantation being of mynds as resolute and of bodyes as able to overcome the difficulties that such aduenturers must at first encounter with as anie other Nation whatsoeuer, and such an enterprise is the more fitt for that our kingdome that it doth craue the transportation of nothing from thence, but only men, women, cattle, and victualls, and not of money, and maie giue a good returne of other commodityes affording the meanes of a new trade at this tyme when traffique is so much decayed For the causes abouespecifeit Wee haue the more willingly harkened to a motion made vnto vs by our trusty and welbeloued Counsellour SIR WILLIAM ALEXANDER knight who hath a purpose to procure a forraine Plantation haueing made choice of lands lying betweene our Colonies of New England and Newfoundland both the Gouernours whereof haue encouraged him thereunto, therefore that he and such as will vndertake with him by getting of good security maie be the better enabled hereunto Our pleasure is that after due consideratione if you finde this course as Wee haue conceaued it to be for the

---

[1] Royal Letters, 1607-1621, General Register House

good of that our Kingdome That yow graunt vnto the sayd Sir William his heires and assignes or to anie other that will joyne with him in the whole or in any part thereof a Signatour vnder our Great Seale of the sayd lands lying betweene New England and Newfoundland as he shall designe them particularely vnto yow To be holden of vs from our kingdome of Scotland as a part thereof vnited therewith by anie such tenure and as freely as yow shall finde vs to haue formerly granted in the like case here, or that yow shall think fitt for the good of the sayd plantation with as great priuiledges and fauours for his and their benefite both by sea and land, and with as much power to him and his heires and their deputyes to inhabite, gouerne, and dispose of the sayds lands, as hath at anie tyme bene graunted by vs heretofore to anie of our subjects whatsoeuer for anie forraine plantation or that hath beene graunted by anie Christian prince of anie other kingdome for the like cause in giueing authority power benefite or hono^r within the bounds to be plaunted to them or by warranting them to conferre the like vpon any particular enterpryser there who shall deserue the samen, adding any further conditiones for the furtherance hereof as yow shall think requisite and that the said Signatour be past and exped with all expedition And likewise Our pleasure is that yow giue all the lawfull ayde that can be afforded for furthering of this enterprise which Wee will esteeme as good seruice done to vs for doing whereof these presents shall be your warrant from Our Court at Beauer the 5th of August 1621.

(*Indorsed*)—

To our Right trusty and welbeloued Cosen and Counsellour The
Earle of Dumfermling oure Chancellour of Scotland And to our
right trusty and welbeloued Counsellours The remanent Earles
Lords and others of our Priuy Councell of our sayd Kingdome.

Proceeding on this authority, the royal warrant or signature for a charter was accordingly prepared, and signed by the King, at Our Castle of Windsor, on the 10th September 1621, and the charter under the Great Seal was duly passed and registered on the 29th of that month, as printed in this collection. Sir William Alexander in this charter is alleged, somewhat gratuitously, to have been the first of our subjects who, at his own expense, endeavoured to plant this foreign colony, on the lands which it describes, while the privileges and liberties conferred on him as the King's hereditary lieutenant-general were almost unlimited. In making this grant the fact was overlooked, or kept altogether out of view, that this region had already been included in the French provinces of Acadie or New France, in virtue of previous settlement, by a grant of Henry IV, of France in the year 1603. Sir William seems to have been aware of this, as he uses the words, "designing the bounds for me *in that part, which hath been questioned by the French*;" but he considered that in his patent the boundaries were clearly enough defined, as "marching upon the West towardes the River of Saint Croix, now Tweed (where the Frenchmen did designe their first habitation) with New England, and on all other parts it is compassed by the great Ocean, and the great River of Canada." Notwithstanding this, it was found, from using the same name for different localities, that the actual boundaries were by no means well ascertained; and it so happened that during the whole of this and part of the following century it became a fruitful source of dispute between France and Britain.[1]

On the 8th of November 1621, a similar charter was granted to Sir Robert Gordon of Lochinvar and his second son Robert, with the view of promoting the great object of colonization. This charter is also included in the present volume. Sir William Alexander having received his patent, the Privy Council passed the following Act in his favour, to have a seal as his Majesty's lieutenant, with the King's portrait and arms

Apud Edinburgh xviij Julij 1622

SIR WILLIAM ALEXANDER.[2]

Forsamekle as in the Patent grantit to SIR WILLIAM ALEXANDER Knght anent the new Plantatioun intendit and vndertane be him of landis lyand betuix his Majesteis Coloneis of New England and the newfundland, thair is a Commissioun of Lieutennandrie Justiciarie and Admiralitie insert and for the gritair solempnitie in useing of the saidis Officeis It is appointit and ordanit be the said Patent that he sall haif ane Scale according to the forme vnderwritten Thairfoir the Lordis of Secreit Counsell ordanis and commandis Charlis Dikkiesoun sinkair of his Maiesteis Irnis, to mak grave and sink in dew and comelie forme Ane scale haueand on the ane syde his Majesteis armes within a sheild, the Scottis armes being in the first

---

[1] As detailed in the voluminous Memorials published by the French Government previously to the Peace of Aix-la-Chapelle in 1763, with regard to the boundaries of New France and Nova Scotia

[2] Acta Reg Secr Concilii, fol. 83 b.

place, with a close crowne aboue the armes, with this circomescriptioun *Sigillum Regis Scotiæ Angliæ Franciæ et Hiberniæ*, and on the other syde of the seale his Maiesteis portrait in armour with a crowne on his heade ane sceptour in the ane hand, and ane globe in the other hand, with this circomescriptioun *Pro Nouæ Scotiæ locum tenente* Anent the makeing graveing and sinking of the whilk seale The extract of this Act salbe vnto the said Charls ane sufficient warrande.

As it became necessary that some active measures should be adopted, Sir William states that, after receiving his patent, he procured a vessel at London, in March 1622, and sent it to Kirkcudbright for men, provisions, &c. that it might sail direct from Scotland. But he enlarges on the delays, the increased expense of provisions, and the difficulty experienced in persuading artisans and other suitable persons[1] to set out for far distant and unknown lands. It was late in the season when the vessel came within sight of the shore near Cape Breton, but, beaten back by contrary winds, no landing was effected, and the company resolved to pass the winter in St John's harbour, Newfoundland, while the vessel was sent home "for a new supply of such things as were needful." The next spring another vessel was freighted, and sailed with not much better success. On arriving, in June, at St John's, they found the former company dispersed, or engaged in various occupations; and after sailing along the coast, making a partial survey of the harbours and adjacent lands, the proposed establishment of a colony there was again postponed, and the company returned to England.

With the hope of exciting a greater interest in the proposed scheme, Sir William Alexander published under the title of "AN ENCOURAGEMENT TO COLONIES," London, 1624, the tract now reprinted page for page with the original, of which some copies have the date 1625. It seems not to have had much success, as six years later, the copies were reissued with the more attractive title of "THE MAPP AND DESCRIPTION OF NEW ENGLAND ; together with A Discourse of Plantation, and Collonies," &c. London, 1630. The two books, excepting the title pages, are precisely

---

[1] Lord Bacon has some useful suggestions on this subject, in his Essay on Plantations, and it would have been well had Sir William completed his arrangements before the vessel had been sent to Kirkcudbright

the same, but the author's dedication "To the most Excellent Prince (Charles)," was cancelled in the later copies, and no other substituted. The engraved map occurs in both, and was also used by Purchase, in the Fourth Part of his Pilgrimes, 1625, where he has a short chapter on the subject. A fac-simile of this Map is given in the present volume. The author concludes his Encouragement to Colonies by acknowledging that no one man could accomplish such an undertaking by his own private fortunes, but if it shall please the King to give his help accustomed, "making it appear to be a work of his own, I must trust to be supplied by some publike helpes, such as hath beene had in other parts," for the advancing of so worthy a work, "which may prove for the credit or benefit of my Nation, to whom I wish all happinesse."

In this expectation Sir William Alexander was not disappointed The scheme which had proved successful in the year 1609 for colonizing certain districts in the province of Ulster, by creating the Order of Knights Baronets in the kingdom of Ireland, and dividing the lands and annexing the title to those who undertook to pay a fixed sum, and furnish a certain number of settlers, suggested the adoption of a similar plan for Scotland, under the title of Knights Baronets of Nova Scotia. Sir William had sufficient influence with the King to persuade him heartily to approve of the scheme, and to write, "We ar so hopefull of that enterprise that we purpose to make it a work of our owne." This project is so well set forth in King James's letter to the Privy Council of Scotland, and in their reply, 18th October and 23d November 1624, that these may here be printed in full, along with the Council's Proclamation on the last of November. It announced the King's resolution on the 1st of April following to proceed to the creating and ranking the one hundred proposed Baronets, and the Knights and Esquires who intended to become undertakers and receive this honour were directed previously to that day to appear and have their names enrolled in the Books of Privy Council. There is also added the letter of Prince Charles, on the 17th, and another of the King's, the 23d of March 1625. But four days before the 1st of April had arrived, and only four days after the King had signed that letter, his reign had come to its termination.

FROM HIS MAJESTIE ANENT BARONETTIS.[1]

[James R.]

Right trustie and welbeloued Counsellour Richt trustie and welbeloued Cosens and Counsello[rs] and trustie and weilbeloued Counsellours We greate you weill The Letter ye sent giving us thankes for renueing of the name of that our ancient Kingdome within America intreateing our favour for the furthering of a Planta-tioun ther, was verie acceptable vnto vs and reposeing vpoun the experience of vthers of oure subiects in the like kinde We ar so hopefull of that enterprise that We purpose to make it a worke of oure Owne And as We wer pleased to erect the honour of Knicht Barronetts within this oure Kingdome for advancement of the Plantatioun of Ireland, So We doe desire to conferr the like honour within that our Kingdome vpoun suche as wer worthie of that degree and will agree for some proportioun of ground within New Scotland furnisheing furth such a num-ber of persones as salbe condiscended vpoun to inhabite there Thus sall both these of the cheife sorte (avoydeing the vsuall contentions at publick meetings) being by this Heredetarie honour preferred to others of meaner qualitie know ther owne places at home and likwyse sall haue ther due abroad from the subiects of our other countreyis accordeing to the course apointed for that our ancient Kingdome And the mentioning of so noble a cause within ther Pattents sall both serue the more by suche a singular merite to honour them and by so goode a ground to iustifie our iudgement with the posteritie But thouch the conferring of honour be meerely Regall and to be done by Vs as We please yet We would proceed in no matter of suche moment without youre advyse Our pleasure is haueing considered of this purpose if ye find it as We conceive it to be both fitt for the credit of that Our Kingdome and for the furtherance of that intended Plantatioun that ye certifie vs your opinione concerning the forme and conveniencis thairof, togither withe your further advyce what may best advaunce this so worthie worke which We doe verie muche affect but will vse no meanes to induce onie man thereunto further then the goodnes of the busines and his awne generous dispositione shall perswade Neither doe We desire that onie man salbe sent for or travelled with by you for being Barronet, but after it is founde fitt will leave it to their owne voluntarie choise, not doubteing (howsoever some for want of knowledge may be averse) but that ther wilbe a greater nomber than we inttend to make of the best sorte to imbrace so noble a purpose whereby bothe they in particular and the whole Natione generally may have honour and profite And We wishe you rather to thinke how

---

[1] Regist. Secr. Concilii.—(Royal Letters, Sept. 19, 1623, May 17, 1632.)

C

remedies may be provyded against any inconveniences that may happin to occure then by conjecturing difficulties to looso so faire and vnrecoucrable occasioun whiche other Nations at this instant are so earnest to vndertake. And for the better directinge of your iudgement We haue appointed ane printed copie of that Order quhiche was taken concerning the Barronettis of this our Kingdome to be sent vnto you as it was publshed by authoritie from Vs.[1] So desireing you to haste back your ansueire that We may signifie our further pleasure for this purpose We bid you Fairweill. From Our Courte at Roystoun the 18 day of October 1624.

TO HIS MAJESTIE ANENT THE BARONETTIS.

Most Sacred Souerane,

We haue considerit of your Maiesties letter concerning the Barronettis and doe therby persaue your Maiesties great affectioun towards this your ancient Kingdome and your Maiesties most iudicious consideratioun in makeing choise of so excellent meanes both noble and fitt for the goode of the same, wherein seing your Maiestie micht haue proceidit without our advyce, and vnacquenting vs with your Maiesties royall resolutioun therein, wo ar so muche the more boundin to rander vnto your Maiestie our most humble thankes for your gracious respect vnto vs not onlie in this but in all vther thinges importeing this estate outher in credito or profit And we humblie wisse that this honour of Barronet sould be conferrit vpoun none but vpon Knichtis and Gentlemen of chiefe respect for their birth, place or fortounes, and we haue taken a course by Proclamatioun to mak this your Maiesties gracious intentione to be publicklie knowen that non heirafter prætending ignorance tako occasion inwardlio to compleyne as being neglected bot may accuse thameselffis for neglecting of so fair ane opportunitie And whereas we ar given to vnderstand that the country of New Scotland being dividit in twa Provinces and eache province in severall Dioceises or Bishoprikis, and eache diocese in thrie Counteyis, and eache countey into ten Baronyis, everie baronie being thrie myle long vpon tho coast and ten myle vp into the countrie, dividit into sex parocheis and eache paroche contening sax thousand aikars of land and that everie Baronett is to be ane Barone of some one or other of the saids Barroneis and is to haif therein ten thowsand aikars of propertie besydis his sax thowsand aikars belongeing to his bur[t] (burgh) of baronie To be holdin free blanshe and in a free baronie of your Maiestie as the barroneis of this Kingdome ffor the onlie setting furth of sex men towardis your Maiesties Royall Colonie armed, apparelld, and

---

[1] This might either be " His Majesties Commission as touching tho creation of Baronets " London, 1611, 4to, or " Three Patents concerning the Honourable Degree and Dignitie of Baronets " London, 1617, 4to

victuald for two yeares And everie Baronet paying SIR WILLIAM ALEXANDER Knicht ane thousand merkis Scottis money only towards his past charges and endevouris Thairfore our humble desire vnto your Maiestie is that care be taken by suirtie actit in the bookis of Secreit Counsall, as was in the Plantatioun of Vlster that the said nomber of men may be dewhe transported thither with all provisions necessar and that no Baronet be maid but onlie for that cause And by some such one particular course onlie as your Maiestie sall appointe And that Articles of Plantatioun may be set furth for encourageing and induceing all others who hes habilitie and resolutioun to transport themsclffis hence for so noble a purpose.

Last we consave that if some of the Englishe who ar best acquainted with such forrayn enterpreises wald joyne with the saids Baronetts heir (as it is liklio the lyker conditioun and proportioun of ground wald induce thame to doe) That it wald be ane grite encouragement to the furtherance of that Royall worke quhilk is worth[ie] of your Maiesties care And we doubte not sindrie will contribute their help heirunto. So exspecting your Maiesties forder directioun and humblie submitting our opinione to your Maiesties incomparable iudgement We humblie tak our leave prayeing the Almichtie God to blisse your Maiestie with long and happie Reigne From Edinbrugh the 23 of November 1624.

(Sic subscribitur)

GEO. HAY.	LAUDERDAILL
MAR.	L ARESKINE.
ST ANDROIS.	CARNEOIE.
MORTOUN.	B. DUMBLANE.
LINLITHGOW.	A. NEPER.
MELROS.	S. [W.] OLIPHANT.

PROCLAMATIOUN ANENT BARONETIS.[1]

Apud Edinburgh ultimo die mensis Novembris 1624.

1624.
November 30

At Edinburgh the last day of November The yeir of God 1600 Tuentie four yearis Our Soverane Lord being formarlie gratiouslie pleased to erect the heritable honnour and title of ane Baronet as ane degree, state and place nixt and immediatlie following the younger sones of Vicounts and Lordis Baronis of Parliament as ane new honnour whairwith to rewaird new meritis Haveing conferrit the same honnour place and dignitie upoun sundrie of the Knights and Esquhyris of Ingland and Ireland to thame and thair airis maill for ever In consideratioun of thair help and assistance toward that happie and successfull plantatioun of ULSTER IN IRELAND To the grite strenth of that his Majesties Kingdome, incresse of his Hienes revenues and help to manie of his Majesties goode subjects And quhairas our said

[1] Regist Secreti Concilii —(Acta, Jan. 1621—Mar. 1625, fol 218.)

Soverane Lord being no les hopefull the plantatioun of NEW SCOTLAND in the narrest pairt of America alreadie discovered and surveyed be some of the subjects of his Majesties Kingdome of Scotland joyning unto NEW INGLAND quhairin a grite pairt of his Hienes nobilitie, gentrie, and burrowis of Ingland ar particularlie interessed and hes actuallie begun thair severall Plantations thairof And for that conceaving that manie his Majesties subjects of this his ancient Kingdome emulating the vertews and industrious interpryssis of utheris And being of bodies and constitutionis most able and fitt to undergo the Plantatioun thairof and propagatioun of Christiane relligioun will not be deficient in anie thing quhilk may ather advance his Majesties Royall intentioun towards that Plantatioun or be beneficiall and honnourable to this his Hienes ancient Kingdome in generall or to thaimeselfis in particular The samyn being ane fitt, warrandable and convenient means to disburding this his Majesties said ancient Kingdome of all such younger brether and meane gentlemen quhois moyens ar short of thair birth worth or myndis who otherwayes most be troublesome to the houses and freindis from whence they ar descendit (the common ruynes of most of the ancient families) Or betak thameselfis to forren warko or baisser chifts to the discredite of thair ancestouris and cuntrey And to the grite losse of manie of his Majesties goode subjects who may be better preservit to his Hienes use, honnour of thair freindis, and thair awne comfort and subsistance Gif transplantit to the said cuntrey of NEW SCOTLAND, most worthie and most easie to be plantit with christiane people and most habill by the fertilitie and multitude of commodities of sea and land, to furnish all things necessarie to manteine thair estaitis and dignitie as Landislordis thairof and subjects to his Majestie to be governed by the Lawis of this his ancient Kingdome of Scotland And our said Soverane Lord being most willing and desyreous that this his said ancient Kingdome participate of all such otheris honnouris and dignities as ar erected in anie of his Majesties otheris Kingdomes To the effect that the Gentrie of this his Hienes said ancient Kingdome of Scotland may both haif thair dew abroad amonge the subjects of utheris his Majesties Kingdomes and at home amonge thameselffis according to thair degree and dignitie As alsua his Majestie being most graciouslie pleasit to confer the said honnour of heretable Baronet as ane speciall mark of his Heighnes princelie favour upoun the Knights and Esquyris of principall respect ffor thair birth worth and fortouns Togidder with large proportionis of Landis within the said cuntrey of NEW SCOTLAND who sall be generouslie pleasit to set furth some men in his Hienes Royal Colonie nixt going thither for that plantatioun THAIRFORE his Majestie ordanis his Hienes lettres to be direct chargeing Herauldis Pursevantis and Messengeris of Armes to pas to the mercat Cros of Edinburgh and vtheris placeis neidfull and thair be oppin proclamatioun to mak publicatioun of the premises And that it is his Majesties princelie

pleasure and expres resolutioun, to mak and creat the nomber of Ane hundreth
heretable Baronettis of this his Hienes Kingdome of Scotland be patentis under
his Majesties grite seale thairof Who and thair airis maill sall haif place and precedencie nixt and immediatlie after the youngest sones of the Vicounts and Lordis
Barrounis of Parliament and the addition of the word Sir to be prefixed to thair
propper name and the style and the title of Baronett subjoyned to the surname
of everie ane of thame and thair airis maill   Togither with the appellatioun of
Ladie, Madame, and Dame, to thair Wyffis in all tyme comeing with precedencie
befoir all others Knights alsweill of the Bath, as Knights Bachelouris and Bannar-
ettis (except these onlie that beis Knighted be his Majestie his airis and successouris in proper persone, in ane oppin feild with banner displayed with new addi-
tioun to thair armes and haill utheris præprogatives formarlie grantit be oure said
Soverane Lord to the saidis Barronettis of Ingland and Ireland Conforme to the
printed patent thairof in all poynts   And that no persone or personis whatsumevir
sall be created and maid Barronetts bot onlie such principall Knights and Esquyris
as will be generouslie pleasit to be Undertakeris of the said Plantatioun of New
Scotland   And for that effect to act thameselfis or some sufficient cautioneris for
thame in the buikis of Secreit Counsaill befoir the first day of Apryll nixt to come
in this insueing year of God 1600 Tuentie fyve yearis To sett furth sex sufficient
men artificeris or laboureris sufficienthe armeit apparrelit and victuallit for tua
yeiris towards his Majesties Royall Colonie to be established God willing thair for
his Hienes use dureing that space   And that within the space of yeir and day efter
the dait of the said Actis under the pane of tua thowsand merkis usuall money of
this realme   As also to pay to Sir Williame Alexander Knight Maister of
Requests of this Kingdome and Lieutenant to his Majestie in the said Cuntrey of
New Scotland the sowme also of ane thowsand merkis money foirsaid for his
past chargeis in discoverie of the said Cuntrey and for surrendering and resigning
his interest to the saidis Landis and Barronies quhilks ar to be grantit be our said
Soverane Lord to the saidis Barronettis and everie one of thame   To be halden
in frie blensh of his Majestie his airis and successouris as frie Barronies of
Scotland in all tyme comeing And as of the Crowne of the samyne Kingdome
and under his Hienes grite seale thairof without onie other fyne or compositioun
to be payit to his Majestie or his hienes thesaurar for the tyme thairfore   Quhilkis
barronies and everie one of thame sal be callit be suche names as seemes meetest
to the saids Barronetts And sall border on the sea coast or some portative river
of the said Cuntrey and conteine threttie thowsand aikers quhairof sextene thowsand aikers is intendit for everie one of the saidis Baronetis thair airis and assignayis quhatsumevir with ane Burgh of Barronie thairupoun   And the remanent
fourtene thowsand aikeris for such other publick use and uses as for the Crowne,

Bishops, Universities, Colledge of Justice, Hospitals, Clargie, Phisitiounis, Schools, Souldiouris and utheris at lenth mentionat in the Articles and Plattforme of the said Plantatioun   And forder that his Majesties will and pleasure is That publict intimatioun be maid as afoirsaid To all the saidis Knights and Esquyris who desyris to accept the said dignitie of Baronett and Baronie of Land upoun the conditionis above exprest that betuix and the first day of Apryle nixt to come they repair in persoun or by some Agent sufficientlie instructed to the Lordis of his Majesties privie Counsall or to suche as sal be nominat be his Hienes and intimat to thame be the saidis Lordis to inroll thair names and ressave forder informatioun fra thame concerning the said plantatioun and for passing of thair infeftmentis and patents accordinglie   And sicklyk that all otheris personis who intendeth not to be Barronetts and that hath suche affectioun to his Majesties service as they will also be Undertakers of some proportionis of Land in NEW SCOTLAND (as the nobilitie gentrie and burrowis of Ingland hath done in New Ingland) may herafter tak notice of the printed Articles[1] of the Plantatioun of New Scotland and informe thameselfis by all laughfull wayes and meanis thairof   With certificatioun to all his Majesties lieges and subjects that immediatlie after the said first day of Apryle nixt to come Our said Soverane Lord will proceid to the creatioun and ranking of the saidis Barronettis, and passing of thair patents and infeftments without respect to ony that sall happin to neglect to cum in before the said day who ar heirby requyrit to tak notice heirof and inroll thair names that thair neglect may be rather imput unto thameselfis then to his Majestie who is so graciouslie pleasit to make offer to thame of so fair ane occasioun of heretable preferment honnour and benefite.

1625
March 17   ANENT BARONETTIS.[2]
              CHARLES P.

Right trustie and right welbeloued Cosens and Counsellouris and right trustie and welbeloued Counsellouris, Whereas it hath pleased the Kingis Majestie in favour of the Plantatioun of NOVA SCOTIA to honnour the Vndertakiris being of the ancientest gentrie of Scotland with the honnour of Barronetts and thairin haif trusted and recommendit SIR WILLIAM ALEXANDER of Menstrie to his Counsell to assist him by all laughfull meanis and to countenance the bussienes by thair authoritie   In like maner We do recommend the said Sir William and the bussines to your best assistance hereby declairing that we favour bothe the bussines and the persone that followeth it in suche sort That your willingness to further it in all you can sall be vnto us very acceptable service   So We bid you hartelie farewell   From the Court at Theobalds, the 17 of Marche 1625.

[1] No copy of these Printed Articles has been discovered
[2] Regist Secr Concilii —(Royal Letters, 1623-1632)

ANENT BARONETTIS.

JAMES R.

Right trustie and welbeloued Counsellour Right trustie and welbeloued Cosens and Counsellours and trustie and welbeloued Counsellours We greete you weele We persave by your letters directit vnto us what care you haif had of that bussienes which We recommendit vnto you concerning the creatting of KNIGHT BARONETTIS within that our Kingdome for the Plantatioun of New Scotland, and ar not onlie weele satisfied with the course that you haif taikin thairin but likewayis it doeth exceidinglie content ws that We haif so happielie fund a meanis for expressing of our affectioun towards that our ancient Kingdome as we find by the consent of you all so much tending to the honnour and proffite thairof, and as we haif begun so we will continue requireing you in like maner to perseuere for the furthering of this Royall work that it may be brought to a full perfectioun And as you haif done weele to warne the auncient Gentrie by Proclamatioun assigneing thame a day for comeing in and that you are carefull to secure that which they sould performe Our pleasure is to this end that this bussienes may be carried with the lesse noice and trouble that everie ane of them that doeth intend to be Baronet give in his name to our trustie and welbeloued SIR WILLIAM ALEXANDER Knight our Lieutennant for that enterprise or in cais of his absence to our trustie and welbeloued Counsellour SIR JOHN SCOTT Knight that one of thame after the tyme appoyntit by the Proclamatioun is expyred may present the names of the whole nomber that ar to be created unto thame whome We sall appoynt Commissionaris for marshalling of them in due ordour And becaus it is to be the fundatioun of so grite a work bothe for the good of the Kingdome in generall and for the particular enterest of everie Baronet who after this first protectionarie Colony is seatled for secureing of the cuntrey may the rather thairefter adventure for the planting of their awne proportioun whiche by this meanis may be maid the more hopefull That the sinceritie of our intentioun may be seen Our further pleasure is that if any of the Baronettis sall chuse rather to pay two thowsand merkis than to furnishe furth sex men as is intendit that then the whole Baronettis mak chois of some certaine persones of thair nomber to concurr with our said Lieutennant taking a strict course that all the said monie be onlie applied for setting furth of the nomber intendit or at the least of so many as it can convenientlie furnishe And as we will esteeme the better of suche as ar willing to imbrace this course so if any do neglect this samine and sue for any other degree of honnour hereafter We will think that they deserve it the lesse since this degree of Baronet is the next steppe vnto a further And so desiring you all to further this purpose als far as convenientlie you can We bid you Farewell, from our Court at Theobaldes, the 23 of Marche 1625.

King James died at Theobalds, London, on Sunday the 27th day of March 1625. At the close of his charter or original patent, granted to Sir William Alexander in October 1621, he engaged that all the privileges and liberties it so bountifully conferred should be ratified, approved, and confirmed in our next Parliament of our said Kingdom of Scotland. No subsequent Parliament was held during his reign; but this scheme was not allowed to drop. King Charles, within three months of ascending the throne, granted a Charter of Novodamus, under the Great Seal, in which the former one is recited, with additional clauses respecting the order of Baronets, and confirming to Sir William Alexander, in the most ample form, the lands and lordship of Nova Scotia, and also engaging to have the same ratified and confirmed by Parliament. The King, however, showed as little inclination to convoke a meeting of Parliament in Scotland as he did in England. But active measures in the meanwhile were pursued for the creation of Baronets, and Sir William, who was appointed, in 1626, one of the Principal Secretaries of State for Scotland, was raised to the peerage by the title of Viscount of Stirling and Lord Alexander, 4th of September 1630. Three years later, at the King's coronation at Holyrood, his Lordship was raised to the dignity of Earl of Stirling, Viscount of Canada, &c., by letters patent, 14th of June 1633.

The Royal Letters and proceedings of the Privy Council of Scotland during the early part of the reign of Charles the First, which relate to Sir William Alexander's various schemes, are too numerous to be given in whole; but the following series, it is believed, includes all that are of any importance in regard to Nova Scotia. They do not require any special comment; but it will be observed that these papers run much more on the creation of Knights Baronets than the enforcing on such undertakers the patriotic scheme of Colonization, and, by the payment of certain fines, they were released from the obligation of sending " out men, women, and provisions " to the intended Colonies, until, in fact, it may be said, the whole matter degenerated into an easy mode of raising money by the sale of hereditary titles. The following documents, unless it may be otherwise stated, are given from either Original letters, the Acts of Privy Council, or the Register of letters kept by

Sir W. Alexander, afterwards Earl of Stirling, while Principal Secretary of State for Scotland.[1] The following Precept may serve as an example of the form or warrant issued for preparing a Charter under the Great Seal, to convey, with the grant of lands, the title and honours of a Nova Scotia Baronet.

PRECEPT OF A CHARTER TO WILLIAM EARL MARISCHAL.   1625
May 2

PRECEPTUM CARTE fact. per S. D. N. Regem predilecto suo consanguineo Willielmo Mariscalli Comiti Dno. Keith et Altrie &c. Regni Scotie Mariscallo heredibus suis masculis et assignatis quibuscunque hrie. [hereditarie] super tota et integra illa parte seu portione regionis et dominii Nove Scotie vt sequitur bondat. et limitat. viz. incipien. a maxima meridionali parte terre ex orientali latere fluvii nunc Tweid appelat. prius autem Sancti Crucis et exinde pergendo orientaliter sex miliaria per maris et littus et exinde pergendo borealiter a maris littore in terra firma ex orien. latere ejusdem fluvii observando semper sex milliaria in latitudine a dicto fluvio orientaliter donec extendat ad numerum quadraginta octo millium acrarum terre cum castris turribus fortalicus &c.   Quequidem terre aliaque in dict. carta ad Dominum Gulielmum Allexander de Menstrie hereditarie pertinuerunt et resignate fuerunt per ipsum in manibus dict. S. D. N. Regis pro hac Nova Carta et infeodatione Prefato predicto suo consanguineo Willielmo Mariscalli Comiti &c. desuper conficienda Preterea cum clausula vnionis in unam integram et liberam baroniam et regalitatem omni tempore futuro Baroniam de Keith Marschell nuncupand. tenen. de dict. S. D. N Rege et successoribus suis de corona et regno Scotie in libera alba firma pro annua solutione vnius denarii vsualis monete dicti regni Scotie super solum et fundum dictarum terrarum nomine albe firme si petatur tantum vel alicujus earundem partis in die festo nativitatis Domini nomine albe firme si petatur tantum Et quod vnica sasina apud Castellum de Edinburgh capienda et erit sufficiens pro omnibus et singulis terris aliisque particulariter et generaliter suprascript. in dicta carta content. et cetera in communi forma cartarum Baronetis concess Apud Aulam de Quhythall vigesimo octavo die mensis Maii Anno Dni. Millesimo sexcentesimo vigesimo quinto.   *Per Signetum.*

[1] This Register consists of three volumes The first and most important is deposited in the General Register House, and contains Letters from January 26, 1626, to last of December 1631. The other volumes are in the Advocates Library they contain, besides a portion of an earlier date, Letters from February 12, 1626, to July 1627 ; and from July 14, 1630, to June 24, 1635, being duplicate copies, so far as the dates correspond, each volume thus supplying portions not in the others.

D

TO THE PRIVY COUNCIL OF SCOTLAND ANENT BARONETTIS

CHARLES R.

RIGHT trustie and right wel-beloued counsellour, right trustie and right wel-beloued cosens and counsellouris, and trustie and wel-beloued counsellouris, WE GREETE YOU WELE. UNDERSTANDING that our late deare Father, after due deliberatioun, for furthering the Plantatioun of NEW SCOTLAND, and for sindrie other goode consideratiounis, did determine the creatting of Knight Baronettis thair, and that a proclamatioun wes maid at the mercatt croce of Edinburgh, to gif notice of this his Royall intentioun, that those of the best sort knowing the same might haif tyme to begin first, and be preferred unto otheris, or than want the said honnour in their awne default · AND UNDERSTANDING likewayes, that the tyme appoyntit by the Counsell for that purpois is expyred, We being willing to accomplisho that whiche wes begun by our said deare Father, haif preferred some to be Knight Baronettis, and haif grantit unto thame signatouris of the said honnour, togither with thrie mylis in breadth and six in lenth of landis within New Scotland, for thair severall proportiounes: AND now that the saidis Plantatiounes intendit thair, tending so much to the honnour and benefite of that our Kingdome, may be advanced with diligence, and that preparatiounes be maid in due tyme for setting furthe a Colonie at the next Spring, to the end that those who are to be Baronettis, and to help thairunto, may not be hinderit by comeing unto us for procureing thair grantis of the saidis landis and dignitie, bot may haif thame there with lesse trouble to themselffis and unto us, We haif sent a Commissioun unto you for accepting surrenderis of landis, and for conferring the dignitie of Baronet upon suche as salbe fund of qualitie fitt for the samine, till the nomber appoynted within the said commissioun be perfited: AND THEREFORE OUR PLEASURE IS, That you exped the commissioun through the sealis with all diligence, and that you, and all otheris of our Privie Counsell thair, give all the lawfull assistance, that you can convenientlie affoord for accomplisheing the said worke, whereby Colonies sould be sett furth; and certifie from us, that as we will respect thame the more who imbrace the said dignitie and further the said plantatioun, so if ony Knight who is not a Baronet presoome to tak place of one who is Baronet, or if ony who is not Knight stryve to tak place of one who hes the honnour from us to be a Knight, inverting the order usuall in all civile pairtis, WE WILL that you censure the pairty transgressing in that kynd, as a manifest contempnar of oure authoritie, geving occasioun to disturbe the publict peace. So recommending this earnesthe to your care, We bid you farewell. Windsore, the 19th of July 1625.

PROCLAMATIOUN CONCERNING BARONNETTIS.

Apud Edinburgh penultimo die mensis Augusti 1625.

Forsameikle as our Souerane Lordis umquhile dearest Father of blissed memorie for diverse goode ressonis and considderationis moveing his Matie and speciallie for the better encouragement of his Hienes subjectis of this his ancient Kingdome of Scotland towardis the plantatioun of New Scotland in America being graciouslie pleased to erect the heretable dignitie and title of Baronet as a degree of honour within the said kingdome (as formerlie he had done in England for the plantatioun of Vlster in Ireland) And being of intention to confer the said title and honnour of Barronet onlie vpoun suche his Ma^tis subjectis of the said ancient Kingdome of Scotland as wald be vndertakeris and furtheraris of the Plantatioun of New Scotland and performe the conditionis appoyntit for that effect Causit publict proclamatioun to be maid at the Mercat Croce of Edinburgh be advise of his Ma^s Counsell of the said Kingdome geving notice to the cheiff gentrie and all his Maties subiectis of that Kingdome of his Royall intention concerning the creating of Barronettis there, and that after a certain day now of a long tyme bypast prescryved be the said proclamatioun his Matie wald proceid to the creating of Barronettis and conferring the said title and honnour vpoun suche personis as his Matie sould think expedient having performed the conditionis appoyntit for the said Plantatioun To the effect the cheifest Knightis and Gentlemen of the Kingdome haveing notice of his Maties princelie resolutioun might (if thay pleasit be Vndertakeris in the said Plantatioun and performe the appoyntit conditionis) be first preferred be his Matie and haue the said heretable honnour and title conferred vpoun thame and there aires maill for ever or otherwayes be there awne neglect and default want the same   And now our Souerane Lord being most carefull and desireous that his said vmquhile deerest Fatheris resolution tak effect for the weele of this his said Kingdome and the better furtherance of the said Plantatioun and otheris good considerationis moveing his Hienes, His Matie hathe already conferred the said heretable honnour and title of Barronet vpoun diverse his Ma^s subjectis of this his said kingdome, of goode parentage, meanis and qualitie and grantit chartouris to thame and there airis maill for evir vnder the Grite Seale of the said kingdome conteining his Ma^s grant vnto thame of the said dignitie and of the particular landis and boundis of New Scotland designit vnto thame of the said dignitie, and of the particular landis and boundis of New Scotland designit vnto thame and diverse liberties and priviledgeis contenit in there saidis patentis and is of the intention to grant the like to otheris   And for the better furtherance of the said

Plantatioun and performe the conditionis appoyntit for that effect and to haif the said honnour and title conferred vpoun thame may not be hinderit nor delayit be going to Court to procure from his Matie there severall patentis and grantis of the said dignity and landis in New Scotland to be grantit to thame but may haif the samo heir in Scotland with lesse truble to his Matie and chargis and expenssis to thame selffis His Matie of his royall and princelie power and speciall favour hathe gevin and grantit a commission and full power to a select nomber of the Nobilitie and Counsell of this Kingdome whose names are particularlie therein insert or ony five of thame the Chancellair Thesaurair and Secretair being thrie of the five to ressaue resignationis of all landis within New Scotland whilk sal happin to be resignit be Sir William Alexander knight Maister of Requestis to his Matie for the said kingdome and his Ma^{s} Lieutennant of New Scotland in favouris of whatsom- evir personis and to grant patentis and infeftmentis thairof againe to thame Together with the said heretable honnour and title thay haveing alwayes first performed to the said Sir William Alexander his aires or assignayis or thair laughfull commissionaris or procuratouris haveing there powers the Conditionis appoyntit for the furtherance of the said Plantatioun and bringing thame a cer- tificat thairof in write vnder the handis of the said Sir Williame or his foirsaidis to be shewn and producit before the saidis commissionaris   And his Matie haveing likewayes gevin informatioun to the Lordis of his Secreit Counsell of this king- dome to certifie his subjectis thereof concerning his princelie will and pleasure anent the place due to the Barronettis and Knightis of the said Kingdome THAIRFORE the saidis Lordis of Secreit Counsell to the effect that nane pretend ignorance Ordanis letteris to be direct chargeing herauldis and officiaris of armeis to pas to the mercat croce of Edinburgh and all otheris placeis neidfull and mak publict intimatioun to all his Ma^{s} leiges and subiectis of this kingdome That all suche as intend to be Barronettis and Vndertakeris in the said Plantatioun and to performe to the said Sir Williame or his foirsaidis the Conditionis appoyntit for the furtherance of the said Plantatioun and haueing a certificat vnder his hand as said is may repair ard resort to the saidis Commissionaris at all tymes convenient and ressave grantis and patentis from thame vnder the Grite Seale of this Kingdome of the landis of New Scotland to be resignit in there favouris to the said Sir Williame or his foir- saidis with the like liberties and priviledgeis and otheris whatsoevir as ar grantit to the Barronettis alreadie maid in thair patentis alreadie past vnder the said Grite Seale, and of the said heretable title and honnour of Barronett to thame and there aires maill for ever and tak place and precedence according to the dates of their severall patentis to be grantit to thame and no otherwayes   And in like maner to mak publicatioun that his Ma^{s} princelie will and pleasure is That the Barronettis of this Kingdome maid and to be maid, haif, hald, tak, and enjoy in

all tyme comeing freelie but ony impediment the place prioritie and precedence
in all respectis grantit to thame in thair severall patentis vnder the said Grite
Scale and that no Knight, Laird, Esquire, or Gentleman whatsoevir who is not a
Barronett presoome in ony conventioun or meeting or at ony tyme place or occasioun whatsoevir to tak place præcedence or præeminence befoir ony who is or
sal heirafter be maid a Baronet neyther ony who is not a Knight tak place befoir
ony who hathe the honnour to be a Knight thereby inverting the ordour vsed in
all civile pairtis Certifieing all his Maⁱ leiges and subjectis of this his kingdome
and everie ane of thame who sall præsoome to do in the contrair heirof That 'thay
sall be most severlie punist be his Maᵗⁱᵉ and the saidis Lordis of his Counsell as
manifest contempnaris of his Maᵗⁱᵉˢ royall power and prærogative and thereby
geving occasioun to disturb the publict peace.

Subscribitur ut supra.

[Geo. Cancell. Roxburgh.
Mortoun. Melros.
Wintoun. Lauderdaill.]
Bugcleugh.

CONVENTIOUN OF ESTATES —ANENT BARONETTIS.

Apud Edinburgh secundo die mensis Novembris 1625.

Anent the Petitioun gevin in be the small Barronis proporting that thay sustenit verie grite prejudice by this new erectit Ordour of Barronettis and the præcedencie grantit to thame befoir all the small Baronis and Freehalderis of this
kingdome whairin thay pretendit grit præjudice in thair priviledgeis and dignityis
possest be thame and thair prædecessouris in all præceding aiges and thairfoir
thay desyrit that the Estaittis wald joyne with thame in thair humble petitioun
that his Maᵗⁱᵉ might be intreatted to suspend the præcedencie grantit to thir
Barronettis vntill the tyme that the Plantatioun for the whilk this dignitie is
conferred be first performed be the Vndertakeris Whairupon Sir William Alexander cheiff vndertaker of this Plantatioun being hard and he having objectit unto
thame his Maⁱ royall prærogative in conferring of honnouris and titles of dignitie
in matteris of this kynd importing so far the honnour and credite of the cuntrey
and that his Maⁱ prærogative wald not admitt ony sort of opposition, and that this
suspensioun of the Vndertakeris præcedencie wald frustratt the whole Plantatioun
After that the small Barronis had most humblie protestit that the least derogation
to his Maⁱ royall prærogative sould never enter in thair hairtis and that thair

Petitioun was in no sort contrair to the same, and that thay acknawledged that
the conferring of honnouris did properlie belong to his Matie as a poynt of his
royall præiogative   And thay undertooke that if it wer fund meete be his Matie
and the Estaittis that this Plantatioun sould be maid that thay vpoun thair awin
chairgis wald vndertak the same without ony retributioun of honnour to be gevin
thairfoir.   The Estaittis haveing at lenth hard both tho paityis It was fund be
pluralitie of voittis that the Estaittis sould joyne with thame in thair petitioun
foirsaid.

EXTRACT FROM THE COUNSALL'S LETTER.[1]

MOST SACRED SOVERANE

The Convention of your Majesties Estaittis, which, by your Ma^s direction
wes callit to the tuentie sevent day of October last being that day verie solemnlie
and with a frequent and famous nomber of the Nobilitie Clergy and Commissionaris for the Shyres and Burrowis præceishe keept, and the Taxatioun grantit,
as our former letter to your Majestie did signifie.

Upon the first second and thrid day of this moneth the Estattis having procceded to
the considderatioun of the Propositions and Articles sende downe be your Matie &c.

.   .   .   .   .   .

After that all thir Articles wer propouned haid discussit and answeirit be the
Estaittis in maner foirsaid Thair wes some petitions gevin in be the small Baronis
and Burrowis whairin thay craved that the Estaittis wald joyne with thame in
thair humble Petitioun to your Matie for obtaining your allowance thairof

.   .   .   .   .   .

Thay had ane other Petitioun and greevance foundit vpon the præjudice alledged
sustenit be thame by this new erectit Ordour of Barronettis and the præcedencie
grantit to thame befoir all the small Barronis and Friehalderis of this Kingdome
whairin thay prætendit grite præjudice in thair priviledgeis and dignityis possest
be thame and thair prædecessouris in all præcceiding aiges   And thairfore thair
desire wes that the Estaittis wald joyne with thame in thair humble Petitioun That
your Matie might be intreatted to suspend the præcedencie grantit to thir Barronettis vntill the tyme that the Plantatioun for the whilk this dignitie is conferred
be first performed be the vndertakeris   Whairupon Sir William Alexander cheif
vndertaker in this Plantatioun being hard and he haveing objectit vnto thame
your Ma^s royall prærogative in conferring of honnouris and tiths of dignitye in
matteris of this kynd importeing so far the honnour and credite of the cuntrey

---

[1] This Letter is printed at length in the Acts of Parliament, vol. v p 185–188.

And that your Ma⁑ prærogative wald not admit ony sort of oppositioun and that this suspensioun of the vndertakeris præcedencie wald frustratt the whole Plantatioun After that the Small Baronis had most humblie protestit that the least derogatioun to your Ma⁑ prærogative sould never enter in thair hairtis and that thair petitioun wes in no sort contrair to the same bot that thay acknowledged that the conferring of honnouris did properlie belong to your Ma⁑⁀ as a poynt of your royall prærogative And thay vndertooke that if it wer fund meete by your Ma⁑⁀ and the Estaittis that this Plantatioun sould be maid That thay vpoun thair awne chargeis wald vndertak the same without ony retributioun of honnour to be gevin thairfoir. The Estaittis haveing at lenth hard bothe partyis It wes fund be pluralitie of voitis that the Estaittis sould joyne with thame in thair Petitioun foirsaid to your Majestie.   .   .

(Sic subscribitur)

Edinburgh	GEO. HAY.	ROXBURGH.
Octavo Novembris 1625.	MAR.	MELROS
	MORTOUN.	B. DUMBLANE.
	WYNTOUN.	ARCᴰ. NAPER.
	LINLITHGOW.	

TO THE COUNSALL.

1626
February 12

[CHARLES R]

Right trustie and weilbeloved Counsellour Right trustie and weilbelovit Cousines and Counsellours Right trustie and weilbeloved Counsellours and trustie and weilbeloved Counsellours We Greet you weill Wheras our late dear Father did determyne the Creating of Knyghts Barronetts within that our Kingdome haveing first had the advyse of his privie Counsall thervnto whoise congratulatorie approbation may appear by a letter of thanks sent vnto him thairefter And sieing the whole gentrie war advertcised of this his Royall resolutioun by publict proclamationis that these of the best sort knowing the same might have tyme to begin first and be preferred vnto vthers or then want the said honour in ther awin default a competent tyme being appoynted vnto them by the said Counsall that they might the more advysedlie resolve with them selffis therein In consideratioun whairof we wer pleased to give a commission vnder our great seall wherby the saidis Knights Barronetts might be created according to the conditions formerlie condescendit vpoun And heirefter hearing that sindrie gentlemen of the best sort wer admitted to the said dignitie we never haveing heard of aney complaynt against the same till the work efter this maner was broght to perfection it could not bot seame strange vnto ws that aney thereifter should have presented such a petition as was gevin to the last Conventioun so much derogatorie to our Royall prerogative and to the hindering of so worthie a work or that the samyne should have bene countenanced or suffered to have bene further prosecuted Now to the effect that the said work may have no hinderance heirefter our pleasur is that the course so advysedlie prescryved by ws to the effect forsaid may be made publictlie knowen of new wairning the said gentrie that they may ather procure the said dignitie for them selffis or not repyne at others for doeing the same And that you have a speciall care that none of the saidis Knyghts Barronetts be wronged in ther priviledges by punisching aney persone who dar presum to doe any thing contrarie to ther grants as a manifest contemner of our authoritie and disturbours of the publict peace And if it shall happin heirefter that the said Commission by the death or change of any persones appoynted Commissioneris to this effect shall neid be renewed Our further pleasur is that at the desyre of our trustie and weilbelovit Counsellour Sir William Alexander kny^t our Secretarie or his aires the same be gevin of new to the Commissioneris of our Excheker the Chancellour Thesaurer or Thesaurer deputie or aney tuo of them being alwyse of the number giveing them such power in all respects as is conteyned in the former Commission with this addition onlie that we doe heirby authorize our Chancellour for the tyme being to knyght the eldest sones of the saidis Knyghts Baronets being of perfyte aige of 21 zeires he being requyred to that effect And we will that a clause bearing the lyk power bo particularlie insert in the said new Commission if vpoun the caussis forsaid it be renewed And that the samyne by our said Chancellour be accordinglie performed. So we bid, &c. Whythall Feb. 12, 1626.

1626
March 24.

TO THE LAIRD OF TRAQUAIR.

Trustie and weilbeloved, &c. We, &c. Thogh ther have bene warning gevin to all the gentrie of that our Kingdome by publict proclamation that they might in dew tyme come to be created Knyght Barronettis and not compleane heirefter of theris befoir whom they might expect to have place wer preferred vnto them yet we have thoght fitt to tak particular notice of yow And the rather becaus it would seame that yow not knowing or mistaking our intention in a matter so much concerneing our Royall prerogative for the furthering of so noble a work did seik to hinder the same Therfor Our pleasur is that you with diligence embrace the said dignitie and performe the conditions as others doe or that yow expect to be heard no more in that purpois nor that yow compleane no more heirefter of others to be preferred vnto yow So not doubting but that both by your selff and with others you will vse your best meanes for furthering of this work wherby yow may doe to ws acceptable service, We bid, &c. Whythall 24 March 1626.

TO THE CHANCELLOUR.

[CHARLES R.]

Right, &c. Wheras we have gevin Ordour by a former letter that the Commission formerlie grantit by ws for creating of knyght Barronettis in that our kingdome might be renewed at the desyre of Sir William Alexander our Livetenent of New Scotland or his Heynes whensoever they should desyre the samyne geving the power in tyme comeing to the Commissioners of our Excheker which the persones nominated in the preceiding Commission formerlie had and that the eldest sones of all Baronettis might be knyghted being of perfite aige of 21 yeirs whensoever they shall desyre the same according to ther patents vnder our greit seall give power to yow or our Chancellour thar for the tyme being to doe the same both for frieing ws from trouble and saveing' them from charges which ther repairing thither for that purpois might procure Our pleasur is that yow caus renew and expeid the said Commission vnder our great seall as said is And in the meane tyme that yow knyght the eldest sones of all and everie ane of such Baronettis who being of 21 yeres of aige shall desyre the same without putting of them to aney charges or expenssis For doeing whairof, &c. So we bid, &c. Whythall 24 March 1626.

TO THE LAIRD OF WAUGHTON.

Trustie, &c. (as in the precedent till this place) Yit we have thoght fitt to tak particular notice of your selff and house desyreing yow to performe the said dignitie of knyght Barronet and to performe the lyk conditions as otheris haveing the lyk honour doe which course we wish the rather to be takin by yow and others in regaird that so noble a wark as the plantation of New Scotland doeth much depend thervpoun and as your willingnes to this our request shall not be a hinderance bot rather a help to ane further place that shalbe thoght fitt to be conferred vpon yow so shall yow heirby doe ws acceptable pleasur. We bid, &c. Whythall 24 March 1626.

TO THE LAIRD OF WEYMES.

Trustie and weilbeloved We, &c. Haveing determined that the Creation of knyght Baronetts should preceid according as our late dear father with advyse of his Counsall had agried vpon Thogh all the gentrie of that our kingdome had warning thairof by publict proclamation yet we ar pleased in regaird of the reputatioun of your house to tak more particular notice of yow And did pass a signatur of the said honour in your name wherin we thoght our favour would have bene acceptable vnto yow Therfoir these presents ar to requyre yow to pass the said signatur

E

and to performe the lyk conditions as others doe Or vtherwayes doe not compleane heirefter of the precedencie of otheis whom we will the rather preferr that by the embraceing of the said dignitie they be carefull to further so worthie a work as doeth depend thervpoun And as it is a nixt stepp to a further title so we will esteame of it accordinglie Thus willing yow to certifie bak your resolution heirin with all diligence to Sir William Alexander our secretarie who will acquaint ws therwith we bid you, &c. Whythall 24th March 1626.

PROCLAMATIOUN ANENT BARONETTIS.

Apud Halyrudhous penultimo Martii 1626.

Forsamekle as our Soverane Lordis umquhile darrest Father of blissed and famous memorie out of his princelie and tender regaird of the honnour and credite of this his ancient kingdome of Scotland And for the better encourageing of the gentrie of the said kingdome In imitation of tho verteous projectis and enterprises of others to undertak the Plantatioun of New Scotland in America determined with advise of the Lordis of his privie Counsell the creating of ane new heretable title of dignitie within the said kingdome callit Knight Barionet and to confer the same vpoun suche personis of goode parentage meanis and qualitie as wald be undertakeris in the said Plantatioun And of this his Royall and princelie resolution Importing so far the honnour and credite of the Kingdome publicatioun and intimatioun wes maid be opin proclamatioun with all solempnitie requisite to the intent those of the best not knawing the same might haif had time first to begin and to haif bene preferrit to otheris And then thrugh thair awne default or negligence the want of the said honnour to haif bene imputt to thameselffis Like as a competent tyme wes appoyntit and assignit be the saidis Lordis vnto thame for that effect whairthrow they might the more advisedlie haif resolved thairin And oure Souerane Lord following his said darrest Fatheris resolutionis in this poynt causit not onlie renew the said Proclamatioun Bot for the ease of his Maˢ subjectis and saulfing of thame from neidles and unnecessair travell chairgeis and expenssis grantit ane commissioun vndei his Grite Seale whairby the saidis Knightis Barronettis might be created and thair patentis exped in this kingdome Like as accordinghe sundrie Gentlemen of the best sort embraced the conditioun of the Plantatioun wer admittit to the said dignitie of Barronet and no question or objection wes moved aganis the same till the worke wes brought to a perfectioun then some of the gentrie repynning at the precedencie done to thir Barronettis whilk proceidit vpon thair awin sleughe and negligence in not tymous imbraceing the conditionis of the said Plantatioun They maid some publick oppositioun aganis the precedencie done to thir Barronettis and so did what in thame lay to haif hinderit the

Plantatioun foirsaid, whairof informatioun being maid to his Matie and his Matie considdering the goode and necessar groundis whairby first his said darrest Father and then himself wer moved to creat the dignitie and ordour foirsaid of Barronettis and his Matie continewing in a firme and constant purpois and resolutioun that the worke foirsaid sall yett go fordward and no hindrance maid thairunto Thairfore his Matie with advyse of the Lordis of his Secreit Counsell Ordanis letters to be direct chargeing Officieris of armes to pas to the Mercat Croce of Edinburgh and otheris placcs neidfull and thair be opin publicatioun mak said publicatioun and intimatioun of his Ma^s royall will and pleasur that the course so advysedlie prescryved be his Matie to the effect foirsaid salbe yitt followit oute And thairfore to wairne all and sundrie the gentrie of this kingdome That thay either procure the said dignitie for thameselffis Or not repyne at otheris for doing of the same And to command, charge and inhibite all and sindrie his Ma^s leiges and subjects that nane of thame presoome nor tak vpoun hand to wrong the saidis Knightis Barronettis in ony of thair priviledgeis nor to doe nor attempt ony thing contrair to thair grantis and patentis Certifieing thame that sall failzie or doe in the contrair That thay salbe punist as contempnaris of his Matie inclination and disturbaris of the publick peace.—

[Followis His Majesties Missive for Warrand of the Act above writtin.]

Right trustie and welbeloved Councellour, &c.—(See *supra*, p. 31.)

.   .   .   .

So We bid you farewell Frome our Courte at Whythall the 12 of Februar 1626.

SIR ROBERT GORDON OF LOCHINVAR.

1626.
May 5.

Wheras the good schip named   of the burden of   tunnes or therabout whairof   Capitan is licenced to pass to the southward of the Equinoctiall lyne These ar therfor to will and command yow and everie of yow to permitt and suffer the said schip with her furnitur and schips company to quhom we doe heirby grant the benefite of our proclamatioun in all respects which was gevin at our house of Hampton Court the 13 of Decr in the first year of our Reigne quyethe and peaciablie to pass by yow without any let stay trouble or impresses of hir men or any vther hinderance whatsumevir whairof yow shall not faill. From the Court at Whythall 5 May of 1626.

To all Officeris of the Admiralty To all Capitanes and
Masteres of schips in the seas And to all others to
whome it may apperteane.

KNIGHTING OF THE ELDEST SONS OF BARONETTIS.

Apud Halyrudhous vigesimo primo die mensis Julij 1626.

The whilk day Sir George Hay of Kinfawnis knight producit and exhibite before the Counsell the missive titles underwrittin signed be the Kingis Matie and direct to him and desired that the same title sould be insert and registrat in the Bookes of Secreit Counsell *ad futuram rei memoriam* Quhilk desire the saidis Lordis finding reasonable They haif ordanit and ordanis the said Letter to be insert and registratt in the saidis bookes to the effect foirsaid Of the quhilk the tenour follows

CHARLES R.

Right trustie, &c.—(See *supra*, p. 33.)

. . . .

So We bid you farewell Whitehall 24 of Marche 1626.

To our Right trustie and welbeloued Counsallour Sir George Hay Knight Our Chancellour of Scotland.

FEES OF BARRONETTIS.

[CHARLES R]

Right, &c. Haveing considered your letter concerning the fees that ar clamed from the knyght Barronets thogh at the first it did appear vnto ws that none could justlie challenge fees of them by vertew of any grant that was gevin befor that ordour was erected yet befoir we would resolve what was to be done heirin we caused enquyre of tho cheff heraulds and other officers within this our kingdome wher the said dignitie of Barronet was first instituted by our late dear Father And doe find that the baronetts ar bund to pay no feyis nor did pay ever any thing at all save that which they did voluntarlie to the heraulds of whom they had present vse And therfor sieing ther creation within that our kingdome is for so good a caus wherby a Colony is making readie for setting furth this next spring to begin a work that may tend so much to the honour and benefite of that kingdome we would have them everie way to be encouraged and not as we wryt befoir putt to neidles charges and our pleasur is that none as Baronetts to be made be bund to pay feys bot what they shalbe pleased to doe out of ther own discretion to the heraulds or to any such officiers of whom they shall have vse And as for ther eldest sones whensoever any of them is cum to perfyte aigo and desyrs to be knighted let them pay the feyis allowed hertofor to be payed by other knights For doeing wherof We, &c. Oatlandis 28 July 1626.

KNIGHTIS BARONNETTIS AND THE HERAULDIS.

Apud Halyrudhous vigesimo Septembris 1626.

The whilk day the Letter underwrittin signed be the Kingis Matie conteneing a declaration of his Royall Will and pleasure anent the fees acclamed be the Herauldis and otheris from the Knyghtis Barronettis and thair eldest sones being presentit to the Lordis of Secreit Counsell and red in an audience They allowit of his Maties will and pleasure thairanent And Sir Jerome Lindsay knight Lyon King at armes being callit upon and he compeirand personalie and his Ma^s will and pleasure in this matter being intimat vnto him he with all humble and deutifull respect promeist that obedience suld be given thairanent. Of the whilk Letter the tennour followis.

CHARLES R.

Right trustie, &c.—(See *supra*, p. 36.)

.   .   .   .

And so We bid you farewell From our Courte at Oatlandis the 28 of Julij 1626.

PLANTATIOUN OF NEW SCOTLAND.

[CHARLES R]

Wheras Sir William Alexander kny^t our Secretarie for Scotland haueing gevin band to the knyght barronetts of that our kingdome that of all such money as he hath or is to receave from them he shall imploy the just two parts thairof for setting furth a Colony for the plantation of New Scotland which is to be estimated and considered according to the conditions agreed vpon betweene him and the said knyghts baronets And the said Sir William haueing for performeing his part prepared a schip with ordinance munition and all other furnitour necessar for hir as lykwyse another schip of great burden which lyeth at Dumbartane togidder with sindrie other provisions necessarie for so far a voyadge and so great work therfoir that the treuth thairof may be publicklie knowen and that all such monnyis as he hath disbursed heirvpon may be trewlie summed vp Our pleasur is that haueing surveyed the said schip yow estimat and value hir to the worth as lykwyes other furniture and provisions that yow find in hir or to be sent with hir for this purpois and with all his charges he hath bene heir for the same and thairefter that yow delyver vnto him a trew Inventure and Estimat therof vnder your hands that it may heirefter serve for clearing his accompts with the said knyght Barronetts and for haueing the same allowed vnto him by them, &c. Whythall 17 Ja^r 1627.

1627.
January 17.

TO THE EARL OF TOTNES.

[CHARLES R]

Wheras Sir William Alexander Knyᵗ our Secretar for Scotland is to buy for the vso of two schipps to be imployed in our service 16 Minner 4 saker and 6 falcor our pleasur is that yow permitt him or his servandis without impediment to transport the same vnto the said kingdome wher for the present one of the said schipps doe by provydeing that the said Sir William find suretie for the right imployment of the saidis Ordinance according to the customo and for so doeing, &c. Whythall 17 Jaʳ 1627.

Direction—

To our right trustie and weilbeloved cousen and counsellour the Earl of Totness Mr of our Ordinance within our kingdome of England.

1627.
January 19.

TO SIR JAMES BAILLIE

CHARLES R.

Whereas Sir William Alexander oʳ Secretarie for Scotland had a warrant from our late dear Father which is ratified by us to oʳ Trer. of England for payment of the soume of Six thousand pounds sterling which lang since was intended to have bane payed here but seeing now it may be more convenientho done out of this casuell commoditie wherewith Weo have apponted you to intromett Our pleasure is and We will you to pay vnto the said Sʳ William or his assignes the said soume of Six thousand pounds sterling and that out of the first readiest moneyes that you haue or shall receaue for our part of the prises taken or to be taken within that our kingdome for doing whereof these pnts. shall be vnto you a sufficient warrant Giuen at oʳ Court at Whitehall the 19 of January 1627.

To oʳ trustie and welbeloued Sʳ James Bailho Treasaurer of oʳ Marine causes within oʳ kingdome of Scotland.

1627
January 26.

TO THE EARLE MARSCHELL OF SCOTLAND.

[CHARLES R.]

Right, &c. Whereas our late dear Father was pleased to creat knyght Barronetts within Scotland as he had done in his vther kingdomes and that for a honorabile cause for enlargeing the Christiane fayth and our dominions And we understand that sindrie of tho most ancient gentrio embraceing the said dignitie having payed these moneyis condiscendit vpon for their part towards the plantation of New

Scotland Thogh ther have bene sufficient warning gevin to all the gentrie of that our kingdome hath in the tyme of our said late dear Father and in ours notwithstanding it be in our power friehe to conferre honour vpon any of our subjects as we in our judgment shall think they deserve yet out of our gratious favour we ar willing that everie ane of the said gentrie have the place which may be thoght due vnto them in so far as can clearlie be discerned or otherways that they be inexcusable by neglecting so fair ane opportunitie as by this meanes is presented vnto them and considering that it doeth most properlie belong to your Charge as Marschell to judge of ranks and precedencie thoght it be difficult to knowe wher so many ar of equal qualitie yet to the effect that they be ranked in some measur as neir as can be that place which may be thoght to be their due Our pleasur is that assumeing to your selff such assessours here present as you shall think requisite you condescend vpon such a number as yow and they shall think fitt to be barronetts ranking them as yow shall think expedient that out of that number the barronetts limited by the Commission may be selected to the effect we may pass ther signatures accordinglie So that by embraceing the said place in due tyme may mak vse of this our gratious favour and otherwyse least our trustie and weil beloved Sir William Alexander our Secretar who is our Lieutenent of the said Cuntrie and who besyds he is now to sett furth in this Spring hath bene at great charges heretofor in the work of that Plantation should be dissabled from prosecuteing of that purpois we ar willing that he proceed with such others as yow shall think fitt to manteane that dignitie for Wee desyre that the ancient gentrie may be first preferred but if they by neglecting so noble ane interpryse shall not mak vse of our favour in this we think it good reasone that these persones who have succeeded to good estates or acquyred them by ther owin industrie and ar generoushe disposed to concurre with our said servand in this Interpryse should be preferred to the said dignitie and to this effect that yow mak them in maner abovespecifeit haueing for your better proceeding heirin appoynted a Roll to be given yow of diverse of the names of the said gentrie as ar knowen to be of qualitie which wher considered by yow in maner foresaid and haueing selected such of them as yow shall find to be most fitt for this purpois that yow sett down a roll for them in ordour and rank vnder your own hand to be schawin vnto ws. And so, &c. Hampton Court the 26 of Jar 1627.

SIR W. ALEXANDER HIS COLONIE IN NEW SCOTLAND.

[CHARLES R.]

Right, &c. Wheras for direction from ws a survey hath bene made of diverse provisions and necessaries to be sent this Spring by our trustie and weilbeloved

Counsellour Sir William Alexander our Secretarie for the vse of a Colony to be planted in New Scotland wherby it doeth evidentlie appear as is reported bak vnto ws by the survegheris that the said Sir William hath bene at much more charges than as yit he hath received moneyis for the knyght Barronetts of that our kingdome who hath condescended according to ther severall bands made to him for advanceing of such moneyis towardis the said plantation so that of the number of persones condescended vpon by our late dear Father and approved by ws to have the style of knyght Barronetts should not be fullie compleit or if that tymelie satisfaction be not gevin according to ther bandis that hopefull work so much recommended to ws by our said Father and ws is lyklie to desert and our said servand who hath bene first and last at so great charges therin vtterlie vndone in his esteat And in regard by reasone of our service heir that his absence from thence wilbe a great hinderance to the bringing of this purpois of the Baronetts to perfection wo have thoght good heirby to desyre yow whois effectuall assistance we ar confident may much conduce to this purpois that yow may vse your best [endeavours] both in privat and publict as yow shall think most fitt for bringing the said purpois to some perfection when we will expect your best endeavours seeing it is a matter we specallie respect. Newmarket, 3 March 1627.

1627
March 10
TO THE TREASURER OF ENGLAND.

[CHARLES R]

Right, &c. Whereas the good shipp called the Eagle, of the burthen of one hundereth and 20 tunnes, or thereabouts, now lying in the River of Thames (whereof Ninian Barclay is captaine), is loaden with powder, ordonance, and other provisions, for the vse of a plantation, ordained to be made in New Scotland, by our speciall direction, and for the vse of ane other shippe, of the burthen of 300 tunnes, now lying at Dumbartan, in Scotland, which is likwise to goe for the said plantation of New Scotland : Our pleasure is, that you give order to all whom it concerneth, that the said shippe, with all her provisions, furniture, and loading, as being for our own particular service, may pass from the river of Thames, without paying custome, subsidie, or any other duetie, and free from any other lett or impediment · And for your so doeing, this shalbe your sufficient warrant. Theobaldes, the 10 of Merche, 1627.

To our right trustie and welbeloved cousin and counsellor,
the Earle of Marleborrough, our heigh Tressurer of
England.

SIR WILLIAM ALEXANDER TO SECRETARY NICHOLLS.[1]

Sr.

There is a Shipp called the Morning Starre which is tyed in consort to attend a Shippe of mine in her intended voyage to Nova Scotia to doe his Mat⁹ Service (which I know you are not ignorant of) the which shipp is now stayed lying in Dover Road, and not willing to depart vntill such tyme as she be released by his Crˢ [Creditors?] · the Mrˢ name is Andrew Baxter who is readie to attend to his Crˢ demands and directions att all occasions. I doe therfore intreate you that you will doe me that favoʳ to move his Crˢ concerninge the release of the said shipp, seeing it concernethe his Matⁱᵉˢ service so much, the staye whereof will be the overthrowne of this voyage: ffor which favor I shall be ready to doe you the like courtesie when any the like occasion of yours shall present In the meane tyme I rest

Yoʳ lovinge ffriend   Wᴹ ALEXANDER.

Whitehall, this 9th of April 1627.

This Shipp was cleered a fortnight before the restraynt to goe in hir intended voyage.

(*In dorso.*) To My very worthy and much respected ffriend
          Mr Edward Nicholls Secretarie ffor the Admiraltie
          for the Lord Duke of Buckinghame.

GRANT TO SIR WILLIAME ALEXANDER.[2]

Grant to Sir Will. Alexander. His patent of 12 July 1625 for all the lands and dominions of Nova Scotia is recited, and Admiralty jurisdiction of those parts granted to him and his heirs, with power to seize vessels belonging to the King of Spain, the Infanta Isabella, or others, His Majesty's enemies. (Latin)

Whitehall, 3d May 1627.

TO THE COUNSELL

[CHARLES R]

Right, &c. Whareas we have conferred the place of cheef Secretarie of that our kingdome vpon our trustie and weelbeloved counsellare, Sir William Alexander, togither with the keeping of the Signet thare, and all feeis and profeits tharevnto belonging, according to our guift granted vnto him tharevpone: Tharefore wee doe heirby require you, from time to time, to be aiding, and assisting vnto the said Sir Williame, and the keepers of the said Signet, for the time, for the

---

[1] Colonial Papers Calendar, p 84.   [2] Ib p 84.

F

better wplifting and enjoying of the feeis thareof, and all such benefittes and privcleges as have bene heirtofore receaved or enjoyed by any of his predecessors, Secretaries for that kingdome, and that in as beneficiall maner as anye of his saids predecessors or keepers of the said Signet formerlie enjoyed the same, at ony time: And for your soe doing these our letters shalbe vnto you and them a sufficient warrant and discharge. Whitehall, the penult day of November 1627.

1627.
December 28

TO SIR JAMES BAILYEE.

[CHARLES R.]

Trustie, &c. Heaveng been informed of the small benefit that doth arise vnto us by the Prises that are taken by the subjects of that our kingdome, and how that some of them have agreed with Sir Williame Alexander, our Secretarie, for a greater proportiono out of the said Prises then was formerlie in vse to be payed vnto us · And in reguard thare are moneyis due long since by a precept granted by our late deir Father vnto the said Sir Williame, for ansuering whareof vnto him out of the said Prises, and according to the said condition, it pleased ws, at our last being heir, to give you directione : Thairefore Oure pleasour is, that, in our name, you wplift the said proportiones of goods, or money soe agreed vpon, betwix him and the said persones ; as likewayis, that you agree with all others, whoe shal happen to tak Prises heerefter, for paying the like proportionable of moneyis or goods ; And tharefter from timo to time, as the said benefite shall happen to arrise, that you pay the same vnto the said Sir Williame, or his assignayis, and that vntill the said precept be complcithe satisfied : ffor doing whareof these presentis shalbe your warrant. Whitehall, the 28 day of December 1627

1628
March 18

ANENT THE SEALE OF ADMIRALITIE OF NEW SCOTLAND.

Apud Halyrudhous decimo octavo die Mensis Martij 1628.

Forsameekle as the Kings Matie by his letters patent vnder the Great Seale hes made and constitute Sir William Alexander knight Admirall of New Scotland ; ffor the better exerceing of which office necessar it is that thair be a Seale of the Admiralitie of the said kingdome Thairfore the Lords of Secreit Counsell ordanis and commands Charles Dickieson, sinkear of his Majesteis yrnes, to make grave and sinke ane Seale of the office of Admiralitie of New Scotland, to be the proper Seale of the said office, The said Seale having a shippe with all her ornaments and apparralling, the mayne saile onelie displayed with the armes of New Scotland bearing a Saltoire with ane scutcheon of the ancient armes of Scotland, and vpon the head of the said shippe careing ane vnicorne sittand and ane savage man standing vpoun the sterne both bearing St Androes Croce And that the great Seale

haue this circumscriptioun, SIGILLUM GULIELMI ALEXANDRI MILITIS MAGNI ADMI-
RALLI NOVI SCOTIÆ: Anent the making graving and sinking of the which Seale
the extract of this Act sall be vnto the said Charles a warrand.

A PASS TO SIR WILLIAM ALEXANDER, YOUNGER.

1628
March 26

[CHARLES R.]

Whereas the four schippis, called the   .   .   .   .   .   .   [1]
belonging to Sir William Alexander knight, sone to Sir Williame Alexander, our
Secretarie for Scotland; whareof the   .   .   .   .   .   .   [2]
are to be set out towards Newfoundland, the River of Cannada, and New Scotland,
for setling of Colonies in those partes, and for other thare laufull effaires: Theis are,
tharefore, to will and require you, and everie one of you, to permitt and suffer the
said schippes, and everie one of them, with thare wholl furneture, goods, merchandice, schips companies, and planters, quietlie and peaceabillie in thare going thither,
returning from thence, or during thare being furthe in any other parte whatsoever,
till they shall happin to returne to any of our dominiones, To pas by you, without any
of your lettes, stayes, troubles, imprestis of ther men, or any other men, or any other
hinderance whatsoever: whareof you shall not faill. Whitehall, the 26 March 1628.

COMMISSION ANENT FUGITIVE SOULDEOURIS.

1628
April 23.

Apud Halyrudhous vicesimo tertio die mensis Aprilis 1628.

Forsameekill as it is vnderstand be the Lords of Secreit Counsell that diuerse
persons who wer conduced and tane on be Sir Williame Alexander knight and his
officiars to have beene transported be thame for the plantatioun of New Scotland
haue most unworthilie abandoned that service and imployment refuising to performe the conditionis of thar agreement To the disappointing of that intendit
Plantatioun which his Majestie so earnesthe affects ffor remedeing of which vndew-
tifull dealing The saids Lords recommends to the Shireffs Justices of peace and
Proveists and Bailleis within burgh, and thairwith all giues thame power and commissione everie ane of thame within thair awin bounds and jurisdictioun, to take
tryell of all and sindrie persouns who haueing covenanted with the said Sir Williame Alexander or his officers to goe with thame to New Scotland, haue abandoned that service and runne away, and ather to compell thame to performe the
conditionis of thair agreement Or otherwayes to doe justice vpon thame according
to the merite of thair trespasse And that the saide Shireffs Justices of peace Pro-
vests and Bailleis within burgh concurre countenance and assist the said Sir Wil-

---

[1] Blank in MS.   [2] Line blank in MS.

hame Alexander and his officers in all and everie thing that may further and aduance the service foresaids And for this effect that the said Shireffs and others foresaids delyuer the said persouns to the said Sir Williame Alexander and his officers, it being first qualified that thay have ressaued money from the said Sir Williame and his officers, or that thay haue beene in service and interteaned by thame.

TO THE EXCHECKQUER.

[CHARLES R.]

Right, &c. Whareas we gave order vnto you formerlie that the mariners, whoe hade been imployed in our service, should be payed out of the first and reddiest moneyis of our Excheq^r, and that all former preceptis should be stayed till they wer first satiefied: Wnderstanding that you have taken a course for payment thareof with the moneyis made of the goods of the Lubeck schip, which, by a former warrant given by ws vnto Sir James Baillie, should have been imployed towards the payment of the soume of 6000 lb. Sterling, first granted vnto our trustie and weelbeloved counsellare, Sir William Alexander, oure Secretarie for that our kingdome, by our late dear Father, and tharefter particularlie appointed by ws to be payed vnto him, out of our parte of what should fall due vnto ws out of any prise: Our plesoure is, that you call Sir James Baillie before you, and, heaving tryed of him what part had he been payed of the said soume, that you give order for payment of the rest, out of the rediest moneyis arrising due vnto ws by the Prises, in maner foirsaid; as likewayis, out of the fines due vnto ws by all such persons whoe haue transgressed the Act of Parliament maid in Anno 1621, against the concellers or wrangous upgivers of moneyis lent by them: ffor doing whareof, these psesents shall be your sufficient warrant and discharge. Given at our Court at Whythall, the 23 of May 1628.

TO THE TREASURER OF ENGLAND.

[CHARLES R.]

Right, &c. Whareas the Lord Naper, our Treasurer Deputie in our kingdome of Scotland, hath informed ws, that divers soumes of money, which, for our service wer payable out of our Excheckq^r heir, have been payed out of our Excheckq^r thare: Our pleasour is, that taking vnto your assistance Sir William Alexander, our Secretarie for that kingdome, you call for such accomptis of that kind as our said Treasurer Deputie shall exhibit vnto you, and after you have perused the same, that you report wnto ws what moneyis you find to have been soe delivered, to the effect we may tharefter giue such order touching the same as we sall think fitt. Soe We, &c. Whythall, the last of June 1628.

TO THE EXCHECKQUER.

1628
July 11

[CHARLES R.]

Right, &c. Heaving hade many prooffes and good experience of the sufficiencie and abilities of our trustie and weelbeloved Counsellare, Sir William Alexander of Menstrie Knight, our principal Secretarie for that our kingdome, and of his good affectione to doe ws service, by performing our trust reposed in him Wee are moved, in regard thareof, and for his better encouragement, and enabling him for our said service, to advance and promove him to be one of the Commissioners of our Excheckq^r in that kingdome. It is tharefore our will and pleasor, and wee doe heirby require you, that, heaving administrat vnto him the oathe accustomed in the like caise, yee admitt him to be one of the Commissioners of our said Excheckq^r, receaving him in that place, as one of your number. ffor doing whareof, these presents shalbe vnto you, and everie of you, a sufficient warrant. Given &c. at Whithall, the 11 of July 1628.

TO THE EXCHECKQUER.

1628
November 7

[CHARLES R.]

Right, &c. Whareas wee were formerlie plessed to assigne the payment of Sax Thousand punds Sterling, granted by our late dear Father to our trustie and weelbeloved counsellare, Sir William Alexander, our Secretarie, his airs and assignais, to be paid out of the benefit arysing to ws out of the Pryses, or concealed moneyis due by the taxationes; heaving hard from you how convenient it wer, that our share of the Pryses, for the incres of our custumes, should be lett out with them, according to that overture made by John Peebles for farming of the custumes, tending soe much to the advancing of our realme, which we wisch to be fordered, We are pleased tharewith; but withall, that the said Sir William be not disapointed of that which doth rest vnto him vnpayed of the said grant, Oure plesour is, that heaving hard from Sir James Bailyee, that the said Sir William have resaved out of the said prises or otherwayis, that you caus our receavers or custumers intromet with the said part of the prises to our vse, after such maner as you shall think expedient, and that you give order, that the said Sir William, his airs and assignais, may be payed out of our rentis, custumes, and casualities, or conceilment forsaids, of the said remainder; as likewayis, in consideration of his long want of the samen of that part of the Prise wines due vnto ws, which he should have hade bot was given for payment of the mariners. ffor doing whareof, and for securing him thareof in any maner you shall think it fitt, these presents shalbe vnto you a sufficient warrant. Whithall, the 7 of November 1628.

TO HIS MAJESTIE IN FAVOURS OF SOME UNDERTAKERS FOR NOVA SCOTIA.

Most Sacred Soverane.

We haue beene petitioned in name of some interrested in New Scotland and Canada holdin of your Matie crowne of this kingdome humblie shewing that by vertew of rights of lands made vnto thame by your Matie or by Sir Wilhame Alexander your Matie leutennent of these bounds they haue alreadye adventured sowmes of money for setting furth of a Colonie to plant there and intending God willing to prosecute the same And that they understand that by reasoun of a voyage made by ane Captaine Kich thither this last Sommer there ar some making sute to your Majestie for a new Patent of the saids lands of Canada and of the trade thairof to be holdin of your Matie Crowne of England; which in our opinion will prove so derogatorie to this your ancient kingdome, vnder the Great Seale whereof your Matie hes alreadie granted a right to the saids bounds And will so exceedinglie discourage all vndertakers of that kynde as we cannot but at thar humble sute represent the same to your Matie humblie intreatting that your Matie may be gratiouslie pleased to take this into your princelie consideration as no right may be heerefter graunted of the saids lands contrarie to your Matie said preceding graunt But that they may be still holdin of the Crowne of this your ancient kingdome according to the purport and trew intentioun of your Matie said former graunt And we ar verie hopefull that as the said Sir William Alexander hes sent furth his Sonne with a Colonie to plant thare this last yeere So it sall be secunded heerefter by manie other Vndertakers of good worth for the advancement of your Matie service increasse of your revenewes and honour of this your said ancient kingdome And so with the continuance of our most humble services and best prayers for your Matie health and happines We humblie take leave as your Matie most humble and faithfull servants

(*Sic Subscribitur.*)

Mar	A. Carre.
Monteith.	Arch. Achesoun.
Hadintoun.	Aduocat.
Wintoun.	Clerk Register.
Linlithgow.	Sir George Elphinstoun.
Lauderdaill.	Scottistarvett.
Tracquair.	

Halyrudhous, 18 *Novembris* 1628.

COMMISSION TO SIR WILLIAM ALEXANDER AND OTHERS to   1629.
make a voyage into the Gulfe and River of Canada, and the parts adjacent, for   February 4.
the sole trade of Beaver Wools, Beaver Skins, Furrs, Hides & Skins of Wild
Beasts. 4 Car. 1. [4 Feb. 1629.[1]]

AN EXTRACT OF THE PATENT GRAUNTED TO S[R] WILLIAM   [1629 ?]
ALEXANDER CONCERNING CANADA.[2]

In the Commission graunted to S[r] William Alexander the Younger & others
(whereof the Preface alleageth the Discovery made by them of a beneficiall Trade
for divers Comoditys to be had in the Gulf & River of Canada & parts adjacent
and his Ma[ties] Resolution thereupon to incorporate them for the sole Trading in
these parts upon further Discovery to be made by them

The said S[r] William Alexander, &c are assigned as Com[ers] for the making of a
Voyage into the said Gulf, River & parts adjacent for the sole Trade, &c. with
Power to settle a Plantation within all the Parts of the said Gulfe & River above
those parts which are over against Kebeck or the south side, or above Twelve
Leagues below Todowsack on the North side.   -

Prohibiting all others to make any Voyage into the said Gulfe or River, or any
the parts adjacent to any the purposes aforesaid upon payne of Confiscation of
their Goods & Shipping so employed, which the Comissioners are authorized to
seize unto their owne use.

Power given them to make Prize of all French or Spanish Ships & Goods at
Sea or Land, &c and to displant the French.

Power of Government amongst themselves.

Covenant of further Letters Patents of Incorporation or otherwise for settling
the Trade & Plantation.

Saving of all former Letters Patents.

TO THE ERLE OF MONTEATH, SIR WILLIAM ALEXANDER, AND   1629
SIR ARCHEBALD ACHESONE.   [May 2]
[CHARLES R.]

Right, &c. Whareas, according to the course begun by our late deare Father,
Wee wer pleased to give order for creating of knight Baronettis within that our
kingdome, for the planting of the Plantatione of New Scotland, as the commissione
given for that effect particularlie beares, and heaveing alwayis a desire that those

---

[1] Colonial Papers, p 96   [2] Ib p. 96

of the most antient families and best estattes might be first preferred; notwithstanding that they had been duelie warrant by proclamatione for that purpos, yet
out of our ernest desire to give them all ressoneabill satisfactione, wee did sign
Patents for sundrie of them, that, in cais they should in due time accept thareof,
they might tak place from the signing the same, notwithstanding that others,
whose patentis wer signed by ws tharefter, had passed our Great Seall before them.
And becaus the most part of those patents being signed by ws at one time, wee
suld not then give order by making of them of severall dates for thare particulare proceedingis as was requirit, Oure Pleasour is, that you, or any twoe of
you, heaveing considered of the qualitie and estate of these for whome such patents
wer signed, doe fill wpp the dates of everie one of them, as yow in your discretione
shall think fitt: for doing whareof, these presents shalbe vnto you a sufficient
warrand, which Wee will you to insert in your books of Counsell or Sessione, iff
yee shall find it expedient.   And soe, &c.   From our Court at Greenwitche.

<table>
<tr><td>1629
October 17</td><td></td></tr>
</table>

TO THE COUNSELL.

[CHARLES R]

Right, &c. Whereas our trustie and weelbeloved Sir William Alexander our
Secretarie, hathe agreet withe some of the heads of the cheef Clannes of the Heigh-
lands of that our kingdome, and with some other persones, for transporting themselves and tharo followers, to setle themselves into New Scotland, as we doe wery
much approve of that course for advancing the said plantatione, and for debordening
that our kingdome of that race of people, which, in former times, hade bred soe
many troubles ther; soe since that purpose may werie much impart the publick
good and quiet thareof, Wee are most willing that you assist the same, by all fair
and laufull wayis; and becaus, as wee are informed, divers are willing to contribute for thare dispatche by thare means, Wee require you to tak the best and
most faire counsel heirin that possibillie you can, that a voluntarie Contributione
may be made for that purpos, in such maner as you shall think most fitt and
that you substitute any persones whom you shall think expedient for the managing and collectione thareof.   Given at Hamptoune Court, the 17 of October 1629.

TO THE CONTRACTERS FOR BARRONETTS.

1629
November 17.

[CHARLES R.]

Right, &c. Whareas wee vnderstand that out of your regard to our service, and
the honor of that our antient kingdome, for forthering the plantatione of New
Scotland, soe oftentimes recommendit by our late dear Father, and by our selff,
you have agreet with our trustie, &c. Sir Williame Alexander, oure secretarie for

Scotland, for advancing great soumes of money for that purpos, taking the benefitt that may arrise by the erectione of Barronettis of the number granted vnto him, as yet to be made for your releef, Wee doe heartlie thank you for the same, and doe accept it as a most singulare service done vnto ws, wishing you to proceed with confidence and diligence, that the nixt supplie may go out in time, ffor wee wilbe werie sorie and loath to sie you suffer for soe generous ane actione, which may tend soe much to our honour, and the good of that our kingdome; and for your better encouragement, and more speedie repayment, whersoever any persone of qualitie fitt for the dignitie of Barronet hath any particulare favor to crave of ws, wee will and allow yow, according to the severall charge that any of yow hath from ws, to require them first to accept of the said dignitie, according to the con-ditiones formerlie condiscendit vpon, with others which shall mak ws the more willing to gratiefie them, ffor wee desire much to have that work brought to per-fectione   Soe willing that this our letter be recorded in the books of our Counsell and Exchecqʳ, We, &c. Whitehall, the 17 Noʳ. 1629.

TO THE COUNSELL

[CHARLES R.]

Right trustie and right well-beloued Cousin and Counsellour, right trustie and well-beloued Cousins and Counsellouris, and right trustie and well-beloued Coun-sellouris, We Groete you well.

Whereas, vpon good consideration, and for the better advancement of the plan-tatione of New Scotland, which may much import the good of our service, and the honor and benefeitt of that our ancient kingdome, oure royall Father did intend, and we since have erected the order and titill of Baronet, in our said ancient Kingdome, which wee have since estabillished, and conferred the same vpon divers gentlemen of good qualitie; and sieing our trustie and well-beloued counsellor Sir Williame Alexander knight, our principall secretarie of that our ancient king-dome of Scotland, and our Leiwetennant of New Scotland, whoe these many yeirs bygone has been at great charges for the discoverie thareof, hath now in end setled a Colonie thare, where his sone, Sir Williame, is now resident; and we being most willing to afford all possible means of encouragement that convenientlie wee can to the Barronettis of that our ancient kingdome, for the furtherance of soe good a wark, and to the effect they may be honored, and have place in all respectis, according to their patents from ws, We have been pleased to authorise and allow, as be theis presents for ws and our successors we authorise and allow, the said Lewetennent and Baronettis, and everie one of them, and thare heirs male, to weare and carry about their neckis in all time coming, ane orange tauney-silk ribbane, whairon shall hing pendant in a scutchion *argent* a saltoire *azeuer*, thairon ane

G

inscutcheeine of the armes of Scotland, with ane imperiall creune above the scutchone, and incircled with this motto, FAX MENTIS HONESTÆ GLORIA · Which cognoissance oure said present Leivetennent shall deliver now to them from ws, that they may be the better knowen and distinguished from other persones · And that none pretend ignorance of the respect due vnto them, Oure pleasure therefore is, that, by oppen proclamatione at the markett crosse of Edinburgh, and all other head borrows of our kingdome, and such other places as you shall think necessarie, you caus intimat our Royal pleasor and intentione herin to all our subjectis : And if any persone, out of neglect or contempt, shall presume to tak place or precedence of the said barronettis, thare wiffes or childring, which is due vnto them by thare Patents, or to wear thare cognoissance, wee will that, vpon notice thareof given to you, you caus punish such offendars, by prisoning and fyning of them, as you shall think fitting, that others may be terriefied from attempting the like : And We ordane that, from tyme to tyme, as occasione of granting and renewing thair patents, or thair heirs succeiding to the said dignitie, shall offer, That the said poware to them to carie the said ribbine, and cognoissance, shalbe tharein particularlie granted and inserted; And Wee likewayis ordaine these presents to be insert and registrat in the books of our Counsell and Excheeq^r, and that you caus registrat the same in the books of the Lyone king at armes, and heraulds, thare to remain *ad futuram rei memoriam*, and that all parties having entres [interest] may have autentick copies and extractis thareof · And for your see doing, These our lettres shalbe vnto you, and everie one of you, from tyme to tyme your sufficient warrant and discharge in that behalf. Given at our Court of Whythall, the seventeinthe of November 1629.

> To our right trustie and right well-beloned cousin and
> counsellour; to our right well-beloued cousins and
> counsellouris; to our right trustie and well-beloued
> counsellouris, and trustie and well-beloued coun-
> sellouris, the Viscount of Dupleine, our Chanceilor
> of Scotland, the Earle of Monteith, the President,
> and to the remanent Earls, Lords, and otheris of
> our Privie Counsell of our said kingdome.

TO THE ERLE OF MONTEATH.

1629
November 26 [CHARLES R.]

Right, &c. Whareas Wee have been delt with for divers persons of that our kingdome, that they might be advanced to titles of honor, some by a new creatione, and others by being raised to a more heigh dignitie then they presently enjoy, Sieing these prefermentis are the cheef markis of a princes favor, whareby the present age and the posteritie tak notice of his judgement, and of the subjectis, as they find them to be conferred, Wee will noe way proceed in that kind but vpon due consideratione: And tharefor it is our pleasor, that you, as one whome wee speciallie trust, informe yourselff, and adverteis us, of the qualitie and service done, or to be done, vnto us, by any whoe desire that favor, and that you have a care to acquent ws whoe of them have any heretable office, shirreffship, baillierie, stewardrie, or regalitie, That they first agrie for the same, for wee will not advance them with whome we are to plead for recovering our right to estabillishe that which wee intend for the good of that our kingdome: But whare non of them have any such thing to demitt, That thare may be some publick service done for thare preferment, It is our forder plesour, that you agree with them for some ressonable number of persons to be furneshit out, vpon thare charges, towards the plantatione of New Scotland, at the sight of our trustie, &c. Sir William Alexander, oure Leivetennent of that bounds, whareby he may be supplied in that great wark, and that our Aduocat, heaving considered those thingis recommendit vnto [you], draw up, and docett the Patents of such as you agrie with, and send them vnto us, that Wee tharefter may proceed as we think fitt. Soe recommending this vnto your care, Wee, &c. Whitehall, the 26 November 1629.

A PRECEPT IN FAVOUR OF SIR W. ALEXANDER.

1629
December 10

[Charles R.]

Wheareas formerlie wee directed a precept vnto Sir James Baillie Knight, that heaving the same charge in our service wharewith you are now entrusted, to pay vnto Sir William Alexander Knight, oure principal secretarie for Scotland, the soume of Sex Thousand pounds sterling, out of our parte of the Prise moneyis, which the saids Sir James was then ordained to resave, and are now appointed to come vnto the Excheckq^r: Tharefore oure plesor is, and wee doe heirby will and require you, vpon the sight heiroff, to pay vnto the said Sir William Alexander, or his assignais, That which you shall find remaining vnpayed of the said precept, and that out of the first and reddiest of our rentis and casualties, or out of any other moneyis belonging vnto ws, presently remaining in your custodie, or that shall nixt come into your hands · And for your soe doing, thes presents shalbe vnto you a sufficient warrand: And [Wee] doe hereby command our treasurer, deputie treasurer, commissioners of our excheq^r, and all others auditors whoe are or shalbe herefter, to allow and defeas vnto you the remanendare of the said Sir William his precept, vpon accompt. Whitehall, the 10 of December 1629.

To our trustie and weelbeloved Mr David Fullertone,
      one of the Receavers of our rentis in Scotland.

1629
December 24 ACT ANENT THE COGNOISSANCE OF THE KNIGHT BARONNETS

Apud Halyrudhous 24 *die mensis Decembris* 1629

The whilk day the missive vnderwrittin signed be the Kingis Matie being presented to the Lords of Secreit Counsell and read in thair audience The saids Lords according to the diectioun of the said missive Ordanes the same to be insert and registrat in the Bookes of Priuie Counsell and Exchecker And siclyke thay ordaned the same to be registrat in the Bookes of the Lyoun King at Armes and Heraulds thairin to remaine *ad futuram rei memoriam* And that all parteis having interesse may have authentick copeis and extracts thairof. Of the whilk missive the tennour followes.

    CHARLES R.

Right trustie and right, &c.   .   .   .   . [See *supra*, p. 49]
Whitehall, the 17 of November 1629.

[In the Acts of Privy Council a copy of the Proclamation is subjoined, which, as usual, is a mere repetition of the King's letter.]

1629
December. TO THE GOVERNOUR OF THE TOUN OF PLIMMOUTH

[CHARLES R.]

Whareas Wee have directed Samuell Jude, post of our toune of Plimmouth, to repair thither for conducting, and bringing hither to our Court, one of the commanders of Cannada, attended by some others of that countree, whoe is directed to ws, in name of the rest, Wee doe heirby will and require you to give vnto him all the laufull fortherance shalbe found requisit for thare conducting and transportatione hither, with all such provisiones as they have to bring along with them, And that you signifie this our pleasour to any others whom it may concern.

    To our trustie and weelbeloved Sir James Bagg knight,
        Governour of our toune of Plymmouthe, and to all
        other our officiars, to whome thes presents doethe or
        may concern.

1630
February 4 TO SIR WILLIAM ALEXANDER.

[CHARLES R.]

Right, &c. Whareas Wee have, by our infeftment vnder the Great Seall of our kingdome of Scotland, granted vnto you, and your heirs, authoritie to be our

Leivetennent of New Scotland, and Cannada, with pouare to confer titles of honour thare vpon such inhabitantis as shalbe aidding and assisting vnto the plantatione thareof; and whareas also, for the better encouragement of our subjectis of our said kingdome, to plant and contribute towards the plantatione of the said country, Wee have erected the Order and dignitie of Knight Baronet in our said kingdome of Scotland, and by our lettres have appointed and licensed the Knight Baronetts of our said kingdome to carie and weare a cognissance, and orange tauney ribbane about thare neckis, Therefore, wee doe alsoe heirby authorise and require you, and your heirs and successors, to authorise, licence, and appoint the Baronetts of New Scotland and Cannada, appointed or heirefter to be appointed, by you, or them, in the said territorie and dominione of New Scotland and Cannada, to wear and carie the like cognissance, and ribbane for thare better distinctione from the others freeholders, and inhabitantis thareof, and that you caus registrat this our warrand in the books of Councell, Sessione, and Excheq^r of our said kingdome, and in the Registers of our said territorie and dominione of New Scotland · And for your soe doing theis our lettres, given vnder our Privie Signett, shalbe vnto you, and your heirs and successors, a sufficient warrand in that behalf. Whitehall, the fourt day of Februar 1630.

MEMOIR OF THE FRENCH AMBASSADOR.[1]

1630
February 1

L'Ambassadeur de France Supplie Sa Majesté de la Grande Bretagne qu'il lui plaise ordonner et conformer à ce que a esté promis et accordé par les articles du xxiiie Auril der^{nr} au Cap^{ne} Querch et au Sieur Guillaume Alexandre et relevans de ses subiects, qui sont ou sejourneront en la Nouvelle France, de s'en retirer et *remettre entre les mains de ceux quil plaira au Roy Son Maistre d'y enuoier, et seront porteurs de sa commission,* tous les lieux et places quilz y ont occupez et habitez depuis ces derniers mouuemens, et par encore la forteresse et habitacion de *Quebec, Costes du Cap Breton, et Port Roial* prins et occupez, scauoir la forteresse de Quebec par le Cap^{ne} Querch, et les costes du Cap Breton et Port Roial par leis Sieur Guillaume Alexandre Ecossois depuis le xxiiii^e Auril der^{er}. Et d'eux remettre en mesme estat quilz les ont trouuez sans desmolir les fortes Creaons, ny bastimens des habitations, ny emporter aucunes armes, munitions, marchandises ny vstencilles de celles qui y estoient lors de la prinse, quilz seront tenuz de rendre et restituer auec touttes les pelletteries quilz ont apportées despuis, ensemble la patache commandée par le Cap^{ne} de Caen qui a esté amenée en Angleterre, comme aussi la nauire nommée la Marie de St Jean de Luz du port de soix^{te} dix tonneaux

---

[1] Colonial Papers, p 107 —The transcript of this letter being in some parts unintelligible, it was found necessary to correct the reading of a few words by conjecture.

qui a esté prins par leis Sieur Alexandre au des baleines coste du Cap Breton, et partie des hommes ramenez ici [par] le Cap^ne Pomercy.

(*In dorso.*) MEMOIRE.—Whereby the French Amb^r desires his Matie to give order for the restitution of all the places taken in Canada by the English and Scotts during these late troubles, Item of all the goods and ships brought from thence hither. All in manner as taken, &c.

1630
February.

A CHARLES ST ESTIENNE BARRON.

Trés chère et bien aymé, vos lettres   .   .   .   .   .

.   .   .   .   .

[A blank space is left at fol. 480 in Sir William Alexander's Register for the continuation of this letter.]   In the margin, "Letters Francois."

1630
February 20

THE LORD OCHILTREE'S INFORMATION.[1]

[The author of the following information was Sir James Stewart of Killeith, eldest son of Captain James Stewart, Earl of Arran. He acquired the Lordship of Ochiltree in 1615, but according to Scotstarvet he only "enjoyed the estate a few years, and was forced to sell all for defraying his debts" This may possibly have induced him to establish a colony at Cape Breton In May 1629 Charles the First authorised the sum of Five hundred Pounds sterling "to be borrowed for the use of Lord Ochiltree, being for his present expedition to Cape Britton for a planting of a colony there." The King on the 10th of December following signed a precept for the repayment of the said sum. But on the 10th September 1629, Lord Ochiltree and many of the settlers were treacherously taken prisoners by Captain Daniel of Dieppe; some were carried to England, while Lord Ochiltree and seventeen others were taken to France, suffering great hardship from the barbarous and perfidious carriage of the French. He estimated his losses at £20,000 The English Ambassador, Sir Thomas Edwards, on the 22d January 1629-30, having made a formal complaint of such usage, his Lordship was set at liberty, as no just cause could be found for his detention —(Colonial Papers, pp 104-106.) On the 24th of April that year, Lord Ochiltree had a patent as a Knight-Baronet. In April 1631, he had renewed his intentions to plant a Colony near the river of Canada [2] But before his patent had passed the Great Seal, in consequence of his being under a criminal process, the King, about the close of 1631, ordered this grant not to be recorded.[3] This process was occasioned

---

[1] Colonial Papers, p 106.   [2] Infra, p 64   [3] See also infra, p 70

by Lord Ochiltree having accused James Marquess of Hamilton of high treason, but when the charge was tried, Crawfurd (Peerage, p. 375) says, "the story appear'd to be a piece of the most notorious folly and forgery that ever was invented; for which he was condemned to perpetual imprisonment in Blackness Castle." Here he was kept till the year 1652 when, being released by the English, he "took himself to be a Doctor of Medicine, by which means he sustains himself and his family."—(Scot of Scotstarvet.) He died in 1659.]

INFORMATION, &c,

1630
February.

The Kinge off France by his commissione doeth assure to himself all that part of America wch lyeth, eleuationne from the fortie too the sixty degree, whereby he doeth incluid the River of Canada, all Acady, wch incluids all New Ingland and New Scotland. Theas lying in lenthe by the sea coast some six hundrithe myllis.

By this he assumis to himself the sole priuiledge and benefitt off fisching, at this tyme the cheef commerce off France whereby in few yeeris he wilbe able to nourissh ane seminary and nurcery off saillers and seamen above ony king in the world And in this land he hathe bothe the commerce as also the occasioun and means off building or causing boold what schips he pleasis, and all thayr furnitur, and the brauest harborys in the world, so that he may frame his schips off what burding he pleases He intends, as Captain Danyell hes publickly confessit and professed, the supplantatioune of theas Colonyes off the Inglis in New Ingland, and the making pryss off all the Inglish schipps going thither; and to this effectt he goeth in ane schipp off the King of Frances this zeir, accompanied with too [two] other smaller schips, and too hundrethe men in euery off them.

That the Kyng of Britane hath as guid right to theas lands as to England I hoop the estate off England knowes it, and I know it can be instructed; and I know it is better then Ingland and Scotland bothe in respect off the climat, the goodnes off ye soylls, and riche contrie, iff it were peopled, wch is easy to the King of Britane to doo hauing alreddy in theas parts above seuen thousand of his Maties subjects.

Captan Danyell is the whol projector of this to the State of France. he is to secound the Jesuits in this cours, he the agent and they the plotters, he is to part from Deep betwix an the twenty off February with theas his thrie schips. Iff he resaue nocht interruptionne in his courss this zeir, it will with moir difficulty and damage both heirefter; for he hathe professed, wch shalbe verified befor Captan Fener and the Lo. Wcheltrie, that the King of France did mynd nothing by the peace with Ingland bot to endur for too zeiris till he secured America and peceably possessed himself therein

(In dorso) The Lo Ewcheltreis Information.

1630
April 15

SECRETARY VISCOUNT DORCHESTER TO SIR ISAAC WAKE, AMBASSADOR IN FRANCE.[1]

In one only point Monsieur de Chasteauneuf seemed to goe away ill satisfyed, that he could not obtayne a direct promise from his Ma^ty for ye restoring of Port Royall, joyning to Canada where some Scottishmen are planted vnder the title of Nova Scotia. This Plantation was authorised by King James of happy memorie vnder Letters Patents of ye Kingdome of Scotland, and severall Priviledges granted vnto some principal Persons of ranke and quality of this Kingdome wth condition to vndertake the same: True it is, it was not begun till towards the end of ye warre wth France, when some of his Maty^s subjects of that Kingdome went to Port Royall, and there seated themselves in a place where no French did inhabite Monsr de Chasteauneuf pretending (rather out of his owne discourse, as wee here conceiue, then by commission) that all should be quitt in state as it was before the warre, and by consequence those men w^thdrawne, hath pressed his Ma^ty earnestly for that purpose, and his Ma^ty w^thout refusing or granting hath taken time to aduise of it letting him know thus much that vnles he found reason as well before, as since the warre, to have that place free for his subjects plantation he would recall them, but in case he shall find the Plantation free for them in time of Peace, the French will have no cause to pretend possession thereof, in regard of the warre, meanwhile Kebec (which is a strong fortified place in the River of Canada, wch the English tooke) his Ma^ty is content should be restored because the French were removed out of it by strong hand and whatsoever was taken from them in that Fort shall be restored likewise, whereby may appear the reality of His Ma^ty^s proceedings; and this I advertise your Lp. for your information, not that it should be needfull for you to treate or negotiate in it, but to ye end, that, if it should be spoken of vpon Mons^er de Chasteauneuf returne, you should not be ignorant how the businesso passed.   DORCHESTER.

Whitehall, 15 Aprill 1630.

(*In dorso.*) Lord of Dorchester to Sr I^c Wake, 15 Aprill
1630 Plantation of Canada, Nova Scotia, Port Royall
and Kebec

TO SIR WILLIAM ALEXANDER, YOUNGER

1630
May 31

[CHARLES R]

Trustie, &c. Heaving vnderstood by your letter, and more ample by report of others, of the good success of your voyage, and of the carefull and provident pro-

---

[1] Colonial Papers, p 113

ceeding for planting of a colonie at Port Royall, which may be a means to settle all that cuntrie in obedience, We give you harthe thanks for the same, and doe wish you (as wee are confident you will,) to continew, as you have begune, that the wark may be brought to the intendit perfectione , which wee will esteem as one of the most singulare services done vnto ws, and of you accordinglie, and of everie one of your company, that have been good instruments in the same, as wee shall have a testimonie of them from you. Soe recommending vnto you that you have a special care before you return, to tak a good coarse for government of the Colonie during your absence Wee bid you farewell. Whitehall, the 13 day of May 1630.

TO EARLES, LORDS, GENTLEMEN, KNYGHTS : GENERAL CONVENTION.

1630
July 3

[CHARLES R.]

Right, &c Being informed of your affection and habilite to doe ws service and desyreing to have a prooff of the same at this tyme wherin sindrie things are to be proponed from ws for the good of that kingdome as will appear by the Articles which we have sent for that effect And that yow may be the better informed we have desyred our trustie and weilbeloved Counsellour Sir William Alexander principall Secretarie for our kingdome of Scotland to acquant yow more particularlie therwith whom yow shall trust in any thing that he doeth delyver vnto yow in our name concerning our service at this tyme and as we find your endeavours to prove we will acknowledge the same accordinglie. Whythall, 3 July 1630.

> Ane Letter to ane Erle and two Lordes and two gentlemen of the tenour and date of the precedent, and ane to Lochinvar, of the tenour and date of the precedent, with this clause more, " As lykwayes in the Treatie with yow concerning your Bailharie and Regalitie."

TO THE COUNSELL· SIR W ALEXANDER IN NEW SCOTLAND.

1630
July 3

[CHARLES R.]

Right trustie and right weilbelouit Cousin and Counsellour, right trustie and right weilbelouit cousins and counsellours, right trustie and weilbelouit counsellours, and trustie and weilbelouit counsellours, We greite yow weill : There being at this tyme some contraversie betwixt Ws and the French, concerneing the title of landes in America, and particularlie New Scotland, it being alledgeit that Port Royall, wher the Scottish Colonie is planted, should be restored as takin since the making of the peace, by reasone of the Articles made concerneing

H

the same: As we ar bund in dewtie and justice to discharge what we owe to everie nyghbour Prince, so we must have a care that none of our subjects doe suffer in that which they have vndertakin, vpon just grounds, to doe ws service, nather would we determine in a matter of so great moment till we vnderstude the trew esteat thairof Thairfoir our pleasur is, that yow tak this bussines into your consideratioun, And becaus we desyre to be certifeid how farre we and our subjects ar interested thairin, and what arguments ar fitt to be vsed when any questioun shall occure concerneing the same for the defence thairof, that efter dew information we may be furnished with reasons how we are bound to manteane the Patents that our late dear Father and We have gevin. So expecting that having informed your selffis sufficientlie of this bussines, yow will returne ws ane answer with diligence. We bid you farewell. Frome our Court at Whitehall, the third July 1630

THE GENERAL CONVENTION.[1]

CHARLES R.

Right trustie, &c. Being informed of your affection and abilitie to doe ws service and desyreing to have a prooff of the same at this tyme wherin sindrie things are to be propounded from ws for the good of that kingdome as will appear by the Articles which we have sent for that effect And that yow may be better informed we have requyred our trustie &c Sir William Alexander our principall secretarie of that our kingdome to acquant yow more particularlie therwith whome yow shall trust in any thing he doeth delyver vnto yow in our name concerneing our service at this tyme And as We find your endeavours to prove we will acknowledge the same accordinglie. At Nonsuche, 14 July 1630.

Ther ar two letters more verbatim ut supra Ther ar four
letters more verbatim, Trustie and Weilbeloved
Thrie Ratifications signed the same tyme, one of the Act
of Interruption One thereof the determinations and
Act of annuitie And the thrid in favours of the Barronetts of the title of Barionett.

DIGNITIE OF KNIGHT BARRONETTS.

CHARLES R.

Right trustie and right weilbelouit cousine and counseller right trustie and weilbelouit cousins and Counsellouis right trustie and weilbelouit counsellours right

---

[1] The proceedings of the Convention of Estates in July 1630 are printed in Acts, vol v p 208, et seq.

trustie and trustie and weilbelouit We greīt you weill Having given furth ane
decree vpon these things q^{lks} wer submitted vnto us in suche sort as after dew
informatioun (having heard all parteis) we conceaved to be best for the publict
good and having given order for making interruptioun that we might no way be
prejudged by the act of præscriptioun, whiche we can never thinke wes at first
intended for anie prejudice of the Crowne, we made choise rather to obviat anie
inconvenient that may come thairby by publict acts in counsell then to trouble a
number of our heges by particular citatiouns Thairfoir we have thought fitt to
recommend the same vnto yow that they may be confirmed by yow our Estaits
conveened by ws at this time And lykewayes where our lait deere Father and we
have erected the dignitie of Baronnets for advancing the Plantatioun of New Scotland, granting lands thairwith for that effect Wee recommend lykewayes the same
in so farre as sall be lawfullie demanded to be confirmed by yow And so not
doubting bot that yow will be carefull both of these and all other things that may
import the honnour of that Kingdome or the good of our service We bid you
farcweill. Frome our court at Nonsuche, the 14 of July 1630

HIS MAJESTIE'S MISSIVE ANENT PORT ROYALL IN NEW SCOTLAND.

Apud Halyrudhous vicesimo die mensis Julij 1630.

The whilk day Sir William Alexander principall Secretar to our Soverane
Lord gave in the missive letter underwritten signed be the King's Majestie and
directed to the saids Lords, of the whilk the tennour followes.

CHARLES R.

Right trustie and right weilbelouit Cousine and Counsellour, &c.   .   .   .
.   .   .   .   [See *supra*, p. 57.]
At Whitehall, the third day of July 1630.

Quhilk letter being read and considderit be the said Lords, They ordaine the
said Sir William Alexander whom this business concernes to attend the Lords
Chancellor, Thesaurair, Præsident, Lord Gordoun and Advocat, and to propone
unto thame the reasouns and arguments for defence of his Majestie's right,
Togidder with the objectiouns moved be the Frenche for recoverie of the same;
To the intent the Counsell upon report thairof, being trewlie informed of the
estait and nature of the bussines may certifie backe to his Majestie thair opinion
thereanent.

1630
July 31

RATIFICATIOUN OF THE ORDER OF KNIGHT BAROUNETS [1]

Apud Halyrudhous Vltimo die mensis Julij 1630

The Estates presentlie conveened all in one voice ratifies allowes approves and confirmes the dignitie and order of Knight Barounets erected be his Matie and his lait deere Father of blessed memorie and conferred by thame vpon sindrie Gentlemen of good qualitie for thair better encouragement and retributioun of thair vndertakings in the Plantatioun of New Scotland with all the acts of Secreit Counsell and proclamatiouns following thairvpon, made for maintening of the said dignitie place and precedence thairof, and ordains the same dignitie place and precedence dew thairto to continew and stand in force in all tyme comming, and that intimatioun be made heirof to all his Ma^teis leiges be opin proclamatioun at the mercat croce of Edinburgh and other places neidfull

Followes his Ma^teis missive for warrand of the Act abouewritten

[See *supra*, pp. 58, 59.]

1630.
July 31

ANENT NEW SCOTLAND. [2]

The Estaits presentlie conveened having dewlie considderit the benefite arysing to this Kingdome by the accessioun of New Scotland and of the successfull plantatioun alreadie made there by the gentlemen vndertakers of the same In regarde whairof and that the saids lands and territoreis of New Scotland ar by the patent thairof made in favours of Sr Wilhame Alexander of Menstrie Knight his Ma^teis Secretarie annexed to the Crowne Thairfoir the saids Estaits all in one voice hes concluded and agreed that his Matie sall be petitioned to mainteane his right of New Scotland And to protect his subjects vndertakers of the said plantatioun in the peaceable possessioun of the same As being a purpose highlie concerning his Ma^teis honnour and the good and credite of this his ancient Kingdome.

1630
September 9

TO HIS MAJESTIE, ANENT NEW SCOTLAND.

MOST SACRED SOUERANE.

We have vnderstood by your Ma^teis letter of the title pretendit by the Frenshe to the Lands of New Scotland, Whiche being communicat the Estaits at thair lait meiting, and they considering the benefite arysing to this kingdome by the accession of these lands to the Crowne and that your Matie is boundin in honnour carefullie to provyde That nane of your Ma^teis subjects doe suffer in that whiche for

---

[1] Acta, vol v p 223   [2] Ib p 224

your Ma^tels service and to thair greit charge they haue warrantablie vndertakin and successfullie followed out We haue thairupoun presoumed by order from the Estaits to make remonstrance thairof to your Matie and on thair behalffe to be humble supplicants to your Matie that your Matie would be gratiouslie pleased seriouslie to take to heart the maintenance of your Royall right to those lands and to protect the Vndertakers in the peaceable possessioun of the same, as being a bussines whiche tuiches your Ma^teis honnour, the credite of this your native kingdome, and the good of your subjects interessed thairin. Remitting the particular reasoun fitt to be vsed for defence of your Ma^tels right to the relatioun of Sir William Alexander your Ma^teis Secretare who is intrusted thairwith, We humblie pray the Almightie God to blesse yor Matie with a long and happie raigne, and wee rest

Your Majesties most humble and obedient Subjects and Seruitours.

MORTOUN	HAMILTON.
WINTOUN	S^R THOMAS HOPE
LAUDERDAILL.	SCOTTISTARVET.

Halyrudhous, 9 *Septembris* 1630.
(*In dorso.*) To the Kings Most sacred and Excellent Maiestie.

REASONS ALLEAGED BY THE SCOTTISH ADUENTURERS FOR THE HOLDING OF PORT ROYAL, &c.[1]

1630.
September 9

Immediatcly about the time that Columbus discoucred the Isle of Cuba, Sebastian Chabot set out from England by Henrie the Seventh did first discouer the continent of America, beginning at the Newfoundland, and thereafter going to the Gulph of Canada and from thence hauing seen Cape Bretton all along the coast to Florida: By which discouery his Matie hath the title to Virginia, New England and New Scotland, as being then first discoucred by Chabot at the charge of the king of England.

The French after this neglecting the knowledge they had thereafter by Jaques Cartier of the river of Canada as a cold climat, or as it may bee in regard it was challenged as first discovered by the English, hauing a great desire to possesse themselves in some part of America, they planted first a colony vnder the charge of Monsr Villegagnon in Brasill, and another vnder the charge of Monsr Laudoñiere in Florida, from both of which they were expelled by the Spaniards.

Then giving ouer all hope of attempting any thing that was belonging to the Spaniards, and pressing by all meanes to haue some interest in America, notwithstanding that the English (though they were not able to possesse the whole at

[1] Colonial Papers, p 119. Annexed is a copy of the preceding letter from the Council of Scotland, September 9, 1630.

first) had possessed themselves of that continent, discouered by them, by a Colonie in the South part thereof was now called Virginia and by another in the north part thereof now called New England and New Scotland, planted by Justice Popham. The French in the time of Henry the fourth, under the charge of Monsieur Pontrincourt, hauing scene all the coasts of New England and New Scotland to both which parts they did then beginne to claim right · They seated themselves in Port Royal, Out of which, as soon as it was made known to the English, they were displanted by Sʳ Samuel Argall, as hauing wrongfully intruded themselues Within those bounds which did belong to this Crowne, both by discouery and possession.

The remainder of this French Collony not hauing occasion to be transported to France stayed still in the contrie Yet they were neglected by the State not owning them any more and hardly supplied in that which was neccessary for them by volontary adventurers, who came to trade in hope of their comodities in Exchange of what they bought And during the time of King James there was no complaint made vpon Sʳ Samuel Argall for hauing displanted them, and they were now lately glad to demand that protection from his Maᵗⁱᵉ which was not afforded them from any other Whereby it may euidentlye appeare, that his Maᵗⁱᵉˢ title was thought good, otherwise it is likely the French King, if any wrong had been done vnto him, would haue sought to haue had the same repaired, either by treatie or otherwise But without making either any priuat complaint, or yet doing any publick Act against the same They went next and seated themselues vpon the north side of the Riuer of Canada at Kibeck, a place whereunto the English by a preceding title might likewise haue claimed right: But small notice was taken thereof till during the time of the late Warre a Commission was given by his Maᵗⁱᵉ to remove them from thence, which was accordingly performed, the place being taken, a little after the peace was concluded, which at that time had not come to the takers knowledge, and a Colonie of Scottish was planted at Port Royal, which had never beene repossessed nor claimed by the French since they were first removed from the same.

This businesse of Port Royal cannot be made lyable to the Articles of the peace, seeing there was no act of hostilitie comitted therebye, a Colonny onely beeing planted vpon his Maᵗⁱᵉˢ owne ground, according to a Patent granted by his Maᵗⁱᵉˢ late deare father and Maᵗⁱᵉ selfe hauing as good right thereto as to any part of that Continent, and bothe the patent and the possession taken thereupon was in the time of his Maᵗⁱᵉˢ late deare Father, as is set downe at length in the Voyages written by Purchas. But neither by that possession nor be the subsequent plantation hath anything beene taken from the French whereof they had any right at all, or yet any possession for the time, and what might haue beene done either before the warre or since the warre, without a breach of peace cannot justly bee complained vpon for beeing done at that time.

After that the Scottish Colonie was planted at Port Royal, they and the French who dwelled there hauing met with the Commanders of the Natiues, called by them Sagamaes did make choice of one of the cheefe of them called Sagamo Segipt to come in name of the rest to his Matie for acknowledging of his title, and to become his Maties subjects crauing only to be protected by his Matie against their enemies, which demand of his was accepted by his Matie, who did promise to protect them, as he reported to the rest at his returne.

Mon^{sr} La Tour who was cheif command^r of the few French then in that Countrie beeing neglected (as is sayd) by his own Countriemen, and finding his Maties title not so much as questioned after their beeing expelled from Port Royal and the coming in of the Scottish necessary for his securitie, did along with the same Sagamo offring and demanding the like in the name of the French who liue there So that his Matie hath a good right to New Scotland by discouery, by possession of his Maties subjects, by removinge of the French, who had seated themselves at Port Royal, and by Mon^{sr} La Tour command^r of them there his turning Tenant and by the voluntarie hauing tenents of the rest to his Matie and that no obstacle might remaine the very Sauages by their Commissioner willingly offring their obedience vnto his Matie So that his Matie now is bound in honor to maintaine them, both in regard of his subjects that haue planted there upon his warrant and of the promises that he made to the Commissioner of the Natiues that came to him from them, as he promised to the Comissioners of the Natiues, And as all the subjects of his Maties ancient kingdome of Scotland did humbly entreat at their last Conuention, as may appeare by a letter to his Matie from his Counsel to that effect.
9 September 1630.

PETITION OF SIR WILLIAM ALEXANDER, CAPTAIN DAVID KIRKE, &c [1]

1631
February .

Petition of Sir Wil. Alexander, Capt. David Kirke, and Others, Adventurers in the Company of Canada, to the Admiralty. The King granted them commission some three years ago to plant colonies in the river of Canada, to displant those who were enemies in those lands, and to trade with the natives. Are informed that divers ships are bound thither, particularly the Whale of London, masters Richard Brewerton and Wolston Goslyn, contrary to that commission and greatly to the petitioners' prejudice. Pray that such vessels may be stayed or sufficient assurance given that they will prosecute no such voyage. Underwritten is a reference to Sec. Dorchester to examine the parties, and if they have intention to go into those parts, to order that they be stayed as is desired.

[1] Colonial Papers, p 128

PROPOSED WARRANT TO STAY CERTAIN SHIPS.[1]

Warrant for the stay of certain ships bound to Canada contrary to a commission granted to Sir Will. Alexander, Jarvis Kirke, and others who have been at great charges in settling and maintaining a colony and fort within those bounds (*Endorsed by Sec. Dorchester*). " Conceit of a letter for
hinderance of men going to Canada, desired by Sir
Wm. Alexander."

JUSTICES OF IRELAND.

[CHARLES R]

Right, &c. Wheras our right trustie and weilbeloved the Lord Ochiltrie Our trustie and weilbeloved Counsellours Sir Peirce Corsbie and Sir Archibald Achiesone kny[ts] and baronets and our trustie and weilbeloved Sir Walter Corsbie kny[t] and baronet intent to plant a Colonie nearer vnto the river of Canada in America Becaus the purpois is honorabill and may conduce to the good of our service our speciall pleasur is that from tyme to tyme as they or any of them shall have occasion yow grant them Commissions and warrants requisit for transporting thither such persones as shalbe willing to be imployed in that plantation And that yow licence and caus licence them and such as shall have ther or any of ther warrants to transport provisions of victuall ordinance munition and all other necessaries whatsoever fitt for ther vse ffor doing wherof as these presents shalbe vnto yow a sufficient warrant so we will accompt your care in forthering of them as good and acceptable service done vnto ws. We bid you farewell. Whythall, 19 Aprill 1631.

TO THE COUNSELL.

[CHARLES R.]

Right, &c. Wheras yow hath recommended to our princelie care the advancement and mantening of the work of Plantation of New Scotland being lykwyse petitioned by our whole Estats convened for taking some course which might best tend for effectuating that interpryse And doing of our selffes daylie more and more sensible how much the prosecution of it concerneth ws in honor and the state of that our antient kingdome many wayes in benefite, considering lykwyse the course which we had layd down for it in conferring a title of honor vpon some deserveing persones who should engadge themselffis for the advancement therof hath made but slow progress and that diverse noblemen and others generoushe

[1] Colonial Papers, p 128

affect have contracted with our trustie and weilbelouit Sir Wm Alexander our Secretarie who is speciallie intrusted by ws to prosecute that work for the more speedie effectuating of our designe in it, the doeing whereof is very acceptable vnto ws Our pleasur is that yow mak choyse of a certane number amonges your selffis of such as haue alreadie testifeid ther ernest affection to the work by contracting in that kynd with our said servand, that they may tak seriouslie vnto ther consideratiouns by what meanes our designes in this may be best accomplisched; that being acquanted therwith we may by your advyse tak such further course as shalbe requisit; ffor there shalbe nothing wanting in ws that may second so just desyres and honorabill designes: which earnesthe recommending vnto your care We bid yow farewell. Whythall, 29 Aprill 1631.

SIGNATURE OF COMMISSION FOR THE BARRONETTS.

1631
May 5.

These conteyne ane Ratificatioun of the two former Commissions of Barronetts and all Patents and Infeftments granted conforme thairto, preceiding the date heirof, with ane new commission gevin power to certane Commissioners above nominat or any fyve of them to receave resignation of lands lyand within the countrie of New Scotland, vpoun the resignation of your Ma^{teis} Secretarie Sir William Alexander Lieutennent of Nova Scotia; and to grant infeftments thairvpon of the saids lands to the persones in whois favours the samyne is made, togidder with the title and dignitie of Bairronett: And also conteynes ane Ratificatioun of the Seall and Armes of New Scotland, with power to the saids Commissioners, with advyse of the said Sir William Alexander, to change the samyne: and last, conteynes ane Ratificatioun of ane warrant gevin by your Matie to the saids Barronetts for bearing and wearing of ane badge, and cognoscence, with a new warrant for bearing and wearing of the samyne in maner above specifeit, dischergeing the vse of the saids former commissions efter the date heirof; and this to indure without revocation ay and whill the full number of ANE HUNDRETH AND FYFTIE BARRONETTS be made and compleit. Greenwich, 5 May 1631.

WILLIAM CLAYBORNE: LICENCE TO TRAFFIC.

1631.
May 16

CHARLES be the Grace of God King of England Scotland France and Ireland Defender of the fayth, &c. Wheras our trustie and weilbeloved William Clayborne, one of our Counsall and Secretarie of state for our Colonie of Virginia, and some other Aduenturers with him, haue condescendit with our trustie and weilbeloved counsellour Sir William Alexander kny^t principall Secretarie of our kingdome of Scotland and others of our loveing subjects who haue charge of our Colonies of New

I

Scotland and New England to keep a course for interchange of trade amongst them as they shall have occasion as also to mak discovereis for increase of trade in these parts, and because we doe verie much approve of all such worthie intentions and ar desyreous to give good encouragment to their proceidingis therin, being for the releiff and comfort of these our subjects and enlargment of our dominions, These ar to licence and authorize the said William Clayborne his associats and companie friehe without interruption from tyme to tyme to trade and traffique for corne furis or any ther commoditeis whatsoever with ther schips men boatts and merchandice, in all seas coasts rivers creiks herbereis landis territoreis in neir or about these parts of America for which ther is not alreadio a patent grantit to others for the whole trade And for that effect we requyre and command yow, and everie of yow, particularlie our trustie and weilbelovit Sir John Hervie knyght governour and the rest of our Counsall of and for our Colonie of Virginia, to permitt and suffer him and them with ther saids schips boats merchandice and cattell mariners servandis and such as shall willinglie accompanie or be imployed by them from tyme to tyme frielie to repair and trade to and agree in all the aforsaids parts and places as they shall think fitt and ther occassins shall requyre, without any stop arreist search hinderance or molestation whatsoever as yow and everie of yow will answer the contrarie at your perrells, giueing and by these presents granting to the said William Clayborne full power to direct and governe correct and punish such of our subjects as shalbe vnder his command, in his waye and discovereis And for your soe doing, these presents shalbe your sufficient warrant. Gevin at our mannor at Greenwich the 16 of May 1631 the sevint year of our regne.

To our trustie and weilbeloved our Governour and Counsall
of Virginia, To all our Livtennents of provinces and
cuntreyis in America, gouernours and vthers haueing
any charge of Coloneis of any of our subjects ther,
and to all Captanes and Masters of schipps, and
generallie to all our subjects whatsoever whom these
presents doe or may concerne.

1631.
June 30

N. BRIOT: FARTHINGS COINING.

[Charles R.]

Wheras we have gevin ordour for coyncing a certane quantitie of copper into farthing tokens in our kingdome of Scotland and for performance of which work yow ar made choyse of These ar therfor to requyre and authorize yow to forge mak and grave or cause to be made and graved in our citie of London or elswher within this our kingdome of England, all kynds of instruments presses engynes yrones stampes coynes with all others provisions necessarie for the fabrication of the saidis farthings, to be delyvered by such as yow shall be directed by our trustie and weilbeloved Counsellour Sir Wm Alexander kny^t, that they may be transported vnto our Mynt of our toun of Edinburgh Within our said kingdome of Scotland For doeing whairof as also for your owin repairing thither for setting vp and establisching the said work, these presents shalbe vnto yow a sufficient warrand. From our Court of Greenwich, the last of Juny 1631.

To our trustie and weilbelovit Nicolas Briot Cheiff graver
of our Mynt within our kingdome of England.

THESAURER AND DEPUTIE.

1631
July 4

[CHARLES R]

Right, &c. Wheras ther hath bene a proposition made vnto ws for coyneing a quantitie of farthingis tokins within that our kingdome such as ar current heir and considering in regard of the scarcitie of money for the present ther, that some such kynd of coyne wer the more necessarie at this tyme for the vse of the meaner sort, and for the smaller sowmes; yet becaus we desyre to proceid heirin as circumspecthe as can be both for the good of our owin subjects and that such correspondencie may be keipit heirin with our other kingdomes as in such caice is requisit Our pleasur is that haveing conferred with them who have the charge of our Mynt as lykwyse with the propounders of this course that yow mak the fayrest and best bargane yow can for our advantage and that yow sequester the moneyis arysing therby to be bestowed as yow shall have a particular warrant from ws for that effect.   Greenwich, fourth July 1631.

PRECEPT TO THE THESAURER AND DEPUTIE.

1631
July 10

[CHARLES R]

In regard of the good and faythfull service done vnto ws by Sir William Alexander our Secretarie, it is Our pleasur that yow delyver vnto him for his vse all and whole the moneyis that doe or shall belong vnto ws (as feyis justhe due being defrayed) for our share by the coyneing of the farthing tokens or of any such copper coyne as yow shall think fitt to be coyned by vertew of our warrant sent vnto yow for that effect and that ye send vnto ws any further warrant that yow think necessarie heirin : ffor doeing wherof in delyverie the same to him by vertew of this warrant or for drawing vp of another these ar to secure yow as a sufficient discharge and warrant.   Greenwich, 10 July 1631.

WARRANT TO SIR WILLIAM ALEXANDER.

[Charles R]

Right, &c. Wheras ther is a finall agreement made betwixt ws and our good brother the French King, and that, amongst other particulariteis for perfecting heirof we haue condescendend that Port Royall shall be putt in the estate it was befor the beginning of the late warre, that no pairtie may have any advantage ther dureing the continuance of the same and without derogation to any preceiding right or title be vertew of any thing done other then or to be done by the doeing of that which we command at this tyme It is our will and pleasur and we command yow heirby that with all possible diligence yow give ordour to Sir George Home knyght or any vther haveing charge from yow ther, to demolisch the Fort which was builded by your Sone ther, and to remove all the people goods ordinance munition cattell and vther things belonging vnto that Colonie, leaveing the boundis altogidder waist and vnpeopled as it was at the tyme when your said Sone landed first to plant ther, by vertew of our commission, and this yow faill not to doe, as yow wilbe answerable vnto ws. Greenwich, 10 July 1631.

TO THE COUNSELL.

[Charles R.]

Right trustie and right weilbelouit Cousine and Counsellour, &c Seeing we have sene, by a letter from yow, the ordour of Barronets erected by our late dear Father and ws, for furthering the Plantation of New Scotland, was approved by the whole Estats of our kingdome at the last Convention, And that we vnderstand, both by ther reports that cam from thence, and by the sensible consideration and notice taken therof by our nyghbour cuntreyis, how well that work is begun, Our right trustie and weilbeloved counsellour Sir William Alexander our Leivtennent ther haueing fullie performed what was expected from him, for the benefite which was intendit for him by these Barronets, being verie desyreous that he should not suffer therin, bot that both he and others may be encouraged to prosecute the good begining that is made, as we hartelie thank all such as hath contribute ther ayde by contracting with him for advanceing of the said work alreadio, Our pleasur is that yow seriouslie consider, either amongst yow all, or by a Committe of such as ar best affectionat towards that work, how it may be best brought to perfection; for we are so far (whatever contraversie be about it) from quyting our title to New Scotland and Canada, that we wilbe verie carefull to manteane all our good subjects who doe plant themselffis there, and lett none of the Barronets anyway be prejudged in the honour and priviledges conteynit in ther Patents, by punisching of all that dare to presume to wrong them therin, that others may be encouraged to tak the lyk course, as the more acceptable vnto ws and the nearer to a title of Nobihtie, whervnto that of Barronets is the next degrie And if the said Sir William as our Livetennent of New Scotland shall convene the Barronetts to consult togidder concerneing that Plantation, we herby authorise him, and will yow to authorise him as far as is requisit for that effect, willing that Proclamatioun be made of what we haue signifeid, or of what yow shall determine for furthering that work, wherof we recomend the care to yow, as a matter importing speciallie our honor and the good of that our ancient kingdome. From our Mannour at Greenwiche, the twelfe day of Julij 1631.

PRO REGE GALLORUM.

1631
July 28.

CAROLUS Dei gratia Magnæ Britanniæ Franciæ et Iliberniæ Rex fideique defensor etc. Omnibus hasce visuris salutem . Quandoquidem omnino justum æquum et bonum judicamus, vt jam tandem pax et concordia nuper inter nos et Regem Christianissimum, fratrem nostrum charissimum conclusa, pristinum vigorem et effectum recuperent, atque adeo omnes contraversiæ et difficultates quæ hactenus hinc inde intercederunt inter nostra regna et subditos mutuo redintegrata et perfecta reconciliatione vtrinque removerantur et aboleantur, In quem finem nos inter alias conditiones ex nostra parte præstandas Consensimus desertionem facere fortalicii seu castri et habitationis Portus Regalis, vulgo *Port Royall*, in Nova Scotia, qui flagrante adhuc bello vigore diplomatis ceu commissionis sub regni Scotiæ sigillo pro derelicto captus et occupatus fuerat, et illud tamen sine vllo prejudicio juris aut tituli nostri aut subditorum nostrorum imposterum · Nos promisserum atque verbi nostri Regii fidem quibuscunque contrariis rationibus et objectionibus hac super re illatis aut inferendis anteferentes, hisce literis asserimus et in verbo Regio promittimus nos præcepturos curatoros et effecturos vt a nostris in dicto fortalicio siue castro et habitatione Portus Regalis, vulgo *Port Royall*, subsistentibus subditis siue ceu milites præsidialii siue ceu Coloni et Incolæ ibidem morentur et habitentur immediate quam primum nostræ jussionis literæ a deputatis vel commissariis qui easdem a prefato nostro fratre charissimo Rege Christianissimo, eo mandandi, habebunt efferendas ipsis erunt exhibitæ et perlectæ, atque redeandi facultas data, dictum castrum seu fortalicium et habitatio in Portu Regali durantur deserentur, relinquanter, denique arma tormenta commeatus armenta bona et vtensilia inde asportentur In cujus rei testimonium has literas nostras manu nostra et magno regni nostri Scotiæ sigillo signare et confirmare volumus: Quæ dabantur ex Palatio nostro Grenovici, die 28 mensis Julij Anno Domini 1631, et nostri regni septimo.

PROCLAMATIOUN ANENT BARONETTIS.

Apud Halyrudhous 28 *July* 1631.

Forsamekle as the order of Barronnets erected by our Soucrane Lord and his lait dear Father of blessed memorie for fordering the plantatioun of New Scotland wes approvin be the whole Estaits of this kingdome at the last Conventioun and his Majesties vnderstanding by many reports that come from hence, and by the sensible consideratioun and notice taken thairof by nighbour countreis how weill that work is begun, His Majesteis right traist cousine and counsellor the Viscount of Stirlnne his Majesteis lieutennent there haueing fullie performed what wes expected from him for the benefite whilk wes intendit by these Baronnets: And His Majestie being verie desirous that he sould not suffer thairin but that both he and others may be encouraged to prosecute the good beginning that is made His Majestie for this effect is so farre (what ever contraversie be anent it) from quitting his title to New Scotland and Cannada that his Majestie will be verie carefull to mainteane all his good subjects who doe plant thameselfes there and will lett none of the Baronnets be anie waye prejudged in the honnour and priviledges conteanit in thair Patents, bot will punische all that darre presoome to wrong thame thairin, for encourageing of others to take the lyke course as the more acceptable to his Majestie and the nearer to ane title of nobilitie whairunto that of Baronnet is the nixt degree And Ordanis letters to be direct chargeing officiaris of armes to pas and make publicatioun heirof be opin proclamatioun at the Mercat Croces of the heid Burrowes of this kingdome and uther places neidfull, quhairthrow nane pretend ignorance of the same.

COMMISSION ANENT BARONNETS

The Lords of Secreit Counsell for the better furderance and advancement of the plantatioun of New Scotland, Gives and grants Commission be thir presents to Thomas Erle of Hadinton Lord Privie Seale, George Erle of Wintoun, Alexander Erle of Linlithgow, Robert Lord Melvill, Johne Lord Tracquair, Archibald Lord Naper, David Bishop of Rosse, Sir Archibald Achesone Secretarie, Sir Johne Hamiltoun of Magdalens Clerk of Register, Sir Thomas Hope of Craighall knicht baronnet Advocat, Sir George Elphinstoun Justice Clerk, Sir Johne Scot of Scotistarvet, and Sir James Baillie, Or anie fyve of thame without excluding of anie others of the Counsell who sall be present To conveene and meit with Wilham Viscount of Stirline and the Knights Baronnets at such tyme and place as the said Viscount of Stirline sall appoint And to conferre with thame upoun the best meanis for the furdering of the said Plantatioun And to make and sett doun Overtures thereanent And to present and exhibit thame to the saids Lords to the intent they may allowe or rectifie the same as they sall thinke expedient.

Followes his Majesteis missive for Warrand of the Act aboue writtin.

CHARLES R.

Right trustie and right weilbelouit Cousine and Counsellour . . . .

. . . . [See *supra*, p. 68].

From our Mannour at Greenwiche, the twelf day of Julij 1631,

TO THE THESAURER DEPUT.

[CHARLES R]

Right, &c. Wheras we wer pleased in July last to send our right trustie, &c. the Viscount of Stirling our principall Secretario for that our kingdome about bussines speciallie importing the good of our service, for which he had no allowance of ws towards the defraying of his charges, and that now vpon the lyk reasone we have thoght good to send him bak agane It is our pleasur that vpon sight heirof yow pay vnto him the sowme of [*blank in MS.*] and the lyk sowme whensoever heirefter he by our speciall direction shalbe imployed by ws thither, out of the first readiest of our rents and casualiteis whatsumever. Greenwich, 28 July 1631.

N. BRIOTT.

[CHARLES R.]

Wheras we have made choyse of our trustie and weilbeloved Nicolas Briott our cheiff gravor of our Mynt of England for the coyneing of a certane quantitie of Copper Coyne, presentlie ordeaned by ws and our Counsall to be coyned in the Mynt of that our kingdome, for which vse we have expresslie directed him thither Our pleasur is, yow permitt him to sett vp and establish in the most convenient place of our said Mynt all engynes and tooles necessarie for that work, and to give vnto him or his deputeis all concurrence and assistance, till the said quantitie of copper be fullie coyned. Whythall, 8 December 1631.

TO THE COUNSELL.

[CHARLES R.]

Right, &c. Wheras vpon our pleasur formerlie signifeid vnto yow tuitching the Copper Coyne yow gave ordour for coyneing of fyftene hundreth stone wecht of copper vnto farthing tokens of the lyk weght and value as thay ar current in this kingdome Being now informed by our right, &c. the Viscount of Stirling our principall Secretarie ther that diverse of our loveing subjects conceave the division of the penney sterling formerlie vsed to be more convenient for exchange and reckonyng then the new division into four farthings and that (for avoyding the danger of counterfitting and for the more exactnesse of the impression) it is thoght fitt to mak the Copper money of a greater proportion of weght Our pleasur is that the said quantitie of Copper be coyned in severall spaces of penny two penny and four penny peices and that a fyftene part therof be coyned into pennyis weying eight granes the peice (being the weght formerlie allowed by yow to the farthings) and the remanent quantitie be equall division into two and four penny peeces of proportionable weght to the penny causing distinguish them be ther bearing on the one syd the figure or number of ther value vnder ane imperiall Croun with our Inscription and on tho vther the Thistle with the vsuall Motto and that ther be made of the said thric peeces the said quantitie of Copper so ordeaned by yow to have bene coyned in farthings with what addition yow shall now or heirefter think fitt in regard of the alteration of the weght of the peices and as the necessitie of the Cuntrie shall requyre Which Coyne we will to have course amongst our subjects for the vse of the poore and change of small commoditeis without any vther imposition in the payment of great sowmes then hath bene formerlie accustomed in the Copper Coyne of that our kingdome or shall from tyme to tyme seme expedient vnto yow And in regard of the necessitie of a speedie returne hither for occasion concerneing our service of Nicolas Bryot our cheiff graver of our Mynt heir whom we direct,t thither for coynceing these moneyis We specialle recommend vnto yow that no farder delay be made in putting that work to perfection.   Whythall, 13 December 1631.

1631
December 29.

TO THE COUNSELL.

[CHARLES R.]

Right, &c. Wheras vpon our pleasur formerlie signifeid vnto yow tuitching the Copper Coyne yow gave ordour for coynceing fyftene hundreth stane weght of Copper into farthing tokens of the lyk weght and value as they ar current in this our kingdome being now informed by our right, &c. the Viscount of Stirling our principall Secretarie ther that diverse of our loveing subjects conceave the division of the penny sterling, &c. [see above] as is forsaid in the vther letter.

1632
February 19

VISCOUNT STIRLING: SIGNATURE £10,000, &c

[CHARLES R]

Right, &c. Wheras we send heirwith inclosed vnto yow a signature of Ten Thowsand pund sterling in favours of our right, &c. the Lord Viscount of Stirling to be past and exped by yow vnder our great Seall; least any mistaking should ensue thervpon we have thought it good to declare vnto yow that (as it may appear by itselff) it is nowayes for quytmg the title ryght or possession of New Scotland or of any part therof, bot onlie for satisfaction of the losses that the said Viscount hath by giveing ordour for removeing of his Colony at our express command for performeing of ane Article of the Treatie betwixt the French and ws, and We ar so far from abandoneing of that busines as We doe heirby requyre yow and everie one of yow to affoord your best help and encouragement for furthering of the same, cheiflie in perswading such to be Baronets as ar in qualitie fitt for that dignitie and come befor yow to seek for favour from ws : but remitting the maner to your own judgment and expecting your best endeavours heirin willing thir presents to be insert in your books of Excheker, and ane act made thervpon, We bid, &c. Whythall, 19 February 1632.

SIR WILLIAM ALEXANDER : LUBEC SHIP.

1632
March 3.

[CHARLES R.]

Right, &c. Wheras we are informed that ther is ane action in Law betweene Sir William Alexander kny^t and some Citizens of Lubec depending befor you concerneing ane schip which they alledge to be wrongouslie takin from them and vnjustlie declared pryse by ane Court of Admiraltie ther, wheranent we directed our warrant to yow two yeres agoe at their desyre Notwithstanding wherof as we ar lykwyse informed they haue delayed till now to prosecute the same befor yow, thoght the said Sir William hath bene severall tymes present ther since that tyme Therfor in regard that his presence for his particular knowledge in that state of the bussines may conduce to the cleiring of it, and that he can not as yit repair thither for occasions speciallie concerning our service Our pleasur is, that all further proceiding therin be delayed till the first day of Jan^{ry} nixt insueing, that he may conveinentlie attend the determination of the same : for doing wherof these presents salbe, &c. Newmerket, 3 March 1632.

SIR JAMES BALFOUR, LYON KING AT ARMES.

1632.
March 15.

[CHARLES R]

Trustie, &c. We haue bene latelie pleased to confer vpon our right, &c. Sir WILLIAM ALEXANDER kny^t our principall Secretarie for Scotland the title of VISCOUNT STIRLING as ane degrie of honour which we have estemed due to his merite And to the effect ther be nothing wanting which is vsuall in this kynd that this our favour and the remembrance of his good and faythfull services done vnto ws may be in record Our pleasur is and We doe heirby requyre yow

K

according to the dewtie of your place to marshall his Coate Armour alloweing it to him quartered with the Armes of Clan Allaster who hath acknowledged him for cheiff of ther familie, in whois armes according to the draught which we send yow heirwith, quartered with his coat, Wo 'ar willing to confirme them Requyreing yow to Register them accordinglie; and we doe further allow to the said Viscount Stirling the armes of the countrie of New Scotland in ane inscutschione as in a badge of his endeavours in the interprysing of the work of that plantation which doe tend so much to our honour and the benefite of our subjects of that our kingdome: and with all to fitt his said Coat with a convenient crest and supporters such as may be acceptable vnto him; ffor doeing whairof, and for registring of this warrand and his Coat in your registers for that purpois, or for drawing such farther warrant as shalbe requisit, these presents shalbe your warrant. Newmerket, 15 March 1632.

1632.
May 29

SIR HENRIE MARTEN: PRYSE OF A LUBEC SCHIP.

[CHARLES R.]

Trustie, &c. Wheras we have bene petitioned concerning a schip of Lubec that some yeres agoe was declared pryse in our Court of Admirahtie in Scotland, We ar desyreous befoir we giue any ordour therin to haue your opinion according to the caee which wo send yow heirwith Therfor our pleasur is that yow pervse it and delyver vnto ws your opinion concerneing the same that we may be the better informed to giue such ordour as shalbe further requysite. Greenwich 29 May 1632.

1632
June 12

RESTITUTION OF QUEBEC TO THE FRENCH.[1]

CHARLES R.

Trusty & well beloved we greete you well, For so much as there is made a finall good agreemt betwixt vs & or brother, the French King, and that allwise as well betwixt or Crownes as subjects are settled by a mutuall & perfect accord, that amongst other particularityes on or side Wee haue consented to the restitution of the fort & habitation of Kebeck in Canada, as taken by force of armes since the peace, howsoeuer the Commision were given out to you duringe the warre betwixt vs & the said King. Wee preferring the accomplishmnt of or Royal words & promises before all whatsoeuer allegations may be made to the contrary in the behalfe, as wee haue obliged or selves to that King for the

---

[1] Colonial Papers, p 151.

due performance thereof by an act passed under the great Seale of this o^r Realme of England, so Wee doe by these o^r letters straightly charge & comaund you, that vpon the first commodity of sending into these parts & meanes for yor people to returne yea we give notice & order to all such subjects of o^{rs} wch are under yor commission & government, as well folouers wch are in garrison in the forsayd fort & habitation of Kebec for defence thereof, as inhabitants wch are there seated & planted, to render according to the said agreem^{nt}, the said fort & habitation into the hands of such as shalbe by o^r sayd brother, the French King, appointed & authorised to comaund & receaue the same from them in the same state it was at the tyme of the taking, wthout demolishing any thing of the fortifications & buildings, wch were erected at the tyme of the taking, or wthout carying away the armes, munitions, marchandises, or vtensills wch were then found therein. And yf anything hathe bene formerly caryed away from thence o^r pleasure is it shalbe restored eyther in specie or value, according to the quality of what hath bene made to appeare vpon oath & was sett downe in a schedule made by mutuall consent of such as had cheife command on both sides at the taking & rendring thereof And for soe doing these o^r letters shall not only serue for warrant, but likewise for such expresse signification of o^r will & pleasure that whosoeuer officer, soldier, or inhabitant, shall not readily obey, but shew himself cross or refractory thereunto, shall incurre o^r highest indignation, & such punishm^{nt} and penalty as shalbe due unto offendo^{rs} of so high a nature. Given under o^r Signett at o^r Mann^{or} of Greenwich the twelft of June in seaventh [eighth] yeare of o^r raygne.

(*In dorso.*) To our trusty and wellbeloved Sir William
    Alexander knight, Robert Charlton and William
    Barkly our Commissioners for the Gulfe & River
    of Canada and parts adjacent & to their partners
    & Deputyes & all others whom it may concern.

SIR WILLIAM ALEXANDER : LUBEC SCHIP.

1632.
June 14

[CHARLES R.]

Right, &c. Haueing heard that there are some actions depending befoir yow for reduceing of decreits that wer gevin by our Admirall vpon pryse schippes dureing the tyme of the late warris, we ar confident that he hath not proceidit in any such processe but vpon verie just groundis and no decreit gevin by our Admirall of this our kingdome can be reduced befoir aney vther judge saue by such as ar especiallie appoynted by ws for that purpois and though we doe not intend to derogate from our Judicatorie in aney thing that is propper object thairof yet in regard that our right, &c. the Duke of Lennox our Admirall is absent for the present, and a minor of whome we have takin charge, and that we would not have any just caus gevin to discourage others heirefter to ondertak in our service in the lyk kynd when they shall sie these to suffer who efter sentence gevin in the ordinarie Court haue disposed of the goodis according thervnto We have thoght fitt to recommend vnto yow that yow proceid the more warelie in any action persewed befor yow of this nature that these our subjects who ar or shalbe interested in that kynd may find all the just favour and encouragement which the practeis of other nationes and the Law is of that our kingdome may allow: which especiallie recommending vnto your care we bid, &c Greenwich, 14 Junij 1632

1632
June 14

ADVOCATE: NEW SCOTLAND.

[Charles R]

Trustie, &c. Wheras vpon the late Treatie betwixt ws and the French King we wer pleased to condescend, that the Colonie which was latelie planted at Port Royall, in New Scotland, should be for the present removed from thence, and have accordinglie gevin ordour to our right, &c. The Viscount of Stirling our principall Secretarie for Scotland, altho, by all our severall ordours and directions concerneing that busines, we have ever expressed that we have no intention to quyt our right title to anie of these boundis, yet, in regard our meaneing perchaunce will not be sufficientlie vnderstude by these our loveing subjects who heirefter shall intend the advancement of that work, ffor ther further satisfaction heirin we doe heirby requyr yow to draw vp a sufficient warrant for our hand to pas vnder our great scall, to our said Right, &c the Viscount of Stirling to goe on in the said work whensoever he shall think fitting wherby for the encouragement of such as shall interest themselffis with him in it he may have full assurance from ws in *verbo principis*, that as we have never meaned to relinquish our title to any part of these cuntreyis which he hath by patents from ws, so we shall ever heirefter be readie by our gracious favour to protect him and all such as have or shall heirefter at aney tyme concurre with him, for the advancement of the plantations in these boundis forsaidis . And if at aney tyme heirefter by ordour from ws they shalbe forced to remove from the saidis boundis or aney part therof wher they shall happin to be planted, we shall fully satisfie them for all loss they shall susteane by aney such act or ordour from ws And for your soe doeing, &c. Greenwich, 14 Junij 1632.

The 20 of Junij a packet went to Scotland direct to Sir
Ar[d] Achiesone, wherin ther was 5 Letteris of his
Ma[tie] To the Advocat, New Scotland: Session, Lubec
Schip· Exchequer, James Dowgles· Chancellour, Sir
Piers Corsbie: Counsell, Mr Ro[t] Williamsone.

SIR WILLIAM ALEXANDER'S NOTE FOR NEW SCOTLAND.[1]

1632
[June 16]

A minute of some points considerable for his Majesties Service in regard of the French their possessing of New Scotland at this time.

The possessing of it by the French immediatelie vpon the late Treatie, though it bee not warranted by the Treatie, if some speidie act do not disproue it, will be held to be authorised by it.

The French pretend title to Virginia & New England as may appeare by their patent graunted to the Canada Companie of all Noua Francia from Florida to the North Pole, To be found in *Mercure Françoise* anno 1627, which tytle may hereafter proue dangerous for his Maties subjects in these pairts if the French become stronge in New Scotland.

It is evident that the French haue a designe more than ordinarie herein for besides there plantacion in Canada for the which there is a reason apparent in the benefite of trade, they haue this yeare sent 300 men to New Scotland where no present benefite can possiblie redound to them in proportion to the charge they are at, and are the next yeare as I am crediblie informed, to sett out ten shippes with planters these that are interested in it haueing bound themselues to a yearlie supplie of a great nomber of planters, which is a certane proofe of some end greater then any persons expectation of proffeit can encourage them into

This then future expectation in my judgement most consist in the use of wood, for building of shippes, and for haueing all materials requisite for shipping such as pitch, tarr, & roset, which are there in abundance, yron oare hath been lykeways formerlie discoucred by the French themselues.

The building of shippes there and the imployment of them in fishing which aboundes vpon that coast especiallie Salt being to be made by the Sunne as in France lykelie to tend infinitlie to the iner case of shipping and of mariners, which apparentlie is the designe of the French besides that if the French doe once in a publie and generall way enter to fish on that coast it can not but vndo the English trade that is by fishinge, sence the French haue Salt at an easier rate than the English, but more if they make salt in the countrie which I am confident they may do.

If his Matie shalbe pleased to appoint some whom he shall thinke fitt for considering these things and the like that may be proponed there may perchance some thing be found expedient to be done either now or hereafter tending to the advancement of his Maties service in these pairts abroad.

These are only in all humble dutie without any priuat end to expresse what in the small experience I haue particularlie had herein I can conceaue may concerne the publick good.

[1] Colonial Papers, p 152.

LORD OCHILTREE'S CRIMINAL PROCESS.

CHARLES R.

Right trusty and right welbeloued Cousin and Counsellour Wee greate yow well Being informed that in regard the Lord Ochiltree is now vnder a criminall processe yow haue stopt the passing of a patent granted vnto him and Sir Peirs Crosbie and other their partners who had long since contracted with our right trustie and welbeloued Counsellour the Viscount of Sterlin for some landes in New Scotland And being willing to secure all such Vndertakers in that plantation and to encourage them to prosecute their vndertakings for the good of our seruice, and encrease of our domyniones Wee for these respects and particularlie calling to mind the good services done vnto Vs by the said Sir Peirs, and conceauing good hopes of his future service in New Scotland are hereby pleased that the said patent be exped vnder our Greate Scale causing raze out the Lo. Ochiltrees name : Otherwayes (if yow find a necessitie) that yow cause draw a patent of new for that purpose to be exped vnder our Cachett and Great Scale without passing other Scales or Registers, for which these shalbe sufficient warrant Wee bid you farewell From our Manour of Greenewich the 7 of June 1632.

Apud Halyrudhouse 28 *July* 1632

Presented read and ordayned to be registrat, and the princ^{ll} to be given bak to My Lo. Chancellour, and ane Act conforme to the letter to be buiked

HADINTON, *I.P.D.*

To our right trustie and right welbeloved Cousin and
    Counsello^r the Viscount of Duplin our Chanceler
    of our kingdome of Scotland,
(*In dorso*) His Maties letter anent Sir Peirce Corsbie, buikit 28 July 1632

TO THE BARRONETS.

[CHARLES R.]

Trustie, &c. Wheras our late dear father out of his pious zeall for the advancement of religion in the remote parts of his dominions wher it had not bene formerlie knowen and out of his royall care for the honour and well of that our ancient kingdome was pleased to annex to the Croun therof the dominion of New Scotland in America that the vse of it might aryse to the benefite of that kingdome we being desyreous that the wished effects might follow by the continuance of so noble a designe wer pleased to confer particular marks of our favour vpon such as should voluntarlie contribute to the furtherance of a plantation to be establisched in these boundis as appeared by our erecting of that order of baronetts wherwith yow ar dignifeid wherunto we have ever since bene willing to add what further we conceaved to be necessarie for the testifeying our respect to these that ar alreadie interested and for encourageing of them who shall heirefter interest themselffis in the advancement of a work which we so reallie tender for the Glorie of God the honour of that nation and the benefite that is lykhe to flow from the right prosecution of it But in regard that notwithstanding the care and diligence of our Right, &c. the Viscount of Stirling whom we have from the beginning entrusted with the prosecution of this work, and of the great charges alreadie bestowed vpon it hath not takin the root which was expected parthe as we conceave by reasone of the incommoditeis ordinarhe incident to all new and remote beginnings, and parthe as we ar informed by want of the tymelie concurrance of a sufficient number to insist in it, bot especiallie the Colonie being forced of late to remove for a tyme by meanes of a Treatie we have had with the French Thairfor We have takin into our royall consideratioun by what meanes agane may this work be establisched and conceaving that ther ar none of our subjects whom it concerneth so much in credit to be affectioned to the progres of it as these of your number for justefieing the groundis of our princelie favours which yow have receaved by a most honorabill and generous way we have thoght fitt to direct the bearer heirof Sir William Alexander knyᵗ vnto yow who hath bene ane actor in the former proceidingis and hath sene the cuntrie and knowen the commoditeis thereof who will communicat vnto yow such propositions as may best serve for making the right vse heirefter of a plantation and trade in these boundis for encouraging such as shall adventure therein And we doubt not bot if yow find the groundis reasonable and fair yow will give your concurrance for the further prosecution of them And as We have alreadie gevin ordour to our Advocat for drawing such warrandis to pass vnder our sealls ther wherby our loveing subjects may be fred from all misconstruction of our proceidingis with the French anent New Scotland and secured of our protection in tyme cuming in ther vndertakeris vnto it So we shalbe readie to contribute what we shall heirefter find we may justlie doe for the advancement of the work and the encouragement of all that shall joyne with yow to that purpois Which recommending vnto your care We bid yow farewell. Beawlie, 15 August 1632.

SIR PEIRCE CORSBIE : WARRANT FOR A SCHIP TO PASS.

1633.
March 4

[CHARLES R.]
Wheras the good schip called the   of the burthen of   is to be sent out by Sir Peirce Corsbie knight and baronet, one of our privie coun-

sell of Irland, towardis America for setting of a Colonie ther according to such particular warrants as he hath from ws to that purpois These ar therfoir to will and requyre yow and euerie ane of yow to permitt and suffer the said schip and her whole furniture goodis merchandice schips companie and planters quyethe and peaciablie in ther goeing thither returneing from thence or dureing ther being furth of any vther part whatsoever till they shal happin to returne to any of our dominions to pas by yow without any your lat stayis troubles imprests of ther men or any vther hindrance whatsoever whairof you shall not faill. Whythall, 4 March 1633.

> To our trustie and weilbelovit The Officers of our
> Admiralitie the Captanes and Masters of our schips
> and to all vther officers and our loveing subjects
> whom these presents doe or may concerne.

1633
March 4

TO SIR PEIRCE CORSBIE · COLONIE IN AMERICA

[CHARLES R.]

Trustie, &c. Wheras we ar informed that yow ar goeing on in preparations for setting furth a Colonie to plant in America according to such warrants as yow have alreadie vnder our hand and which ar past vnder our great seall of our kingdome of Scotland, your endeavours heirin ar verie acceptable vnto ws And we doe heirby allow yow to proceid and for your further encouragement and all such as ar therin entrusted with yow we doe heirby assure yow that we shalbe euer readie to protect yow in this your vndertaking aganst all persones whatsumever, and as occasion shall offer we will giue yow such further testimonie of our favour as may stirr vp vthers to the lyk generous vndertakingis So recommending the serious prosecution of a work so much concerneing our service We bid, &c. Whythall, 4 March 1633.

1633.
April 24

COMMISSIONERS FOR THE PLANTATION OF NEW SCOTLAND.

[CHARLES R.]

Trustie, &c Wheras our late dear Father for the honour of that his ancient kingdome did grant the first Patent of New Scotland to the Viscount of Stirling and was willing to conferr the title of Knyght Baronet on such of his weill deserving subjects as should contribute to the advancement of the work of the plantation in the said cuntrey we wer pleased to giue ordour for the effectuating of the same according to our Commission direct to yow for that purpois And vnderstanding perfectlie (as we doubt not is weill knowen vnto yow all) that the said Viscount did begin and prosecute a plantation in these parts with a far greater charge then could be suppleyed by the meanes forsaid And the rather in regard of the late discouragement of some by our commanding him to remove his Colonie from Port Royall for fulfilling the Articles of ane treattie betwixt our brother the French King and ws to mak everie thing betwixt ws be in the esteat wherin it was befor the warre hearing that ther was a rumour gevin out by some that we had totallie left our purpois to plant in that cuntrey as haveing surrendred our right therof Least any further mistakings should aryse heirvpon we thoght good heirby to clear our intention therin which is That our said Viscount with all such as shall adventure with him shall prosecute the said work and be encouraged by all lawfull helps thervnto alsweill by compleiting of the intendit number of Knyght Baronetts as other wayes And being informed that some of our subjects of good qualitie in this our kingdome and Ireland who have taken Land in New Scotland holdin from ws did accept of the said dignitie ther and more obliged to contribute as much towardis the said Plantatioun as any vther in that kynd war putt to far greater charges at the passing of ther rights then the natives of the kingdome wer at in the lyk caice It is our pleasur that whosoever aney of our subjects of qualitie fitt for that dignitie within this our kingdome or of Ireland haveing takin landis holdin of ws in New Scotland And having agried with our said Viscount for ther part of a supplie towardis the said plantation and that it is signifeid so by him vnto yow that till the number of Barronettis formerlie condescendit vpon be compleit yow accept of them and giue ordour that ther Patents be passed at as easie a rate as if they wer naturall subjects of that our kingdome and this yow mak knowen to such persones and in such maner as yow in your judgments shall think fitt, for doing wharof, &c. Whythall, 24 Aprill 1633.

PATENT TO SIR WILLIAM ALEXANDER KNIGHT AND OTHERS for the sole trade in all & singular the Regions, Countreys Dominions & all places whatsoever adjacent to the River & Gulf of Canada, & the sole Traffick from thence and the places adjoyning, for beaver skins & wooll, and all other skins of wild beasts for 31 yeares. 9 Car. 1.[1]

1633 May 11

ACT XXVIII. RATIFICATION IN FAVOUR OF THE VISCOUNT OF STERLING, of the infeftments and signature granted to him of the Dominions of New Scotland and Canada in America, and Priviledges therein contained, and of the dignity and order of Knight Baronets, and Act of Convention of Estates made thereanent.

1633 June 28

Our Soveraigne Lord, and Estates of this present Parliament, Ratifie and

---

[1] Colonial Papers, p. 165.

L

approve all letters Patents, and Infeftments granted by King Iames the Sixth of blessed memorie, or by our said Soveraigne Lord, unto William Viscount of Sterling, and to his heires and assignes of the Territories and Dominions of new Scotland and Canada in America; and especially the Patent, Charter, and Infeftment granted by his Majesties umwhile dearest Father of worthie memorie, of new Scotland, of the date the tenth day of September, the yeare of God 1621.[1] Item, another charter of the same, granted by his Majestie, under the great Seale, of the date the twelfth day of July, 1625 years.[2] Item, another Charter and infeftment granted by his M^{tie} of the Countrie and Dominion of new Scotland under the great Seale, of the date the third day of May, 1627 yeares[3] Item, another Charter and Infeftment granted by his Majestie under the great Seale, of the River and gulf of Canada, bounds, and priviledges thereof, mentioned in the said Patent, of the date the second day of Februarie, 1628 years.[4] Item, a Signature past under his Majesties hand of the said Countrie and Dominion, which is to be with all diligence exped through the Seales, of the date at Whitehall the twenty fourth day of Aprill, 1633 years.[5] With all liberties, priviledges, honours, jurisdictions, and dignities *respective* therein mentioned. Together also with all execution, precepts, instruments of seasings, and seasings following, or that shall happen to follow thereupon. And also ratifies and approves the Act of general Convention of Estates; at Holy-rude-house, the sixth day of July, the year of God 1630.[6] Whereby the said Estates have ratified & approved the dignities & order of Knight Baronet, With all the Acts of Secret Counsell, and Proclamations following thereupon, made for maintaining of the said dignitie, place and precedencie thereof. And his Majestie and Estates foresaid, will, statute, and ordaine, that the said letters Patents, Charters, and Infeftments; and the said dignitie, title, and order of Baronets, and all letters patents and infeftments of Lands, and dignities granted therewith, to any person whatsoever, shall stand and continue in full force; with all liberties, priviledges and precedencies thereof, according to the tenour of the same. And in als ample maner as if the bodies of the said letters patents, infeftments, and signature above mentioned were herein particularly ingrost and exprest. And ordaine intimation to be made hereof by open proclamation to all his Majesties lieges, at the market crosse of Edinburgh, and other places needfull, that none pretend ignorance hereof[7]

---

[1] Printed infra, among the Charters, p 3   [2] Ib. p. 27.
[3] This charter apparently is not recorded.   [4] Infra, p. 46.
[5] Supra, p 80   [6] Supra, p 58   Acts of Parl, vol v, p 208, *et seq*
[7] Acts 1 Parl. Charles I., p 60.; Edinb. 1633. Acts of Parl, vol. v., p. 43.

TO THE COUNSELL AND COMMISSIONERS APPOYNTED FOR PASSING THE PATENTS OF KNIGHT BARRONETS, AND IN- FEFTMENTS OF LANDS IN NEW SCOTLAND.

1633
September

A Letter concerneing New Scotland was past 27 September 1633, verbatim, lyk vnto that which was past 24 Aprill 1653   [See p. 80.]   .   .   .

.   .   .   .

TO THE COUNSELL.

1633
September

[Charles R]

Right trustie and right weilbelouit Cousine and Counseller, right trustie and weelbelouit Cousines and Counsellers, trustie and weilbelouit Counsellers, and trustie and weilbelouit We greit you weill Whereas our lait deir Father for the honnour of that his ancient Kingdome did grant the first patent of New Scotland to our right trustie and right weilbelouit Cousine and Counsel- ler Williame Erle of Stirline, and wes willing to conferre the title of Knight Baronnet on suche of his weill deserving subjects as sould contribute to the ad- vancement of the worke of the plantation in the said countrie We wer pleased to giue order for effectuating of the same, according to our commissioun directed to you for that purpose And understanding perfytehe (as We doubt not bot is weill knowne to yow all) that the said Erle did begin and prosecute a Plantation in these parts with a farre greater charge than could be supplied by the meanes fore- said, and the rather in regarde of the late discouragement of some by our com- manding him to remove his colonie frome Port Royall for fulfilling of ane article of the Treatie betuix Our Brother the Frenche King and Ws, To make everie thing betuix Ws be in the estait wherein it wes before the warre, hearing that there wes a rumour givin out by some that We had totallie left our purpose to plant in that Countrie as having surrendered our right thereof, least anie further mistaking sould arise heerupon Wee thought good heerby to cleere our intentioun therein: Whiche is, That our said Erle with all suche as sall adventure with him sall prosecute the said worke and be encouraged by all lawfull helpes thereunto als weill by compleitting of the intended nomber of Knights Baronnets as other- wayes And being informed that some of our subjects of good qualitie in this our Kingdome and Ireland, who having takin land in New Scotland haldin frome ws did accept of the said dignitie there and wes obliged to contribute als muche to- ward the said Plantation as anie other in that kynde wes putt to greater charges in passing of thair ryghts than the natives of this kingdome wer in the like caise It is Our pleasure that whensoever anie of our subjects of qualitie fitt for that dignitie within this Our kingdome or of Ireland having takin lands holdin of Ws in New Scotland, and having agreed with our said Erle for thair part of a supplee toward the said Plantation, and that it is signified so by him vnto yow That till the nomber of Baronnets formerlie condescended vpon be compleit yow accept of thame and give order that thair Patents be past at als easie a rate as if they wer naturall subjects of that Our kingdome And this yow [sall] make knowne to suche persons and in suche maner as yow sall in your judgements thinke fitt for doing whairof these presents sall be your sufficient warrand Frome Our Court at St James the 27 of September 1633.

THE EARL OF STIRLING.

[CHARLES R.]

It is our pleasur that yow examyne what part of the moneyis due by ws vnto our right, &c. the Earle of Stirling hath bene payed vnto him, and the accompt of the Copper Coyn being dewlie made, that yow certifie what is lyklie entend vnto for his vse that ane vther course may be takin for his payment wher it may not by that meanes be due And if he cannot be convenientlie payed at this tyme nor particular assignement be made vnto him for the same, lest his creditours at this tyme mistrusting our intention to pay him may persew him or your frendis whom we vnderstand to be bund as sureties for him · It is our pleasur to the effect he may not suffer for so much as is due by ws yow certifie ws what course ye think best for the tyme ather for payment of the principall to his creditours or of some part therof, and that yow tak such course as yow shall think best to satisfie them for ther forbearing the same that they may not charge him till we appoynt his payment some other way which We warrand yow heirby to allow out of the benefite arrysing out of the Copper Coyne that he may reap the benefite We intend for him according to our warrand : for doeing whairof, &c. Whythall, 18 October 1633.

ANENT NEW SCOTLAND.

Apud Edinburgh 15 February 1634.

Forsamekle as his Majesteis laite deir Father of blessed memorie for the honnour of this his ancient kingdome of Scotland did grant the first patent of New Scotland to his Majesteis right traist cousine and counsellour Williame Erle of Stirline and wes willing to conferre the title of Knight Barronet upon suche of his weill deserving subjects as sould contribute to the advancement of the worke of Plantation in the said countrie His Majestie wes pleased to give order for effectuating of the same, according to his commission directed to the Lords of Privie Counsell for that purpose And His Majestie understanding perfytelie that the said Earle did begin and prosecute a Plantation in these parts with a faire greater charge than could be supplied by the means forsaid and the rather in regard of the late discouragement of some by His Majestie commanding the said Erle to remove the Colonie from Port Royall for fulfilling of ane article of the Treatie betuix His Majestie and his Brother the Frenche King to make everiething betuix thame to be in the estait wherein it wes befoir the warre, hearing that there wes a rumour given out by some that His Majestie had totallie left his purpose to plant in that countrie as having surrendered his right thairof And thairfoir least anie further mistaking sould arise heerupon His Majestie hes thought good heirby to cleere his intention heerin, which is, that the said Erle with all suche as sall adventure with him sall prosecute the said worke and be encouraged by all lawfull helpes thereunto als weill by compleating the intended nomber of Barronets as otherwayes And whereas some of the subjects of the Kingdome of England and Ireland of good qualitie who having takin land in New Scotland haldin of his Majestie did accept of the said dignitie ther and wes obliged to contribute als much toward the said Plantation as anie others in that kynde, wes putt to greater charges at the passing of thair rights than the natives of this Kingdome wer at in the like caises Thairfor His Majestie hes thought meet heirby to declare His Royall will and pleasure that whensoever anie of His Majesteis subjects of qualitie fitt for that dignitie within the Kingdoms of England or Ireland having takin land haldin of his Majestie in New Scotland and having agreed with the said Erle for part of a supplee towards the said Plantation, and that it is signified so by him to the saids Lords of Privie Counsell That till the nomber of Baronnets formerlie condescended upon be compleit the saids Lords sall accept of thame and give order that thair patents be past at als easie a rate as if they wer naturall borne subjects of this kingdome And the saids Lords Ordanis letters to be direct chargeing Officers of armes to pas and make publication hereof be open proclamation at the mercat croces of the heid burrowes of this kingdome and others places neidfull Wherethrow nane pretend ignorance of the same.

Followes his Majesteis missive for warrand of the Act aboue writtin.

Right trustie and right weilbelouit, &c.　　　.　　.　　.　　.　　.　　.

[See p. 83]

.　　.　　.　　.　　.　　.　　.　　.　　.　　.
From our Court at St James, the 27 of September 1633.

ACCEPTATION OF A COMMISSION FOR PASSING INFEFTMENTS OF NEW SCOTLAND.

Apud Edinburgh 15 *Februarÿ* 1634.

The whilk day, George Erle of Kinnoull Lord High Chancellor William Erle of Morton Lord High Thesaurer and Thomas Erle of Hadingtoun Lord Privie Scale of this Kingdome William Erle Marishell Robert Erle of Roxburgh Johne Erle of Annerdaill Sir Johne Hay Clerk of His Majesteis Registers and Sir Thomas Hope of Craighall His Majesteis Advocat accepted upon thame the Commission granted vnto thame vnder His Majesteis Great Scale, dated at Theobalds, 14 Septembris 1633, for passing of Infeftments of New Scotland.

SIR ROBERT FILIBERT'S WARRANT.

[Charles R]

Trustie, &c. Wheras we ar informed by our right trustie the Erle of Stirling our principall Secretarie for Scotland that yow ar goeing in a course with him towards the advancement of the work of the Plantatioun of New Scotland the good whairof we exceidinglie tender we cannot bot approve of your affection in this as in your other former publict vndertakings for the good of our servise, and as we ar willing to naturalise yow in that our kingdome of Scotland, and to conferre vpon yow the lyk honors and priviledges as vther Knyght Barronetts vndertakeris in the forsaid Plantation doe enjoy, so we shalbe euer readie to encourage yow and all vthers that shall tak the lyk courses with further testimonie of our gratious favour as occasion shall offer. Newmerket, 18 March 1634.

TO THE THESAURER AND DEPUTIE.

[Charles R.]

Right, &c. Wheras in consideratioun of a precept of 6000 lib Stg. granted be our late dear Father to our right trustie and weilbeloved Cousen and Counsellour the Erle of Stirling our principall Secretarie for Scotland for good and faythfull service done by him and of a warrant of Ten Thowsand punds granted by ws vnto him vpon verie good considerations as may appear by the same, We wer pleased to grant vnto him the benefite arysing by the coynage of the Copper money within that our kingdome for the space of nyne yeres and furder till he should be compleithe payed of all sowmes whatsumever due by ws vnto him · Now to the effect our said servant may have the more assurance to mak bargane with others anent the said benefite for his releiff, and that ther may be a certane tyme appoynted for his payment, and for our haveing the benefite of the said Coyne to returne into ws We doe heirby ratifie vnto him his grant of the whole benefite arysing dew vnto ws of that Copper Coyneage during the tyme yit to rin of that his patent And it is our speciall pleasur that yow grant a warrant such as shalbe requisite of Coynadge of sex thowsand stane weght of Copper without intromission immediatlie efter the ending of the Coynadge of 1500 staine weght presentlie in hand and for continewing of the Coynadge efter the full perfyteing of the said 6000 stane from yeir to yeir for the accustomed quantitie as we coyned these two yeires past and that dureing the whole tyme yit to rin of his patent if ther sall any of it remane efter the full perfyteing of the Coynadge of the 6000 stane And that yow give ordour to our Advocat for drawing vp a sufficient discharge of the saids two precepts to be signed by our said servant with a discharge to him from ws of his intromission with any benefite arysing with the Coynadge dureing the tyme past or to cum of his patent (of the which we doe lykwayes heirby discharge him) and that without any accompt to be made vnto ws or any in our name for the same in regard of his discharge of his saids two precepts And caus registrat this our letter and mak such farder in Counsell & Exchequer as may be most expedient for the farder securitie and satisfaction of our said servant of such as he shall have occasion to treat or bargane with for making the best advantage of this our gratious intention towards him for doeing wherof ther presents shalbe vnto yow ane sufficient warrant. Theobalds, 18 September 1634.

LORD ALEXANDER, SESSIONER.

[CHARLES R.]

1634
December 2

Right, &c. It being fitt and necessarie for the good of our service that the extraordinarie place in our Session appoynted for our right, &c. the Erle of Stirling our Secretarie for that our kingdome (who necessarlie most attend our service about our persone) be supplied in his absence and vnderstanding the abiliteis and affection to our service of our right trustie and weilbeloved Counsellour the Lord Alexander whom we hold fitt to supplie that place and charge It is our pleasur that haveing administred vnto him the oath accustomed in the lyk caices yow admitt him to the said Extraordinarie place in Session[1] and that he enjoy all the priviledges and liberteis belonging thervnto for which these presents shalbe your warrant. Hampton Court, 20 December 1634.

[1] William Lord Alexander was admitted one of the Extraordinary Lords of Session (upon his father's resignation) on the 27th January 1635. (Brunton and Haig's Senators, p 295.)

TO SIR FERDINANDO GEORGE [GORGES] KNICHT

[CHARLES R]

Trustie, &c. Haveing fund it of late necessarie that some good courso be establisched for right prosecution of the work of the Plantation of New Scotland in such kynd as may be most for the advancement thairof and the encouragment of such as vndertak therin And haveing (in regard of your affection and long endeavours in that work from the beginning, and your experience therin) bene pleased to mak choyse of yow for vndertaking the chieff chaige in mangeing of such things as shalbe for the good of that cuntrie and the government to be establisched therin, We have thoght good at this tyme to requyre yow so soone as yow can convenenthe to repair to our Court that We may have your opinion and yow receave our direction in such things We shalbe pleased to requyie and appoynt tuitching this bussines. Whythall, 5 January 1634 stylo Anglicano.

COMMISSIONERS FOR SURRENDERS

His Majestie was pleased, by a Letter of his Heynes to his Commissioneris for Surrenders, vpon the 9 January 1635 to requyre them to admitt the Lord Alexander to be ane of their number.

TO SIR JAMES BALFOUR.

[CHARLES R]

Trustie, &c. Wheras we did formerlie signifie our pleasur vnto yow that our right trustie, &c. the Erle of Stirling our Secretarie for Scotland should haue the Armes of New Scotland in ane Inscutchion with his own paternall coat and that other coat (which we lykwayes allow him to bear for reasones signifeid at that tyme vnto yow as by our letter may particularlie appear) now considering that he hath in particular and singular maner deserved the said augmentatioun of the Armes of New Scotland and to the effect he may bear it in a way propper vnto him selff and different to all others who ar authorized for bearing of it we ar pleased to allow it vnto him to be quartered in the first quarter with his other coats and thairfor it is our pleasur that yow draw such further warrant for this purpois as shalbe expedient and withall that yow register this our letter in your Books of Office to remane therin according to the custome in the lyk kynd to the effect no other may tak vpon them to bear the said agumentatioun in this maner to the prejudice of the gracious favour which We doe heirin intend to him alone ffor the which these presents, &c. Whythall, 28 January 1635

COMMISSIONERS FOR PLANTATIONS.[1]

1634-5
January 29

Att a Meeting, att the Lord Gorges' House in St Martin's Lane, January 29 1634—Present, Lord Maltreuers, Ld Gorges, Sr Ferd. Gorges, Capt. John Mason. This day the Earle of Stirling and the Lord Alexander were receaved into the New England Company as Councellours and Patentees.

Moreover it was ord^d att the same Meeting, that the Duke of Lenox, the Marques of Hamilton, and the Earle of Carlisle (being admitted of the Councill before this booke was received from Mr Dickenson Clerke of the Councell of State [and agent?] of the Lord Commissioners for the Plantations,) should be registered here as Pattentees and Councellours of the New England Company.

COUNCIL FOR NEW ENGLAND: GRANT OF LAND TO WILLIAM LORD ALEXANDER [2]

1635
April 22.

Grant of the Council for New England to William Lord Alexander, of all that part of the main land in New England from St Croix, adjoining New Scotland, along the sea coast to Pemaquid, and so up the river to the Kinebequi [Kenebeck] to be henceforth called the County of Canada; also the island of Matowack, or Long Island, to the west of Cape Cod, to be hereafter called the Isle of Sterling; to be holden of the Council and their successors, *per Gladium Comitatus*, that is to say, to find four able men, armed for war, to attend upon the Governor of New England for the public service, within fourteen days after warning given. [Copy on parchment.]

To all Christian people vnto whom theis presents shall come The Councell for the Affaires of New England send greetinge in our Lord God everlastinge. Whereas our late Souraigne Lord Kinge James of blessed memory by his highnes Letters Patente vnder the greate seale of England, bearing date att Westminster the Thirde daye of November in the eighteenth yeare of his Maties raigne ouer his highnes Realme of England, for the consideration in the said Letters Patente expressed and declared hath absolutely given graunted and confirmed vnto the said Counsell and theire successors for euer all the lands of Newe England in America lyinge and beinge in breadth from fortie degrees of Northerly latitude from the Equinoctiall lyne to fortie eight degrees of the said Northerly latitude inclusivelie and in length of and within all the breadth aforesaid throughout the maine land from Sea to Sea. Together alsoe with all the ffirme lands, soyles,

1635
April 22.

---

[1] Colonial Papers, p. 195.   [2] Ib. p. 204.

M

grounde, havons, ports, rivers, waters, fishinge, mynes, and mineralls, as well
Royall mynes of Gold & Silver as other mynes and mineralls pretious stones
quarries and all and singular other commodities jurisdictions royalties previledges,
ffranchises, and preheminences both within the said tracte of land vppon the
Maine and alsoe within the Islands and Seas adjoininge (as by the said Letters
Patents amongst diuers other things therein conteyned more att large it doth and
may appeare) Now Knowe all men by these presents that the said Counsell of New
England in America beinge assembled in publique Courte, accordinge to an acte
made and agreed vppon the thirde day of ffebruary last past before the date of theis
presents for diuers good causes and consideracions them herevnto especially move-
inge have given, graunted, aliened, bargayned, and sold And in and by theis presents
doe for them and theire Successors give, graunt alien bargaine sell and confirme
vnto the right honorable William Lord Alexander his heires and assignes, All that
part of the Maine Land of Newe England aforesaid beginninge, from a certaine
place called or knowne by the name of Saint Croix next adjoininge to New Scotland in America aforesaid and from thence extendinge alonge the sea coast vnto
a certaine place called Pemaquid, and soe vpp the River thereof to the furthest
head of the same as it tendeth Northwarde and extendinge from thence att the
nearest vnto the River of Kinebequi and soe upwards alonge by the shortest
course which tendeth vnto the River of Canada ffrom henceforth to be called and
knowne by the name of the Countie of Canada.   And allsoe all that Island or
Islands heretofore comonly called by the severall name or names of Matowack or
Longe Island and hereafter to be called by the name of the Isle of Starlinge situate
lyinge and beinge to the westward of Cape Codd or the Narohiganlets within the
latitude of fffortie or fortie one degrees or thereabouts abuttinge vpon the Maine-
land betweene the two Rivers there knowne by the severall names of Conectecutt
and Hudsons River and conteyninge in length from East to West the whole length
of the Sea Coast there betweene the said two Rivers.   Together with all and
singular havens, harbours creckes, and Islands, imbayed and all Islands and
Iletts lyinge within ffive leagues distance of the Maine beinge opposite and
abuttinge vpon the premises or any part thereof not formerly lawfully graunted to
any by speciall name And all mynes mineralls quarries, soyles and woods,
marishes, rivers, waters, lakes, ffishings, hawkinge, huntinge and ffowlinge and all
other Royalties Jurisdiccions, priviledges, prehementes, proffitts, commodities and
hereditaments whatsoeuer with all and singular there and euery of theire appurte-
nentes.   And together alsoe with all Rents reserued and the benefitt of all proffitts due to them the said Counsell and their Successors and precincts aforesaid to
be exercised and executed accordinge to the Lawes of England as neere as may
be by the said William Lord Alexander his heires or assignes or his or theire

Deputies Lieutenents, Judges, Stewards, or officers therevnto by him or them or theire assignes deputed or appointed from time to time with all other priviledges, franchises, liberties, immunities, escheates, and casualties thereof arriseing or which shall or may hereafter arise within the said limitte and precincts, with all theire intrest right title claime and demand whatsoever, which the said Councell and there successors, now of right have or ought to have or claime or may haue or acquire hereafter in or to the said portion of Lands or Islands, or any the premises and in as free ample large and beneficiall manner to all intents constructions and purposes what so euer as the said Councell by vertue of his Maties said Letters Patent may or can graunt the same· Saueing and allwayes reseruinge vnto the said Councell and there Successors power to receaue heare and determine all and singular appeale and appeales of euery person and persons whatsoeuer dwellinge or inhabitinge within the said Territories and Islands or any part thereof soe graunted as aforesaid of and from all judgements and sentences whatsoeuer given within the said lands and Territories aforesaid To haue and to holde all and singular the lands and premises aboue by theis presents graunted (excepte before excepted) with all and all manner of proffitts commodities and hereditaments whatsoeuer within the lands and precincts aforesaid to the said lands, Islands and premises or any of them in any wise belonginge or apperteyninge vnto the said William Lord Alexander his heires and assignes To the only proper use and behoofe of him the said William Lord Alexander his heires and assignes for euer To be holden of the said Councell and theire successors, per *Gladium Comitatus,* that is to say by findeinge foure able men conveniently armed and arrayed for the warre to attend vppon the Governor of New England for the publique seruice within ffourteene dayes after any warninge given; yieldinge and payinge vnto the said Councell and theire Successors for euer one fift part of all the . . . . .
are of the mynes of gold and silver which shalbe had possessed or obteyned within the limitte or precincts aforesaid for all rents seruices dueties and demaunds whatsoeuer due vnto the said Councell and their successors from plantacion within the precincts aforesaid The same to be deliuered vnto his Maties Receiver or deputie or deputies Assignes . . . . to the use of his Matie his heires and successors from . . . . the Lands precincts and Territories of New England atoresaid . . . .
the two and twentie day of [Aprill 1635] and 11th yeare of the Raigne.

ANENT KNIGHTING OF BARONNETS SONNES.

Apud Edinburgh 16 *Junij* 1636.

Forsamekle as the Kings Majestie having formerlie upon verie good considerations both for freithing his Matie frome truble and saving of the parties whome it concernes frome charges Give warrand and direction to his Ma^{teis} Chanceller for the time being That the eldest sonnes of all Baronnets being of the age of 21 yeeres sould be knighted whensoever thay sould desire the same according to thair patents under the Great Seale And his Matie being yett willing upon the same consideratiouns that the said course be continued His Majestie for this effect hes gevin warrand to the Lord High Chanceller of this kingdome to knight the eldest sonnes of all and everie ane of suche Baronnets who being of the perfyte age of 21 years compleit sall desire the same without putting thame to anie charges and expensses As in the said warrant presentit and exhibite this day before the Lords of Secreit Counsell at lenth is conteanit Quhilk being read heard and considderit be the saids Lords and thay with all humble and dewtifull respect acknowledgeing his Majesteis gratious will and pleasure in this mater They ordaine the said warrand to be insert and registrat in the bookes of Priuie Counsell and to haue the force of ane act of Counsell in time comming To the end the said Lord Chanceller may knight the saids eldest sonnes of all Baronnetts without forder warrand and that all whome it may concerne may take notice of his Majesteis Royall pleasure heerin and ordanis letters to be direct to make publication heirof wherthrow nane pretend ignorance of the same.

Followes His Majesteis missive for warrand of the Act foresaid.

1636
May 10   CHARLES R

Right Reverend Father in God We greit you weill Whereas We wer pleased by our letter unto our lait Chanceller to give power unto him or anie other for the time being that the eldest sonnes of all Baronnetts might be knighted being of the perfyte age of 21 yeeres whensoever they sould desire the same according to thair patents under our Great Seale both for freing Ws from trouble and saving thame frome charges whiche thair repairing hither for that purpose might procure and now being willing upon the like consideration that the same sould be continued We have thought fitt heirby to renew our pleasure unto yow for that effect and thairfoir We will that yow knight the eldest sonnes of all and euerie one of suche Baronnetts who being of the perfyte age of twenty-one yeeres sould desire the same, without putting thame to anie charges or expensses And Our further pleasure is that yow make ane Act of Counsell herrupon That your successors in your charge of Lord Chanceller doe the same without anie further warrand and that all others whome it may concerne may take notice of our Royall pleasure heerin for doing whairof these presents sall be your warrand We bid you farewell Frome our Courte at Whitehall, the 10 of Maye 1636.

Sir William Alexander
to my lord Viscount of Stormonth.

Right honorable my verie good lord
as I have manie wayes beene beholding
to your Lo: favoure so I have dealt earnest-
lie with his Majestie for you as you
may perceave by his letter which I send
herewith for I love to approve rather
rather by effectes than by professiones
I think my self verie much beholding to your
Lo: favoure in welcoming your cousin Sir William
Murray barronet but it is likelie to doe me
a greate deale of harme if your Lo: help
it not by other moving some chief barrons
of Fyfe to come after him, or by moving
him to give place unto some of them because
I feare this makes them all not come in
a bushe I referre this to your Lo: discretion
and be assured that in anie thing that
may tend to your good there is no man
with a true affection more carefull for you
then I am
to serve your Lo:

Whitehall the
23 of November

W Alexander

In the preceding documents it will be seen that Sir William Alexander was nominated His Majesty's Lieutenant-General, and Admiral of New Scotland. The great importance of such an appointment, with the view of successfully promoting this scheme of colonization, was not duly considered, as no obligation was exacted for personal services in the colony; and there is no evidence to shew that Alexander himself ever set his foot on the soil. When we hear so much said of his advancing large sums in setting forth this scheme, it should be remembered that he was bound to expend two-thirds of the money received from the newly created Knight Baronets in carrying on the Plantation. We know that he fitted out two vessels in 1622 and 1623, and also that his son Sir William the younger sailed with other vessels in 1627 and 1628; yet it may be asserted, that from various causes SIR WILLIAM NEVER WAS ABLE TO FULFIL THE GREAT AND AVOWED OBJECT OF THE ROYAL GRANTS IN HIS FAVOUR BY ACTUALLY ESTABLISHING ANY PERMANENT SETTLEMENT WHATEVER IN NOVA SCOTIA. In his engraved map of 1624, and reissued in 1630, there is no indication of any such settlements in that country, while so many English names appear in the adjoining districts of New England. Had any effectual measures been employed, the majority of the Convention of Estates in November 1625 would never have supported the lesser Barons when they complained of the precedency granted to the newly created Order of Knight Baronets, and prayed the Estates to join in a humble petition to the King to suspend at least this precedency *until the tyme that the Plantatioun, for the whilk this dignitie is conferred, be first performed.* These small Barons went still farther, and offered that *if this Plantatioun should be made,* they, "upoun their own charges, would undertake the same, without any retribution of honour to be given therefor."[1]

In the measures actually pursued, Sir William Alexander appointed his eldest son to act as Deputy-Lieutenant; and he appears on two, or perhaps three, occasions to have visited some portions of North America. The first occasion was in 1627, as we may infer from this

[1] See *supra*, pp. 29-31; also the King's reply in February following, pp. 31-32.

entry in the Kirk-session Register of Stirling:—"1627, December 25.—The whilk day Sir William Alexander, *after his return from his sea voyage,* gave to the poor of Stirling fifty-aucht pounds money." [1] Either in 1628 or the following year Sir William Alexander younger had made a second voyage, as the King, in writing to the Privy Council, 17th November 1629, mentions him as being "now resident in Nova Scotia," [2] and the King addressed to him a letter while at Port Royal, on the 13th May 1630, [3] where he and his attendants had effected a settlement, as will be afterwards noticed.

In the Roll of Knight Baronets of Nova Scotia the first name is Sir Robert Gordon. He was the second son of Alexander, Earl of Sutherland, and was the founder of the family of Gordonstoun, in Morayshire. His charter of the Barony of Gordon is recorded in the Register of the Great Seal, 28th May 1625, [4] and is given at full length in Douglas's Baronage of Scotland. [5] In a work which has recently appeared, "Social Life in Former Days: Second Series. Illustrated by Letters and Family Papers," the author has a chapter on "The Plantation of Nova Scotia, and the Knight Baronets thereof, 1625," [6] in which he inserts from the Gordonstoun papers copies of some contracts or bonds of agreement with Sir William Alexander, connected with this subject. The price paid for a baronetcy, it appears, was 3000 merks, two-thirds of which Sir William engaged should be expended "in setting forth a colonie of men, furnished with necessarie provisioun, to be planted by me, my aires, or our deputies, within the said country (and dominion of New Scotland) be the advyse of the said Sir Robert Gordon and the remanent Barronetts of Scotland, adventurers in the plantation of the same," dated at London the 4th of June 1625. This is followed by a similar engagement, on the last of the month, in the name of Sir Donald Gorme of Slait, knight.

In the Scottish records no notice is taken of a fact, which seems to be undisputed, although the details are not clearly ascertained, that Sir William Alexander, by some private arrangements in the year 1629 or

---

[1] That is, £2, 18s sterling. (Extracts in Miscellany of the Maitland Club, vol. i, p. 467.)
[2] Supra, p 49.   [3] Supra, p 56.   [4] Lib. ii, No. 34.   [5] Edinb., 1798, p. 2.
[6] By E. Dunbar Dunbar, pp 8-21, Edinb., 1864, 8vo.

1630, transferred to Claude St Estienne, Seigneur de La Tour, a French Huguenot, the whole of his territorial rights and possessions of Nova Scotia, still to remain subject to the Crown of Scotland. From this bargain a special exception was made of Port Royal. The name of Claude, and of his son Charles, both occur in the List of Baronets, November 30, 1629, and May 12, 1630. La Tour was of a temporising spirit, and changing his religion, he succeeded in having his acquisitions confirmed by the King of France in 1634. This may have given rise to Scotstarvet's vague report that Sir William "got also a large sum of money from the King of France to quit his interest in Nova Scotia." Sir Thomas Urquhart is more entitled to credit when he alleges, that this transaction was completed without Sir William having either informed or obtained the concurrence of the Knight Baronets, who undoubtedly possessed by their several charters the same territorial rights as himself.

After this period, at least, we hear but little of Nova Scotia and of Alexander's colonial schemes, except in general terms, and always connected with urgent endeavours to fill up the prescribed number of Baronets. In a subsequent page will be given a roll of the names of Baronets of Nova Scotia, as they appear in the public records. During the Earl of Stirling's time the dates of these Patents extend from May 28, 1625 to December 17, 1638, to the number of about one hundred and thirteen individuals.

The following passage from Sir Thomas Urquhart's Jewel (pp. 208-211, Lond. 1652), although well known, may be quoted, as it contains, with some rash, but amusing statements, a good deal of truth relating to this subject:

" SIR WILLIAM ALEXANDER.—It did not satisfie his ambition to have a laurel from the Muses, and be esteemed a King amongst Poets, but he must be King of some New-found-land; and like another Alexander indeed, searching after new worlds, have the soveraignity of *Nova Scotia*. He was born a Poet, and aimed to be a King; therefore would he have his royal title from King James, who was born a King, and aimed to be a Poet. Had he stopped there, it had been well: but the flame of his honour must have some oyle wherewith to nourish it. Like another King Arthur, he must have his Knights, though nothing limited to so small a number; for how many soever that could have looked out but for one day like gentlemen, and given him but one hundred and fifty pounds sterlin, . . . they had a scale from him whereby to ascend unto the platformes of vertue, &c. . . .

they immediately hung out the Orange colours, to testifie their conquest of the honour of Knight-Baronet.

" Their King nevertheless, not to staine his Royal dignity, or to seem to merit the imputation of selling honor to his subjects, did for their money give them land, and that in so ample a measure, that every one of his Knight-Baronets had for his hundred and fifty pounds sterlin heritably disponed unto him six thousand good and sufficient acres of *Nova Scotia* ground, which being but at the rate of sixpence an acre, could not be thought very dear, considering how prettily in the respective parchments of disposition they were bounded and designed fruitful corne-land, watered with pleasant rivers, running alongst most excellent and spacious meadows; nor did there want abundance of oaken groves in the midst of very fertil plaines (for if they wanted anything, it was the Scrivener or Writer's fault; for he gave order, as soon as he received the three thousand Scots marks, that there should be no defect of quantity or quality, in measure or goodness of land) and here and there most delicious gardens and orchards, with whatever else could in matter of delightful ground, best content their fancies, as if they had made purchase amongst them of the *Elysian fieldes;* or *Mahumets Paradise.*

" After this manner my Lord Sterlin for a while was very noble, and according to the rate of Sterlin money, was as twelve other Lordes in the matter of that frankness of disposition, which not permitting him to dodge it upon inches and ells, better and worse, made him not stand to give to each of his champions territories of the best and the most. and although there should have happened a thousand acres more to be put in the Charter or writing of disposition, then was agreed upon at first, he cared not; half a piece to the Clerk was able to make him dispense with that. But at last, when he had inrolled some two or three hundred knights, who, for their hundred and fifty pieces each, had purchased amongst them several millions of *New Caledonian* Acres, confirmed to them and theirs for ever, under the great seal, the affixing whereof was to cost each of them but thirty pieces more, finding that the society was not like to become any more numerous, and that the ancient gentry of Scotland esteemed of such a whimsical dignity as of a disparagement rather than addition to their former honor, he bethought himself of a course more profitable for himself, and the future establishment of his own state; in prosecuting whereof, without the advice of his Knights (who represented both his Houses of Parliament, Clergy and all) like an absolute King indeed, disponed heritably to the French, for a matter of five or six thousand pounds English money both the dominion and propriety of the whole continent of that kingdom of Nova Scotia, leaving the new Baronets to search for land amongst the Selenits in the Moon, or turn Knights of the Sun. so dearly have they bought their Orange Riban, which (all circumstances considered) is and will be no more honorable to them or their posterity, then it is or hath been profitable to either.''

No part of the American continent was more favourable for an English settlement, and the encouragement of the fisheries, than Nova Scotia; but no settlement has been more subject to be disputed, or has so often changed its master. An attempt had been made in 1602 to settle an English colony here; but this not succeeding, the French, in 1604, concluding it to be abandoned, took possession of it under the title of Acadia, as forming part of New France or Canada.

Henry the Fourth of France in 1603 had appointed Mons. de Monts Governor-general of the country, extending between the 40th and 46th degrees of north latitude,—that is, from Virginia to near the head of Hudson's Bay,—which then obtained the name of Acadie. De Monts was accompanied in his voyage of discovery by a personal friend, Poutrincourt, who received from him a grant of that part of the district where they found the large and spacious harbour near the Bay of Fundy, then called *La baye François*, and to which he gave the name of Port Royal. The King of France afterwards confirmed to Poutrincourt this grant, and the place became the headquarters of the French colonists. In 1613, on the ground of some alleged encroachment on the English limits of Virginia, Captain Argall, with some armed vessels, succeeded in obtaining possession of the fort, and dislodging the French. But, as Judge Haliburton observes, "it does not appear that this transaction was either approved of by the Court of England or resented by the Crown of France." Port Royal, since named as Annapolis Royal, in Nova Scotia, is situated on the south side of the bay and river of Annapolis, which runs into the Bay of Fundy; and except for the extraordinary rise and fall of the tides, was reckoned one of the finest harbours in the world. Unless it may have been by some of the first settlers and other stragglers, the place remained deserted for several years. No reference to these proceedings occur in the Nova Scotia grants made to Sir William Alexander, who was authorized to divide the country into portions, and assign them to the Knight Baronets on the conditions prescribed. But this was still a disputed territory, which the French claimed in virtue of previous discovery and possession. After various changes, Charles the First,

N

instigated probably by Sir William Alexander, had given a commission to Captain David Kertch or Kirk, a French Calvinist, for the recovery to England of the possession of Nova Scotia. Having fitted out an armament for that purpose in 1627, he captured 18 French transports, with 135 pieces of ordnance, destined for the fortifications of Port Royal and Quebec. Next year he had retaken Port Royal, and proceeded up the river St Lawrence to attack Quebec, the capital of New France; but the lateness of the season caused him to defer this till 1629, when it was forced to capitulate. In this manner the English regained possession of Nova Scotia, Port Royal, and most part of Canada.

It was at this time that Sir William Alexander the younger, and those who accompanied him, landed at Port Royal, and succeeded in effecting a straggling settlement in that locality. They built a fort on the west side of the haven (Granville), nearly opposite to Goat Island, the remains of which are still visible, and retain the name of the Scottish Fort. But the successes of Captain Kirk proved of no avail, in consequence of the negotiations between Charles the First and his brother-in-law the King of France. During the first winter thirty of the Scots settlers died, and the hopeless expense and numerous difficulties connected with this infant colony induced the younger Sir William Alexander to return home, and must have had no small influence on the elder Sir William in his negotiations with Claude de La Tour, by which he conveyed to him his title to the whole of Nova Scotia (with the exception of Port Royal) to be held of the Crown of Scotland. The precise terms of this transference are not recorded. It is alleged by Chalmers, and repeated by Haliburton and others, that Sir William Alexander, finding that neither considerable profit nor honour were soon or easily to be acquired from the further prosecution of this colonial undertaking, in the year 1630 conveyed his title to the whole of Nova Scotia (with the above exception) to Claude St Estienne, Seigneur de la Tour, upon this condition, that the inhabitants should continue to be subjects of the Scottish Crown. It is also said that La Tour had influence enough to have this transference confirmed by Louis XIII.; and this may have given rise to Sir John

Scot's unfounded assertion[1] that Lord Stirling "got also a great sum of money from the King of France to quit his interest in Nova Scotia." Sir Thomas Urquhart's statement on the same head is already quoted.[2]

By the Treaty of St Germain-en-laye, concluded in March 1632,[3] the English monarch absolutely restored to Louis XIII. of France the sovereignty of Acadia, New France, and Canada generally, and without limits,—and particularly Port Royal, Quebec, and Cape Breton. In terms of this treaty, Charles sent peremptory instructions for the settlers at Port Royal to dispossess themselves, and transfer the place to the French authorities; but instead of stipulating that a sum should be awarded for what had been spent on the fort and other buildings erected in this place, these were ordered to be razed to the ground and the place left desolate, as when first occupied by Sir William Alexander younger and his followers. The King, however, in compensation for the money and labour that had been expended, and for the hardships they had to suffer in quitting this settlement, gave a warrant to pay the Viscount Stirling the sum of £10,000.

The site of this fort is well ascertained, and a stone having the date 1606 indicates the earlier French settlement, the fort having been erected by the Scottish settlers on the site of the French corn-fields previous to the treaty of St Germains. "The remains of this fort," says Judge Haliburton, "may be traced with great ease; the old parade, the embankment and ditch, have not been disturbed, and preserve their original form. It was occupied by the French for many years after the peace of 1632, and near the eastern parapet a large stone has been found, with the following monumental inscription, LEBEL, 1643."[4]

"The French" (says Chalmers) "gloried at a future day, not that they had recovered without consideration what the bravery of Englishmen had won, but that, in these transactions, the name of Nova-Scotia did not appear. Colonial historians, with an inattention or interestedness of which there are few examples, have always insisted, that, not-

---

[1] Staggering State, p 74. [2] *Supra*, pp 95, 96. [3] Corps Diplomatique, Rymer's Fœdera, &c.
[4] An Historical and Statistical Account of Nova Scotia, by Thomas C. Haliburton, vol. ii., p 156, Halifax, 1829, 2 vols., 8vo.

withstanding the absolute restitution before mentioned, certain rights, with regard to that territory, still remained in England: And her statesmen, with a credulity and want of wisdom equally unexampled, have implicitly adopted their sentiments. But in what consists the justice or policy of preserving latent pretensions, which cannot be defended by candid discussion? The law of nations reprobates whatsoever contributes to disturb their repose." [1]

A later author of a valuable work on British America says, that the vast importance of such possessions " should be estimated less by their territorial extent than by the resources they offer, the capabilities of improvement, the great increase of which their commerce is susceptible, and the extensive field they present for emigration." [2]

But the connexion of the Alexanders with North America extended beyond the boundaries of Nova Scotia. At a later period, when New Scotland, so far as they were concerned, might be said to have ceased to exist, William Lord Alexander obtained from the Council for New England one of those indistinct or conflicting grants of land, which had become so common; in other words, which "were couched in vague language, and were made in hasty succession, without deliberation on the part of the Council of Plymouth, and without any firm purpose of establishing colonies on the part of those for whose benefit they were issued." [3] It consisted of the Province of Maine, or that part of the mainland of New England extending from Piscataqua River, adjoining New Scotland, along the sea-coast to Sagadahoc, and up the river to Kenebek, to be called the country of Canada; also Long Island, &c. The date was April 1635. [4]

The Colonial Papers, now rendered accessible, throw some light on such transactions, having reference to extensive districts of which the proper boundaries were not strictly defined, and which proved, as might be expected, a fruitful source of dispute. Towards the end of January 1635

---

[1] Chalmers' Political Annals, p. 93, Lond, 1780, 4to, a work containing an immense mass of information. It is to be regretted that no second volume (with an index) ever appeared.

[2] The British Dominions in North America, by Joseph Bouchette, vol. 1, p. vii.

[3] Bancroft's United States, vol 1, p 335.   [4] See page 89

the Earl of Stirling and his son Lord Alexander were admitted Councillors and Patentees. On the 3d of February it was proposed, upon obtaining separate personal grants of the lands, laid out in eight divisions, upon the sea-coast of New England, to be held immediately of his Majesty, to resign their great patent into the King's hands. Preliminary to this, deeds of feoffment were made, and leases drawn out in their own favour for the term of three thousand years (which sounds very like perpetuity) in virtue of the original charter to the patentees, adventurers and Council of New England.

At a meeting of the Council for New England, held in the Earl of Carlisle's chamber, Whitehall, 25th April 1635, a declaration was prepared for the intended resignation of their great charter. " *Present,*—Lord Gorges, President; Capt. Mason, Vice-President; Marquis of Hamilton; Earls of Arundel and Surrey, Southampton, Lindsey, Carlisle, Sterling; Lords Maltravers, Alexander ; Sirs Ferdinando Gorges, Kenelm Digby, Robert Mansel, Henry Spilman, James Bagg, and Mr Montague. They have found, by long experience, that their endeavours to advance the plantation of New England have been attended with frequent troubles and great charges; that they have been deprived of near friends and faithful servants employed in that work; assaulted with sharp litigious questions before the Privy Council by the Virginia Company, who complained to Parliament that their plantation was a grievance to the Commonwealth, and that they have been much disheartened by the loss of the 'most noble and principal props thereof,' as the Duke of Lenox, Marquis of Hamilton, and many other 'strong stays to this weak building ;' and also by the claims of the French Ambassador, taking advantage of the divisions of the sea-coast, which have been satisfactorily answered. These crosses only left a 'carcass in a manner breathless,' until some lands in Massachussets Bay were granted to certain persons, who surreptitiously obtained a second grant of lands justly passed to Captain Robert Gorges and others long before." [1]

Accordingly, on the 25th of April that year, when this declaration was adopted, Edward Lord Gorges, President, in name of himself and other members of the Council of New England, presented a

[1] Calendar of State Papers, Colonial, 1574-1660, pp 204-205

petition to Charles the First, on the 1st of May, respecting a voluntary surrender of the great patent of their Corporation, and praying for a royal confirmation of the proposed division of the saids lands. These arrangements seem to have been favourably received, and were probably carried into effect. The new patents were designedly extended both north and south, for the purpose of keeping up the English claims to New Netherlands in possession of the Dutch, to the southward, and to l'Acadie or Nova Scotia, then in possession of the French, to the northward.

On the 1st of November 1638 a meeting of the late Council for New England was held at London in Lord Stirling's house. The object of this meeting was to request the King for an augmentation of a degree more in latitude and longitude to such of themselves who should declare whether they would have it to the northward or westward,—these Councillors being Lord Maltravers, Lord Gorges, Sir Ferdinando Gorges, and the Earl of Stirling.[1]

It has been remarked by an old and intelligent writer that "Royal grants of lands if not occupied, and, in process of time, if another grant (with occupancy) is made to others, the first grant becomes void. Thus Duke Hamilton's grant in the Naraganset country, Mr Mason's grant of New Hampshire, and many grants in the northeast parts of New England, are become void."[2] The obsolete grants to Sir William Alexander of Nova Scotia, as well as to his son of lands in New England, might have been specified in the instances of original holders who had neglected or relinquished their territorial acquirements.

Having in some measure traced the progress and termination of the Earl of Stirling's Colonial schemes, a brief notice may be given of the latter period of his life. He was sworn a privy counsellor, and appointed Secretary of State for Scotland in 1626. He was created Viscount of Stirling, Lord Alexander of Tullibody, 4th September 1630; he was admitted an extraordinary Lord of Session in 1631; and raised to the Earldom in 1633. He obtained at various times from the King several grants, which, although they promised to be lucrative, proved to be

---

[1] Colonial Papers, Calendar, p 282.   [2] Douglass, vol 1 p. 111   See also pp 366, 373

otherwise. One was a license under the Privy Seal for the space of thirty-one years to print "The Psalms of King David, translated by King James," 28th December 1627. This metrical version, published in the King's name, was to a great extent the work of Sir William Alexander. It was not completed or published until the year 1636; but the expectation of having it introduced into general use, so as to supersede the old version of Sternhold and others, which would have insured its circulation to an incalculable extent, and been a lucrative speculation, proved a complete failure.[1] Another grant to Lord Stirling was to authorize the coinage of 6000 stones weight of an inferior kind of copper money. Sir John Scot, when he alludes to this permission to coin base money, far under the value of the weight of copper, says, that "this brought great prejudice to the kingdom,"[2] and rendered him so unpopular that it was said he durst not come to Scotland to attend to the King's affairs. In April 1631 he had a patent under the Privy Seal,[3] "granted be his Majestie to William, Earle of Stirlne, and John Alexander, his sone, and the longer liver of thame twa, to be maisters of all mineralls and metals within this kingdome." The embarrassed state of the Earl's affairs at the time of his decease is sufficient to prove that with all his schemes and speculations he had not succeeded in the ultimate object of acquiring wealth. "He conquest to his old heritage of Menstrie, the baronie of Tillicultrie and Gogar,—all which were comprised from his heirs instantly after his decease: And of six or seven sons none but one or two are remaining. The house of Menstrie was burnt by command of his superior the Earl of Argyle, because his sons were favourers of James Graham (Marquess of Montrose) and his party."[4] If so, this must have been four years after the Earl of Stirling's death. In 1632 Lord Stirling had erected a larger edifice for himself, beautifully situated, with terrace walks, at the head of the Castle Wynd in Stirling. After his death this was also seized by his creditors. It became the property of the Marquess of Argyle, who caused the Earl's armorial bearings and other ornaments to be

---

[1] See Bannatyne Miscellany, vol. i., p. 227-250, and Appendix to Baillie's Letters and Journals, vol iii., pp 525-532.

[2] Sir John Scot's Staggering State.   [3] Regist. Secret. Concilii   [4] Scot s Staggering State

taken down, and replaced with those of his own family.[1] It was long known as Argyll's Lodging, but has in late years been converted into a military hospital for the garrison.

The Earl of Stirling died at London in February 1640. By his wife, Janet Erskine, daughter of Sir William Erskine, Knight, he had a large family of seven sons and three daughters Sir James Balfour says,—"His body was embalmed, and by sea transported to Streveling, and there privatly interr'd by night in Bowie's Iyle [aisle], in Streveling Church, the 12th of Apryle 1640."[2] His patent as Earl in 1633 carries the title to himself and his heirs-male bearing the surname and arms of Alexander. His two eldest sons having predeceased him, it was alleged, with the view of supporting some false claims to succession, that the Earl, fearing the extinction of his male issue, resigned his honours in the King's hands, for the purpose of obtaining a new charter, changing the destination, failing heirs-male, in favour of heirs-female. But such resignation is a mere assumption, without a particle of evidence; and the alleged charter of Novodamus never existed except as a forged document.

It is not required in a volume like the present to trace in minute genealogical detail the descendants of William, Earl of Stirling. It is admitted on all hands, and we presume the matter was well ascertained at the time, that the male succession terminated in the person of Henry, fifth Earl of Stirling, who died at London on the 4th of December 1739.

WILLIAM ALEXANDER, the eldest son, was knighted, and, as presumptive heir of the Viscount and Earl of Stirling, he himself became Lord Alexander in 1630, and Viscount Canada in 1633. From the previous pages it will be seen that on more than one occasion he visited Nova Scotia, and resided for some time in the colony as Deputy-Lieutenant. He afterwards received an extensive grant of territory from the Council for New England on April 1635, as already noticed at page 89. He died during his father's life at London in March 1638, and his body was embalmed and brought to Scotland for interment in the church of Stirling. By his wife, Lady Margaret,

---

[1] An excellent view of the house will be found in Billings's Antiq , vol iv
[2] Balfour's Hist. Works, vol ii , p 427.

daughter of William, Marquess of Douglas, he left one son, William, and two daughters. The lady survived till January 1, 1660.

WILLIAM, second Earl of Stirling, succeeded his grandfather in 1640, when about eight years of age, but he died that year, within a few months of his succession. Both his sisters were married, and their descendants are not extinct.

SIR ANTHONY ALEXANDER, the Earl of Stirling's second son, in July 1626 had a pass allowing him to travel for three years in foreign parts.[1] On the 1st April 1629 he was joined with James Murray of Kilbaberton (who had held the office since 26th December 1607), as joint Master of the King's Works and Buildings in Scotland. He married a daughter of Sir Henry Wardlaw of Pitreavie, but died at London, without issue, in August 1637, and was interred in the family vault in the church of Stirling. Drummond of Hawthornden honoured his memory in a poem of great beauty: "To the Exequies of the Honorable Sr. Antonye Alexander, Knight, &c., A Pastorall Elegie." Edinb., 1638, 4to. Sir James Balfour says,—" About the latter end of August (1637) Sir Anthony Alexander, knight, second son of William, Earl of Stirling, and Master of Works, &c., departed this lyffe at London, from whence his corps, being embalmed, was brought by sea, and, by torche light, privatly interred in Bowes Iyle, in the church of Striveling." [2]

HENRY ALEXANDER, the third son, on the death of his nephew, succeeded as third Earl of Stirling in 1640; but he did not long enjoy his honours, having died about August 1644. By his wife, Mary, daughter of a wealthy London merchant, Sir Peter Vanlore, he had a son Henry, the fourth Earl of Stirling, who survived till 1690, and two daughters, Mary and Jane Alexanders. His widow, the Countess of Stirling, married for her second husband Colonel John Blount, who, after the Restoration of Charles II., presented a memorial respecting the claim, which is added on a subsequent page.

JOHN ALEXANDER, of Over Gogar, the fourth son. He married a daughter of Sir John Graham of Gartmore, leaving one daughter.

CHARLES ALEXANDER, the fifth son. He was witness in December

---

[1] Sir W. Alexander's Register of Letters.   [2] Balfour's Hist. Works, vol. ii , p. 251.

1642 to the testament of his sister Lady Elizabeth Alexander. He is said to have left a son, who died without issue.

Mr LUDOVICK ALEXANDER, the sixth son, had a pass to go to France in December 1634. He died without issue.

JAMES ALEXANDER, the seventh son, was a witness to his sister Lady Elizabeth's testament in December 1642. James Alexander and Grissell Hay had a daughter, Margaret, born 23d June 1669.

The place or vault where the Earl of Stirling and so many of his family were interred was in the Cross Kirk or High Church of Stirling. From its former proprietor it had been known as Bowye's Isle, but belonged to Thomas Craigengelt of that ilk, who, on the 26th February 1618, "resigned his right to that Ile in the Rude Kirk of Stirling, callit of auld the Bowey's Ile, and now Craigengeltis." The Kirk-session, on the 4th October 1631, granted the seat or loft within the said Kirk of Stirling to William, Viscount of Stirling; and on the 4th September 1632 the Session ratified to his Lordship the disposition by the Maister of the Hospital (with consent of the Provost), "of their Isle, situat on the south syde of their kirk, sometyme callit Bowye's or Craigingelt's Iyle, &c."[1] In 1656, when the church was divided into two distinct places of worship, the vault may have been injured. It remained at least long neglected; and the leaden coffins, it is supposed, were abstracted by Cromwell's soldiers. The only inscription of which we have any notice was that erected by the first Countess of Stirling to the memory of her parents, Sir William and Lady Erskine. In 1825, when the assumed Earl of Stirling visited the possessions of his alleged ancestors, and was welcomed by the Provost and Magistrates, with the church bells ringing on such an auspicious event, he presented the family vault to Mr Wright, a writer in the town, who caused it to be enclosed, and appropriated, when it should be required, for his own use. This insured the complete destruction of every vestige of the Alexanders of Menstrie, including the Erskine monument, but a copy of the inscription was fortunately preserved by a local antiquary.[2]

---

[1] Extracts from Maitland Miscellany, vol i, pp 455, 471, 472

[2] See Mr Turnbull's Preface, pp 42-44, to his Report on the Stirling Peerage Trial; where the inscription is printed. Edinb, 1839, 8vo.

IV.—SIR ROBERT GORDON OF LOCHINVAR.

The author of the spirited proposals contained in the "Encourage-ments, &c. by mee, Lochinvar," in 1625, was SIR ROBERT GORDON, in Galloway. The family from which he was descended is traced back, in the Peerage, to the time of King Robert Bruce. Having at a subsequent date acquired this property in Kirkcudbright, Robert, the eldest son of Sir John Gordon of Lochinvar, was served his heir, 5th November 1604 ; and is described "as one of the strongest and most active men of his time." He had occasion to display his bodily power in the Border feuds between the inhabitants of Galloway and Annan-dale. He had the less enviable distinction of being selected, or accused, for the slaughter of James Gordon, his page, on the 29th of June 1608 ; but by a warrant signifying his Majesty's pleasure, signed by the Lord Chancellor, and the Secretary, George, Earl of Dunbar, "the dyet," or day fixed for his trial, was deserted [1] Sir James Balfour, in his Annals, connects the murder of his servant with some scandalous reports, which he admits were unfounded, but uncharitably insinuates that Sir Robert was desirous to have got rid of his wife.[2] In the Court festivities at Prince Henry's Barriers (or tilting match), on the Twelfth Night, Sir Robert was one of the three successful champions to whom prizes were delivered by the Princess Elizabeth in January 1609-10. A contemporary writer indeed says that Gordon's success as a Scot was owing "more in favour of the nation, than for any due desert." [3]

When the proposed establishment of Colonies in America was sanc-tioned by the Crown, Sir Robert Gordon was among the first to embark in the scheme with a proper spirit. He obtained a Charter under the Great Seal, with ample privileges, of certain lands to be erected into the Barony of New Galloway in Nova Scotia, 8th November

---

[1] Pitcairn's Criminal Trials, vol. ii. p. 558.   [2] Balfour's Hist. Works, vol. ii. p. 20
[3] R. Johnstoni Historia, p. 714, Nicholl's Progresses of King James, vol. ii p 283.

1621. This Charter is printed in the present volume.[1] He appears to have engaged in this undertaking with more patriotic zeal and less selfish motives than his precursor, " the Lieutenant Generall to his Majestie in the Kingdome of New Scotland," to whom he dedicates his " Encouragements," in 1625. This tract, which is now of great rarity, is highly honourable to the author, who assigns for his MOTIVES, the propagation of the Gospel among the Heathen; the service of his Prince and native Country, by enlarging its dominions; and the gain to be derived by those who should engage in such an enterprize. His OFFERS to Ministers of the Gospel, Gentlemen, and others who were inclined to become Undertakers, were most liberal and praiseworthy.

Gordon had also a similar Charter under the Great Seal of the barony and lordship of Charles's Island (INSULA CAROLI), dated 1st May 1626.[2] Four days later he obtained the pass for a ship which he was to dispatch to America.[3] In the Signature to Sir Robert Gordon of Lochinvar for this Charter, he is honourably mentioned, as " being one of the first of this Nation who hath projected and undertaken *at his owne charge* to procure a forraine Plantation."[4]

In the Acts of Privy Council, 12th July 1627, we find that Sir Robert had personally appeared before the Lords of Council, and made the following declaration in regard to prizes, then a frequent subject of dispute. But Gordon's death in November that year brought all his schemes of Colonization to a premature close.

LOCHINVAR HIS DECLARATIOUN.

Apud Halyrudhous duodecimo Julij 1627.

The whilk day in presence of the Lords of Secreit Counsell compeirit personallie Sir Robert Gordoun of Lochinvar Knight and declairit that notwithstanding of the Commissioun grantit and exped vnto him this day for his furtherance and advancement in the Kingis Ma[ties] service against the enemie, he was content, of his awne consent, that all the prysses that sall be tane be him, or be utheris having warrant and power from him, on this syde of the Equinoctiall Lyne sall be judged

---

[1] Charters, &c., p. 16.—Line 10, for *desuperet* should read *desuper et*
[2] Reg. Magni Sig. Lib. li No. 126.   [3] Printed supra, p 35
[4] Register of Signatures, &c , vol. xlix   July 8, 1626

in no countrie but in this kingdome be the Admirall of this kingdome, and that he sall make payment to the Kingis Matie and the Admirall of the proportioun dew to thame out of the prysses And that this Declaratioun and Act sall stand in force so long as his Commissioun stands, and ay and whill he give up the same to the saidis Lords

Dr Robert Johnston, who belonged to that part of the country, and was no doubt personally acquainted with Sir Robert Gordon, in mentioning his death says, " Calculo extinctus est. Qui excelsi corporis robore, et animi magnitudine, in omni ætate conspicuus viguerat. Unde singularem gratiam apud magnanimum Principem Henricum promeruerat ; solennique Armorum exercitatione, in Aula victor evaserat ; ac præmium meritæ palmæ tulerat : Henricoque mortuo, fabricatis navibus, ultra Æquinoctialem Scotici nominis famam propagare destinaverat. Verum, morte ejus tam laudabilis conatus evanuit." [1]

Sir Robert Gordon married Lady Elizabeth Ruthven,[2] one of the daughters of William, first Earl of Gowrye ; and had issue, two sons and two daughters. They were divorced about the year 1609, and she became the second wife of Sir Hugh Campbell of Loudon, first Lord Loudoun. She died in January 1617.[3] The eldest son, Sir John Gordon, who seems to have taken no special share in this project of colonization, was served heir of his father 29th March 1628. He was created Viscount of Kenmore and Lord of Lochinvar, by patent, dated 8th January 1633 ; but he did not long enjoy his honours, having died on 12th September 1634, aged thirty-five. The second son, Robert Gordon of Gilston, was joined with his father in the Royal Charter of 1621, containing the grant of the barony of New Galloway in Nova Scotia ; and he appears to have taken the most active share in this enterprise, by visiting the Colony, and superintending its affairs. He died without issue.

[1] Rerum Britannicarum Historiæ, Lib xxii., p. 714 Amstel. 1655, folio.
[2] In the Peerages this Lady is always called Isabella It would appear, however, from her Confirmed Testament, that her name was Elizabeth (Paterson's Ayrshire Families, vol. ii. p 306)
[3] Douglass' Peerage, by Wood, vol ii p 147.

V.—JOHN BURNETT, ABERDEEN.

Although not specially connected with the Collections in the present volume, the following warrant "to traffique with Virginia," preserved among the Colonial Papers, may be added in illustration of the traffic, to a limited extent, which was carried on at this period from some of the ports in Scotland. Of Burnett himself we have no information.

1638.
July 2

[Charles R]

Whereas the Bearer hereof John Burnett of Aberdeene being the sole Marchant of o^r Kingdome of Scotland, that hath supplied the Plantacion of that o^r Colony of Virginia, & become o^r tenant there, hath by occasion of our late proclamation of the fourteenth of March in the thirteenthe yeare of o^r reigne apprehended that some stopp or impeachment of his trade into Scotland may be made by o^r officers there in regard of o^r demand in the said proclamation expressed that all the Tobacco of that Plantacion should be vnloaded and brought into o^r Port of London, whereas the same is only exclusive of other Ports wthin o^r Dominions of England, Ireland and Wales, and no wayes intended to impeach the freedome of commerce and traffique into o^r Kingdome of Scotland by the Natiues thereof: These are therefore to will and require you upon sight hereof to permitt vnto the said John Burnett and his factors a free commerce and traffique from o^r kingdome of Scotland to that o^r Colony, and from thence back againe, as well to importe and vnloade any Marchandize in any port or haven of the said Colony, as likewise to loade and exporte Tobacco or any other Marchandize from thence into any port or ports of o^r said Kingdome, And that without any stop or hindrance or impeachment from you or any other o^r officers or louing subjects as ye or they will answere the contrarey at your perill providing alweis that they pay o^r usuall customes, and enter into bond that he shall not vnloade any where other than in the ports of o^r Kingdome of Scotland, and at every returne shew good Certificates of soe doing before the said Bonds to be released And for his better security in the premisses it is o^r pleasure that this o^r warrant be by you putt vpon public record. Given under o^r hande and seale att o^r Courte att Greenwich the second day of July in the fourteenth yeare of our reigne.

To o^r Trusty and Wellbeloved the Govern^r of o^r Colony of
Vuginia or any other o^r officers that are for the present
or that shall be hereafter, whome it may concerne

VI.—NOVA SCOTIA PAPERS SUBSEQUENT TO THE YEAR 1640.

The following papers are added, with no design of tracing the history of Nova Scotia subsequent to the death of the Earl of Stirling, but simply as throwing some light on transactions with which he had been connected. The name of New Scotland no longer appearing in our Parliamentary or Privy Seal Records; but Acadia and Nova Scotia continued to be mixed up in the contests between the French and English settlers. Perhaps no clearer account is to be found of this period of its history than is given by a late popular writer, Judge Haliburton, in his work entitled, "An Historical and Statistical Account of Nova-Scotia," 1829. Sir Charles St Estienne, or Stephen de La Tour, son and heir of Claude de La Tour, having proved his right to the proprietory of this country by virtue of his father's purchase from Sir William Alexander in 1630, and the subsequent confirmation of his title by the French King, in the fresh disputes which arose after the country was once more regained by the English, the Protector adjudged these lands to La Tour, and granted a charter in his favour, along with Sir Thomas Temple and William Crowne, of the territory under the designation of Acadia, and part of the country commonly called Nova Scotia, extending south-westward to the river St George.

Dr William Douglass, author of "A Summary, Historical and Political, of British Settlements in North America," has a chapter on Nova Scotia or L'Accadie, in which he says,—"Hitherto, it cannot be called a Colony; it is only an impotent British garrison in an ill-regulated French settlement." He adds,—

"There have been many revolutions in the property and dominion of Nova Scotia.

" 1. Anno 1627 and anno 1628, Sir David Kirk and associates, upon a private adventure, but by commission from the King or Crown of

England, conquered the French settlements in Canada and Nova
Scotia; and patents were obtained from the Court of England, by which
the lands called Canada, north of the river St Laurence were granted
to Sir David Kirk, and the lands called Nova Scotia south of the said
river were confirmed to Sir William Alexander.

" 2. Sir William sold the property to M. Claude de la Tom
d'Aunay, a French Protestant, and anno 1632, March 29, by treaty
King Charles quit-claim'd it to France.

" 3. Cromwell sent Col Sedgwick; he reduced it anno 1654, and it
was confirmed to England by treaty in the year following; M. St
Estienne, son and heir of the above Claude de la Tour, came to England, made out his claim, and had the property surrendered to him; this
La Tour sold the property to Sir Thomas Temple, who was governor
and in possession of the property until anno 1662; it was then delivered up to the French by King Charles II. (that race ought to be
called sons of France, not sons of Great Britain) who agreed with the
Temples for a sum of 10,000l sterl. to be paid them (but it never was
satisfied) upon account of their right

" Menival was appointed Governor, and built a small stockaded fort,
called Port-Royal, upon a bason, nine miles from the bay of Fundy;
Nova Scotia was confirmed to the French by the Breda treaty, anno
1667, in the manner of a quit-claim. La Tour, a French Protestant,
upon his returning to the Roman Catholic way of worship, had it confirmed (as to property) to him by the Court of France. La Tour in
the various vicissitudes, was Protestant when the country was under the
dominion of England, and Roman Catholic when it was subject to the
King of France "[1]

In the successive changes that took place, when Nova Scotia, Canada,
and the islands on their coasts, had been ceded to France, and afterwards
regained by the English, the name of New Scotland never appears; and
it is certain that no claims were preferred, nor any reservations made
of rights of superiority supposed to be inherited by the Earl of Stir-

[1] A Summary, Historical and Political, of the First Planting, Progressive Improvements,
and Present State of the British Settlements in North America By William Douglass, M D.,
vol 1, p 306 Boston, 1755, London, reprinted 1755, 2 vols, 8vo

ling's representatives; and, in fact, Henry fourth Earl of Stirling, in his Case submitted to Charles the Second in the year 1660, became an applicant for a continuation of the former grant of Nova Scotia, being in the King's hands, or for payment of the £10,000, also claimed for his Sisters; but neither of them seem to have been successful.[1]

When Major-General Robert Sedgwick, as Lieutenant to the Lord Protector in 1654, took possession of these territories, Cromwell never contemplated restoring the conquered countries to the French, while negotiating the peace of Westphalia. Sir Charles St Estienne, having succeeded his father, presented a memorial setting forth his claims in virtue of the purchase from Sir William Alexander by his father Claude de La Tour. His rights were fully recognized in the following documents:—

1656. July 14.—Warrant for Articles of Agreement between Oliver, Lord Protector, and Sir Charles St Stephen, Lord Delatour, Bart. of Scotland, Thos. Temple, and Will. Crowne, to pass the Great Seal. Letters Patent to be granted on or before 10th of August next, for all those lands in America called Acadia and that part of the country called Nova Scotia, the boundaries of which are particularly described, with reservation of lands already granted to any colony in New England. Some articles or conditions are specified which it is not necessary here to recapitulate.[2]

1656. August 9.—Patent containing a grant to Sir Charles St Stephen, Baron Delatour, Thomas Temple, and William Crowne, of the country and territories called Laccady and Nova Scotia, with reservation of powers and privileges as in the above articles of agreement.[3]

A month later (20th September) La Tour is said to have made a conveyance of his rights to Temple and Crowne. Colonel Temple was not allowed to retain peaceable possession of the country, being exposed to French aggressions, as we learn from the Colonial Papers of 1658 and 1659.[4] He, however, was in possession at the Restoration, and was one of the competing parties who endeavoured to obtain from Charles the Second either a new grant of Nova Scotia, or to be reimbursed for the heavy charges they had severally incurred.

[1] See infra, p. 119.　　[2] Colonial Papers, p 444.　　[3] Ib., p. 447.　　[4] Ib., pp. 469-478

1660
(end of) EXTRACT FROM SEVERALL PROCEEDINGS RELATING TO THE TITLE TO
NOVA SCOTIA.

Anno 1606. That Monsr De la Tour first discouei'd that country neare 60 years agoe, and built for his owne habitation on the place called St Johns Fort vpon the river of St Johns.

1621 Monsr de la Tour comeing in to Scotland engaged Sr Willm Alexander then Sec^{ty} of state to King James to support his right in it, and for that end to take part of the Interest & in order thereto Sir Willm Alexander obtained a Grant of it from K. James 1621.

1625 This grant was by K. Ch. I. confirmed to Sir Willm Alexander (now Earle of Sterline) 1625.

1630 In the yeare 1630 the Ea of Sterline for consideracion conveyed part of Nova Scotia to M^r De la Tour with all rights, &c. and this was confirmed vnder the Great Scale of Scotland

1632 In the year 1632 the Earle of Sterline at the Kings perswasion did (inter alia) surrender into the hands of the French by vertew of a Treaty of that yeare, Fort Royal which was not contained in his grant to La Tour (for which surrender the K. gave the La. a Pr. Scale for 10,000 li. issueable out of the Realme of Scotland, which grant was neuer paid the Earle And thus the pretencions of the Earles Widdow marryed to Col^l Blount, and of the Earles heires (Daughters & Sonnes). In the Earles right come in Sir Lewis Kirke, Mr Fran. Barkly, &c. who bestowed vast sums in planting that Countrey vpon contract with the Earle & who having vpon the said Treaty surrendred their Interest to the French for 60,000 li wch was neuer satisfyed by the French. Kirke and Barkly think they have a equitable pretencion in the matter.

After the yeare 1632 the French that were in possession of Fort Royal make warre vpon La Tour at St John's Fort, whereby La Tour was constrained to goe to New England for succour, for obtaining of wch he mortgages his Fort of St Johns to Mr Gibbons but when La Tour returned to Nova Scotia he finds the French vnder one Douey had seized his Fort St Johns and committed severall other outrages. Of this he complains to the K. of France who disowns the action, & gives La Tour a power to seize Douey whereuer he finds him, in order to satisfaction: La Tour returning to Nova Scotia finds Douey dead, and marrying his widdow enters into possession of Port Royal which he now holds by that right.

1655 Att length in 1655 Sedgwicke having a designe of attempting something in America vpon the Manhattans, the Dutch, & the Peace with Holland having diuerted him; turnes without order his force vpon the French in Nova Scotia seizes La Tour's Forts & brings himselfe pretencions to Cromwell. But Cromwell thought fitt to restore that Countrey to La Tour & with him (vpon Articles agreed between them) to Tho. Temple and Crowne by a Deed, 1656 · And so it remained when the King returned. It may be doubted

1. In which Prince the R^t of Souerainty, and the proprietry is, the King of England or the French King?
2. If in his Ma^{ty} and his subjects, then whether in Temple & Crowne, &c. by Cromwell's Grant? or which pretentions are to be allowed?

1. Kirke ⎱ Baikley⎰ for their 60,000 li, &c.
2. Gibbons for his Mortgage.
3. Earle of Sterline's heires & for their 10,000 li.

To the Right Honble the Lords of his Maties most Hono^{rable} Privy Councill the humble Petition of Charles St Stephens Lord De la Tour Baronet of Nova Scotia, Thomas Temple, and William Crowne, Esqr.

1661 March

Humbly Shewing,

That whereas the Right Honb^{le} Lord Sterlin Secretary of State to King James for the Kingdome of Scotland and one of his said Maties Privy Councill had not only in the yeare 1621 a ffeofm^t and grant of all Nova Scotia to him his heures and assignes for euer, but also power to create Baronets there; which was comfirmed by his late Matie of blessed memory in the yeare 1625 And whereas the said Lord Sterline as well out of affection to yor Pet^r De la Tour's father and himselfe, as also in lieu & recompence of theire great paines and expences, Together with the hazard of theire lives in adventureing first into the Wildernes among the Savages to discover the Country for the service of his said Matie and the publique good and other consideration haueing settled there above 15 yeares before any grant from either of the said Kings, Was pleased to grant a part of the said bordering towards New England vnto your said Pet^{trs} father and himselfe theire heires and assignes for euer, and created them Baronetts of the said Country as a further acknowledgement of theire said service, as by the said grants more fully appeares of which said Countree yor said Pet^{rs} and his Father were quietly possessed duringe the Raigne of the aforesaid Kings without any interruption, as relating vnto the Crowne of England or Scotland. But in the yeare 1654 by strength of forces of the late Cromwells vnder the command of one Major Generall Sedgwick your said Pet^{trs} was by violence forced out of possession and his goods plundred and taken away to the value of about £10,000, and was carried to the said Cromwell where your said Pet^rs waited nere a yeare before he could be heard. And then no releife without paying Cromwells Souldiers and other Debts to the value of about £5000 as by the said Articles dothe appeare. And your Pet^rs Temple and Crowne's right being by purchase from your Pet^r De La Tour upon valuable consideration as by theire covenants fully appeareth, And whereas wee have been lately informed that some not knowing the true state of the right which your Pet^rs have to the said Country, haue endeavoured to obtaine a grant from his now Matie thereof Wee doe not doubt your Lo^pps clemency and justice but that when the evidence of your Pet^rs foresaid right and title shall appeare, wee shall receive a gratious confirmation therein.

> Your Pet^rs humble suit to your Lo^pps is That in tender consideration of the premises they may be admitted to make theire said Titles appeare And that in the interem nothing may be done to theire prejudice.

And your Pet^rs (as in duty bound) shall pray, &c.

(*In dorso.*) The Petition of Charles St Stephens Lord
de La Tour Baronet of Nova Scotia, Thomas Temple
and Wm Crowne. Received first of March 166⅘.
Read at Committee the 12 March 1660[1].

1660
March

THE STATE OF THE CASE OF COLONEL TEMPLE AS TO HYS INTEREST IN NOVA SCOTIA.

These parts of North America called Nova Scotia or Nova Francia, and the severall p^ts thereof Canada & La Cadia have been continually disputed between the subjects of the 2 Crownes of England & France, sometimes the one and sometimes the other haueing possession thereof

About 1632 they were wholly or for the moste part in the possession of the English in which yeare by treatye between the 2 Crownes dated 29th March they were all to be restored to the French and satisfaction in money was agreed to be given to some English, not ffor the said Countreys and fforts but ffor certaine shipps, goods and equipage thereof (wch some interested therein say was never performed) viz. 64,246 liuers 4 solz, trois deniers tournois pour le merchandizes du Vassicu de Jaques & 69,896 liuers neufe solz deuz deniers tournois pour les merchandizes du Vassicu le Benediction le tout temp du Roy et satisfacion pour le regard du naive Le Bride au la Espousse les Counsels

But the French were putt in possession of the ffortes & Countreyes and the Countrey of L'Cadia (with part whereof Col Temple is nowe possessed) was in the hands of Monsʳ Sᵗ Etienne Signeur de La Tour, who the better to secure himself on all sides tooke a grant thereof from Sir William Alexander to whom K. James 10th September 1621 granted a pattent thereof and alsoe ffrom the Frenche Kinge) And built Sᵗ Johns fforte (now the cheife if not the onely ffort) att his owne chardge ffor that Port Royall which was one of those surrendered 1632, was lately demolished soone after itt & all the Countrey & fforts of L'Cadia were taken ffrom de La Tour by Major Sedgwicke in Oliver's time wherevpon he being brought into England solicited the restitution of the fforts and Countrey to him as holding them by a pattent ffrom the Crowne of England , and came to an agreeᵐᵗ wᵗʰ Col. Temple and William Crowne and made over his interest to them by deed dated 20th of Sepʳ 1656 upon a valuable consideration p. vᵗ in the deed videlicet, 3,379 li to Margarett Gibbons the Relict of Major Edward Gibbons ffor wᶜʰ La Tour had some yeares before engaged the said fforts.

Besides Temple could not have the fforts and Country out off the handes off Sedgwickes officers & ffrom the power then in being, untill he had paid 1,800 li to them, besides he is out of purse many thousand poundes to mainteyne them from the Frenche who assaulted him and tooke them But were retaken by Col Temple, though by the Treatye made betweene France and the Protectour that together with other differences considering damages received on the one side & the other, stood reffered to arbitrage wᶜʰ is not yett determined.

So his Case Col. Temple is able to make out by such pattents and evidences as he hath wᵗʰ him in New England.

Ro Nelson

(*In dorso*) Col Temples Case, Mr R. Nelson received
    20th Augˢᵗ 1660.

To the King's most Excellent Majfstie the humble Petition of Col. John   1660
    Blount, the Ladys Mary and Jane Alexander daughters of the late December 1
    Earle of Sterline.

Sheweth,

That Willᴹ late Earle of Sterline Principal Secretary of Scotland having to his vast Expence & the Wastenge of his whole estate in Scotland Planted a Colony in Nova Scotia, and a peace beinge concluded between his late Maᵗⁱᵉ of euer blessed memory & the late French King, Nova Scotia was included in the Articles of peace to be rendered to the French by which the said Earles whole fortune there was lost for reparation whereof His late Maᵗⁱᵉ was graciously pleased to thinke himselfe bound in equity to relieve him & grant his pattents for the reimbursement and payment of £10,000 to him & his assignes out of the Excheq^r and all other the proffits in Scotland whatsoever that should first arise : But the warres ensuing there, and afterwards here the said Earle and his Son, ffather to your petitioners Mary, and Jane, dyed before payment of the said £10,000 & your Pet^r John marryed Dame Mary Countesse of Sterlinge and disbursed for her necessitys and preservation of her Estate and her children £2500.

In tender consideration whereof and for that £10,000 is all the expectancie & subsistance of your Pet^{rs} Mary and Jane & to reimburse your Pet^r John who faithfully served his late Matie & your Matie ever since the first warre in Scotland and commaunded your Maties owne Regiment of Horse That your Matie will be graciously pleased to grant your Letters Pattents for the satisfaction of the said £10,000 in proportion to your Pet^{rs} out of your Maties Receipts in Scotland or other wayes as your Matie shall thinke fitt.

And your Pet^{rs} shall ever pray, &c.

Whitehall, 4 December 1660.

1661
March

His Maty^e being sensible of the Pet^{rs} condition and sufferings is gratiously inclined to releiv them, and is pleased to refer their case to the right Honble the Lord Chambirlane of his Matie hous, that he may consider of their pretensions in equity to Nova Scotia, and to report what he conceaves fit to be done therein whereupon his Maty^e will declare his further pleasure.

LAUDERDAILL.

(*In dorso*) Petⁿ of Coll. John Blount, &c.   Read at the
Committee the 12 March 1661.

May it please yor most Excellent Matie

According to your Maties reference to me vpon the Petition annexed I see find by the patent therein mentioned, of the late King Charles your Royall Father of blessed memory That William late Earle of Sterlino did by speciall order and command from his said Matie According to Articles with the French King render back to the French his plantation of Nova Scotia in consideration whereof His said Matie conceived himselfe bound to relieve him, and gave him the said Patent for Tenne thousand pounds payable out of the first profitts of the Revenue of Scotland, which the Petitio^r affirms to bee yett unsatisfyed And therefore humbly conceive it equitable that the Petitio^{rs} may be paid the same, And in all humilty submit it to y^{or} Maties Royal consideration.

MANCHESTER

THE CASE OF THE RIGHT HON^{BLE} HENRY EARLE OF STERLINE TOUCHING NOVA SCOTIA IN AMERICA.

1660
(end of)

King James by his Letters Patents vnder the Greate Seale of Scotland beareing date 10th Dec 1621 did give and grant vnto Sir William Alexander afterwards EARLE OF STERLINE and his heires All that County of New Scotland.

King Charles by his Infeoffment under the Great Seale of Scotland of the 12th of July 1625, did give graunt and dispose vnto the said Sir William Alexander his heires and assignes, All and singular the lands and dominion of the Signo^r of New Scotland in America.

King Charles by his Letters Patents vnder the great Seale of Scotland beareing date the 3d of May 1627 recitcing the Infeoffm^t afores^d did graunt vnto the said Sir William Alexander and his heires the Admiraltie of New Scotland in America. Sir William Alexander afterwards dyed Henry Earle of Sterline beinge his sonne and heire who is likewise dead Henry now Earl of Sterline being his sonne and heire. It is said that Sr William Alexander did in his lifetime by the Kings generall command withdraw his Plantations in New Scotland. But if any such thing was, it was done vpon consideration of £10,000 to be paid vnto him by the King haueing expended in setthng the Plantation there above £20,000 which 10,000 are to this day vnpaid.

It is humbly prayed by the now EARLE OF STERLINE that in regards the 10,000 li remaine vnpaid and that the Sig^{re} of New Scotland is now in the possession of his Majestie that his Majestie would be pleased to continue vnto him the graunt of that Countrie.

(*In dorso.*) The Case of the Earle of Sterline touching Nova Scotia.

VII.—ROLL OF BARONETS OF NOVA SCOTIA who had Territorial Grants from Sir William Alexander, Earl of Stirling.

The numbers at the right hand side refer to the pages of a volume in the General Register House, containing Precepts of Charters to the several Baronets of Nova Scotia It is titled on the back " Regist Precep Cart pro Baronettis Nov Scoti r" 1625-1630. The Precepts are entered not in strict Chronological order, but probably according to the time of their Registration The names having no references are given on the authority of former lists

Several of the above are included in the Register of the Great Seal, and also, at great length, in the "Register of Signatouris in the Office of Comptrollerie," but others, probably from not having paid the fees, seem not to have been registered.

In drawing these Collections to a close, a few words may be added in reference to the extraordinary claims to Territorial possessions and Superiority supposed to be attached to the Earldom of Stirling. Unless for the assumption that the royal grants to Sir William Alexander of vast territories were inalienable, and remained in full force, to be resumed with the title, we might never have heard of claimants whose pretensions were utterly baseless. That the direct male succession to the Earldom became extinct in 1739 is admitted on all hands. Supposing, however, there had been a continuous and undisputed succession, before any such Superiority could be reclaimed in virtue of grants made by Kings James and Charles, the following questions would remain to be solved:—

First, Whether Sir William Alexander fulfilled all or any of the obligations contained in his grants, by undertaking the Conversion of the infidel natives to the Christian faith,[1] or by the actual Plantation of colonies in New Scotland?

Secondly, Whether Sir William, about the time when raised to the Peerage, had not actually divested himself of whatever right or title he possessed to the Superiority and lordship of his lands in Nova Scotia in terms of his arrangements with Claude St Estienne, Seigneur de la Tour? And

---

[1] In all the early Signatures, the similar words are repeated "for Propagation of Christiane religion within the bounds, countrey, and dominion of New Scotland, lyand within the bounds of America." But not a single instance is on record of either the King, Sir William Alexander, or his adventurers having, I will not say sent, but even of having proposed to send, a minister or missionary for such a purpose. Had the King set his sons Charles II. and James II an example of "banishing to the Plantations" some of the obstreporous clergy, who opposed his innovations in the church, he might have unintentionally rendered the cause of religion a good service. It is to the undying credit of the Protector, that Cromwell, in 1649, ordered a general collection to be made in all the parishes of England and Wales for erecting a Corporation for the propagation of the Gospel in New England.

Thirdly, Whether Charles the First could be said to have exceeded his royal prerogative when, by the treaty of St Germain-en-laye, in March 1632, the whole British possessions in Nova Scotia and Canada, and places adjacent, were ceded and transferred to France, with no reservation in favour of Viscount Stirling and the other proprietors of lands in these territories, which had previously been conveyed to them by charters under the Great Seal of Scotland?

Charles the First indeed admitted that Lord Stirling was entitled to compensation for money that his son Lord Alexander and friends had spent in erecting a fort at Port Royal, before the settlers in that colony were, by the King's peremptory command, in a summary way, dispersed. The sum allotted was £10,000 sterling, but this, as we learn from the petitions of Henry Earl of Stirling,[1] and of Colonel John Blount, the husband of the Countess of Stirling, on behalf of himself and her two daughters,[2] remained unpaid at the Restoration in 1660.

No doubt the King, in his letter to the Privy Council of Scotland, in June 1632, says that this sum of £10,000 of indemnification was not to interfere with the Earl of Stirling's territory in Nova Scotia, &c. But these were mere soothing words of course, signifying nothing, or only a permission to retain an empty titular distinction; for what rights could his Lordship or any other British subject not resident possess in a country which was ceded unconditionally to France? Again, the King, in his letter to the Privy Council, September 27, 1633, says, " hearing that there was a rumour given out by some that *We had totallie left our purpose to plant in that countrie, as having surrendered our right thereof*, leist anie further mistaking sould arise heirupon, We thought good heerby to cleare our intention therein : Which is, That our said Erle, with all such as sall adventure with him, *sall prosecute the said worke*, and be encouraged by all lawfull helpes *as weill by compleitting of the intended number of Knight Baronets* as otherwise." Such vague language conveys no other meaning than that *prosecuting the said worke* extended no further than endeavours to increase the proposed number of Baronets, the King engaging still to maintain the dignity and privileges of the Order, but giving no assurance either for securing the

[1] Supra, p. 119   [2] Ib. p. 117.

lands conveyed to them by their patents, or for any active measures to be pursued towards the plantation of a country which no longer was subject to the British Crown.

The individual claims of the earlier Knight Baronets of Nova Scotia should also form no unimportant element in regard to the Territorial rights claimed for the Earldom of Stirling, although this in a great measure has been ignored or overlooked. In 1625, when this Order was instituted, Nova Scotia was nominally divided into so many baronies, with a certain allotment of land attached to each; and Sir William Alexander was empowered to dispose of these, along with the hereditary dignity, to persons of rank or distinction, upon payment of a stipulated sum. The number of persons was not to exceed One hundred and fifty;[1] and the sum payable by each was three thousand merks[2] (the equivalent to £166, 13s. 4d. sterling). Of this sum one-third was to go into Alexander's pocket, he engaging that the remaining two-thirds should be expended in setting forth the Plantation. Had it been exacted, as in the case of the Ulster settlers, that each Baronet, with a stated number of colonists, should take personal possession, it is certain the number of applicants would have been scanty indeed. To obviate this difficulty it was held, by a fiction of the law, that the usual legal form of taking possession by an instrument of seisin, or infeftment of lands on the other side of the Atlantic, should take place within the Castle of Edinburgh. Yet it appears that during the first four years the applicants who received patents were only about sixty, while during the next ten years about fifty more were induced to avail themselves of this hereditary title;[3] and thus the object remained unaccomplished during the reign of Charles, although its original sphere was so enlarged as to render persons not connected with Scotland admissible to this dignity.

[1] Supra, p. 65, May 5, 1631.   [2] Supra, p 21.

[3] It is no easy matter to prepare a very accurate or satisfactory List of these Knight Baronets The earliest List I have met with is contained in "A Catalogue of the Dukes, Marquesses, Earles, Viscounts, Bishops, Barons of the Kingdomes of England, Scotland, and Ireland, &c" Collected by T W. London, 1640, 12mo At p 71 we find "The names of Knight Baronets of Scotland," amounting in all to ninety-five, including Sir Henry Gib (of St Martin's), but the dates of the patents are not given. Of this Catalogue by T. W. or Thomas Walkely, Lowndes quotes several editions

Such were the immediate results of this scheme, notwithstanding the interest taken by the King in his repeated and urgent appeals to have the number of Baronets completed, as if his own personal advantage was concerned, rather than that of merely serving a favourite in promoting a scheme which had promised to establish his personal dignity and interest.

The precept for a charter to each Knight Baronet was granted in the name of Sir William Alexander, who surrendered to the Crown the respective proportions of his said Lordship of New Scotland to be attached to the Baronetcy, with all the privileges of regality. It is thus clear that the Knight Baronets, according to the extent of their several Baronies, holding of the Crown, were placed on precisely the same footing with the lord superior, and consequently his individual rights, while these remained in force, must have become more and more contracted by each successive resignation.

In the later patents the locality of the lands attached to each new grant of the dignity of Knight Baronet ceased to be defined. This may be reckoned a matter of the smallest importance. Should the representative of any one of the first Nova Scotia Baronets, on the faith of his original patent, conveying to him and his heirs in perpetuity a certain extent of land, to form a distinct Barony in that country, with its boundaries described with seeming minuteness and accuracy, set out on a voyage of discovery, to ascertain its locality, and claim his right to possession, we may presume he would soon find that his prospects of success were by no means very encouraging.

DAVID LAING.

April 30, 1867.

CHARTERS UNDER THE GREAT SEAL

GRANTED TO

SIR WILLIAM ALEXANDER OF MENSTRIE

AND

SIR ROBERT GORDON OF LOCHINVAR,

OF LANDS IN NOVA SCOTIA.

M.DC.XXI.—M.DC.XXVIII

CHARTERS.

CARTA DOMINI WILLELMI ALEXANDRI EQUITIS DOMINII ET BARONIÆ NOVÆ SCOTIÆ IN AMERICA. 10 SEPTEMBRIS 1621.

JACOBUS Dei gratia Magnae Britanniae Franciae et Hiberniae Rex &c. Fideique Defensor Omnibus probis hominibus totius terrae suae clericis et laicis salutem. SCIATIS nos semper ad quamlibet quae ad decus et emolumentum regni nostri Scotiae spectaret occasionem amplectendam fuisse intentos nullamque aut faciliorem aut magis innoxiam acquisitionem censere quam quae in exteris et incultis regnis ubi vitae et victui suppetunt commoda novis deducendis coloniis facta sit; praesertim si vel ipsa regna cultoribus prius vacua vel ab infidelibus quos ad Christianam converti fidem ad Dei gloriam interest plurimum insessa fuerunt; sed cum et alia nonnulla regna et haec non ita pridem nostra Anglia laudabiliter sua nomina novis terris acquisitis et a se subactis indiderunt quam numerosa et frequens Divino beneficio haec gens hac tempestate sit nobiscum reputantes quamque honesto aliquo et utili cultu eam studiose exerceri ne in deteriora ex ignavia et otio prolabatur expediat plerosque in novam deducendos regionem quam coloniis compleant operae pretium duximus qui et animi promptitudine et alacritate corporumque robore et viribus quibuscunque difficultatibus si qui alii mortalium uspiam se audeant opponere hunc conatum huic regno maxime idoneum inde arbitramur quod virorum tantummodo et mulierum jumentorum et frumenti non etiam pecuniae transvectionem postulat neque incommodam ex ipsius regni mercibus retributionem hoc tempore cum negotiatio adeo imminuta sit possit reponere hisce de causis sicuti et propter bonum fidele et gratum dilecti nostri consiliarii Domini Willelmi Alexandri equitis servitium nobis praestitum et praestandum qui propriis impensis ex nostratibus primus externam hanc coloniam ducendam conatus sit diversasque terras infra-designatis limitibus circumscriptas incolendas expetiverit NOS IGITUR ex regali nostra ad

Christianam religionem propagandam et ad opulentiam prosperitatem pacemque naturalium nostrorum subditorum dicti regni nostri Scotiae aequirendam cura sicuti alii principes extranei in talibus casibus hactenus fecerunt cum avisamento et consensu praedilecti nostri consanguinei et consiliarii Joannis Comitis de Mar Domini Erskin et Garcoch summi nostri thesaurarii computorum rotulatoris collectoris ac thesaurarii novarum nostrarum augmentationum hujus regni nostri Scotiae ac reliquorum dominorum nostrorum commissionariorum ejusdem regni nostri Dedimus concessimus et disposuimus tenoreque praesentis cartae nostrae damus concedimus et disponimus praefato Domino Willelmo Alexander haeredibus suis vel assignatis quibuscunque haereditarie omnes et singulas terras continentis ac insulas situatas et jacentes in America intra caput seu promontorium communiter Cap de Sable appellatum jacens prope latitudinem quadraginta trium graduum aut eo circa ab equinoctiali linea versus septentrionem a quo promontorio versus littus maris tendentes ad occidentem ad stationem Sanctae Mariae navium vulgo *Sanctmaries Bay* et deinceps versus septentrionem per directam lineam introitum sive ostium magnae illius stationis navium trajicientes quae excurrit in terrae orientalem plagam inter regiones Suriquorum et Etechemmorum vulgo *Suriquois* et *Etechemines* ad fluvium vulgo nomine Sanctae Crucis appellatum et ad scaturiginem remotissimam sive fontem ex occidentali parte ejusdem qui se primum praedicto fluvio immiscet unde per imaginariam directam lineam quae pergere per terram seu currere versus septentrionem concipietur ad proximam navium stationem fluvium vel scaturiginem in magno fluvio de Cannada sese exonerantem et ab eo pergendo versus orientem per maris oras littorales ejusdem fluvii de Canada ad fluvium stationem navium portum aut littus communiter nomine de Gathepe vel Gaspie notum et appellatum et deinceps versus euronotum ad insulas Bacalaos vel Cap Britton vocatas relinquendo easdem insulas a dextra et voraginem dicti magni fluvii de Canada sive magnae stationis navium et terras de Newfundland cum insulis ad easdem terras pertinentibus a sinistra et deinceps ad caput sive promontorium de Cap Britton praedictum jacens prope latitudinem quadraginta quinque graduum aut eo circa et a dicto promontorio de Cap Britton versus meridiem et occidentem ad praedictum Cap Sable ubi incepit perambulatio includendo et comprehendendo intra dictas maris oras littorales ac earum circumferentias a mari ad mare omnes terras continentis cum fluminibus torrentibus sinubus littoribus insulis aut maribus jacentibus prope aut infra sex leucas ad aliquam earundem partem ex occidentali boreali vel orientali partibus orarum littoralium et praecinctuum earundem et ab euronoto (ubi jacet Cap Britton) et ex australi parte ejusdem (ubi est Cap de Sable) omnia maria ac insulas versus meridiem intra quadraginta leucas dictarum orarum littoralium earundem magnam insulam vulgariter appellatam Yle de Sable vel Sablon includendo jacentem versus Carban

vulgo *south-south-eist* circa triginta leucas a dicto Cap Britton in mari et existentem
in latitudine quadraginta quatuor graduum aut eo circa   Quaequidem terrae praedictae omni tempore affuturo nomine NOVAE SCOTIAE IN AMERICA gaudebunt quas
etiam praefatus Dominus Willelmus in partes et portiones sicut ei visum fuerit dividet
iisdemque nomina pro beneplacito imponet   Unacum omnibus fodinis tam regalibus auri et argenti quam aliis fodinis ferri plumbi cupri stanni aeris ac aliis mineralibus quibuscunque cum potestate effodiendi et de terra effodere causandi purificandi et repurgandi easdem et convertendi ac utendi suo proprio usui aut aliis
usibus quibuscunque sicuti dicto Domino Willelmo Alexander haeredibus suis vel
assignatis aut iis quos suo loco in dictis terris stabilire ipsum contigerit visum fuerit
(reservando solummodo nobis et successoribus nostris decimam partem metalli
vulgo *oore* auri et argenti quod ex terra in posterum effodietur aut lucrabitur)
Relinquendo dicto Domino Willelmo suisque praedictis quodcunque ex aliis metallis
cupri chalibis ferri stanni plumbi aut aliorum mineralium nos vel successores nostri
quovismodo exigere possumus ut eo facilius magnos sumptus in extrahendis praefatis
metallis tollerare possit   Unacum margaritis vulgo *pearle* ac lapidibus praetiosis
quibuscunque aliis lapicidinis silvis virgultis mossis marresiis lacubus aquis piscationibus tam in aqua salsa quam recenti tam regalium piscium quam aliorum venatione aucupatione commoditatibus et haereditamentis quibuscunque   Unacum plenaria potestate privilegio et jurisdictione liberae regalitatis capellae et cancellariae
imperpetuum cumque donatione et patronatus jure ecclesiarum capellarum et
beneficiorum cum tenentibus tenandriis et liberetenentium servitiis earundem una
cum officiis justiciariae et admiralitatis respective infra omnes bondas respective
supra mentionatas   Una etiam cum potestate civitates liberos burgos liberos portus
villas et burgos baroniae erigendi ac fora et nundinas infra bondas dictarum terrarum
constituendi curias justiciariae et admiralitatis infra limites dictarum terrarum fluviorum portuum et marium tenendi una etiam cum potestate imponendi levandi et
recipiendi omnia tolonia custumas anchoragia aliasque dictorum burgorum fororum
nundinarum ac liberorum portuum devorias et eisdem possidendi et gaudendi adeo
libere in omnibus respectibus sicuti quivis baro major aut minor in hoc regno nostro
Scotiae gavisus est aut gaudere poterit quovis tempore praeterito vel futuro cum
omnibus aliis praerogativis privilegiis immunitatibus dignitatibus casualitatibus proficuis et devoriis ad dictas terras maria et bondas earundem spectantibus et pertinentibus et quae nos ipsi dare vel concedere possumus adeo libera et ampla forma sicuti
nos aut aliquis nostrorum nobilium progenitorum aliquas cartas patentes literas infeofamenta donationes aut diplomata concesserunt cuivis subdito nostro cujuscunque
qualitatis aut gradus cuivis societati aut communitati tales colonias in quascunque partes extraneas deducenti aut terras extraneas investiganti in adeo libera et ampla forma

sicuti eadem in hac praesenti carta nostra insereretur   Facimus etiam constituimus
et ordinamus dictum Dominum Willelmum Alexander haeredes suos aut assignatos
vel eorum deputatos nostros HÆREDITARIOS LOCUMTENENTES GENERALES ad repre-
sentandum nostram personam regalem tam per mare quam per terram in regionibus
maris oris ac finibus praedictis in petendo dictas terras quamdiu illic manserit ac
redeundo ab eisdem ad gubernandum regendum et puniendum omnes nostros subditos quos ad dictas terras ire aut easdem inhabitare contigerit aut qui negotiationem cum eisdem suscipient vel in eisdem locis remanebunt ac eisdem ignoscendum
et ad stabiliendum tales leges statuta constitutiones directiones instructiones formas
gubernandi et magistratuum ceremonias infra dictas bondas sicut ipsi Domino Willelmo Alexander aut ejus praedictis ad gubernationem dictae regionis et ejusdem
incolarum in omnibus causis tam criminalibus quam civilibus visum fuerit et easdem
leges regimina formas et ceremonias alterandum et mutandum quoties sibi vel suis
praedictis pro bono et commodo dictae regionis placuerit ita ut dictae leges tam
legibus hujus regni nostri Scotiae quam fieri possunt sint concordes   Volumus etiam
ut in casu rebellionis aut seditionis legibus utatur militaribus adversus delinquentes
vel imperio ipsius sese subtrahentes adeo libere sicuti aliquis locumtenens cujusvis
regni nostri vel dominii virtute officii locumtenentis habent vel habere possunt excludendo omnes alios officiarios hujus regni nostri Scotiae terrestres vel maritimos qui in
posterum aliquid jurisclamei commoditatis authoritatis aut interesse in et ad dictas
terras aut provinciam praedictam vel aliquam mihi jurisdictionem virtute alicujus
praecedentis dispositionis aut diplomatis praetendere possunt   Et ut viris honesto
loco natis sese ad expeditionem istam subeundam et ad coloniae plantationem in
dictis terris addatur animus nos pro nobis nostrisque haeredibus et successoribus
cum avisamento et consensu praedicto virtute praesentis cartae nostrae damus et
concedimus liberam et plenariam potestatem praefato Domino Willelmo Alexander
suisque praedictis conferendi favores privilegia munia et honores in demerentes cum
plenaria potestate eisdem aut eorum alicui quos cum ipso Domino Willelmo suisque
praedictis pactiones vel contractus facere pro eisdem terris contigerit sub subscriptione sua vel suorum praedictorum et sigillo infra mentionato aliquam portionem vel
portiones dictarum terrarum portuum navium stationum fluviorum aut praemissorum
alicujus partis disponendi et extradonandi erigendi etiam omnium generum machinas
artes facultates vel scientias aut easdem exercendi in toto vel in parte sicuti ei pro
bono ipsorum visum fuerit   Dandi etiam concedendi et attribuendi talia officia
titulos jura et potestates constituendi et designandi tales capitaneos officiarios
balivos gubernatores clericos omnesque alios regalitatis baroniae et burgi officiarios
aliosque ministros pro administratione justiciae infra bondas dictarum terrarum aut
in via dum terras istas petunt per mare et ab eisdem redeunt sicuti ei necessarium

videbitur secundum qualitates conditiones et personarum merita quos in aliqua coloniarum dictae provinciae aut aliqua ejusdem parte habitare contigerit aut qui ipsorum bona vel fortunas pro commodo et incremento ejusdem periculo committent et eosdem ab officio removendi alterandi et mutandi prout ei suisque praescriptis expediens videbitur Et cum hujusmodi conatus non sine magno labore et sumptibus fiunt magnamque pecuniae largitionem requirant adeo ut privati cujusvis fortunas excedant et multorum suppetiis indigeant ob quam causam praefatus Dominus Willelmus Alexander suique praescripti cum diversis nostris subditis aliisque pro particularibus periclitationibus et susceptionibus ibidem qui forte cum eo suisque haeredibus assignatis vel deputatis pro terris piscationibus mercimoniis aut populi transportatione cum ipsorum pecoribus rebus et bonis versus dictam Novam Scotiam contractus inibunt volumus ut quicunque tales contractus cum dicto Domino Willelmo suisque praescriptis sub ipsorum subscriptionibus et sigillis expedient limitando assignando et affigendo diem et locum pro personarum bonorum et rerum ad navem deliberatione sub pena et forisfactura cujusdam monetae summae et eosdem contractus non perficient sed ipsum frustrabunt et in itinere designato ei nocebunt quod non solum dicto domino Willelmo suisque praedictis poterit esse praejudicio et nocumento verum etiam nostrae tam laudabili intentioni obstabit et detrimentum inferet tunc licitum erit praefato Domino Willelmo suisque praedictis vel eorum deputatis et conservatoribus inframentionatis in eo casu sibi suisve praedictis quos ad hunc effectum substituet omnes tales summas monetae bona et res forisfactas per talium contractuum violationem assumere Quod ut facilius fiat et legum prolixitas evitetur dedimus et concessimus tenoreque praesentis cartae nostrae damus et concedimus plenariam licentiam libertatem et potestatem dicto Domino Willelmo suisque haeredibus et assignatis praedictis eligendi nominandi assignandi ac ordinandi libertatum et privilegiorum per praesentem nostram cartam sibi suisque praedictis concessorum conservatorem qui expeditae executioni leges et statuta per ipsum suosque praedictos facta secundum potestatem ei suisque praedictis per dictam nostram cartam concessam demandabit volumusque et ordinamus potestatem dicti conservatoris in actionibus et causis ad personas versus dictam plantationem contrahentes spectantibus absolutam esse sine ulla appellatione aut procrastinatione quacunque quiquidem conservator possidebit et gaudebit omnia privilegia immunitates libertates et dignitates quascunque quae quivis conservator Scoticorum privilegiorum apud extraneos vel in Gallia Flandria aut alibi hactenus possiderunt aut gavisi sunt quovis tempore praeterito Et licet omnes tales contractus inter dictum Dominum Willelmum suosque praedictos et praedictos periclitatores per periclitationem et transportationem populorum cum ipsorum bonis et rebus ad statutum diem perficientur et ipsi cum suis omnibus pecoribus et bonis ad littus

illius provinciae animo coloniam ducendi et remanendi appellent et nihilominus postea
vel omnino provinciam Novae Scotiae et ejusdem confinia sine licentia dicti Domini
Willelmi ejusque praedictorum vel eorum deputatorum vel societatem et coloniam
praedictam ubi primum combinati et conjuncti fuerant derelinquent et ad agrestes indigenas in locis remotis et desertis ad habitandum sese conferent quod tunc amittent
et forisfacient omnes terras prius iis concessas omnia etiam bona infra omnes praedictas bondas et licitum erit praedicto Domino Willelmo suisque praedictis eadem fisco
applicare et easdem terras recognoscere eademque omnia ad ipsos vel eorum aliquem
quovismodo spectantia possidere et suo peculiari usui suorumque praedictorum convertere   Et ut omnes dilecti nostri subditi tam regnorum nostrorum et dominiorum
quam alii extranei quos ad dictas terras aut aliquam earundem partem ad mercimonia contrahenda navigare contigerit melius sciant et obedientes sint potestati et
authoritati per nos in praedictum fidelem nostrum consiliarum Dominum Willelmum
Alexander suosque praedictos collatae in omnibus talibus commissionibus warrantis
[et] contractibus quos quovis tempore futuro faciet concedet et constituet pro decen-
tiori et validiori constitutione officiariorum pro gubernatione dictae coloniae concessione terrarum et executione justiciae dictos inhabitantes periclitantes deputatos factores vel assignatos tangentibus in aliqua dictarum terrarum parte vel in navigatione
ad easdem terras nos cum avisamento et consensu praedicto ordinamus quod dictus
Dominus Willelmus Alexander suique praedicti unum commune sigillum habebunt ad
officium locumtenentis justiciariae et admiralitatis spectans quod per dictum Dominum Willelmum Alexander suosque praedictos vel per deputatos suos omni tempore
affuturo custodietur in cujus uno latere nostra insignia insculpentur cum his verbis in
ejusdem circulo et margine Sigillum Regis Scotiae Angliae Franciae et Hyber-
niae et in altero latere imago nostra nostrorumque successorum cum his verbis (Pro
Novae Scotiae Locumtenente) cujus justum exemplar in manibus ac custodia
dicti conservatoris remanebit quo prout occasio requiret in officio suo utetur   Et cum
maxime necessarium sit ut omnes dilecti nostri subditi quotquot dictam provinciam
Novae Scotiae vel ejus confinia incolent in timore Omnipotentis Dei et vero ejus
cultu simul vivant omni conamine nitentes Christianam religionem ibi stabilire
pacem etiam et quietem cum nativis incolis et agrestibus aboriginibus earum terrarum colere (unde ipsi et eorum quilibet mercimonia ibi exercentes tuti cum
oblectamento ea quae magno cum labore et periculo acquisiverunt quiete possidere
possint) nos pro nobis nostrisque successoribus volumus nobisque visum est per
praesentis cartae nostrae tenorem dare et concedere dicto Domino Willelmo Alexander suisque praedictis et eorum deputatis vel aliquibus aliis gubernatoribus officiariis et ministris quos ipsi constituent liberam et absolutam potestatem tractandi
et pacem affinitatem amicitiam et mutua colloquia operam et communicationem cum

agrestibus illis aboriginibus et eorum principibus vel quibuscunque aliis regimen et potestatem in ipsos habentibus contrahendi observandi et alendi tales affinitates et colloquia quae ipsi vel sui praedicti cum iis contrahent modo foedera illa ex adversa parte per ipsos silvestres fideliter observentur quod nisi fiat arma contra ipsos sumendi quibus redigi possunt in ordinem sicuti dicto Willelmo suisque praedictis et deputatis pro honore obedientia et Dei servitio ac stabilimento defensione et conservatione authoritatis nostrae inter ipsos expediens videbitur   Cum potestate etiam praedicto Domino Willelmo Alexander suisque praedictis per ipsos vel eorum deputatos substitutos vel assignatos pro ipsorum defensione [et] tutela omni tempore et omnibus justis occasionibus in posterum aggrediendi ex inopinato invadendi expellendi et armis repellendi tam per mare quam per terram omnibus modis omnes et singulos qui sine speciali licentia dicti Domini Willelmi suorumque praedictorum terras inhabitare aut mercaturam facere in dicta Novae Scotiae provincia aut quavis ejusdem parte conabuntur et similiter omnes alios quoscunque qui aliquid damni detrimenti destructionis laesionis vel invasionis contra provinciam illam aut ejusdem incolas inferre praesumunt quod ut facilius fiat licitum erit dicto Domino Willelmo suisque praedictis eorum deputatis factoribus et assignatis contributiones a periclitantibus et incolis ejusdem levare in unum cogere per proclamationes vel quovis alio ordine talibus temporibus sicuti dicto Domino Willelmo suisque praedictis expediens videbitur omnes nostros subditos infra dictos limites dictae provinciae Novae Scotiae inhabitantes et mercimonia ibidem exercentes convocare pro meliori exercituum necessariorum supplemento et populi et plantationis dictarum terrarum augmentatione et incremento   Cum plenaria potestate privilegio et libertate dicto Domino Willelmo Alexander suisque praedictis per ipsos vel eorum substitutos per quaevis maria sub nostris insigniis et vexillis navigandi cum tot navibus tanti oneris et tam bene munitione viris et victualibus instructis sicuti possunt parare quovis tempore et quoties iis videbitur expediens ac omnes cujuscunque qualitatis et gradus personas subditi nostri[1] existentes aut qui imperio nostro sese subdere ad iter illud suscipiendum voluerint cum ipsorum jumentis equis bobus ovibus bonis et rebus omnibus munitionibus machinis majoribus armis et instrumentis militaribus quotquot voluerint aliisque commoditatibus et rebus necessariis pro usu ejusdem coloniae mutuo commercio cum nativis inhabitantibus earum provinciarum aut aliis qui cum ipsis plantatoribus mercimonia contrahent transportandi et omnes commoditates et mercimonia quae iis videbuntur necessaria in regnum nostrum Scotiae sine alicujus taxationis custumae aut impositionis pro eisdem solutione nobis vel nostris custumariis aut eorum deputatis inde portandi eosdem ab eorum officiis in hac parte pro spatio septem annorum diem datae

---

[1] Sic in Reg —should be *subditos nostros*

praesentium immediate sequentium inhibendo quamquidem solam commoditatem per spatium tredecim annorum in posterum libere concessimus tenoreque praesentis cartae nostrae concedimus et disponimus dicto Domino Willelmo suisque praedictis secundum proportionem quinque pro centum postea mentionatam   Et post tredecim illos annos finitos licitum erit nobis nostrisque successoribus ex omnibus bonis et mercimoniis quae ex hoc regno nostro Scotiae ad eandem provinciam vel ex ea provincia ad dictum regnum nostrum Scotiae exportabuntur vel importabuntur in quibusvis hujus regni nostri portubus per dictum Willelmum suosque praedictos tantum quinque libras pro centum secundum antiquam negotiandi morem sine ulla alia impositione taxatione custuma vel devoria ab ipsis imperpetuum levare et exigere quaquidem summa quinque librarum pro centum sic soluta per dictum Dominum Willelmum suosque praedictos aliisque nostris officiariis ad hunc effectum constitutis exinde licitum erit dicto Domino Willelmo suisque praedictis eadem bona de nostro hoc regno Scotiae in quasvis alias partes vel regiones extraneas sine alicujus alterius custumae taxationis vel devoriae solutione nobis vel nostris haeredibus aut successoribus aut aliquibus aliis transportare et avehere proviso tamen quod dicta bona infra spatium tredecim mensium post ipsarum in quovis hujus regni nostri portu appulsionem navi rursus imponantur   Dando et concedendo absolutam et plenariam potestatem dicto Domino Willelmo suisque praedictis ab omnibus nostris subditis qui colonias ducere mercimonia exercere aut ad easdem terras Novae Scotiae et ab eisdem navigare voluerint praeter dictam summam nobis debitam pro bonis et mercimoniis quinque libras de centum vel ratione exportationis ex hoc regno nostro Scotiae ad provinciam Novae Scotiae vel importationis a dicta provincia ad regnum hoc nostrum Scotiae praedictum in ipsius ejusque praedictorum proprios usus sumendi levandi et recipiendi et similiter de omnibus bonis et mercimoniis quae per nostros subditos coloniarum ductores negotiatores et navigatores de dicta provincia Novae Scotiae ad quaevis nostra dominia aut alia quaevis loca exportabuntur vel a nostris regnis et aliis locis ad dictam Novam Scotiam importabuntur ultra et supra dictam summam nobis destinatam quinque libras de centum   Et de bonis et mercimoniis omnium extraneorum aliorumque sub nostra obedientia [minime] existentium quae vel de provincia Novae Scotiae exportabuntur vel ad eandem importabuntur ultra et supra dictam summam nobis destinatam decem libras de centum dicti Domini Willelmi suorumque praedictorum propriis usibus per tales ministros officiarios vel substitutos eorumve deputatos aut factores quos ipsi ad hunc effectum constituent et designabunt levandi sumendi ac recipiendi   Et pro meliori dicti Domini Willelmi suorumque praedictorum aliorumque omnium dictorum nostrorum subditorum qui dictam Novam Scotiam inhabitare vel ibidem mercimonia exercere voluerint securitate et commoditate et generaliter omnium aliorum qui nostrae authoritati et potestati sese subdere non gravabuntur nobis visum est volumusque quod licitum erit dicto Domino Willelmo suisque praedictis unum aut plura munimina propugnacula castella loca fortia specula armamentaria *lie blokhouss* aliaque aedificia cum portubus et navium stationibus aedificare vel aedificari causare unacum navibus bellicis easdemque pro defensione dictorum locorum applicare sicut dicto Domino Willelmo suisque praedictis pro dicto conamine perficiendo necessarium videbitur proque ipsorum defensione militum catervas ibidem stabilire praeter praedicta supramentionata et generaliter omnia facere quae pro conquaestu augmentatione populi inhabitatione preservatione et gubernatione dictae Novae Scotiae ejusdemque orarum et territorii infra omnes hujusmodi limites pertinentias et dependentias sub nostro nomine et authoritate quodcunque nos si personaliter essemus praesentes facere potuimus licet casus specialem et strictum magis ordinem quam per praesentes praescribitur requirat cui mandato volumus et ordinamus strictissimeque praecipimus omnibus nostris justiciariis officiariis et subditis ad loca illa sese conferentibus ut sese applicent dictoque Domino Willelmo suisque praedictis in omnibus et singulis supra mentionatis earum substantiis circumstantiis et dependentiis intendant et obediant eisque in earum executione in omnibus adeo sint obedientes ut nobis cujus personam representat esse deberent sub pena disobedientiae et rebellionis Et quia fieri potest quod quidam ad dicta loca transportandi refractarii sint et ad eadem loca ire recusabunt aut dicto Domino Willelmo suisque praedictis resistent nobis igitur placet quod omnes vicecomites senescalli regalitatum ballivi pacis justiciarii praepositi et urbium ballivi eorumque officiarii et justiciae ministri quicunque dictum Dominum Willelmum suosque deputatos aliosque praedictos in omnibus et singulis legitimis rebus et factis quas facient aut intendent ad effectum praedictum similiter et eodem modo sicuti nostrum speciale warrantum ad hunc effectum haberent assistent fortisficient et eisdem suppetias ferant Declaramus insuper per praesentis cartae nostrae tenorem omnibus christianis regibus principibus et statibus quod si aliquis vel aliqui qui in posterum de dictis coloniis vel de earum aliqua sit in dicta provincia Novae Scotiae vel aliqui alii sub eorum licentia vel mandato quovis tempore futuro piraticam exercentes per mare vel terram bona alicujus abstulerint vel aliquod injustum vel indebitum hostiliter contra aliquos nostros nostrorumve haeredum et successorum aut aliorum regum principum gubernatorum aut statuum in foedere nobiscum existentium subditos quod tali injuria sic oblata aut justa querela desuper mota per aliquem regem principem gubernatorem statum vel eorum subditos praedictos nos nostri haeredes et successores publicas proclamationes fieri curabimus in aliqua parte dicti regni nostri Scotiae ad hunc effectum magis commoda ut dictus pirata vel piratae qui tales rapinas committent stato tempore per praefatas proclamationes limitando plenarie restituent quaecunque bona sic ablata et pro dictis injuriis omnimodo satisfaciant ita ut dicti principes aliique sic conquaerentes satisfactos se esse reputent et quod si talia facinora committent bona ablata non restituent aut restitui faciant infra limitatum tempus quod tunc in posterum sub nostra protectione et tutela minime erunt et quod licitum erit omnibus principibus aliisque praedictis delinquentes eos hostiliter prosequi et invadere Et licet neminem nobilem aut generosum de patria hac sine licentia nostra decedere statutum sit nihilominus volumus quod praesens hoc diploma sufficiens erit licentia et warrantum omnibus qui se huic itineri committent qui laesaemajestatis non sunt rei vel aliquo alio speciali mandato inhibiti atque etiam per praesentis cartae nostrae tenorem declaramus volumusque quod nemo patria hac decedere permittatur versus dictam Novam Scotiam nullo tempore nisi ii qui juramentum supremitatis nostrae primum susceperint ad quem effectum nos per praesentes dicto Domino Willelmo suisque praedictis vel eorum conservatori vel deputatis idem hoc juramentum omnibus personis versus illas terras in ea colonia sese conferentibus requirere et exhibere plenariam potestatem et authoritatem damus et concedimus Praeterea nos cum avisamento et consensu praedicto pro nobis et successoribus nostris declaramus decernimus et ordinamus quod omnes nostri subditi qui ad dictam Novam Scotiam proficiscentur aut eam incolent eorumque omnes liberi et posteritas qui [quos] ibi nasci contigerit aliique omnes ibidem periclitantes habebunt et possidebunt omnes libertates immunitates et privilegia liberorum et naturalium subditorum regni nostri Scotiae aut aliorum nostrorum dominiorum sicuti ibidem nati fuissent Insuper nos pro nobis et successoribus nostris damus et concedimus dicto Domino Willelmo Alexander suisque praedictis liberam potestatem stabiliendi et cudere causandi monetam pro commercio liberiori inhabitantium dictae provinciae cujusvis metalli quo modo et qua forma voluerint et eisdem praescribent Atque etiam si quae quaestiones aut dubia super interpretatione aut constructione alicujus clausulae in hac presenti carta nostra contentae occurrent ea omnia sumentur et interpretabuntur in amplissima forma et in favorem dicti Domini Willelmi suorumque praedictorum Praeterea nos ex nostra certa scientia proprio motu authoritate regali et potestate regia fecimus univimus annexavimus ereximus creavimus et incorporavimus tenoreque praesentis cartae nostrae facimus unimus annexamus erigimus creamus et incorporamus totam et integram praedictam provinciam et terras Novae Scotiae cum omnibus earundem limitibus et maribus[1] ac mineralibus auri et argenti plumbi cupri chalibis stanni aeris ferri aliisque quibuscunque fodinis margaritis lapidibus praeciosis lapicidinis silvis virgultis mossis marresiis lacubus aquis piscationibus tam in aquis dulcibus quam salsis tam regalium piscium quam aliorum civitatibus liberis portubus liberis burgis urbibus baroniae burgis maris portubus anchoragiis machinis molendinis officiis et jurisdictionibus omnibusque aliis gene-

<hr>

[1] In Reg Mag Sigilli *maris*

raliter et particulariter supra mentionatis in unum integrum et liberum dominium et baroniam per praedictum nomen Novae Scotiae omni tempore futuro appellandum Volumusque et concedimus ac pro nobis et successoribus nostris decernimus et ordinamus quod unica sasina nunc per dictum Dominum Willelmum suosque praedictos omni tempore affuturo super aliquam partem fundi dictarum terrarum et provinciae praescriptae stabit et sufficiens erit sasina pro tota regione cum omnibus partibus pendiculis privilegiis casualitatibus libertatibus et immunitatibus ejusdem supramentionatis absque aliqua alia speciali et particulari sasina per ipsum suosve praedictos apud aliquam aliam partem vel ejusdem locum capienda penes quam sasinam omniaque quae inde secuta sunt aut sequi possunt nos cum avisamento et consensu praescripto pro nobis et successoribus nostris dispensavimus tenoreque praesentis cartae nostrae modo subtus mentionato dispensamus imperpetuum TENENDAM ET HABENDAM totam et integram dictam regionem et dominium Novae Scotiae cum omnibus ejusdem limitibus infra praedicta maria mineralibus auri et argenti cupri chalibis stanni ferri aeris aliisque quibuscunque fodinis margaritis lapidibus praeciosis lapicidinis silvis virgultis mossis marresus lacubus aquis piscationibus tam in aquis dulcibus quam salsis tam regalium piscium quam aliorum civitatibus liberis burgis liberis portubus urbibus baroniae burgis maris portubus anchoragiis machinis molendinis officiis et jurisdictionibus omnibusque aliis generaliter et particulariter supra mentionatis cumque omnibus aliis privilegiis libertatibus immunitatibus casualitatibus aliisque supra expressis praefato Domino Willelmo Alexander haeredibus suis et assignatis de nobis nostrisque successoribus in feodo haereditate libero dominio libera baronia et regalitate imperpetuum modo supramentionato per omnes rectas metas et limites suas prout jacent in longitudine et latitudine in domibus aedificiis aedificatis et aedificandis boscis planis moris marresiis viis semitis aquis stagnis rivolis pratis pascuis et pasturis molendinis multuris et eorum sequelis aucupationibus venationibus piscationibus petariis turbariis carbonibus carbonariis cuniculis cuniculariis columbis columbariis fabrilibus brasinis brueriis et genistis silvis nemoribus et virgultis lignis lapicidus lapide et calce cum curiis et curiarum exitibus herezeldis bludewetis et mulierum marchetis cum furca fossa sok sak thole thame infangtheiff outfangtheiff vert wrak wair veth vennysoun pitt et gallous ac cum omnibus aliis et singulis libertatibus commoditatibus proficuis asiamentis ac justis suis pertinentiis quibuscunque tam non nominatis quam nominatis tam subtus terra quam supra terram procul et prope ad praedictam regionem spectantibus seu juste spectare valentibus quomodolibet in futurum libere quiete plenarie integre honorifice bene et in pace absque ulla revocatione contradictione impedimento aut obstaculo aliquali   Solvendo inde annuatim dictus Dominus Willelmus Alexander suique praedicti nobis nostrisque haeredibus et successoribus unum

denarium monetae Scotiae super fundum dictarum terrarum et provinciae Novae
Scotiae ad festum Nativitatis Christi nomine albae firmae si petatur tantum   Et
quia tentione dictarum terrarum et provinciae Novae Scotiae et alba firma praedicta
deficiente tempestivo et legitimo introitu cujusvis haeredis vel haeredum dicti
Domini Willelmi sibi succedentium quod difficulter per ipsos praestari potest ob
longinquam distantiam ab hoc regno nostro eaedem terrae et provincia ratione
non-introitus in manibus nostris nostrorumve successorum devenient usque ad
legitimum legitimi haeredis introitum et nos nolentes dictas terras et regionem
quovis tempore in non-introitu cadere neque dictum Dominum Willelmum suosque
praedictos beneficiis et proficuis ejusdem eatenus frustrari idcirco nos cum avisamento praedicto cum dicto non-introitu[1] quandocunque contigerit dispensavimus
tenoreque praesentis cartae nostrae pro nobis et successoribus nostris dispensamus
ac etiam renunciavimus et exoneravimus tenoreque ejusdem cartae nostrae cum
consensu praedicto renunciamus et exoneramus dictum Dominum Willelmum
ejusque praescriptos praefatum non-introitum dictae provinciae et regionis quandocunque in manibus nostris deveniet aut ratione non-introitus cadet cum omnibus
quae desuper sequi possunt proviso tamen quod dictus Dominus Willelmus suique
haeredes et assignati infra spatium septem annorum post decessum et obitum
suorum praedecessorum aut introitum ad possessionem dictarum terrarum aliorumque praedictorum per ipsos vel eorum legitimos procuratores ad hunc effectum potestatem habentes nobis nostrisque successoribus homagium faciant et dictas terras dominium et baroniam aliaque praedicta adeant et per nos recipiantur secundum leges et
statuta dicti regni nostri Scotiae   Denique nos pro nobis et successoribus nostris
volumus decernimus et ordinamus praesentem hanc nostram cartam et infeofamentum supra scriptam praedictarum terrarum dominii et regionis Novae Scotiae privilegia et libertates ejusdem in proximo nostro parliamento dicti regni nostri Scotiae
cum contigerit ratificari approbari et confirmari ut vim et efficaciam decreti imbi
habeat penes quod nos pro nobis et successoribus nostris declaramus hanc nostram
cartam sufficiens fore warrantum et in verbo principis eandem ibi ratificari et approbari promittimus atque etiam alterare renovare et eandem in amplissima forma
augere et extendere quoties dicto Domino Willelmo ejusque praedictis necessarium
et expediens videbitur   Insuper nobis visum est ac mandamus et praecipimus
dilectis nostris
vicecomitibus nostris in hac parte specialiter constitutis quatenus post hujus cartae
nostrae nostro sub magno sigillo aspectum statum et sasinam actualem et realem
praefato Domino Willelmo suisque praedictis eorumve actornato vel actornatis terrarum dominii baroniae aliorumque praedictorum cum omnibus libertatibus privilegiis

---

[1] In Reg Mag Sigilli *introitu.*

immunitatibus aliisque supra expressis dare et concedere quam sasinam nos per praesentis cartae nostrae tenorem adeo legitimam et ordinariam esse declaramus ac si
praeceptum sub testimonio nostri Magni Sigilli in amplissima forma cum omnibus
clausulis requisitis ad hunc effectum praedictum haberet penes quod nos pro nobis et
successoribus nostris imperpetuum dispensamus In cujus rei testimonium huic
praesenti cartae nostrae magnum sigillum nostrum apponi praecepimus testibus
praedilectis nostris consanguineis et consiliariis Jacobo Marchione de Hammiltoun
comite Arranie et Cambridge domino Aven et Innerdaill[1] Georgio Mariscalli comite
domino Keyth &c. regni nostri mariscallo Alexandro comite de Dumfermeling
domino Fyvie et Urquhart &c. nostro cancellario Thoma comite de Melros domino
Binning et Byres nostro secretario dilectis nostris familiaribus consiliariis dominis
Ricardo Cokburne juniore de Clerkingtoun nostri secreti sigilli custode Georgio
Hay de Kinfawnis nostrorum rotulorum registri ac consilii clerico Joanne Cokburne
de Ormestoun nostrae justiciariae clerico et Joanne Scot de Scotstarvett nostrae
cancellariae directore militibus　Apud castellum nostrum de Windsore decimo die
mensis Septembris anno Domini millesimo sexcentesimo vigesimo primo regnorumque nostrorum annis quinquagesimo quinto et decimo nono.

> Per signaturam manu S. D. N. Regis suprascriptam ac manibus Can-
> cellarii Thesaurarii Principalis Secretarii ac reliquorum Dominorum
> nostrorum Commissionariorum ac Secreti Consilii ejusdem Regni Sco-
> tiae subscriptam.

Writtin to the Great Seall,
　29 Septemb. 1621.
　　　　J. Scott,
　　　　　gratis.
　Sigellat Edinburgi,
　29. Septemb. 1621,
　　　　Ja. Raithe,
　　　　　grs.

---

[1] In the Regist Mag Sigilli the names of the witnesses are not given, but only a reference, as
specified in an earlier Charter in the Record. The indorsement of the Charter, "Writtin, &c ," of
course is not found in the Register itself.

CARTA DOMINI ROBERTI GORDOUN DE LOCHINVAR MILITIS BARONIE DE GALLOWAY IN NOVA SCOTIA IN AMERICA. 8 NOVEMBRIS 1621.

Jacobus Dei gratia Magne Britannie Francie et Hibernie Rex Fideique Defensor Omnibus probis hominibus totius terre sue clericis et laicis salutem Sciatis quia nos per nostrum infeofamentum et patentes literas nostro sub magno sigillo regni nostri Scotie de data   dedimus concessimus et disposuimus nostro fideli et predilecto consiliario Domino Willhelmo Allexander de Menstri militi heredibus suis et assignatis hereditarie totas et integras terras dominium et baroniam Nove Scotie in America jacentes et bondatas modo in dicto infeofamento mentionato Cujusquidem regionis plantationem cum omnino deserta vel ad minimum ab infidelibus inhabita sit dictus Dominus Willhelmus Allexander aggressus est Que plantatio cum privati cujusvis conatus et vires desuperet dictus Dominus Willhelmus Allexander plerosque subditorum nostrorum ad ibidem periclitandum commovit ac presertim dilectum nostrum Dominum Robertum Gordoun de Lochinvar militem qui rogatu prefati Domini Willielmi magnum opus subiturus magnosque sumptus et expensas in dicta periclitatione impensurus est in quorum sumptuum et expensarum compensationem per contractum et appunctuamentum inter memoratum Dominum Willielmum Allexander de Menstri militem ab una et prefatum Dominum Robertum Gordoun de Lochinvar militem pro seipso ac onus in se suscipientem pro Roberto Gordoun ejus filio legitimo secundo genito ab altera partibus initum et confectum de data apud Edinburgum et vigesimo secundo et   diebus Septembris et anno Domini millesimo sexcentesimo vigesimo primo predictus Dominus Willielmus Alexander ad concurrendum cum prenominato Domino Roberto Gordoun seipsum astrinxit et obligavit pro acquisitione et procuratione in et ad favorem dicti Roberto Gordoun heredum suorum et assignatorum hujus presentis infeofamenti illius partis et portionis dicti dominii et baronie Nove Scotie in America postea modo subsequenti nominate prout in dicto contractu et appunctuamento de data prescripta latius continetur Nos igitur cum avisamento et consensu prefidelis et predilecti nostri consanguinei et consiliarii Joannis Marrie comitis Domini Erskene et Gareoche &c principalis nostri thesaurarii computorum rotulatoris collectoris novarumque nostrarum augmentationum dicti regni nostri Scotie thesaurarii ac etiam cum avisamento et consensu reliquorum Dominorum nostri secreti consilii ejusdem regni nostri nostrorum commissionariorum dedimus concessimus et disposuimus tenoreque presentis carte nostre damus concedimus et disponimus prefato Roberto Gordoun heredibus suis et assignatis hereditarie totam et integram illam partem et portionem predicti dominii et baronie Nove Scotie bondatam ut sequitur videlicet Incipiendo a capite seu promontorio nomine de Caip Brettoun noto et appellato et inde pergendo versus occidentem per oras maritimas insule seu insularum de Caip Brettoun ad stationem navium fretum fluvium aut scaturiginem de Campseaw et ad mediam partem ejusdem que dictas oras maritimas et insulas de Caip Brettoun a continenti regionis Suriquorum (que Nove Scotie provincia est) dividere supponitur ac inde pergendo per mediam partem dicte scaturiginis freti aut fluvii versus septentrionem ad stationem navium Chaleur mediculleum[1] ejusdem perpetuo tenendo et deinceps ad voraginem sive magnum fluvium de Canada relinquendo insulas Cape Brettoun predicto pertinentes a dextra et oras maritimas ex boreali parte continentis Nove Scotie ubi stationes navium de Chaleur et Gaspie jacent a sinistra et deinceps versus septentrionem et orientem ad regionem terre nove vulgo Newfundland et ad caput Ray partem ejusdem et infra decem leucas ejusdem et ab hinc pergendo versus meridiem et occidentem ad caput et promontorium de Caipe Brettoun predictum ubi perambulatio incepit et sex leucas a continenti ad mare ab ulla parte predictarum terrarum infra borealem et australem partes limitum earundem inclusum aut eisdem pertinens aut in dicto contractu contentum inter Badischaleur et portum seu introitum scaturiginis predicte de Campseaw aut juxta eandem ex boreali australi et orientali partibus esse reputatum Quequidem pars et portio dicti dominii et baronie Nove Scotie omni tempore affuturo BARONIA DE GALLOWAY in Nova Scotia in America nuncupabitur et nominabitur Quam etiam prefatus Robertus suique predicti sicuti ipsum expedientissimum videbitur in partes dividet easdem nominibus suis distinguent unacum omnibus fodinis tam regalibus auri et argenti quam aliis fodinis ferri plumbi cupri stanni æris ac aliis mineralibus quibuscunque cum potestate effodiendi aut de terra effodere et extrahere causandi purificandi et repurgandi eadem in suos proprios usus aliosve usus quoscunque convertendi et utendi sicuti dicto Roberto Gordoun heredibus suis et assignatis vel iis quos suo loco in dictis terris stabilire ipsum contigerit visum fuerit RESERVANDO solummodo nobis et successoribus nostris decimam partem metalli vulgo *Oore* auri et argenti quod e terra imposterum effodietur aut lucrabitur Relinquendo

---

[1] This word stands in the Reg *meditulleu* or *mediculleu*—i. e. *meditulleum* or *mediculleum*, probably it should be *medialveum*. The boundary evidently runs northward through the gulf or strait of *Canso*, and then westward through Northumberland strait to the Bay of *Chaleurs*

prenominato Roberto suisque predictis quodcunque ex aliis metallis cupri chalybis
ferri stanni plumbi aut aliorum minerabum nos vel successores nostri exigere
possumus ut eo facilius magnos sumptus in extrahendis metallis tollerare posset
unacum omnibus margaritis vulgo *pearls* ac lapidibus preciosis lapicidinis sylvis
virgultis mossis marresiis lacubus aquis piscationibus tam in aquis dulcibus quam
in salsis tam regalium quam aliorum piscium venatione aucupatione commoditatibus et hereditamentis quibuscunque unacum plenarie potestate privilegio et jurisdictione libere regalitatis capelle et cancellarie imperpetuum cumque donatione et juro
patronatus ecclesiasticarum capellaniarum et beneficiorum cum tenentibus tenandriis
et liberetenentibus servitiis earundem unacum officiis admiralitatis et justiciarie infra
omnes bondas respective supra mentionatas una etiam cum potestate civitates liberos
burgos liberos portus villas et burgos baronie erigendi ac fora et nundinas infra
bondas terrarum et baronie predictarum constituendi curias justiciarie et admiralitatis
infra limites dictarum terrarum fluviorum portuum et niarium tenendi una etiam cum
potestate imponendi levandi et recipiendi omnia tolonia custumas anchoragia aliasque dictorum burgorum fororum nundinarum et liberorum portuum devorias eisdemque fruendi et gaudendi adeo libere in omnibus respectibus sicuti quivis baro major
aut minor in hoc regno nostro Scotie gavisus est aut gaudere poterit quovis tempore
preterito aut futuro cum omnibus aliis privilegiis prerogativis dignitatibus immunitatibus casualitatibus proficuis et devoriis ad predictam baroniam maria et bondas ejusdem quovismodo spectantibus et pertinentibus et que nos ipsi dare vel concedere possumus in adeo libera et ampla forma sicuti nos aut aliquis nostrorum progenitorum aliquas alias literas cartas patentes infeofamenta donationes aut diplomata concesserunt
cuivis subdito nostro cujuscunque qualitatis aut gradus aut cuivis societati et communitati periclitanti aut tales colonias in quascunque partes extraneas deducenti ter-
rasve extraneas investiganti ac in tam libera et ampla forma sicuti eadem hac presenti carta nostra insererentur cum plena potestate prefato Roberto Gordoun suisque
predictis gubernandi regendi et puniendi omnes nostros subditos quos sub mandato
dicti Roberti ad dictam partem et portionem dominii et baronie Nove Scotie predicti profiscisci aut eandem habitare contigerit aut qui in aliqua parte ejusdem
negotiabuntur et remanebunt et stabiliendi ejusmodi leges statuta constitutiones
directiones instructiones formas et ceremonias regiminum et magistratuum infra
dictas bondas sicuti prefato Roberto ejusque predictis pro gubernatione dicte regionis
et ejusdem incolarum in omnibus causis criminalibus et civilibus visum fuerit ac
easdem leges regimina formas et ceremonias alterandi et mutandi quoties sibi
suisque predictis pro bono et commodo dicte regionis placuerit proviso tamen quod
dicte leges legibus hujus regni nostri Scotie quam maxime fieri possint sint concordes   Ac etiam quod prefatus Robertus Gordoun suique predicti sint subjecti et
obedientes legibus tam ecclesiasticis quam civilibus per nos aut successores aliosve

potestatem a nobis habentes statuendis pro gubernatione dicti dominii et baronie de Galloway in Nova Scotia tam ecclesiasticarum quam communitatum ejusdem nostrorumve subditorum ibidem remanentium ac aliorum quovis tempore futuro eo proficiscentium et frequentantium   Et ut viris honesto loco natis sese suosque expeditionem conferant in et ad colonie plantationem in predicta baronia de Galloway faciendam et stabiliendam addatur animus nos pro nobis nostrisque successoribus cum avisamento et consensu predicto tenore presentis carte nostre damus et concedimus liberam et plenariam potestatem prefato Roberto Gordonn suisque predictis approbandi conferendi et consignandi iis eorumque alicui aut aliis quos cum ipso Roberto suisque predictis pactiones vel contractus facere pro eisdem contigerit sub subscriptione sua et sigillo suorumve predictorum aliquam portionem seu portiones terrarum portuum navium stationum fluviorum aut alicujus partis predicte baronie de Galloway omnium etiam generum machinas artes facultates et scientias erigendi aut easdem coercendi in toto vel in parte vel qualibet alia mensura sicuti ipsis pro bono ipsorum expedientissimum videbitur ejusmodi etiam officia titulos jura et potestates dandi concedendi et attribuendi ac tales capitaneos officiarios ballivos gubernatores clericos omnesque alios regalitatum baroniarum et burgorum officiarios aliosque ministros constituendi et designandi pro administratione justicie infra bondas predicte baronie aut in via dum eo per mare proficiscuntur et inde rediunt sicuti ei necessarium videbitur secundum qualitates conditiones et personarum merita quas in aliqua coloniarum dicte baronie aut aliqua ejusdem parte habitare contigerit aut qui ipsorum fortunas aut bona pro commodo et incremento ejusdem in ista expeditione periculo committent ac eosdem ab officio removendi alterandi et mutandi prout ei suisque predictis expediens videbitur   RESERVANDO tamen nostro fideli et predilecto consiliario Domino Willelmo Alexander militi nostro in predicta baronia locumtenenti heredibus suis et assignatis de predictis terris et bondis de Cape Brettoun sive baronia de Galloway prescripta et ejusdem limitibus insulam seu talem partem continentis dicte insule seu insularum de Cape Brettoun predictarum que littoribus terre nove proxime adjacent in optione prefati Domini Willelmi Allexander suorumque predictorum   PROVISO tamen quod viginti quinque miliaria mensure Scotie in circuitu non excedant cum integris privilegiis officiis jurisdictionibus libertatibus et immunitatibus infra bondas predicte insule aut partem continentis jacentibus sicuti nos eadem per patentes nostras literas sub nostro magno sigillo regni nostri Scotie predicti Domino Willelmo heredibus suis et assignatis perprius concessimus   Et licet omnes ejusmodi contractus inter dictum Robertum Gordoun suosque predictos et dictos periclitatores per periclitationem et populorum transportationem cum ipsorum bonis et fortunis ad diem et locum prius statutos perficientur et ipsi cum suis populis bonis et fortunis ad quamlibet partem predicte baronie de Galloway coloniam deducendi et ibidem remanendi gratia appellent   Et nihilominus postea vel omnino predictam baroniam de Galloway in Nova Scotia et ejusdem confinia sine licentia prefati Roberti suorumve predictorum vel eorum deputatorum aut societatem suam et coloniam predictam ubi primum combinati et conjuncti fuerant derelinquent et deserent et ad agrestes indigenas et in locis remotis et desertis sese conferent quod tunc omnes terras prius iis concessas aut concedendas omniaque bona et fortunas infra quamlibet partem bondarum predictarum forisfactura perdent et amittent ac prefato Roberto Gordoun suisque predictis licitum erit ad fiscum redigere et recognoscere omnes ejusmodi terras bona et fortunas eademque omnia iis quovismodo spectantia et pertinentia recipere et possidere et in suum suorumque predictorum particulares usus convertere Et cum maxime necessarium erit ut omnes dilecti nostri subditi quotquot dictam baroniam de Galloway incolent in timore omnipotentis Dei et vero ejus cultu simul vivant cunctis viribus nitentes christianam religionem ibidem stabilire et pacem et quietem civilem cum nativis incolis et agrestibus aboriginibus illarum terrarum colere unde ipsi ipsorumque quilibet mercimonia ibi exercentes tuti et cum majori oblectamento et commoditate ea que magno labore et periculo acquirent possidere possint SIMILITER nos pro nobis nostrisque successoribus volumus nobisque beneplacitum est ac per presentis carte nostre tenorem damus et concedimus prefato Roberto Gordoun suisque predictis eorumque deputatis vel aliis hujusmodi gubernatoribus officiariis et ministris quod ipsi constituent liberam et absolutam potestatem pacem amicitias et affinitatem foedera mutua colloquia et communicationem cum agrestibus aboriginibus et eorum principibus vel quibuscunque aliis regimen et potestatem in ipsos habentibus tractandi et contrahendi hujusmodi foedera et affinitates que ipsi vel sui predicti cum iis contrahent alendi observandi et magna cura retinendi modo ipsi sylvestres foedera illa ex sua parte fideliter observent quod nisi fiat arma contra ipsos sumendi eosque in talem ordinem redigendi sicuti dicto Roberto suisque predictis eorumve deputatis pro honore obedientia et Dei servitio nostreque authoritatis inter ipsos stabilimento protectione et conservatione expediens videbitur cum potestate dicto Roberto Gordoun suisque predictis per ipsos vel eorum deputatos substitutos et assignatos pro ipsorum defensione et tutela omni tempore omnibusque justis occasionibus imposterum aggrediendi ex inopinato invadendi expellendi et armis repellendi tam per mare quam terram omnibus modis omnes et singulos qui sine licentia speciali prefati Roberti Gordoun ejusque predictorum dictam baroniam de Galloway in Nova Scotia vel quamlibet ejusdem partem inhabitare aut ibidem mercaturam facere conabuntur et similiter omnes alios quoscunque qui aliquid damni detrementi destructionis lesionis vel invasionis contra dictam baroniam ejusdemque incolas inferre presument Ac pro meliori ipsorum adversus ejusmodi personas munitione et fortificatione prenominato Roberto Gordoun suisque predictis eorumque deputatis factoribus et assignatis licitum erit periclitantibus et ejusdem incolis contributiones levare ac etiam omnibus nostris subditis infra dictos limites baronie de Galloway predicte inhabitantibus et mercimonia ibidem exercentibus pro meliori copiarum eidem necessariarum supplemento imperare eosque per proclamationes vel quemvis alium ordinem (ejusmodi temporibus et locis sicuti prefato Roberto ejusque predictis visum fuerit) in unum cogere et convocare Ac pro majori populi et plantationis coloniarum in dicta baronia incremento cum plenaria potestate privilegio et libertate supradicto Roberto Gordoun ejusque predictis per ipsos eorumve substitutos per quevis maria sub nostris insignibus navigandi tantis onere munitione viris et victualibus oneratis et instructis sicuti quovis tempore et quoties ipsis videbitur expediens emittere possunt et a quovis dominiorum seu regnorum nostrorum omnes cujuscunque qualitatis status aut gradus personas subditos nostros aut qui imperio nostro subdere ad iter illud suscipiendum voluerint cum ipsorum jumentis equis equabus bobus ovibus bonis et fortunis munitionibus machinis majoribus armis et instrumentis militaribus quotquot voluerint aliisque commoditatibus et rebus necessariis pro usu colonias deducendi ac cum nativis incolis dicte baronie de Galloway aliisque qui cum ipsis coloniarum ductoribus ibidem mercimonia exercebunt mutuo commercio ad dictam baroniam de Galloway transportandi et omnes commoditates et merces que ipsis necessarie videbuntur in regnum nostrum Scotie sine alicujus taxationis custume aut impositionis pro eisdem solutione nobis custumariis nostris eorumve deputatis inde portandi eos ab eisdem ipsorumque in hac parte officiis pro spatio septem annorum diem date presentium sequentium inhibendo Quarumquidem solam commoditatem per spatium tredecim annorum imposterum libere concessimus et disposuimus tenoreque presentis carte nostre concedimus et disponimus prefato Roberto Gordoun ejusque predictis secundum proportionem quinque de centum postea mentionatam Et post tredecim illos annos finitos nobis heredibus et successionibus nostris licitum erit ab omnibus bonis et mercimoniis que ex hoc regno nostro Scotie ad baroniam predictam exportabuntur vel inde ad quosvis portus dicti regni nostri Scotie per perfatum Robertum Gordoun ejusque predictos importabuntur quinque libras tantummodo de centum secundum antiquam negotiandi consuetudinem sine aliqua alia impositione taxatione custuma aut devoria ab ipsis imperpetuum levanda Quaquidem summa quinque librarum de centum per dictum Robertum ejusque predictos nostris officiariis ad hunc affectum constitutis soluta exinde prefato Roberto suisque predictis licitum et liberum erit eadem bona e hoc regno nostro Scotie in quasvis alias partes vel regiones extraneas sine alicujus alterius custume taxationis vel devorie solutione nobis vel heredibus et successoribus nostris alisve quibuscunque transportare et avehere Proviso tamen quod dicta bona infra spatium tredecim mensium post ipsorum in quovis hujus regni nostri portu appulsionem navi rursus imponantur dando et concedendo absolutam et plenariam potestatem prefato Roberto suisque predictis ab omnibus nostris subditis qui colonias deducere mercaturam facere aut ad dictam baroniam de Galloway et ad eadem navigare voluerint preter dictam summam nobis solvi statutam pro bonis et mercibus ut predicitur quinque libras de centum vel ratione exportationis ex hoc regno nostro Scotie ad dictam baroniam de Galloway vel importationis a dicta baronia ad hoc regnum nostrum Scotie predictum in ipsius suorumque prescriptorum proprios usus sumendi levandi et recipiendi et similiter de omnibus bonis et mercimoniis que per nostros subditos coloniarum deductores negotiatores et navigatores a dicta baronia de Galloway ad quevis nostra dominia aut alia quevis loca exportabuntur vel a regnis nostris et aliis locis ad dictam baroniam importabuntur preter et ultra summam nobis destinatam quinque libras de centum ac etiam de bonis et mercimoniis omnium extraneorum aliorumque sub nostro imperio minime existentium que vel de predicta baronia de Galloway exportabuntur vel ad eandem importabuntur preter et ultra summam nobis destinatam decem libras de centum in dicti Roberti suorumque predictorum proprios usus per tales ministros officiarios et substitutos eorumve substitutos factores et assignatos quales ipsi constituent et designabunt levandi recipiendi et colligendi Et pro meliori prefati Roberti ejusque predictorum aliorumque omnium dilectorum nostrorum subditorum qui dictam baroniam de Galloway inhabitare vel ibidem mercaturam exercere voluerint et generaliter omnium aliorum qui ibidem nostre authoritati et regie potestati sese subdere minime gravabuntur securitate et commoditate nos volumus et damus licentiam prefato Roberto Gordoun ejusque predictis unum aut plura presidia propugnacula loca fortia munitoria turres excubitorias asyla hospitia aliaque edificia cum portubus et navium stationibus edificare seu edificari causandi navesque bellicas extruendi easdemque pro dictorum locorum defensione collocandi sicuti dicto Roberto suisque predictis pro dicto conamine perficiendo utile et necessarium videbitur et pro eorum protectione presidia ponendi et ultra et supra ea que in hac presenti carta nostra mentionata sunt et generaliter omnia faciendi que pro dominatione populi frequentatione inhabitatione preservatione et gubernatione dicto baronie de Galloway et omnium orarum et pomeriorum infra precinctum ejusdem et pertinentiarum et dependentiarum ejusdem sub nostro nomine et authoritate quecunque legitime fieri possunt exceptis iis que ad officium generalis nostri locumtenentis totius et integri dicti dominii et baronie in America spectant quod officium cum privilegiis et libertatibus eidem pertinentibus predicto Domino Willelmo Alexander ejusque predictis expresse reservatur PRETEREA nos mandamus et ordinamus strictissimeque precipimus omnibus officiariis justiciariis et subditis ad loca predicta sese conferentibus ut sese accommodent et predicto Roberto Gordoun ejusque predictis in omnibus et singulis predictis eorum substantiis circumstantiis et dependentiis attendant et obediant sub pena contumacie et rebellionis Et quia fieri potest quod sunt quidam licentiosi et dissoluti ad dictam baroniam de Galloway transportandi qui forsan dicto Roberto Gordoun usque

[ejusque] predictis renuent et resistent NOBIS IGITUR beneplacitum est quod omnes
vicecomites senescalli ballivi regalitatum pacis justiciarii prepositi et ballivi burgorum eorumque officiarii et justicie ministri quicunque prefato Roberto ipsius deputatis aliisque predictis in omnibus et singulis rebus quas ad effectum prescriptum intendent aut efficient similiter ac eodem modo ac si nostrum speciale warrantum ad hunc
effectum scriptum haberent assistant auxilientur protegant et suppetias ferant IN-
SUPER per presentis carte nostre tenorem declaramus omnibus christianis regibus
principibus et statibus quod si aliquis vel aliqui qui coloniam dicte baronie de Galloway vel quamvis aliam imposterum incolet vel aliqui alii sub eorum licentia de
mandato quovis tempore futuro piraticam exercentes per mare vel terram bona alicujus diripuerint et abstulerint vel aliquod injustum vel illegitimum facinus hostiliter contra aliquos nostros nostrorumve heredum vel successorum aut aliorum regum
principum aut statuum nobiscum et heredibus nostris confederatorum subditos
patraverint quod tali injuria sic oblata ac justa querela desuper mota per aliquem
regem principem gubernatorem statum vel eorum subditos predictos nos nostri heredes et successores publicas proclamationes fieri curabimus infra aliquam partem
regni nostri Scotie ad hunc effectum magis commodam ut dictus predator vel pre-
datores qui tales rapinas commiserint stato tempore per dictas proclamationes limitando quecunque bona sic ablata plenarie restituant et pro dictis injuriis omnino satisfaciant ita ut dicti principes aliique sic conquerentes sese plenarie satisfactos et
contentos esse reputent Et si aliquis vel aliqui talia facinora patrantes bona ablata
restituere aut congruam et condignam satisfactionem infra ejusmodi tempus limitandum facere recusaverint quod tunc nostra protectione et tutela omnino imposterum privabuntur et cunctis principibus aliisque predictis licitum erit ejusmodi pre-
datores eorumve singulos hostiliter prosequi et invadere Et licet neminem nobilem
aut generosum de hac sua patria sine permissione et licentia nostra decedere
statutum sit nihilominus volumus hoc presens diploma sufficientem fore licentiam
et warrantum omnibus qui expeditionem hanc suscipient nisi fuerint lesemajestatis
rei vel aliquo speciali mandato inhibiti AC ETIAM per presentis carte nostre tenorem
volumus et declaramus quod nemo versus dictam baroniam de Galloway de hac
sua patria decedere permittatur nisi qui juramentum supremitatis nostre prius
susceperint ad quem effectum nos per presentes damus et concedimus plenariam
potestatem et licentiam prefato Roberto Gordoun suisque predictis vel privilegiorum
Nove Scotie conservatoribus eorumve deputatis idem hoc juramentum omnibus quos
versus illam coloniam expeditionem facere et ibidem remanere contigerit requirendi
et exhibendi PRETEREA nos cum avisamento predicto pro nobis et successoribus nostris declaramus decernimus et ordinamus quod omnes nostri subditi qui ad dictam
baroniam de Galloway proficiscentur aut eam incolent omnesque eorum liberi et
posteritas quos infra ejusdem limites nasci contigerit et similiter omnes qui ibidem

periclitabuntur omnes libertates immunitates et privilegia liberorum et naturalium
subditorum dicti regni nostri Scotie aut quorumvis aliorum nostrorum dominiorum
possidebunt et gaudebunt ac si ibidem nati fuissent Et preterea nos pro nobis et
successoribus nostris damus et concedimus prefato Roberto Gordoun et suis predictis
cotumve successoribus pro faciliori et meliori commercio et coemptione bonam et
usualem monetam inter incolas stabiliendi et cudere causandi ex quovis metallo iis
modo et forma quos ipsi limitabunt et designabunt ac etiam volumus si que ques-
tiones aut dubia super interpretatione aut constructione alicujus clausule in hac presenti carta nostra occurrant ea omnia in amplissima et optima forma in favorem dicti
Roberti Gordoun ejusque prescriptorum accipi et interpretari Insuper nos ex nostris
certa scientia proprioque motu authoritate regali et regia potestate fecimus univimus
annexavimus creavimus et incorporavimus tenoreque presentis carte nostre facimus
unimus annexamus creamus et incorporamus totam et integram dictam partem et
portionem dicti dominii et baronie Nove Scotie in America cum omnibus fodinis
auri et argenti plumbi cupri chalybis stanni aeris ferri aliisque fodinis et mineralibus
quibuscunque cum omnibus margaritis lapidibus preciosis lapicidinis sylvis virgultis
mossis mariesiis lacubus aquis piscationibus tam in aquis dulcibus quam salsis tam
regalium quam aliorum piscium civitatibus liberis burgis liberis portubus urbibus
baronarum burgis portubus marinis anchoragiis machinis molendinis officiis et jurisdictionibus omnibusque aliis generaliter et particulariter supra expressis in unam
integram et liberam baroniam baroniam de Galloway omni tempore affuturo nuncupandam Volumusque et concedimus ac pro nobis et successoribus nostris decernimus et ordinamus quod unica sasina nunc per prefatum Robertum Gordoun heredes suos et assignatos predictos omni tempore futuro super fundo alicujus partis
predicte partis et portionis dicti dominii et baronie Nove Scotie in America capienda stabit et sufficiens erit sasina pro tota et integra predicta parte et portione
dicti dominii et baronie Nove Scotie cum omnibus partibus pendiculis privilegiis
casualitatibus libertatibus et immunitatibus ejusdem supra mentionatis absque aliqua
alia speciali aut particulari sasina per ipsum suosque predictos apud aliquem aliam partem seu locum ejusdem capienda penes quam sasinam omniaque inde sequuta aut que
desuper sequi possunt nos cum avisamento et consensu prescripto pro nobis et successoribus nostris dispensavimus tenoreque presentis carte nostre dispensamus imperpetuum modo subtus specificato Tenendam et habendam totam et integram predictam partem et portionem predicti dominii et baronie Nove Scotie in America nunc
unitam creatam et incorporatam in unam integram et liberam baroniam baroniam de
Galloway ut predicitur nuncupandam cum omnibus fodinis auri et argenti plumbi
cupri chalybis stanni æris ferri aliisque fodinis et mineralibus quibuscunque cum
omnibus margaritis lapidibus preciosis lapicidinis sylvis virgultis mossis marresiis
lacubus aquis piscationibus tam in aquis dulcibus quam salsis tam regalium quam

aliorum piscium civitatibus liberis burgis liberis portubus urbibus baroniarum burgis
portubus marinis anchoragiis machinis molendinis officiis et jurisdictionibus omnibusque aliis generaliter et particulariter supra expressis ac cum omnibus aliis privilegiis
immunitatibus casualitatibus aliisque supramentionatis sepefato Roberto Gordoun
heredibus suis et assignatis predictis nobis et successoribus nostris in libera baronia
et regalitate imperpetuum modo supra expresso per omnes rectas metas suas antiquas et divisas prout jacent in longitudine et latitudine in domibus edificiis boscis
planis moris marresiis viis semitis aquis stagnis rivolis pratis pascuis et pasturis
molendinis multuris et eorum sequelis aucupationibus venationibus piscationibus
petariis turbariis carbonibus carbonariis cuniculis cunicularus columbis columbariis
fabrilibus brasinis brueriis et genestis sylvis nemoribus et virgultis lignis tignis
lapicidiis lapide et calce cum curiis et earum exitibus herezeldis bluduitis et mulierum merchetis ac cum furca fossa sok sak thole them infangtheiff outfangtheiff
wrak wair wraith vert et vennessoun pit et gallowis ac cum omnibus aliis et singulis libertatibus commoditatibus proficuis asiamentis ac justis suis pertinentiis quibuscunque tam non nominatis quam nominatis tam subtus terra quam supra terram
procul et prope ad predictas terras et baroniam aliaque predicta cum pertinentiis
spectantibus seu juste spectare valentibus quomodolibet in futurum libere quiete
plenarie integre honorifice bene et in pace sine aliquo revocatione impedimento aut
obstaculo quocunque SOLVENDO inde annuatim prefatus Robertus Gordoun ejusque
predicti nobis et successoribus nostris unum denarium monete Scotie super solo dictarum terrarum et baronie de Galloway ad festum Nativitatis Christi nomine albe
firme si petatur tantum   Et quia tentione dicte baronie de Galloway et alba firma
predicta deficiente tempestivo et legitimo introitu cujusvis heredis aut heredum prefati Roberti Gordoun vel sibi in eisdem succedentium (quod difficulter ab iis prestari
potest ob longinquam distantiam dictarum terrarum ab hoc regno nostro) eedem terre
et baronia predicta ratione nonintroitus in manibus nostris nostrorumve successorum
devenient et earundem commoditas et proficua nobis et successoribus nostris redunda-
bunt usque ad legitimum legitimi heredis introitum   Et nos nolentes dictam baroniam
quovis tempore futuro in nonintroitum cadere neque dictum Robertum ejusque predictos proficuis et emolumentis ejusdem baronie catenus frustrari   IDCIRCO nos cum
avisamento predicto cum dicto nonintroitu quandocunque contigerit dispensavimus
ac pro nobis et successoribus nostris tenore presentis carte nostre dispensamus   Ac
ETIAM renunciavimus et exoneravimus tenoreque presentis carte nostre cum consensu
prescripto renunciamus [et] exoneramus dictum Robertum Gordoun ejusque predictos de predicto nonintroitu terrarum et baronie de Galloway prescriptarum quandocunque in manibus nostris devenire contigerit cum omnibus proficuis earundem ac
omnibus que desuper sequi possunt pro nunc et imperpetuum   PROVISO tamen quod
prefatus Robertus heredes sui et assignati predicti infra spatium septem annorum post

decessum et obitum suorum predicessorum aut introitum ad possessionem dictarum terrarum aliorumque predictorum per ipsos vel eorum legitimos procuratores ad hunc effectum potestatem habentes nobis successoribus nostris pareant seu homagium prae-stent et ad dictas terras et baroniam aliaque predicta intrentur et secundum leges et statuta dicti regni nostri Scotie per nos recipiantur DENIQUE nos pro nobis et suc-cessoribus nostris volumus decernimus et ordinamus presentem hanc nostram cartam et infeofamentum suprascriptum predictarum terrarum et baronie de Galloway pri-vilegiorum et libertatum earundem in proximo parliamento dicti regni nostri Scotie cum contigerit ratificare approbare et confirmare ut vim et efficaciam decreti et acti inde habeat penes quas nos pro nobis et successoribus nostris declaramus hanc pre-sentem cartam nostram sufficiens fore wariantum et in verbo Principis eandem rati-ficare et approbare promittimus ac etiam alterare renovare et eandem in amplissimam formam augere et extendere quoties dicto Roberto suisque predictis necessarium et expediens videbitur INSUPER volumus mandamus et precipimus dilectis nostris

vicecomitibus nostris in hac parte specialiter constitutis quatenus post hujus carte nostre sub nostro magno sigillo aspectum statum et sasinam actualem et realem prefato Roberto Gordoun suisque predictis eorumve actornato vel actornatis terrarum et baronie de Galloway aliorumque pre-dictorum cum omnibus libertatibus privilegiis immunitatibus aliisque supra expressis sine dilatione tradant et concedant quam sasinam nos per presentis carte nostre tenorem tam legitimam et ordinariam fore declaramus quam si preceptum sub testi-monio magni nostri sigilli in amplissima forma cum omnibus clausulis requisitis ad hunc effectum predictum haberent penes quod nos pro nobis et successoribus nostris imperpetuum dispensamus IN CUJUS REI testimonium huic presenti carte nostre magnum sigillum nostrum apponi precepimus TESTIBUS predilectis nostris consan-guineis et consiliariis Jacobo Marchione de Hammiltoun Comite de Arrania Domino Even &c. Georgio Mariscalli Comite Domino Keith &c. regni nostri mariscallo Alex-andro Comite de Dumfermling Domino Fyvie et Urquhart &c. nostro cancellario Thoma Comite de Melrois Domino Binning et Byris &c. nostro secretario dilectis nostris familiaribus consiliariis Dominis Richardo Cokburne juniore de Clerkingtoun nostri secreti sigilli custode Georgio Hay de Kinfawinis nostrorum rotulorum regis-tri ac consilii clerico Joanne Cokburne de Ormestoun nostre Justiciarie clerico et Joanne Scott de Scottistarvet nostre cancellarie directore militibus Apud Theobaldis octavo die mensis Novembris anno Domini millesimo sexcentesimo vigesimo primo regnorumque nostrorum annis quinquagesimo quarto et decimo nono.

CARTA DOMINI WILLELMI ALEXANDER DE MENSTRIE MILITIS TERRARUM BARONIE ET DOMINII NOVE SCOTIE IN AMERICA. 12 JULII 1625.

CAROLUS Dei gratia Magnae Britanniae Franciae et Hiberniae Rex Fideique Defensor Omnibus probis hominibus totius terrae suae clericis et laicis salutem SCIATIS nos semper ad quamlibet quae ad decus et emolumentum regni nostri Scotiae spectaret occasionem amplectendum fuisse intentos nullamque aut faciliorem aut magis innoxiam acquisitionem censere quam quae in exteris et incultis regnis ubi vitae et victui suppetunt commoda novis deducendis coloniis facta sit praesertim si vel ipsa regna cultoribus prius vacua vel ab infidelibus quos ad Christianam converti fidem ad Dei gloriam interest plurimum insessa fuerunt sed cum et alia nonnulla regna et haec non ita pridem nostra Anglia laudabiliter sua nomina novis terris acquisitis et a se subactis indiderunt quam numerosa et frequens Divino beneficio haec gens hac tempestate sit nobiscum reputantes quamque honesto aliquo et utili cultu eam studiose exerceri ne in deteriora ex ignavia et otio prolabatur expediat plerosque in novam deducendos regionem quam coloniis compleant operae pretium duximus qui et animi promptitudine et alacritate corporumque robore et viribus quibuscunque difficultatibus si qui alii mortalium uspiam se audeant opponere hunc conatum huic regno maxime idoneum inde arbitramur quod virorum tantummodo et mulierum jumentorum et frumenti non etiam pecuniae transvectionem postulat neque incommodum ex ipsius regni mercibus retributionem hoc tempore cum negotiatio adeo imminuta sit possit reponere Hisce de causis sicuti et propter bonum fidele et gratum dilecti nostri consiliarii Domini Willhelmi Alexander equitis servitium nobis praestitum et praestandum qui propriis impensis ex nostratibus primus externam hanc coloniam ducendam conatus sit diversasque terras infradesignatis limitibus circumscriptas incolendas expetiverit Nos IGITUR ex regali nostra ad Christianam religionem propagandam et ad opulentiam prosperitatem pacemque naturalium nostrorum subditorum dicti regni nostri Scotiae acquirendam cura sicuti alii principes extranei in talibus casibus hactenus fecerunt cum avisamento et consensu praedilecti nostri consanguinei et consiliarii Joannis Comitis de Mar Domini Erskene et Garioche &c. summi nostri thesaurarii computorum rotulatoris collectoris ac thesaurarii novarum nostrarum augmentationum hujus regni nostri Scotiae ac reliquorum dominorum nostrorum commissionariorum ejusdem regni nostri

Dedimus concessimus et disposuimus tenoreque piaesentis cartae nostrae damus concedimus et disponimus praefato Domino Willielmo Alexander haeredibus suis vel assignatis quibuscunque haereditarie OMNES et singulas terras continentis ac insulas situatas et jacentes in America juxta caput seu promontorium communiter *Cap de Sable* appellatum jacens prope latitudinem quadraginta trium graduum aut eo circa ab equinoxiali linea versus septentrionem a quo promontorio versus littus maris tendendo ad occidentem ad stationem navium Sanctae Mariae vulgo *St Maries Bay* et deinceps versus septentrionem per directam lineam introitum sive ostium magnae illius stationis navium transeundo quae excurrit in terrae orientalem plagam inter regiones Suriquorum et Etecheminorum vulgo *Suriquois* et *Etechemines* ad fluvium vulgo Sanctae Crucis appellatum et ad scaturiginem remotissimam sive fontem ex occidentali parte ejusdem qui se primum praedicto fluvio immiscet unde per imaginariam directam lineam quae pergere per terram seu curiere versus septentrionem concipietur ad proximam navium stationem in fluvium vel scaturiginem in magno fluvio de Cannada sese exonerantem et ab eo pergendo versus orientem per maris oras littorales ejusdem fluvii de Cannada ad fluvium stationem navium portum aut littus communiter nomine de *Gathepe* vel *Gaspie* notum et appellatum et deinceps versus euronotum ad insulas Bacalaos vel *Cap Brittoun* vocatas reliquendo easdem insulas a dextra et voraginem dicti magni fluvii de Cannada sive magnae stationis navium et terras de Newfundland cum insulis ad easdem terras pertinentibus a sinistra et deinceps ad caput sive promontorium de Cap Brittoun praedictum jacens prope latitudinem quadraginta quinque graduum aut eo circa et a dicto promontorio de Cap Brittoun versus meridiem et occidentem ad praedictum Cap Sable ubi incepit perambulatio includendo et comprehendendo intra dictas maris oras littorales ac earum circumferentias a mari ad mare omnes terras continentis cum fluminibus torrentibus sinubus littoribus insulis aut maribus jacentes prope aut infra sex leucas ad aliquam earundem partem ex occidentali boreali vel orientali partibus orarum littoralium et praecinctuum earundem et ab euronoto (ubi jacet Cap Brittoun) ex australi parte ejusdem (ubi est Cap de Sable) omnia maria et insulas versus meridiem intra quadraginta leucas dictarum orarum littoralium earundem magnam insulam vulgariter appellatam *Ile de Sable* vel *Sablon* includendo jacentem versus Carbane vulgo *south-south-eist* circa triginta leucas a dicto Cap Brittoun in mari et existentem in latitudine quadraginta quatuor graduum aut eo circa Quaequidem terrae praedictae omni tempore affuturo nomine NOVAE SCOTIAE IN AMERICA gaudebunt quas etiam praefatus Dominus Willielmus in partes et portiones sicut ei visum fuerit dividet eisdemque nomina pro beneplacito imponet Unacum omnibus fodinis tam regalibus auri et argenti quam aliis fodinis ferri plumbi cupri stanni aeris ac aliis mineralibus quibuscunque cum potestate effodiendi et ex terra effodere causandi purificandi et repurgandi easdem ac convertendi ac utendi suo proprio usui aut aliis usibus quibuscunque sicuti dicto Domino Wilhelmo Alexander haeredibus suis et assignatis aut iis quos suo loco in dictis terris stabilire ipsum contigerit visum fuerit RESERVANDO solummodo nobis et successoribus nostris decimam partem metalli vulgo *ure* auri et argenti quod ex terra imposterum effodietur aut lucrabitur Relinquendo dicto Domino Wilhelmo suisque praedictis quodcunque ex aliis metallis cupri chalybis ferri stanni plumbi aut aliorum mineralium nos vel successores nostri quovismodo exigere possumus ut eo facilius magnos sumptus in extrahendis praefatis metallis tolerare possint Unacum margaritis vulgo *pearle* ac lapidibus praeciosis quibuscunque aliis lapicidinis silvis virgultis mossis marresiis lacubus aquis piscationibus tam in aqua salsa quam recenti tam regalium piscium quam aliorum venatione aucupatione commoditatibus et haereditamentis quibuscunque Unacum plenaria potestate privilegio et jurisdictione liberae regalitatis capellae et cancellariae imperpetuum cumque donatione et jure patronatus ecclesiarum capellaniarum et beneficiorum cum tenentibus tenandriis et libere tenentium servitus earundem Unacum officiis justiciariae et admiralitatis respective infra omnes bondas respective supra mentionatas Una etiam cum potestate civitates liberos burgos liberos portus villas et burgos baroniae erigendi ac fora et nundinas infra bondas dictarum terrarum constituendi curias justiciariae et admiralitatis infra limites dictarum terrarum fluviorum portuum et marium tenendi Una etiam cum potestate imponendi levandi et recipiendi omnia tolonia custumas anchoragia aliasque dictorum burgorum fororum nundinarum et liberorum portuum devorias et eisdem possidendi et gaudendi adeo libere in omnibus respectibus sicuti quivis baro major vel minor in hoc regno nostro Scotiae gavisus est aut gaudere poterit quovis tempore praeterito vel futuro Cum omnibus aliis praerogativis privilegiis immunitatibus dignitatibus casualitatibus proficuis et devoriis ad dictas terras maria et bondas earundem spectantibus et pertinentibus Et quae nos ipsi dare et concedere possumus adeo libere et ampla forma sicuti nos aut aliquis nostrorum nobilium progenitorum aliquas cartas patentes literas infeofamenta donationes aut diplomata concesserunt cuivis nostro subdito cujuscunque gradus aut qualitatis cuivis societati aut communitati tales colonias in quascunque partes extraneas deducenti aut terras extraneas investiganti in adeo libera et ampla forma sicuti eadem in hac praesenti carta nostra insererentur FACIMUS ETIAM constituimus et ordinamus dictum Dominum Wilhelmum Alexander haeredes suos et assignatos vel eorum deputatos nostros haereditarios locumtenentes generales ad repraesentandum nostram personam regalem tam per mare quam per terram in regionibus maris oris et finibus praedictis in petendo dictas terras quamdiu illic manserit ac redeundo ab eisdem ad gubernandum regendum puniendum et remittendum omnes nostros subditos quos ad dictas terras ire aut easdem inhabitare contigerit aut qui negotiationem cum eisdem suscipient vel in eisdem locis remanebunt ac eisdem ignoscendum et ad stabiliendum tales leges statuta constitutiones directiones instructiones formas gubernandi et magistratuum caeremonias infra dictas bondas sicuti ipsi Domino Wilhelmo Alexander aut ejus praedictis ad gubernationem dictae regionis aut ejus-dem incolarum in omnibus causis tam criminalibus quam civilibus visum fuerit et easdem leges regimina formas et caeremonias alterandum et mutandum quoties sibi vel suis praedictis pro bono et commodo dictae regionis placuerit ita ut dictae leges tam legibus dicti regni nostri Scotiae quam fieri possunt sint concordes VOLUMUS etiam ut in casu rebellionis aut seditionis legibus utatur militaribus adversus delinquentes vel imperio ipsius sese subtrahentes adeo libere sicuti aliquis locumtenens cujusvis regni nostri vel dominii virtute officii locumtenentis habent vel habere possunt Excludendo omnes alios officiarios hujus regni nostri Scotiae terrestres vel maritimos qui imposterum aliquid jurisclamei commoditatis authoritatis aut interesse in et ad dictas terras aut provinciam praedictam vel aliquam inibi jurisdictionem virtute alicujus praecedentis dispositionis aut diplomatis praetendere possunt Et ut viris honesto loco natis sese ad expeditionem istam subeundam et ad coloniae plantationem in dictis terris addatur animus nos pro nobis nostrisque haeredibus et successoribus cum avisamento et consensu praedicto virtute praesentis cartae nostrae damus et concedimus liberam et plenariam potestatam praefato Domino Willielmo Alexander suisque praedictis conferendi favores privilegia munia et honores in demerentes Cum plenaria potestate eisdem aut eorum alicui quos cum ipso Domino Willielmo suisque praedictis pactiones vel contractus facere pro eisdem terris contigerit sub subscriptione sua vel suorum praedictorum et sigillo inframen-tionato aliquam portionem seu portiones dictarum terrarum portuum navium stationum fluviorum aut praemissorum alicujus partis disponendi et extradonandi Erigendi etiam omnium generum machinas artes vel scientias aut easdem exercendi in toto vel in parte sicuti ei pro bono ipsorum visum fuerit Dandi etiam et con-cedendi et attribuendi talia officia titulos jura et potestates constituendi et desig-nandi tales capitaneos officiarios balivos gubernatores omnesque alios regali-tatis baroniae et burgi officiarios clericos aliosque ministros pro administratione justiciae infra bondas dictarum terrarum aut in via dum terras istas petunt per mare et ab eisdem redeunt sicuti ei necessarium videbitur secundum qualitates conditiones et personarum merita quos in aliqua coloniarum dictae provinciae aut aliqua ejusdem parte habitare contigerit aut qui ipsorum bona et fortunas pro com-modo et incremento ejusdem periculo committent et eosdem ab officio removendi alterandi et mutandi prout ei suisque praescriptis videbitur expediens ET QUUM hujusmodi conatus non sine magno labore et sumptibus fiunt magnamque pecuniae largitionem requirant adeo ut privati cujusvis fortunas excedant et multorum suppetiis indigeant   Ob quam causam dictus Dominus Willielmus Alexander suique praescripti cum diversis nostris subditis aliisque pro particularibus periclitationibus et susceptionibus ibidem qui forte cum eo suisque haeredibus assignatis vel deputatis pro terris piscationibus mercimoniis aut populi transportatione cum ipsorum pecoribus rebus et bonis versus dictam Novam Scotiam contractus inibunt Volumus ut quicunque tales contractus cum dicto Wilhelmo suisque praedictis sub ipsorum subscriptionibus et sigillis expedient limitando assignando et affigendo diem et locum pro personarum bonorum rerumque deliberatione in navim imponendorum sub forisfactura cujusdam monetae summae et eosdem contractus non perficient sed ipsum frustrabunt et in itinere designato ei nocebunt quod non solum dicto Domino Wilhelmo suisque praedictis poterit esse praejudicio et nocumento verum etiam nostrae tam laudabili intentioni obstabit et detrimentum inferet tunc licitum erit dicto Domino Wilhelmo suisque praedictis vel eorum deputatis et conservatoribus inframentionatis in eo casu sibi suisve praedictis quos ad hunc effectum substituet omnes tales summas monetae bona et res forisfactas per talium contractuum violationem assumere   Quod ut facilius fiat et legum prolixitas evitetur dedimus et concessimus tenoreque praesentium damus et concedimus plenariam potestatem nostri consilii dominis ut eos in ordinem redigant et talium contractuum vel foederum violatores pro transportatione populorum factorum puniant   Et licet omnes tales contractus inter dictum Dominum Wilhelmum suosque praedictos et praedictos periclitatores per periclitationem et transportationem populorum cum ipsorum bonis et rebus ad statutum diem perficientur et ipsi cum suis omnibus pecoribus et bonis ad littus illius provinciae animo coloniam ducendi et remanendi appellent et nihilominus postea vel omnino provinciam Novae Scotiae et ejusdem confinia sine licentia dicti Domini Willielmi suorumque praedictorum vel eorum deputatorum aut societatem et coloniam praedictam ubi primum combinati et conjuncti fuerant derelinquent et ad agrestes indigenas in locis remotis et desertis habitandum sese conferent quod tunc amittent et forisfacient omnes terras prius iis concessas omnia etiam bona infra omnes praedictas bondas licitumque erit praedicto Domino Wilhelmo suisque praescriptis eadem fisco applicare et easdem terras recognoscere eademque omnia ad ipsos vel eorum aliquem quovismodo spectantia possidere et suo peculiari usui suorumque praedictorum applicare et convertere   Et ut omnes dilecti nostri subditi tam regnorum nostrorum et dominiorum quam alii extranei quos ad dictas terras aut aliquam earundem partem ad mercimonia contrahenda navigare contigerit melius sciant et obedientes sint potestati et authoritati per nos in praedictum fidelem nostrum consiliarum Dominum Wilhelmum Alexander suosque praedictos collatae in omnibus talibus commissionibus warrantis et contractubus quos quovis tempore futuro

faciet concedet et constituet pro decentioi i et validiori constitutione officiariorum pro
gubernatione dictae coloniae concessione terrarum et executione justiciae dictos inhabitantes periclitantes deputatos factores vel assignatos tangentes in aliqua dictarum
teriarum parte vel in navigatione ad easdem terras nos cum avisamento et consensu
praedicto ordinamus quod dictus Dominus Wilhelmus Alexander suique praedicti
unum commune sigillum habebunt ad officium locumtenentis justiciariae et admiral-
tatis spectans quod per dictum Dominum Wilhelmum Alexander suosque praedictos
vel per suos deputatos omni tempore affuturo custodietur in cujus uno latere nostra
insignia insculpentur cum his verbis in ejusdem circulo et margine SIGILLUM REGIS
SCOTIE ANGLIE FRANCIE ET HIBERNIE et in altero latere imago nostra nostrorumque successorum cum his verbis PRO NOVE SCOTIE LOCUMTENENTE cujus justum
exemplar in manibus ac custodia conservatoris privilegiorum Novae Scotiae
remanebit quo ut occasio requiret in officio suo utatur. ET QUUM maxime necessarium sit ut omnes dilecti nostri subditi quotquot dictam provinciam Novae Scotiae
vel ejus confinia incolent in timore Omnipotentis Dei et vero ejus cultu simul vivant
omni conamine intendentes Christianam religionem ibi stabilire pacem etiam et
quietem cum nativis incolis et agrestibus aboriginibus earum terrarum colere (unde
ipsi et eorum quilibet mercimonia ibi exercentes tuti cum oblectamento ea quae
magno cum labore et periculo acquisiverunt quiete possidere possunt) nos pro nobis
nostrisque successoribus volumus nobisque visum est per presentis cartae nostrae
tenorem dare et concedere dicto Domino Wilhelmo Alexander suisque praedictis et
eorum deputatis vel aliquibus aliis nostris gubernatoribus officiariis et ministris
quos ipsi constituent liberam et absolutam potestatem tractandi et pacem affinitatem
amicitiam mutua colloquia operam et communicationem cum agrestibus illis aboriginibus et eorum principibus et quibuscunque aliis regimen et potestatem in ipsos
habentibus contrahendi observandi et alendi tales affinitates et colloquia quae ipsi
vel sui praedicti cum iis contrahent modo foedera illa ex adversa parte per ipsos
silvestres fideliter observentur quod nisi fiat arma contra ipsos sumendi quibus
redigi possunt in ordinem sicuti dicto Domino Wilhelmo suisque praedictis et deputatis suis pro honore obedientia et Dei servitio ac stabilmento defensione et conservatione authoritatis nostrae inter ipsos expediens videbitur. Cum potestate
etiam praedicto Domino Wilhelmo Alexander suisque praescriptis per ipsos vel
eorum deputatos substitutos vel assignatos pro eorum defensione et tutela omni
tempore et omnibus justis occasionibus imposterum aggrediendi ex inopinato
invadendi expellendi et armis repellendi tam per mare quam per terram omnibus
modis omnes et singulos qui sine speciali licentia dicti Domini Willielmi suorumque
praedictorum terras eas inhabitare aut mercaturam exercere in dicta provincia Novae
Scotiae aut quavis ejusdem parte conabuntur et similiter omnes alios quoscunque

qui aliquid damni detrimenti destructionis laesionis vel invasionis contra provinciam illam aut ejusdem incolas inferre praesumunt Quod ut facilius fiat licitum erit dicto Domino Willielmo suisque praedictis eorum deputatis factoribus et assignatis contributiones a periclitantibus et incolis ejusdem levare in unum cogere per proclamationes vel quovis alio ordine talibus temporibus sicuti dicto Domino Willielmo suisque praedictis expediens videbitur omnes nostros subditos infra dictos limites dictae provinciae Novae Scotiae inhabitantes et mercimonia ibidem exercentes convocare pro meliori exercitio necessariorum supplemento et populi ac plantationis dictarum terrarum augmentatione et incremento Cum plenaria potestate privilegio et libertate dicto Domino Willielmo Alexander suisque praescriptis per ipsos vel eorum substitutos per quaevis maria sub nostris insigniis et vexillis navigandi cum tot navibus tanti oneris et tam bene munitione viris et victualibus instructis sicuti possunt parare quovis tempore et quoties iis videbitur expediens ac omnes cujuscunque qualitatis et gradus personas subditos nostros existentes aut qui imperio nostro sese subdere ad iter illud suscipiendum voluerint cum ipsorum jumentis equis bobus ovibus bonis et rebus omnibus munitionibus machinis majoribus armis et instrumentis militaribus quotquot voluerint aliisque commoditatibus et rebus necessariis pro usu ejusdem coloniae mutuo commercio cum nativis inhabitantibus earum provinciarum aut aliis qui cum ipsis plantatoribus mercimonia contrahent ti ansportandi et omnes commoditates et mercimonia quae iis videbuntur necessaria in regnum nostrum Scotiae sine alicujus taxationis custumae et impositionis pro eisdem solutione nobis vel nostris custumariis aut eorum deputatis inde portandi eosdemque ab eorum officiis in hac parte pro spatio septem annorum diem datae praesentis cartae nostrae immediate sequentium inhibendo Quamquidem solam commoditatem per spatium tredecim annorum imposterum libere concessimus tenoreque praesentis cartae nostrae concedimus et disponimus dicto Domino Willielmo suisque praedictis secundum proportionem postea mentionatam Et post tredecim illos annos finitos licitum erit nobis nostrisque successoribus ex omnibus bonis et mercimoniis quae ex hoc regno nostro Scotiae ad eandem provinciam Novae Scotiae vel ex ea provincia ad dictum regnum nostrum Scotiae exportabuntur vel importabuntur in quibusvis hujus regni nostri portubus per dictum Dominum Willielmum suosque praedictos tantum quinque libras pro centum secundum antiquum negotiandi modum sine ulla alia impositione taxatione custuma vel devoria ab ipsis imposterum levare et exigere quaquidem summa quinque librarum pro centum sic soluta per dictum Dominum Willielmum suosque praedictos aliisque nostris officiariis ad hunc effectum constitutis exinde licitum erit dicto Domino Willielmo suisque praedictis eadem bona de hoc regno nostro Scotiae in quasvis alias partes et regiones extraneas sine alicujus alterius custumae taxationis vel devoriae solutione nobis vel nostris haeredibus aut

e

successoribus aut aliquibus aliis transportare et avehere Proviso tamen quod dicta bona infra spatium tredecim mensium post ipsarum in quovis hujus regni nostri portu appulsionem navi rursus imponantur Dando et concedendo absolutam et plenariam potestatem dicto Domino Williclmo suisque praedictis ab omnibus nostris subditis qui colonias deducere mercimonia exerceie aut ad easdem terras Novae Scotiae et ab eisdem navigare voluerint practer dictam summam nobis debitam pro bonis et mercimoniis quinque libras de centum vel ratione exportationis ex hoc regno nostro Scotiae ad dictam provinciam Novae Scotiae vel importationis a dicta provincia ad hoc regnum nostrum Scotiae praedictum in ipsius ejusque praedictorum proprios usus sumendi levandi et recipiendi Et similiter de omnibus bonis et merci-moniis quae per nostros subditos coloniarum ductores negotiatores et navigatores de dicta provincia Novae Scotiae ad quaevis nostra dominia aut alia quaevis loca exportabuntur vel a nostris regnis et aliis locis ad dictam Novam Scotiam importa-buntur ultra et supra dictam summam nobis destinatam quinque libras de centum Et de bonis et mercimoniis omnium extraneorum aliorumque sub nostra obedientia minime existentium quae vel de dicta provincia Novae Scotiae exportabuntur vel ad eandem importabuntur ultra et supra dictam summam nobis destinatam decem libras de centum dicti Domini Willielmi suorumque praedictorum propriis usibus per tales ministros officiarios vel subditos eorumve deputatos aut factores quos ipsi ad hunc effectum constituent et designabunt levandi sumendi ac recipiendi Et pro meliori dicti Domini Willielmi suorumque praedictorum aliorumque omnium dictorum nostrorum subditorum qui dictam Novam Scotiam inhabitare vel ibidem mercimonia exercere voluerint securitate et commoditate et generaliter omnium aliorum qui nos-trae authoritati et potestati sese subdere non gravabuntur nobis visum est volumusque quod licitum erit dicto Domino Willielmo suisque praedictis unum vel plura muni-mina propugnacula castella loca fortia specula armamentaria lie blokhousa aliaque aedificia cum portubus et navium stationibus aedificare vel aedificari causare una-cum navibus bellicis easdemque pro defensione dictorum locorum applicare sicuti dicto Domino Willielmo suisque praedictis pro dicto conamine perficiendo necessarium videbitur proque ipsorum defensione militum catervas ibidem stabilire praeter praedicta supramentionata et generaliter omnia facere quae pro conquaestu augmentatione populi inhabitatione preservatione et gubernatione dictae Novae Scotiae ejusdemque terrarum et territorii infra omnes hujusmodi limites pertinentias et dependentias sub nostro nomine et authoritate quodcunque nos si personaliter essemus praesentes facere potuimus licet casus specialem et strictum magis ordinem quam in hac praesenti carta nostra praescribitur requirat cui mandato volumus et ordinamus strictissimeque praecipimus omnibus nostris justiciariis officiariis et subditis ad loca illa sese conferentibus ut sese applicent dictoque Domino Willielmo suisque praedictis in omnibus et singulis supramentionatis earum substantiis et dependentiis intendant et obediant eisque in earum executione in omnibus adeo sint obedientes ut nobis cujus personam representat esse deberet sub poena disobedientiae et rebellionis DECLARAMUS insuper per praesentis cartae nostrae tenorem omnibus Christianis regibus principibus et statibus quod si aliquis vel aliqui qui imposterum de dictis coloniis vel de earum aliqua sit in provincia Novae Scotiae predicta vel aliqui alii sub eorum licentia et mandato quovis tempore futuro piraticam exercentes per mare vel terram bona alicujus abstulerint vel aliquod injustum aut indebitum hostiliter contra aliquos nostros nostrorumve haeredum aut successorum seu aliorum regum principum gubernatorum aut statuum in foedere nobiscum existentium subditos quod tali injuria sic oblata aut justa querela desuper mota per aliquem regem principem gubernatorem statum vel eorum subditos predictos nos nostri haeredes et successores publicas proclamationes fieri curabimus in aliqua parte dicti regni nostri Scotiae ad hunc effectum magis commoda ut dicti pirata vel piratae qui tales rapinas committent stato tempore per prefatas proclamationes limitando plenarie restituant quaecunque bona sic ablata et pro dictis injuriis omnimodo satisfacient ita ut dicti principes aliique sic conquirentes satisfactos se esse reputent et quod si talium facinorum commissores neque satisfactionem condignam facient nec fieri infra tempus limitandum curabunt quod tunc is vel ii qui tales rapinas commiserint neque sunt nec imposterum sub nostra obedientia et protectione erunt quodque licitum et legitimum erit omnibus principibus aliisque quibuscunque tales delinquentes eorumve quemlibet omni cum hostilitate prosequi et invadere ET LICET neminem nobilem et generosum de patria hac sine licentia nostra discedere statutum sit nihilominus volumus quod hoc presens nostrum diploma sufficiens erit licentia et warrantum omnibus qui se huic itineri committent nisi laesaemajestatis sint rei aut aliquo alio speciali mandato sint inhibiti atque per praesentis cartae tenorem declaramus volumusque quod nemo patria hac discedere permittatur et ad dictam regionem Novae Scotiae tendere nisi qui juramentum nostrae supremitatis primum susceperint ad quem effectum nos tenore praesentis cartae nostrae dicto Domino Wilhelmo suisque praedictis vel eorum conservatoribus et deputatis idem hoc juramentum omnibus personis versus illas terras in ea colonia sese conferentibus requirere et exhibere plenariam potestatem et authoritatem damus et concedimus PRAETEREA nos cum avisamento et consensu praedicto pro nobis et successoribus nostris declaramus decernimus et ordinamus quod omnes nostri subditi qui ad dictam Novam Scotiam proficiscentur aut eam incolent eorumque omnes liberi et posteritas qui ibi nasci contigerint aliique omnes ibidem periclitantes habebunt et possidebunt omnes libertates immunitates et privilegia liberorum et naturalium subditorum regni nostri Scotiae aut aliorum nostrorum dominiorum sicuti ibidem nati fuissent INSUPER nos pro nobis et successoribus nostris damus et concedimus dicto Domino Wilhelmo suisque praedictis liberam potestatem stabiliendi et cudere causandi monetam pro commercio liberiori inhabitantium dictae provinciae cujusvis metalli quomodo et qua forma voluerint et easdem praescribent Atque etiam si quae quaestiones aut dubia super interpretatione et constructione alicujus clausulae in hac praesenti carta nostra contentae occurrent ea omnia sumentur et interpretabuntur in amplissima forma et in favorem dicti Domini Wilhelmi suorumque praedictorum PRAETEREA nos ex nostra certa scientia proprio motu authoritate et potestate regali fecimus univimus annexavimus ereximus creavimus et incorporavimus tenoreque praesentis cartae nostrae facimus unimus annexamus erigimus creamus et incorporamus totam et integram dictam provinciam et terras Novae Scotiae cum omnibus earundem limitibus et maribus in unum integrum et liberum dominium et baroniam per praedictum nomen NOVAE SCOTIAE omni tempore futuro appellandum Volumusque et concedimus ac pro nobis nostrisque successoribus decernimus et ordinamus quod unica sasina nunc per dictum Dominum Wilhelmum suosque praedictos omni tempore affuturo modo subsequente sumenda stabit et sufficiens erit sasina pro tota dicta regione cum omnibus partibus pendiculis privilegiis casualitatibus et immunitatibus ejusdem supramentionatis absque aliqua alia speciali aut particulari sasina per ipsum suosque praedictos apud aliquam aliam partem capienda penes quam sasinam omniaque quae inde sequuta sunt aut sequi possunt nos cum avisamento et consensu praescripto pro nobis et successoribus nostris dispensavimus tenoreque praesentis cartae nostrae modo subtus mentionato dispensamus imperpetuum TENENDAM ET HABENDAM totam et integram dictam regionem et dominium Novae Scotiae cum omnibus ejusdem limitibus infra praedicta maria cunctisque aliis privilegiis libertatibus immunitatibus casualitatibus aliisque supra expressis praefato Domino Wilhelmo Alexander haeredibus suis et assignatis de nobis et successoribus nostris in feodo haereditate libero dominio libera baronia et regalitate imperpetuum modo supra mentionato per omnes rectas metas et limites suos prout jacent in longitudine et latitudine in domibus aedificiis aedificatis et aedificandis boscis planis moris marresiis viis semitis aquis stagnis rivolis pratis pascuis et pasturis molendinis multuris et eorum sequelis aucupationibus venationibus piscationibus petariis turbariis carbonibus carbonariis cuniculis cuniculariis columbis columbariis fabrilibus brasinis brueriis et genestis silvis nemoribus et virgultis lignis tignis lapicidiis lapide et calce cum curiis et earum exitibus herezeldis amerciamentis bluidwitis et mulierum merchetis cum communi pastura liberoque introitu et exitu cum furca fossa sok sake thoile theme vert venisoun infangtheiff outfangtheiff pit et gallows ac cum omnibus aliis et singulis libertatibus commoditatibus proficuis asiamentis ac justis suis pertinentiis quibuscunque tam non nominatis

quam nominatis tam subtus terra quam supra terram procul et prope ad praedictum
dominium baroniam et regalitatem spectantibus seu juste spectare valentibus quomodolibet in futurum libere quiete plenarie integre honorifice bene et in pace sine ulla
revocatione contradictione impedimento aut obstaculo quocunque REDDENDO inde
annuatim dictus Dominus Wilhelmus Alexander suique praedicti nobis nostrisque
haeredibus et successoribus unum denarium monetae regni nostri Scotiae super
fundo dictarum terrarum et provinciae Novae Scotiae ad festum Nativitatis Christi
nomine albae firmae si petatur tantum ET QUIA tentione dictarum terrarum et provinciae Novae Scotiae in alba firma ut praedicitur deficiente tempestivo et legitimo
introitu cujusvis haeredis vel haeredum dicti Domini Wilhelmi sibi succedentium quod
difficulter per ipsos praestari potest ob longinquam distantiam ab hoc regno nostro
eaedem terrae et provincia ratione non-introitus in manibus nostris nostrorumve
successorum devenient usque ad legitimum legitimi haeredis introitum et nos
nolentes dictas terras et regionem quovis tempore in non-introitu cadere neque
dictum Dominum Wilhelmum suosque praedictos beneficiis et proficuis ejusdem
eatenus frustrari idcirco nos cum avisamento praedicto cum dicto non-introitu
quandocunque contigerit dispensavimus tenoreque praesentis cartae nostrae pro
nobis et successoribus nostris dispensamus ac etiam renunciavimus et exoneravimus
tenoreque ejusdem cartae nostrae cum consensu praedicto renunciamus et exoneramus dictum Dominum Wilhelmum suosque praedictos de prefato non-introitu dictae
provinciae et regionis cum omnibus beneficio et commoditate earundem firmis proficuis censibus et devoriis hujusmodi cum omnibus quae desuper sequi possunt quandocunque in manibus nostris devenient aut ratione non-introitus cadent Proviso tamen
quod dictus Dominus Wilhelmus suique haeredes et assignati infra spatium septem
annorum post decessum et obitum suorum praedecessorum aut introitum ad possessionem dictarum terrarum aliorumque praedictorum per ipsos vel eorum legitimos
procuratores ad hunc effectum potestatem habentes nobis nostrisque successoribus
homagium faciant et dictum dominium terras et baroniam aliaque praedicta adeant
et per nos recipientur secundum leges et statuta dicti regni nostri Scotiae In quo-
quidem casu haeredes et assignati dicti Domini Wilhelmi Alexander non obstante
praedicto non-introitu gaudebunt et possidebunt omnes et singulas praedictas terras regionem et dominium Novae Scotiae cum omnibus et singulis proficuis commoditatibus beneficiis privilegiis et libertatibus earundem ac si dictus non-introitus
non fuisset vel ac si in non-introitum nunquam cecidissent QUAEQUIDEM terrae
regio et dominium Novae Scotiae tam terra firma quam insulae infra omnes et
singulas dictas bondas et maria earundem cum silvis piscationibus tam in aquis salsis
quam dulcibus tam piscium regalium quam aliorum cum margaritis praeciosis
lapidibus venis mineralibus regiis auri et argenti aliis mineralibus ferri chalybis

plumbi cupri aeris stanni orichalci aliisque quibuscunque ac omnibus privilegiis libertatibus immunitatibus praerogativis officiis et jurisdictionibus aliisque specialiter et generaliter supra-recitatis perprius ad dictum Dominum Wilhelmum Alexander suosque haeredes et assignatos pertinuerunt et per ipsum suosque procuratores suo nomine in manibus nostris debite et legitime resignatae fuerunt et hoc pro novo nostro haereditario infeofamento earundem in favorem dicti Domini Wilhelmi suorumve haci edum et assignatorum praedictorum in debita et competenti forma ut congruit concedendo TENENDARUM ut dictum est cum dispensatione non-introitus modo praescripto cum contigerit INSUPER nos cum avisamento praescripto pro bono fideli et gratuito servitio nobis per dictum Dominum Wilhelmum Alexander praestito et impenso et respectu habito magnarum et multarum expensarum et sumptuum confei endarum et impendendarum in plantatione dictarum bondarum dominii et regionis Novae Scotiae et earundem sub nostra obedientia reductione aliisque gravibus et causis onerosis DE NOVO dedimus concessimus et disposuimus tenoreque praesentis cartae nostrae damus concedimus et disponimus praefato Domino Wilhelmo Alexander suisque haei edibus et assignatis haereditarie Omnes et singulas praedictas terras dominium et regionem Novae Scotiae unacum omnibus et singulis castellis turribus fortaliciis manci ici um locis domibus aedificiis exstructis et exstruendis hortis pomariis plantatis et plantandis toftis croftis pratis pascuis sylvis virgultis molendinis multuris tei ris molendinai iis piscationibus tam i ubrorum quam alborum piscium salmonum piscium tam magnorum quam minutorum tam in aquis salsis quam dulcibus unacum omnibus et singulis decimis garbalibus earundem inclusis tam magnis quam minutis cum advocatione donatione beneficiorum ecclesiarum et capellaniarum et juribus patronatuum earundem annexis connexis dependentiis tenentibus tenandriis et liberetenentium sei vitiis earundem Unacum omnibus et singulis pracciosis lapidibus gemmis cristallo alumine corallio et aliis cum omnibus et singulis mineralibus venis et lapicidis earundem tam metallorum et mineralium regalium et regiorum auri et argenti infia dictas bondas et dominium Novae Scotiae quam aliorum mineralium tei i chalybis stanni plumbi cupri aeris orichalci aliorumque mineralium quorumcunque cum omnibus et singulis partibus pendiculis pertinentiis privilegiis libei tatibus et immunitatibus omnium et singularum praedictarum teri arum dominii et regionis Novae Scotiae Cum plena potestate et privilegio dicto Domino Wilhelmo Alexander haeredibus suis et assignatis tentandi et investigandi fodiendi et scrutandi fundum pro eisdem et extrahendi eadem purgandi et repurgandi purificandi eadem utendi convei tendi ac suis propi iis usibus applicandi (i eservata solummodo nobis nostrisque successoribus decima parte regalium metallorum vulgo appellatoi um *the ure* auri et ai genti inveniendorum et extrahendorum imposterum de ductis terris et regione) et reliqua dictoi um metallorum mineralium pracciosorum lapidum

gemmarum ac aliorum quorumcunque dicto Domino Willielmo Alexander suisque
haeredibus et assignatis pertinebunt cum ipsis perpetuo remanenda eorumque propriis usibus convertenda cum omnibus proficuis et devoriis earundem   Cum potestate dicto Domino Willielmo Alexander suisque hacredibus et assignatis condendi
exstruendi et erigendi in et infra omnes bondas dictae regionis sicuti iis videbitur expediens civitates liberos burgos baroniae villas villulas sinus portus stationes navium
et designandi nundinas et macella tam in villis quam extra et imponendi levandi
et recipiendi omnes et quascunque tolonias custumas anchoragia aliasque devorias
earundem civitatum burgorum baroniae villarum villularum nundinarum macellorum
liberorum portuum sinuum navium stationum cum omnibus et singulis casualitatibus proficuis et devoriis quibuscunque easdem civitates et burgos adornandi tam
infra burgos quam extra cum sufficientibus et habilibus magistratibus pacis justiciariis praepositis balliviis senioribus constabulariis aliisque officiariis civibus burgensibus liberis et manufactoribus artificibus omnium generum cum decanis ipsorum
aliisque ad hoc requisitis   Cum plenaria potestate privilegio et libertate iis eorumve
liberis civibus et burgensibus vendendi vinum et ceram salmones haleces aliaque
stapuli bona et mercimonia tam magna quam minuta et exstruendi ecclesias
capellas xenodochia *lie hospitallis and maisoun dieuis* cruces forales campanilia
campanas aliaque omnia ornamenta ordinaria eisdem spectantia et plantandi et
sufficienter providendi easdem ecclesias cum sufficientibus doctoribus praedicatoribus
pastoribus et ministris   Et similiter erigendi fundandi et exstruendi scholas triviales
collegia et universitates sufficienter provisas cum habilibus et sufficientibus magistris
rectoribus regentibus professoribus omnium scientiarum literarum linguarum et
sermonum et providendi pro sufficiente alimento stipendiis et victu pro eisdem ad hunc
effectum ac etiam erigendi praelatos archiepiscopos episcopos rectores et vicarios
parochiarum et ecclesiarum parochialium et distribuendi et dividendi omnes praedictas bondas dictae regionis in diversis et distinctis vicecomitatibus provinciis et paro-
chiis pro meliori provisione ecclesiarum et ministerii divisione vicecomitatuum et
omni alia civili politia   Et similiter fundandi erigendi et instituendi senatum justiciae
loca et justiciae collegia consilii et sessionis senatores earundem membra pro
justiciae administratione infra dictam regionem aliaque justiciae et judicaturae loca
praeterea erigendi et designandi tam secreta et privata consilia et sessiones pro
publico bono et commodo dictae regionis et dandi et concedendi titulos honores et
dignitates membris earundem et creandi clericos et earundem membra et designandi
sigilla et registra cum ipsorum custodibus ac etiam erigendi et instituendi officiarios status cancellarium thesaurarium computorum rotulatorem collectorem secre-
tarium advocatum vel actornatum generalem clericum vel clericos registri et
rotulorum custodes justiciariae clericum directorem vel directores cancellariae

conservatorem vel conservatores privilegiorum dictae regionis advocatos procuratores causarumque patronos earundemque solicitatores et agentes aliaque membra necessaria Et similiter convocandi congregandi et constituendi conventiones et congregationes ecclesiasticorum praelatorum tam generales synodales vel provinciales conventiones quam alias pro politia et disciplina ecclesiastica et authorizandi ratificandi et confirmandi easdem conventiones consilia et congregationes cum actis statutis et decretis inibi conclusis pro eorundem meliori authoritate PRAETEREA fecimus constituimus et ordinavimus tenoreque praesentis cartae nostrae facimus constituimus et ordinamus dictum Dominum Willielmum Alexander suosque haeredes et assignatos nostros nostrorumve haeredum et successorum locumtenentes generales ad repraesentandum nostram regalem personam tam per mare quam terram totius et integrae dictae regionis et dominii Novae Scotiae tam durante spatio quo ibi remanebit quam in itinere ipsius vel eorum ad dictam regionem vel ab eadem et post ipsorum reditum continuo sine intervallo temporis aut loci Excludendo omnes alios vel per mare vel per terram ab usurpatione hujus contrarii vel ab acclamatione alicujus juris beneficii authoritatis et interesse infra dictas bondas et dominium Novae Scotiae vel alicujus judicaturae aut jurisdictionis eatenus virtute alicujus praecedentis aut subsequentis juris aut tituli cujuscunque Et cum speciali potestate dicto Domino Wilhelmo Alexander suisque praedictis gubernandi regendi puniendi et condonandi omnes nostros subditos aliosque dictarum bondarum et regionis Novae Scotiae inhabitantes aut ibi proficiscentes pacis aut legum dictae regionis transgressores ac faciendi sanciendi et stabiliendi ibidem leges tam civiles quam criminales cum legibus justiciariae admiralitatis senescallatus regalitatis et vicecomitatus pro eorum beneplacito modo eaedem leges tam conformes sint legibus Scotiae quam convenienter fieri potest respectu habito circumstantiarum loci regionis personarum et qualitatum earundem Et similiter designandi gubernatores imperatores et ductores omnium et singularum praedictarum civitatum burgorum portuum navium stationum et sinuum et capitaneos etiam castrorum fortaliciorum et propugnaculorum tam per mare et prope littus quam per terram bene et sufficienter munitas instructas et fortificatas militum turmis et copiis pro manutentione defensione et praeservatione earundem et repulsione omnium tam domesticarum quam extranearum invasionum earundem et convocandi congregandi et convenire faciendi omnes inhabitantes dictae regionis ad effectum praescriptum omnibus occasionibus necessariis ac pro repulsione et resistantia omnium aliarum virium et violentiarum quarumcunque Et pro meliori fortificatione dicti dominii et regionis Novae Scotiae cum potestate dicto Domino Wilhelmo Alexander suisque praedictis transportandi de dicto regno aliisve bondis convenientibus omnia genera munitionis magna et minuta tormenta majora media vulgo *cannonis demi-cannonis zetlingis falconis* aeris et ferri sclopetos atque alia instrumenta et belli machinas cum sclopetis minoribus vulgo *muskettis hagbuittis half haggis* bombardis vulgo *pistolettis* pulvere globulis aliisque necessariis victualibus et armis tam offensivis quam defensivis et gerendi et utendi talibus armis tam infra dictam regionem Novae Scotiae quam in eorum transitu et cursu vel ad easdem terras vel ab eisdem cum eorum comitibus sociis et dependentibus Nos etiam cum avisamento praedicto fecimus constituimus et ordinavimus tenoreque praesentis cartae nostrae facimus constituimus et ordinamus dictum Dominum Willhelmum Alexander suosque haeredes et assignatos haereditarie nostros justiciarios generales in omnibus causis criminalibus infra dictam regionem et dominium Novae Scotiae magnum admirallum et Dominum regalitatis et admiralitatis infra dictam regionem haereditarios etiam senescallos ejusdem omniumque et singularum regalitatum hujusmodi Cum potestate sibi suisque haeredibus et assignatis utendi exercendi et gaudendi omnibus et singulis praefatis jurisdictionibus judicaturis et officiis cum omnibus et singulis privilegiis praerogativis immunitatibus et casualitatibus earundem similiter et adeo libere quam aliquis alius justiciarius vel justiciarii generales senescalli admiralli vicecomites aut domini regalitatis habuerunt vel habere possunt aut possidere et gaudere iisdem jurisdictionibus judicaturis officiis dignitatibus et praerogativis in aliquibus nostris regnis bondis et dominiis nostris quibuscunque Cum potestate dicto Domino Willielmo Alexander suisque haeredibus et assignatis constituendi eligendi nominandi et creandi clericos officiarios serjandos adjudicatores omniaque alia curiae membra omnium et singularum praefatarum judicaturarum et jurisdictionum respective cum omnibus feodis devoriis et casualitatibus eisdem spectantibus prout iis videbitur expediens sine praejudicio omnimodo omnium aliorum infeofamentorum jurium vel dispositionum per nos nostrosve praedecessores cuicunque personae vel quibuscunque personis qui participes sunt vel erunt dictae plantationis Novae Scotiae procedentium supra resignationem dicti Domini Willhelmi Alexander solummodo et non aliter de quibuscunque partibus aut portionibus dictae regionis et dominii Novae Scotiae cum privilegiis et immunitatibus in ipsorum infeofamentis mentionatis Et QUUM ratione longi intervalli et distantiae dictae regionis et dominii Novae Scotiae a dicto antiquo regno nostro Scotiae et quod eadem regio neque facile neque commode nisi aestatis tempore peti potest quodque eadem regio publicis tabellionibus et notariis requisitis pro sasinis sumendis omnino est destituta adeo ut sasina commode super fundum dictae regionis omnibus temporibus capi non potest atque etiam respectu habito magnorum et multifariorum incommodorum quae cadere possunt in defectu tempestivae sasinae sumendae super hoc praesens diploma et super alias cartas et similia infeofamenta concessa et concedenda de praedictis terris et dominio Novae Scotiae vel aliqua earundem parte igitur ut

f

praesens haec nostra carta magis sit efficax et ut sasina desuper magis commode capi possit necessarium est ut sasina sumatur omnium et singularum praedictarum terrarum dictae regionis et domini Novae Scotiae infra dictum regnum nostrum Scotiae et super fundia et terras ejusdem in magis eminente ejusdem loco quod nec convenienter nec legitime fieri potest sine expressa unione dictae regionis et dominii Novae Scotiae dicto regno Scotiae Quocirca et pro facilitate commodo et convenientia antedictae sasinae nos cum avisamento praedicto annexavimus univimus et incorporavimus tenoreque praesentis cartae nostrae unimus annexamus et incorporamus dicto regno nostro Scotiae totam et integram praedictam regionem et dominium Novae Scotiae cum decimis et decimis garbalibus earundem inclusis et omnibus et singulis partibus pertinentiis privilegiis jurisdictionibus et libertatibus earundem aliisque generaliter et specialiter supra mentionatis Et per praesentis cartae nostrae tenorem volumus declaramus decernimus et ordinamus quod unica sasina nunc capienda apud castellum nostrum de Edinburt tanquam maxime eminentem et principalem locum dicti regni nostri Scotiae de omnibus et singulis dictis terris regione et dominio Novae Scotiae vel aliqua earundem parte cum decimis et decimis garbalibus earundem respective inclusis est et erit sufficiens sasina pro totis et integris praedictis terris regione et dominio Novae Scotiae cum decimis et decimis garbalibus earundem inclusis vel aliqua earundem parte terrarum et regionis prescriptarum et omnibus privilegiis jurisdictionibus et libertatibus ejusdem respective aliisque specialiter et generaliter supramentionatis non obstante quod eaedem terre regio et dominium Novae Scotiae longe distent et discontigue jaceant a dicto regno nostro Scotiae penes quod nos cum avisamento et consensu praedicto dispensavimus tenoreque praesentis cartae nostrae dispensamus imperpetuum sine praejudicio et derogatione omnimodo dicti privilegii et praerogativae praefato Domino Wilhelmo Alexander suisque haeredibus et assignatis concessi pro confectione et stabilimento legum actorum et constitutionum omnium et singularum praedictarum terrarum regionis et dominii Novae Scotiae tam per mare quam per terram Et per praesentis cartae nostrae tenorem declaramus quod non obstante dicta unione (quae concedi solummodo declaratur pro commoditate et convenientia sasinae) eadem regio et dominium Novae Scotiae judicabitur regetur et gubernabitur per leges et constitutiones factas fiendas constituendas et stabiliendas per dictum Dominum Wilhelmum Alexander suosque haeredes et assignatos spectantes ad dictam regionem et dominium Novae Scotiae similiter et adeo libere in eo respectu sicuti eadem unio nunquam fuisset facta nec eatenus concessa Et praeterea non obstante praedicta unione licitum erit praedicto Domino Wilhelmo Alexander suisque haeredibus et assignatis dare concedere et disponere aliquas partes vel portiones dictarum terrarum regionis et dominii Novae Scotiae iis haereditarie spectantes ad et in favorem quarumcunque personarum eorum haeredum et assigna-

torum haereditarie cum decimis et decimis garbalibus earundem inclusis (modo nostri
sint subditi) tenendas de dicto Domino Wilhelmo Alexander vel de nobis et nostris
successoribus vel in alba firma feudifirma vel warda et relevio pro eorum beneplacito et intitulare et denominare easdem partes et portiones quibuscunque stilis
titulis et designationibus iis visum fuerit aut in libito et optione dicti Domini
Wilhelmi suorumque praedictorum Quaequidem infeofamenta et dispositiones per
nos nostrosve successores libere sine aliqua compositione propterea solvenda appro-
babuntur et confirmabuntur Insuper nos nostrique successores quascunque
resignationes per dictum Dominum Wilhelmum Alexander suosque haeredes et
assignatos fiendas de totis et integris praefatis terris et dominio Novae Scotiae vel
alicujus earundem partis in manibus nostris nostrorumque successorum et commissionariorum praedictorum cum decimis et decimis garbalibus earundem inclusis aliisque generaliter et specialiter supra mentionatis recipiemus ad et in favorem cujuscunque personae aut quarumcunque personarum (modo nostri sint subditi et sub nostra obedientia vivant et desuper infeofamenta expedient) tenendis in libera alba firma
de nobis haeredibus et successoribus nostris modo supra mentionato libere sine ulla
compositione QUASQUIDEM terras regionem et dominium Novae Scotiae cum decimis
garbalibus earundem inclusis omnesque et singulas partes pendiculas et pertinentias
privilegia jurisdictiones praerogativas et libertates earundem aliaque specialiter et
generaliter supra mentionata unacum omni jure titulo interesse jurisclameo tam
petitorio quam possessorio quae nos nostrive praedecessores aut successores habui-
mus habemus vel quovismodo habere clamare aut praetendere potuimus ad easdem
vel aliquam earundem partem aut ad census firmas proficua et devorias earundem de
quibuscunque annis aut terminis praeteritis pro quacunque causa vel occasione NOS
eum avisamento praedicto pro rationibus supra mentionatis DE NOVO damus concedimus et disponimus praedicto Domino Wilhelmo Alexander suisque haeredibus et
assignatis haereditarie imperpetuum Renunciando et exonerando iisdem simpliciter
cum omni actione et instantia eatenus competenti ad et in favorem dicti Domini
Wilhelmi Alexander suorumque haeredum et assignatorum tam pro non solutione
devoriarum in ipsorum originalibus infeofamentis contentarum quam pro non praesta-
tione debiti homagii eisdem conformiter aut pro non perimpletione alicujus puncti
dicti originalis infeofamenti aut pro commissione alicujus culpae aut facti omissionis
vel commissionis iisdem praejudiciabili et unde idem originale infeofamentum legitime impugnari aut in questionem duci imposterum quovismodo possit Aequietando
et remittendo iisdem simpliciter cum omni titulo actione instantia et interesse
eatenus competenti aut quae nobis nostrisque haeredibus et successoribus compe-
tere potest Renunciando iisdem simpliciter juri liti et causae cum pacto de non
petendo ac cum supplemento omnium defectuum tam non nominatorum quam nomina-

totum quae nos tanquam pro expressis in hac praesenti carta nostra haberi volumus Tenendas in libera alba firma ut dictum est et dispensando cum non-introitu quandocunque contigerit modo praedicto Insuper nos pro nobis et successoribus nostris cum avisamento praedicto damus concedimus et committimus potestatem dicto Domino Wilhelmo Alexander suisque haeredibus et assignatis habendi et legitime stabiliendi et cudere causandi monetam currentem in dicta regione et domino Novae Scotiae et inter inhabitantes ejusdem pro faciliori commercii et pactionum commodo talis metalli formae et modi sicuti ipsi designabunt aut constituent et ad hunc effectum damus concedimus et committimus iis eorumve haeredibus et assignatis dictae regionis locumtenentibus privilegia monetam cudendi cum instrumentis ferreis et officiariis ad hunc effectum necessariis Praeterea nos pro nobis et successoribus nostris cum avisamento praedicto dedimus concessimus ratificavimus et confirmavimus ac per praesentis cartae nostrae tenorem damus concedimus ratificamus et confirmamus dicto Domino Wilhelmo Alexander suisque haeredibus et assignatis omnia loca privilegia praerogativas praeeminentias et praecedentias quascunque data concessa et reservata vel danda concedenda et reservanda dicto Domino Wilhelmo Alexander suisque haeredibus et assignatis ejusque successoribus locumtenentibus dictae regionis et domini Novae Scotiae per equites auratos baronettos reliquosque portionarios et consortes dictae plantationis adeo ut dictus Dominus Wilhelmus Alexander suique haeredes masculi de corpore suo descendentes tanquam locumtenentes praedicti sument et sumere possunt locum praerogativum praeeminentiam et praecedentiam tam ante omnes armigeros barones minores et generosos vulgo *squyis lairdis and gentilmen* dicti regni nostri Scotiae quam ante omnes praedictos equites auratos baronettos ejusdem regni nostri omnesque alios ante quos dicti equites aurati baronetti locum et praecedentiam virtute privilegii dignitatis iis concessi habere possunt pro cujus plantationis et coloniae Novae Scotiae adjumento et ejus praecipue respectu dicti equites aurati baronetti cum ipsorum statu et dignitate cum avisamento praedicto in dicto regno nostro Scotiae creati fuerant tanquam indicium speciale nostri favoris super tales generosos et honesto loco natos collati praedictae plantationis et coloniae participes cum hac expressa provisione omnimodo quod numerus praefatorum baronettorum nunquam excedat centum et quinquaginta Denique nos cum avisamento praedicto pro nobis haeredibus et successoribus nostris volumus decernimus et ordinamus quod hoc nostrum diploma et infeofamentum ratificari approbari et confirmari cum omnibus ejusdem contentis in proximo nostro parliamento regni nostri Scotiae et ut habeat vim robur et efficaciam acti statuti et decreti ejusdem supremae judicaturae penes quod nos pro nobis nostrisque successoribus declaramus et ordinamus praesentem hanc nostram cartam dominis articulorum dicti nostri parliamenti pro ratificatione et confirmatione ejusdem

modo praescripto sufficiens fore warrantum INSUPER dilectis nostris
et vestrum cuilibet conjunctim
et divisim vicecomitibus nostris in hac parte specialiter constitutis salutem Vobis
praecipimus et mandamus quatenus praefato Domino Wilhelmo Alexander vel suo
certo actornato latori praesentium statum et sasinam haereditariam pariter et possessionem corporalem actualem et realem totarum et integrarum praedictarum
terrarum regionis et dominii Novae Scotiae cum omnibus et singulis partibus pendiculis privilegiis commoditatibus immunitatibus aliisque tam generaliter quam
particulariter superius expressatis apud dictum castrum nostrum de Edinburt
tradatis et deliberetis sine dilatione et hoc nullo modo omittatis Ad quod faciendum
vobis et vestrum cuilibet conjunctim et divisim vicecomitibus nostris in hac parte
antedictis nostram plenariam et irrevocabilem tenore praesentis cartae nostrae committimus potestatem Quamquidem sasinam nos cum avisamento praedicto pro nobis
nostrisque successoribus tenore praesentis cartae nostrae volumus declaramus et
ordinamus tam fore legitimam et sufficientem quam si praecepta sasinae separatim
et ordinarie e nostra cancellaria ad eum effectum super dicta nostra carta fuissent
directa penes quam nos cum avisamento praedicto pro nobis haeredibus et successoribus nostris dispensavimus ac per praesentis cartae nostrae tenorem dispensamus
imperpetuum IN CUJUS REI testimonium huic praesenti cartae nostrae magnum
sigillum nostrum apponi praecepimus Testibus predilectis nostris consanguineis et
consiliariis Jacobo marchione de Hammiltoun comite Arranio et Cambridge domino
Aven et Innerdaill &c Georgio Mariscalli comite domino Keyth &c regni nostri
mariscallo predilecto nostro consiliario Domino Georgio Hay de Kynfawns milite
nostro cancellario predilecto nostro consanguineo et consiliario Thoma comite de
Melros domino Byning &c. nostro secretario dilectis nostris familiaribus consiliariis
Dominis Ricardo Cokburne de Clerkingtoun nostri secreti sigilli custode Joanne
Hamiltoun de Magdalenis nostrorum rotulorum registri ac consilii clerico Georgio
Elphingstoun de Blythiswod nostrae justiciariae clerico et Joanne Scott de Scottistarvett nostrae cancellariae directore militibus Apud aulam nostram de Otlandis
duodecimo die mensis Julii anno Domini millesimo sexcentesimo vigesimo quinto et
regni nostri primo.

CARTA WILLELMI ALEXANDER DE MENSTRIE MILITIS
DE DOMINIO CANADAE &c.   2 FEBRUARII 1628.

CAROLUS Dei Gratia Magne Britannie Francie et Ihbernie Rex Fideique Defensor omnibus probis hominibus totius terre seu clericis et laicis salutem SCIATIS quia nos perfecte diligentes quo pacto fidelis ac praedilectus noster consiliarius Dominus Willielmus Alexander de Menstrie miles noster principalis secretarius pro regno nostro Scotiae ac haereditarius locumtenens regionis et dominii nostri Novae Scotiae in America variis suis susceptis navium machinarum bellicarum tormentorum et munitionum provisione deductione coloniarum necnon in dicta regione perspicienda peragranda et possidenda magnos sumptus et impensas sustinuerit et quo melius ipse ceterique nostri subditi dictae regionis inhabitationem secum experturi corroborentur pro ulteriore nostrorum in istis partibus dominiorum dilatatione Christianae religionis imbi propagatione viaeque seu transitus sperabili relevatione et detectione ad ista maria quae Americae ab occidente incumbunt vulgo *he South Sea* nuncupata unde magni istius fluminis seu sinus Canadae vel alicujus in eundem defluentis fluvii caput seu scaturigo non procul distare existimatur Ac quoniam ex specimine per dictum Dominum Willielmum in dictae regionis Novae Scotiae ad praefatum sinum et fluvium Canadam terminantis perspectione et peragratione hactenus exhibito spectata plantationis in istis partibus mitia ad propagationem dictae religionis magnumque antiqui regni nostri Scotiae decus et emolumentum tantum tendentia sibi stabilienda proposuit ex quo fieri potest ut dictae coloniae per ipsum suosque successores plantandae hac ope praefatam viam seu transitum ad dicta maria multum huc usque praegravibus considerationibus desideratum totiesque per varias personas susceptum processu temporis detegant IGITUR ac pro dicti Domini Willielmi haeredum suorum assignatorum suorumque participum et associatorum ad ulteriorem in tali tantoque suscepto progressum flagrantioribus accendendis animis NOS cum specialibus avisamento et consensu prefidelis et praedilecti nostri consanguinei et consiliarii Joannis Comitis Marriae Domini Erskene et Garcoch magni nostri thesaurarii nostrorum computorum rotulatoris collectoris et thesaurarii novarumque nostrarum augmentationum regni nostri Scotiae fidelis et praedilecti nostri consiliarii Archibaldi Domini Naper de Merchingstoun nostri in dictis officiis deputati ac reliquorum dominorum nostri secreti consilii nostrorum commissionariorum dicti regni nostri Scotiae dedimus concessimus et disposuimus tenoreque praesentis cartae nostrae damus concedimus et disponimus praefato Domino Willielmo Alexander haeredibus suis et assignatis haereditarie imperpetuum Omnes et singulas insulas infra sinum Canadae jacentes inter Novam Scotiam et Terram Novam ad ostium et introitum praedicti magni fluminis Canadae ubi decidit et intrat in dictum sinum (includendo imibi magnam insulam *Anticosti*) Necnon dedimus concessimus et disposuimus tenoreque praesentis cartae nostrae damus concedimus et disponimus praenominato Domino Willielmo Alexander suisque praedictis omnes et singulas insulas infra dictum fluvium Canadam jacentes a dicto ostio et introitu ad caput usque primum ortum et scaturiginem ejusdem ubicunque sit aut lacum unde fluit (qui putatur esse versus magnum sinum Californiae a quibusdam Mare Vermeio nuncupatum) aut infra quosvis alios fluvios in dictum fluvium Canadam defluentes vel in quibuscunque lacubus aquis sive fretis per quae vel dictus magnus fluvius Canada vel aliqui alii dictorum fluviorum decurrunt aut in quibus exeunt Ac praeterea dedimus et concessimus tenoreque praesentis cartae nostrae damus et concedimus praefato Domino Willielmo suisque antedictis quinquaginta leucas bondarum ab utroque latere antedicti fluvii Canadae a dicto ostio et introitu ad dictum caput fontem et scaturiginem ejusdem necnon ab utroque latere dictorum aliorum fluviorum in eundem defluentium ac etiam ab utroque latere dictorum lacuum fretorum seu aquarum per quas quilibet dictorum fluviorum decurrunt aut in quibus exeunt Et similiter dedimus et concessimus tenoreque praesentis cartae nostrae damus et concedimus praefato Domino Willielmo Alexander suisque praedictis totas et integras bondas et transitus tam in aquis quam in terra a praedicto capite fonte et scaturigine Canadae ubicunque sit aut a quocunque lacu unde labitur ad praefatum sinum Californiae quantacunque comperta fuerit esse distantia cum quinquaginta leucis omnimodo ab utroque latere ejusdem transitus inter dictum caput Canadae et sinum Californiae et similiter omnes et singulas insulas infra eundem sinum Californiae jacentes ac etiam totas et integras terras et bondas eidem sinui ab occidente et austro adjacentes sive reperiantur pars continentis sive terrae firmae sive insula (ut putatur esse) quae Californiae nomine vulgo nuncupatur et indigitatur Insuper dedimus et concessimus tenoreque praesentis cartae nostrae damus et concedimus ac pro nobis et successoribus nostris cum avisamento et consensu praedicto pro perpetuo confirmamus prefato Domino Willielmo Alexander haeredibus suis et assignatis quibuscunque haereditarie omnes et singulas alias terras bondas lacus fluvios freta silvas forrestas aliaque per ipsum suosve successores eorum participes associatos aut alios eorum nomine seu potestatem ab his habentes quocunque tempore futuro invenienda conquerenda seu detegenda super utroque latere integrarum bondarum et transitus antedictarum ab ostio et introitu dicti fluvii Canadae ubi in dictum sinum Canadae se exonerat ad dictum sinum Californiae aut insulas in maribus eidem adjacentibus quae per alios nostros subditos aut subditos alterius alicujus Christiani principis seu ordinum nobiscum in foedere et amicitia constitutorum hactenus realiter et actualiter possessa non sunt Cum plena et absoluta potestate ipsi dicto Domino Willielmo Alexander suisque praedictis (nullisque aliis) eorum factoribus servis et aliis eorum nomine colonias stabiliendi ac utendi commercio in praenominatis locis seu bondis vel qualibet earundem parte particulariter designata omnesque alios ab iisdem arcendi seu prohibendi necnon proportiones terrarum earundem cuicunque personae seu quibuscunque personis prout sibi commodum videbitur elocandi ac super iisdem terminis conditionibus restrictionibus et observationibus infra omnes praenominatas bondas sicut in Nova Scotia per quascunque literas patentes seu diplomata ipsi per quondam nostrum charissimum patrem vel nosmetipos concessas facere potest cum talibus etiam et tantis privilegiis libertatibus et immunitatibus in omnibus praedictis locis seu bondis insulis aliisque suprascriptis tam in mari aqua dulci quam in terra quales quantasque dictus Dominus Willielmus Alexander habet in Nova Scotia per priores suas literas patentes seu diplomata de Nova Scotia de data apud

Quaequidem privilegia in dictis prioribus literis patentibus contenta et unumquodque eorum adeo sufficientia et valida fore ordinamus ac si singula hic particulariter et sigillatim concessa et expressa fuissent de verbo in verbum ejusdem omnimodo roboris fortitudinis et efficaciae fore volentes penes quorum particularem hic non insertionem nos pro nobis et successoribus nostris dispensavimus tenoreque praesentis cartae nostrae dispensamus imperpetuum Declarando etiam sicut nos cum avisamento et consensu praedicto ordinamus et declaramus pro nobis et successoribus nostris quod hae praesentes nostrae literae patentes seu diploma nullatenus erit praejudiciabile nec derogativum quibuscunque juribus cartis seu diplomatibus praefato Domino Willielmo Alexander suisve antedictis de aut super Nova Scotia quocunque tempore datam praesentium praecedente concessis aut alicui capiti clausulae articulo seu conditioni in iisdem expressis ac etiam sine praejudicio prioris alicujus literae patentis per nos antehac quibuscunque baronettis infra Scotiam de regione Novae Scotiae concessae seu concedendae quovis tempore futuro Prohibendo et vetando prout nos tenore praesentis cartae nostrae specialiter prohibemus et vetamus omnes et singulos nostros subditos cujuscunque gradus seu conditionis in quolibet nostrorum regnorum seu dominiorum ne ullam faciant plantationem nec ullo utantur commercio in dictis locis seu bondis sinubus fluviis lacubus insulis et fretis suprascriptis aut in aliqua earundem parte absque specialibus avisamento licentia et consensu praefati Domini Willielmi Alexander suorumve praedictorum ac cum speciali potestate dicto Domino Willielmo

Alexander suisque praedictis attachiandi arrestandi et deprehendendi omnes et singulas personas quae negotiari et commercio uti in aliqua dictorum locorum seu bondarum parte contra hanc prohibitionem inventae fuerint eorumque naves et bona confiscandi ac desuper in suos proprios usus pro libito disponendi absque ullo computo seu ratione de eisdem vel aliqua earundem parte reddenda quomodolibet omniaque alia adeo libere et large in omnibus intentionibus propositis et instructionibus faciendi infra totas et integras praenominatas bondas seu spatia sicuti praefatus Dominus Willielmus Alexander suique praedicti infra dictam regionem Novae Scotiae seu dictum regnum nostrum Scotiae fecisse potuit seu facere potest virtute cujuslibet dictarum literarum patentium priorum cartarum seu diplomatum TENENDAS et HABENDAS totas et integras praenominatas terras spatia seu bondas insulas aliaque generaliter et particulariter expressa cum singulis suis privilegiis immunitatibus et commoditatibus quibuscunque generaliter et particulariter supramentionatis praefato Domino Willielmo Alexander suisque praedictis de nobis et successoribus nostris de corona et regno nostro Scotiae in libera alba firma imperpetuum per omnes rectas metas antiquas suas et divisas prout jacent in longitudine et latitudine in domibus aedificiis boscis planis moris marresiis viis semitis aquis stagnis rivolis pratis pascuis et pasturis molendinis multuris et eorum sequelis aucupationibus venationibus piscationibus petariis turbariis carbonibus carbonariis cuniculis cunicularis columbis columbariis fabrilibus brasinis brueriis et genistis silvis nemoribus et virgultis lignis tignis lapicidiis lapide et calce cum curiis et earum exitibus herezeldis bludevitis et mulierum merchetis cum communi pastura liberoque introitu et exitu ac cum omnibus aliis et singulis suis libertatibus commoditatibus proficuis asiamentis ac justis suis pertinentiis quibuscunque tam non nominatis quam nominatis tam subtus terra quam supra terram procul et prope ad praedictas terras cum pertinentiis spectantibus seu juste spectare valentibus quomodolibet in futurum libere quiete plenarie integre honorifice bene et in pace cum furca fossa sok sak thole thame wert wraik wair weth vennysoun infangtheif outfangtheif pit et gallous sine aliquo impedimento revocatione contradictione aut obstaculo aliquali REDDENDO inde annuatim dictus Dominus Willielmus suique praedicti nobis et successoribus nostris unum denarium monetae Scotiae super solo dictarum terrarum aut alicujus partis earundem ad festum Nativitatis Domini nomine albae firmae si petatur tantum   Quasquidem totas et integras praenominatas terras spatia seu bondas insulas aliaque generaliter et particulariter supra expressa ut dictum est nos cum specialibus avisamento et consensu praedicto pro nobis et successoribus nostris ereximus et univimus tenoreque praesentis cartae nostrae erigimus et unimus in unum integrum et liberum [dominium] DOMINIUM DE CANADA nuncupandum ad memoratum Dominum Willielmum Alexander suosque praedictos haereditarie spectans et pertinens imperpetuum   NOBIS etiam tenore praesenti cartae nostrae gratiose

9

placet quod quandocunque dictus Dominus Wilhelmus Alexander suique antedicti vel
aliquis eorum hanc praesentem nostram cartam cum omnibus et singulis beneficialibus
clausulis et conditionibus quae in dictis prioribus literis patentibus cartis seu diplomatibus de Nova Scotia renovari voluerit et desideraverit vel prout ipse sui antedicti
vel eorum quilibet ex advocatorum consultatione aut speciali aliqua ulterioris seu
certioris [citerioris?] dictorum locorum seu bondarum fluviorum lacuum fretorum seu
transituum aliorumque supra mentionatorum detectionis cognitione magis commodum
et expediens videbitur tunc et in eo casu nos dictam cartam praefato Domino Wilhelmo Alexander suisque antedictis in optima et amplissima quae comminisci poterit
forma renovaturos et translaturos promittimus in verbo principis Insuper nos tenore
praesentis cartae nostrae cum avisamento et consensu praedicto decernimus declaramus et ordinamus quod sasina per dictum Dominum Wilhelmum Alexander suosve
praedictos apud castrum nostrum de Edinburgh tanquam eminentissimum et principalem dicti regni nostri Scotiae locum aut super solo et fundo praefatarum terrarum
bondarum et insularum vel cujuslibet earundem partis ad placitum et libitum ejusdem
Domini Wilhelmi suorumque praedictorum capienda omni tempore futuro sufficiens
erit pro totis et integris praenominatis terris bondis insulis aliisque supra specificatis
aut aliqua parte seu portione earundem et quod haeredes praefati Domini Wilhelmi
suorumque praedictorum in omnibus et singulis praenominatis terris bondis insulis
aliisque praedictis vel per praecepta e cancellaria dicti regni nostri Scotiae aut cancellaria per dictum Dominum Wilhelmum suosque antedictos in praefata regione et
domino de Canada instituenda pro libito sasiantur aut etiam prout haeredes sui per
dictas priores suas concessiones in Nova Scotia sasiri possunt penes quod nos cum
avisamento et consensu praedicto pro nobis et successoribus nostris dispensavimus
tenoreque praesentis cartae nostrae dispensamus imperpetuum ac penes omnia et
singula prenominata privilegia aliaque generaliter et particulariter supra mentionata
Et praeterea fecimus et constituimus tenoreque praesentis cartae nostrae facimus
et constituimus

et eorum quemlibet conjunctim et divisim ballivos nostros in hac parte dando et concedendo iis et eorum cuilibet nostram plenam potestatem et speciale warrantum
statum et sasinam haereditariam pariter et possessionem actualem realem et corporalem praefato Domino Wilhelmo Alexander suisque antedictis vel suis certis
actornatis hanc praesentem cartam nostram habentibus seu producentibus dandi
concedendi et deliberandi de omnibus et singulis praenominatis terris bondis fluviis
lacubus insulis fretis seu transitibus aliusque quibuscunque generaliter et particulariter supra expressis dictae regionis et domini de Canada apud dictum castrum nostrum de Edinburgh vel super solo et fundo cujuslibet partis praedictarum terrarum
et bondarum seu locorum vel uti oque modo ad placitum dicti Domini Wilhelmi Alexander suorumque praedictorum Mandando iisdem et eorum cuilibet quatenus visis

praesentibus indilate statum et sasinam haereditariam pariter et possessionem actualem realem et corporalem omnium et singularum praenominatarum terrarum locorum seu bondarum insularum fluviorum lacuum aliorumque praedictorum generaliter et particulariter supra expressorum praefato Domino Wilhelmo Alexander suisque praedictis vel suis certis actornatis hanc praesentem cartam nostram habentibus seu producentibus super qualibet parte fundi dictarum terrarum vel apud castrum nostrum de Edinburgh vel utroque modo prout ipsi suisque praedictis melius apparebit dent tradant et deliberent seu aliquis eorum det tradat et deliberet per terrae et lapidis deliberationem praefato Domino Wilhelmo suisque antedictis vel eorum actornatis hanc praesentem nostram cartam habentibus seu producentibus apud dictum castrum vel super solo et fundo dictarum terrarum aliorumque suprascriptorum vel utroque modo pro libito dicti Domini Wilhelmi suorumque praedictorum   Quamquidem sasinam ita per dictos nostros ballivos in hac parte praefato Domino Wilhelmo suisque antedictis vel eorum actornatis hanc praesentem cartam nostram habentibus seu producentibus tradendam nos pro nobis et successoribus nostris decernimus et ordinamus bonam legitimam validam et sufficientem fore in omni tempore futuro dispensando sicuti nos tenore praesentis cartae nostrae dispensamus penes omnia quae adversus eandem objici possunt sive in forma sive in effectu Denique nos pro nobis et successoribus nostris cum avisamento et consensu praedicto volumus decernimus declaramus et ordinamus hanc praesentem cartam nostram cum omnibus et singulis privilegiis libertatibus clausulis articulis et conditionibus supradictis in proximo nostro parliamento regni nostri Scotiae seu quolibet alio ejusdem regni parliamento posthac tenendo ad libitum et placitum dicti Domini Willielmi Alexander suorumque praedictorum ratificandam approbandam et confirmandam roburque fortitudinem et efficaciam decreti ejusdem supremi fore habituram ad quod faciendum nos pro nobis et successoribus nostris volumus et declaramus eandem nostram cartam et clausulas imibi contentas sufficiens fore mandatum seu warrantum idem ita fieri et perfici promittentes in verbo regis In cujus rei testimonium huic praesenti cartae nostrae magnum sigillum nostrum apponi praecepimus Testibus nostris consanguineis et consiliariis Jacobo marchione de Hammiltoun comite Aranie et Cantabrigie domino Aven et Innerdaill Wilhelmo Mariscalli comite domino Keyth &c regni nostri mariscallo Georgio vicecomite de Duplin domino Hay de Kinfawnis nostro concellario Thoma comite de Hadingtoun domino Bynning et Byris &c nostri secreti sigilli custode dilectis nostris familiaribus consiliariis Dominis Wilhelmo Alexander de Menstrie nostro secretario principali Jacobo Hammiltoun de Magdalenis nostrorum rotulorum registri ac consilii clerico Georgio Elphingstoun de Blythiswod nostrae justiciariae clerico et Joanne Scot de Scottistarvett militibus nostrae cancellariae directore Apud regiam nostram de Quhythall secundo die mensis Februarii anno Domini millesimo sexcentesimo vigesimo octavo et regni nostri tertio

C Race
Trepassa
C de pene
Glamorgan
Vaughans Coue.
Pembrok
Cardigan
Brechonia
Rhenus
Cambriola
Fretum
Placentiæ
Formofa
Golden
South Falkland
Placentia
harbor
Ferriland
S. George Caluert
Lord Baltemor de
Baltimor
Caplin bay
C Broyle
Iles efperv
B. of Bulls
Petit harbor
St. Jhons
Torbay
Cuports
coue
I Ruge
C S. Francis
Bay of Contion
Brigushops
Trinite bay
NORTH FAYLKLAD
Bona Vista a Caboto
primum reperta
Bay of flowers
Broad hauen
Bay of foggs
Penguin Ins
Bay Noterdam
Port Flourdelice
C S Iohn
Groy
Bellile
Port St. Iulian
C de Grote
Bellile

Banck Androes
IS. Peter
Lacus incognitus
difcouered in Anno 1617 by Captaine Mafon
Insula of
Terra
The Ile

NEWFOVND
defcribed by Captaine Iohn Mafon
who fpent feuen years in the

A Scale of
5 10 15 20

Infula olim appellata Noua Terra a Caboto Veneto primu
reperta Anno Dm 1499 fub aufpicys et fumptibus Henrici
7 Anglorum Regis; per literas patentes a Regina
Elizabetha conceffa 1577 Dno Humphredo Gilbert
Equiti Aurato Anno 1609 a Iacobo Magnæ Brittanniæ
Monarcha Societati Nobilis quorundu et Mercatorum
Lonadmenfu et Briftotienfis concefsa fub Magno Sigillo:
Angliæ Cutus pars Auftralis de Captini portu vfq ad Placentiæ Fretum data et afsignata fuit fub Cambriola noine
Gulielmo Vaughanno Cambrobritano 1616 cura et labore Io:
hanis Slany Societatis Trefaurary Hominis de Repub op
time meriti Hanc parte Auftralis Vaughanus primus incolere
cæpit 1617 Et poftea portiones cuifde Terræ de Septentrioah
parte Rheni Fluminis vfq ad Captini Portu Vico Falklædie
D: Georgio Caluert Baroni de Baltimore afsignauit

C Brittaine

NOUA
SCOTIA

...nuc tissimo Carolo Magnæ
Brittanniæ Monarchæ
...nouum Regnum, cuius fundamina
...
...in Australi, Rex tibi sixit huno

Ile St Paule

Peirges
C Veirges
CRay

St Ihons riuer

Ile Brion

Ile Ramea

ta Noua

ed of olde:

ND

us Gent:

THE GRAND

BAYE

The Gulfe of
the Riuer of
Canada

South

East   West

North

35   40

Ile of Diamonds

PART OF NOUA FRANCIA

A

BRIEFE DISCOVRSE
of the Nevv-found-land,

with the situation, temperature,
and commodities thereof,

inciting our Nation to goe
forward in that hope-
full plantation begunne.

Scire tuum nihil eſt, niſi te ſcire hoc ſciat alter.

EDINBVRGH,
Printed by *Andro Hart.* 1620.

TO THE RIGHT
WORSHIPFVLL SIR
IOHN SCOTT
of Scots-Tarvet,
KNIGHT, &c.

IR, you are like to haue none other accompt for the prefent than fuch as Marchant-Factors, after bad markets returne, that is, papers for paymēt, for liuers lines. The which though not fo acceptable as more folide returnes, yet giues fome fatiffactiõ for the expenfes of time queftionable. I haue fent you a difcourfe of our Countrie penned at the requeft of friends, for the better fatisfaction of our Nobilitie, vnpolifhed and rude, bearing the countries badge where it was hatched, onely clothed with plainneffe and trueth. I intreat your fauourable acceptation thereof, as your wonted clemencie hath beene to the Author, if you thinke it may doe good by incouraging any of your Countrie to the interprife, I am willing you publifh it, other wife let it bee buried in filence as you fhall thinke meeteft, and efteeme mee ftill one of whome you haue power to difpofe.

IOHN MASON.

To the Reader.

OR as much as there bee fundrie relations of the New-foundland and the commodities thereof, Some too much extolling it, some too much debafing it, preferring the temperature of the aire thereof before ours, the hopes of commodities there without paines and mineralles, as if they were apparent (which as I deny to bee a veritie, yet I affirme not to bee impofsible) with other narrations diffenting from the trueth, the which although done out of a good affection, yet had they better beene vndone. I haue therefore (gentle Reader) hoping of thy fauourable conftruction, fet downe in few and plaine tearmes out of that experience I haue gained in three yeares and feuenth monthes refidence there, the trueth, as thou fhalt finde by proofe thereof, to the which I recommend thee and vs all to his Grace, that is able and will plant thofe that feare him in a better Kingdome.   Farewell.

Thine and his Countries in
part, not whollie his owne.

IOHN MASON.

A BRIEF DISCOVRSE

of the Newfoundland, with the
Situation, temperature, and commodities there-
of, inciting our Nation to goe forward in
that hopefull plantation begunne.

HE Countrie commonly knowne
and called by the name of Newfoundland, albeit it is fo much
frequented and reforted yearely to,
by thoufands of our Nation and
others, which haue fcarcely fo
much as a fuperficiall knowledge
thereof (onely fo much as concerneth their fifhings excepted) is
an Iland or Ilands as fome plats
haue defcribed it, fituate on the front of *America*, betwixt
46. and 52. degrees of Northerly latitude, of the bignes
of *Ireland*. the Eaftermoft fide thereof bounded with the
Ocean extendeth it felfe neareft North and South: the
variation allowed 100. Leagues, the fouth face deuided
from the Iles of *Cap*. Bretone by the Gulfe of Sainct Low-
rence a ftraigth of 27. Leagues ouer lyeth Weft. and
by North northerly, and Eaft and by South Southerly in
length 77. Leagues, on the Weft part inbraced by the
Grand-bay ftretching it felfe Northeaft and Southweft 75.
Leagues. and on the North confined by the Norther arme
of the Grand-bay which feparateth it from the continent of
Noua

A difcourfe of

Noua Fiancia, making a fret of 7. Leagues wide, & is defcribed by the Rhombe of W. and by North and E. and by S. 25. Leag. Almoft of a Triangular forme fauing that many bays & Inlets making incroachment haue diffigured the face thereof with Scars, eating into the land into 40 leagues fpace on the South part where we haue fearched 30 as good Harbours as the world affords. The longitude thereof reackoned from the weftermoft part of the *Infulæ fortunatæ* is 330 degrees, diftant in the Line of Weft & by the South from our *Meridian* 45. degrees by cōmon account which in the midle parallell of the differēce the Latitude betwixt the lāds end of *England* & the bodie of Newfoundland at 39 one halfe miles anfwerable to each degree in the fame maketh 1764. miles or 588 Leagues. The aire fubtle & wholefome, the Summer feafon pleafant conforme to the like latitude in Europe, fauing that ye woodie places in Iune & Iulie are fomewhat peftered with fmall Flies bred of the rottenes of ruined woode & moyfture like as in *Rufsia*. The Winter degenerating therfrom, being as cold & fnowy as 60 degrees in Europe, & of the like temperature in December, Ian Febr. March, as the northermeft parts in *Scotland* viz. The Hebrides and the Orcades wherin I haue twife wintered, or of the Coaft betwixt *Hamburgh* & the mouth of the *Sownd* or *Nofe* of *Norway* · yet more comfortable for the length of the day in Winter, which exceedeth theirs three houres at the leaft And albeit it be thus cold in the Winter feafon by accidentall meanes, contrarie to the naturall pofition thereof in the Spheare, yet is it tollerable, as by experience, fo that there needs no Stoaues as in *Germanie:* Likewife fruitefull enough both of Sommer and Winter corne, an example for our confirmation thereof we haue in *Poland* one of the greateft corne Countries of Europe & yet as cold and fubject to freizing as Newfoundland, as alfo our owne experience both in Wheate, Rye, Barlie, Oates, and Peafe, which haue growen and ripened there as well and als timely as in *Yorkfhire* in *England* And for grouth of Garden herbes of diuers forts as Hyfope, Time, Parfely, Clarie, Nepe,
trench

french Mallowes, Bugloffe, Collombines, Wormewood, &c
There is at this present of 3. yeares old of my fowing, likewife Rofemary, Fenell, Sweet marierim, Baffell, Purfelyn,
Lettife, and all other Herbes & Rootes: as torneps, Paf-
nepes, Caretts, and Radifhes we haue found to growe well
there in the Sommer feafon. The common wild herbes of the
Countrie are Angelica, Violets, Mints, Scabius, Yarrow,
Ferne, Sarfaparilla, with diuers other forts whereof I am
ignorant; But fuppofe would for variety and rariety compofe
another Herball; of thefe kinds we haue only made vfe of
certain great green leaues plētifully growing in the woods,
and a great Roote growing in frefh water ponds, both good
againft the Skiruye, and an other prettie Roote with a blew
ftalke and leaues of the nature of a Skirret growing in a dry
Beachy ground, good meate boyled: The Countrie fruites
wild, are cherries fmall, whole groaues of them, Filberds
good, a fmall pleafant fruite, called a Peare, Damaske Rofes fingle very fweet, excellēt Ҫtiaberries, and Hartlebeiries
with aboundance of Rafberries, and Goofeberries fomewhat
better than ours in *England*, all which replanted would be
much inlarged. There is alfo a kinde of wild Coranies, wild
Peafe or Feetches in many places which we haue both found
good meat and medecine for the Skiruy; The Land of the
North parts moft mountanye & woodye very thick of Firre
trees, Spruce, Pine, Lereckhout, Afpe, Hafill, a kinde of ftin-
king wood, the three formeft goodly Timber and moft con-
ueniēt for building. No Oakes, Afhe, Beech, or Ellmes, haue
we feene or heard of; the greateft parts of the Plaines are
marifh and boggs, yet apt to be drawen dry by meanes of
many frefh Lakes intermixt which paye tribute to the Sea;
and on the brinks of thefe Lakes, through which the water
draines away from the rootes of the Graffe, it florifheth, in
the other parts of the Plaines where the water ftandeth and
killeth the growth of the Graffe with his coldneffe it is
rufhie and feggy; in fome parts is barien, & mosfie ground,
but that that is firme and dry beareth good graffe   The
                                                    Springs

A difcourfe of

Spring beginneth in the end of Aprill, & Harueft continueth
while Nouember, I haue feene September and October
much more pleafant than in *England*, The South part is not
fo mountanous nor fo woodie, for being a little paffed vp
from the Sea coaft the continent hath champion ground for
40. miles together in North and South extent of the like
nature of the former, hauing pretty Groues and many frefh
laks replenifhed with Eeles & Salmon-Trontes great, and in
great plentie. The Beaftes are Ellans, Follow-deare, Hares,
Beares harmeles, Wolues, Foxes, Beauers, Catnaghenes excellent, Otteres, and a fmall beaft like a Ferret whofe excre-
ment is Muske And the Plantations haue prettie ftoare
of Swine and Goates. The Fowles are Eagles, Falcons, Taf-
fills, Marlins, a great Owle much deformed, a leffer Owle,
Buffards, Gripes, Ofprayes which diue for Fifhes into the
Water, Rauens, Crowes, wild Geefe, Snipes, Teales, Twil-
lockes, excellent wilde Duckes of diuers forts and aboundance, fome whereof rare and not to be found in Europe,
Their particulars too tedious to relate, all good meate, Par-
triches white in Winter, and gray in Summer, greater thã
ours, Butters, blacke Birds with redd breaftes, Phillidas,
Wrens, Swallowes, Iayes, with other finall Birds, and 2. or
3. excellent kinds of Beach Birds very fat and fweet, & at the
plãtations Englifh Pigeons. The fea fowles, are Gulles white
and gray, Penguins, Sea Pigeons, Ice Birds, Bottle nofes,
with other fortes ftrange in fhape, yet all bowntifull to vs
with then Egges as good as our Turkie or Hens, where with
the Helands are well replenifhed. But of all, the moft admirable is the Sea, fo diuerfified with feuerall forts of Fifhes a-
bounding therein, the confideration whereof is readie to
fwallow vp and drowne my fenfes not being able to compre-
hend or expreffe the riches therof For could one acre therof be inclofed with the Creatures therein in the moneths of
Iune, Iulie, and Auguft, it would exceed one thoufand acres
of the beft Pafture with the ftocke thereon which we haue
in *England*. May hath Herings on equall to 2. of ours, Lants
and

and Cods in good quantity. Iune hath Capline, a fifh much re-
fembling Smeltes in forme and eating, and fuch aboundance
dry on Shoare as to lade Carts, in fome partes pretty ftore
of Salmond, and Cods fo thicke by the fhoare that we heard-
lie haue beene able to row a Boate through them, I haue killed of them with a Pike; Of thefe, three men to Sea in a
Boate with fome on Shoare to dreffe and dry them in 30.
dayes will kill commonlie betwixt 25. and thirty thoufand,
worth with the Oyle arifing fiom them 100 or 120. pound.
And the fifh and Traine in one Harbour called Sainct Iohns
is yearly in the Sommer worth 17, or 18. thoufand pounds.
Iulie, and fo till Nouember, hath Macrill in aboundance:
one thereof as great as two of ours, Auguft hath great large
Cods but not in fuch aboundance as the fmaller, which continueth with fome little decreafing till December; What
fhould I fpeake of a kinde of Whales called Gibberts, Dog-
fifh, Porpofes, Hering-Hogges, Squides a rare kinde of fifh,
at his mouth fquirting mattere forth like Inke, Flownders,
Crabbes, Cunners, Catfifh, Millers, thunnes &c. Of al which
there are innumerable in the Summer feafon; Likewife of
Lobfters plentie, and this laft yeare ftoare of Smelts not
hauing beene knowne there before. I haue alfo feene Tonnie
fifh in Newland; now of fhell fifh there is Scalupes, Mufфеles,
Vrfenas, Hens, Periwinkles &c. Here we fee the chiefe fifhing
with his great commoditie expreffed, which falleth fo fitly
in the Summer feafon betwixt feed-time and Harueft that it
cannot be any hinderance to either. I haue heard fome
countries commended for their two fowld Harueft, which
heare thou haft, although in a different kinde, yet both as
profitable, I (dare fay) as theirs fo much extolled, if the right
courfe be taken; & well fareth, that country fay I, which in
one months time with reafonable paines, wil pay both land-
lords rent, feruants wages, and all Houfhold charges. But
peraduenture fome fqueayfie ftomake will fay, Fifhing is a
beaftly trade & vnfeeming a Gentleman, to whom I anfwere
(*Bonus odor luti cū lucro*) & let them propound the Holanders

B   to

to themfelues for example whofe Countrie is fo much in-
riched, by it; others fay the Countrie is barren, but they
are deceiued, for *Terra quæ tegit feipfam tegit Dominum*, and
the great aboundance of Woodes and wilde Finites which
excedingly florifh there proue the contrary. And what thogh
the fertility of the foyle and temperature of the Climate
be inferiour to *Virginia*, yet for foure maine Reafons to be
laid downe it is to be parallelled to it, if not preferred before it, the which we will heere propound.

1 The firft reafon is the nearenes to our owne home, which
naturally we are fo much addicted vnto, being but the halfe
of the way to *Virginia*, hauing a conuenient paffage for three
feafonable monthes, March, Aprill, and May, which alwayes
accomodate faire windes to paffe thether, fometime in 14.
or 20. dayes, feldome in thirtie dayes. Likewife the commodious returne in Iune, Iulie, Auguft, September, October, and Nouember, fometimes in 12. 16. 20. and now and
then in thirtie dayes.

2. The great intercourfe of trade by our Nation thefe
threefcore years and vpwards, in no fmall numbers frequen-
ting the New-found land, and daylie increafing, with the
likelineffe thereof to continue, fifh being a ftaple commoditie with vs, and fo fellable in other countries yearlie im-
ploying 3000. thoufand Sea-men and breeding new daylie,
alfo fraighting three hundreth Ships in that voyage, and
releuing of 20000. people moe here in *England* (for moft
of thefe fifhers are maried and haue a charge of Children,
and liue by this ineanes not being able to gaine halfe fo
much by another labour) furthermore the reuenew that
groueth to the King by the cuftomes of *French*, *Spanifh*
and Straights goods imported, from the proceede of this
fifh trade fuppofe at the leaft to the value of ten thoufand
pounds yearely.

3 The conueniency of tranfporting plantors thether at the
old rate, ten fhillings the man, and twentie fhillings to find
him victual thether, likewife other commodities by fhippes
that

that goe fackes at ten fhilling per tunne out, and thirtie fhillings home, whereas *Virginia* and *Birmooda* fraightes, are fiue pound the man and three pound the tunne.

4 Fourthly and laftly, Securitie from foraine and domefticke enemies, there being but few Saluages in the north, and none in the fouth parts of the Countrie; by whom the planters as yet neuer fuffered damage, againft whom (if they fhould feeke to trouble vs,) a fmall fortification will ferue being but few in number, and thofe onely Bow men. Alfo if any Warres fhould happen betwixt vs and other Nations, wee neede not feare rooting out. For the Yce is a Bulwarke all Aprill commonlie and after that during the whole Summer wee haue a garifon of 9. or 10. 1000 of our owne Nation with many good and warlike Shippes, who of necefsitie muft defend the fifhing feafon for their huings fake, as they alwayes formerlie haue done in the Warres with *Spaine*. And afterwards in the monthes of Harueft and Winter the winds are our friends and will hardlie fuffer any to approach vs, the which if they fhould, the cold oppofite to the nature of the Spainard will giue him but cold Intertainement; neither will the Plantours be altogether puffed vp with careleffe fecuritie, but fortifie in fome meafure knowing that *Non funt fecuri qui dant fua Colla fecuri*

Nowe hauing formerly layed downe the temperature of the Aire and difpofition of the Weather in the Winter feafon to be cold and confequently different from other places of the fame fituation vnder the fame Parallel in Europe, and by experience anfwerable to 59. or 60. degrees thereof. It will be expected that I fhould fhew fome reafons concerning the fame which according to mine opinion (fubmitting my felfe to better Iudgements) I will fet downe; It being a generall rule approued through *America* that any place vnder the fame Parallel of another place in Europe is as cold as thofe places which are fituate in 12. or 13. degrees to the North wards therof, and the fame rule holdeth alike on either fide

either ſide of the Equinoctiall. For example, the ſtraigths
of *Magelan* in 54 to the South of the Equinoctiall, are
more cold, ſnowie and boyſterous than any part of Europe
in 65. Likewiſe on this ſide the Line, the Country about
the Riuer *Orenoaque* and *Trinidade* in 9. or ten degrees is
found as temperate as *Gualata* vnder 23. degrees of more nor-
therlie latitude in *Africa*. So likewiſe Sainct *Auguſtine* in *Florida* vnder 31 degrees is anſerable to *Valadulid* in 42. degrees
in *Spaine*, alſo the plantations vnder 37. degrees in *Virginia*
are correſpondent in the Winter to the temperature of *Deuen-
ſhire* or *Cornewall* vnder 50. degrees heare in *England*, and
although their Summer bee ſome what hotter in regard of
the nearenes of the Sunne, being then in *Cancer* within 15. degrees of their Zenith, the Radius therof then ſtriking neare
at a right Angle, cauſing a ſtrange reflection, yet would it be
much hotter if the Sun in his paſſage ouer the great *Oceane*
3000. miles broad vnder that Paralel, betwixt Europe & *America*, by the exhalation of wateriſh vapours & much moiſture
thereout, into the middle region of the Aire, did not coole
the ſame, which being made more groſſe & thick with miſty
Clouds, his Beames cannot pearce through with their pro-
pre vigor and force, to heate the Earth; To this cooling of
the Sunnes heate helpeth alſo all thoſe great freſh ponds
and lakes ſo abounding in *America*. Freſh waters being more
naturally cold than ſalt, and both colder than the Earth, of
like qualitie alſo are the mariſh and Boggie groundes,
the Lands not manured and therefore more naturally cold,
the Country ſlenderly peopled, voide of Townes and Cities,
whereof Europe is full; the ſmoake whereof and heate of
fires much qualifieth the coldneſſe of the Aire. Laſtly the
chiefeſt reaſon of the coldneſſe in New-found-land in the
VVinter ſeaſon is the Yce which beeing congealed into
great firme Lands, euen from the North Pole, all alongſt
the Coaſt of *Gronland, Grenland,* The North-weſt paſſage
Terra de laberador & ſo towardes the Grand bay, all that tract
hauing many Inlets and broken Lands apt as vnnaturall
wombes

wombes to breede and bring foorth fuch Monfters, which being nurfed in their ruder armes, till the VVinter feafon paft, are turnde foorth of doores in the Spring to fhift for themfelues, and being weary of their imprifonments in thofe angrie Climes with one accord as if they had a-greed with winde and ftreame take Ferrie into New-found-land, which immuring vs in the months of Febru. & March, both which are fubject to northeaft winds & blowing from this Yce caufeth it very cold. The currant ftil fetting it fouth-ward as a Iaylor to bring it before the Iudge, neuer leaueth it till with the helpe of the outfet of Sainct *Lawrence* Gulfe it be prefented nearer the Sun to be broild by his fcorching Beames and confumed. I cannot deny but in fome VVinters betwixt Chriftmas and March, Yce is bred in the Harbors and bayes of New-foundland, by reafon of the calmeneffe of the winds there incident, And the want of ftreames not cauf-ing motion in the Waters, and when it is fo frozen, it is none otherwife then the Texfell or Inner Seas in Holand of 15 or 18. Inches thickneffe, and breakes and confumes in the Spring; all frefh Lakes frozen opens in the end of March or the beginning of Aprill, which brings with it many fhowers to wafh away Snow, and bare the ground; and in the midle of the Month many Ships arriue of the *Englifh*, fome *French*, and in the mideft of May fome *Portingalls*. All which as fo many Reapers come to the Harueft, gathering in aboun-dance the wonderfull blefsings of the Loid.

I might heare further difcourfe of our difcoueries, confe-rence with the Saluages by Mafter *Iohn Gye*, their maner of life: Likewife of the managinge our bufineffe in our Planta-tions, with the defcriptions of their fituations in 2. places 16. miles diftant from other, on the northfide the bay of Concep-tion; of the manner charge and benefite of our fifhings with the feuerall ftrange formes, and natures of Fifhes, pro-jects for making Yron, Salt, Pitch, Tarre, Tirpintine, Frank-Incenfe, Furres, Hope of trade with Saluages and fuch like, with many accidents and occurences in the time of
my

my gouerment there, but thefe may fuffice as *Verbum fapienti;* being of fufficient trueth to remoue errours of conceiuing the Countrie more pleafant by reafon of his naturall fight in the Spheare, then it is indeede, alfo to convince and take away malicious and fcandelous fpeeches of maligne perfons, who out of enuy to G O D and good Actions (inftructed by their father the Deuill) haue fought to dif-poile it of the dewe, and blamifh the good name thereof.

And laftlie to induce thee, gentle Reader, to the true confideration thereof as a thing of great con- fequence to our Nation not only at prefent, but like to bee much more benefici- all when the plaintations there fhall increafe, which God grant to his owne glo- rie and the good of our Common- Wealth.

FINIS.

NOVA SCOTIA.

The Kings Patent to
Sir William Alexander Knight,
for the Plantation of New Scotland,
in America, and his Proceedings
therein.

From the Fourth Part of
PURCHASE HIS PILGRIMES:
London, 1625.

NOVA SCOTIA.

THE KINGS PATENT TO SIR WILLIAM ALEXANDER *Knight*,

for the Plantation of New Scotland *in* America,

and his Proceedings therein.

I ACOBUS Dei gratia Magnæ Brittanniæ, Franciæ, & Hiberniæ Rex fideique defenſor : Omnibus probis hominibus totius terræ suæ Clericis & laicis ſalutem. Sciatis nos ſemper ad quamlibet quæ ad deciis & emolumentum regni nostri Scotiæ ſpectaret occaſionem amplectendum fuiſſe intentos, nullamque aut faciliorem aut magis innoxiam acquiſitionem censere, quàm quæ inexteris & incultis regnis vbi vitæ & victui suppetunt commodo nouis deducendis Colonijs facta ſit; præſertim ſi vel ipsa regna cultoribus prius racua, vel ab infidelibus, quos ad Christianam conuerti fidem & Dei gloriam intereſt plurimum, inſeſſa fuerint. Sed cum & alia nonnulla regna, & hæc non ita pridem nostra Anglia laudabiliter ſua nomina nouis terris acquiſitis ſed in ſe ſubactis indiderunt, quam numerosa & frequens Diuino beneficio hæc gens, hac tempestate ſit nobiscum reputantes, quamque honesto aliquo & vtili cultu eam ſtudioſe exerceri ne in deteriora ex ignauia & otio prolabatur expediat pleroſque in nouam deducendos regionem quam Colonijs compleant, operæpretium duximus qui & animi promptitudine & alacritate corporumque robore et viribus quibuſcunque difficultatibus, ſi qui alij mortalium vſpiam ſe audiant opponere, hunc conatum huic regno maxime idoneum inde arbitramur quod virorum tantummodo & mulierum iumentorum & frumenti, non etiam pecuniæ tran-

C

ſuectionem

ſuectionem poſtulat, neque incommodam ex ipſius regni mercibus retributionem hoc tempore cum negotiatio adeo imminuta ſit, poſſit reponere. Hiſce de cauſis ſicuti & propter bonum fidele & gratum dilecti noſtri conſilarij Domini WILLELMI ALEXANDRI equitis ſeruitium nobis prœſtitum & prœstandum, qui proprijs impenſis ex nostratibus primus externam hanc coloniam ducendam conatus ſit, diuerſaſque terras infra deſignatis limitibus circumſcriptas incolendas expetiuerit. NOS IGITUR ex Regali nostra ad Christanam religionem propagandam & ad opulentiam, prosperitatem, pacemque naturalium nostrorum ſubditorum dicti regni nostri Scotiœ acquirendam cura, ſicuti alij Principes extranei in talibus caſibus hactenus fecerunt, cum auiſamento & conſenſu prœdilicti nostri conſanguinei & consilarij Ioannis Comitis de Marr Domini Erskene & Garrioche ſummi nostri Theſaurarij computorum rotulatoris collectoris ac Theſaurarij nouarum nostrarum augmentationum huius Regni nostri Scotiœ, ac reliquorum dominorum noſtrorum Commiſſionariorum eiuſdem Regni nostri, Dedimus conceſſimus & diſpoſuimus, tenoreque prœſentis chartœ noſtrœ damus concedimus & diſponimus prœfato Domino Willelmo Alexandro, hœredibus ſuis vel aſſignatis quibuſcunque hœreditariè Omnes & ſingulas terras continentis ac inſulas ſituatas & iacentes in America, intra caput ſeu promontorium conmuniter Cap. de Sable appellatum iacens prope latitudinem quadraginta trium graduum aut ab eo circa, ab œquinoctiali linea verſus ſeptentrionem, à quo promontorio verſus littus maris tendentis ad occidentem ad ſtationem Sanctœ Mariœ nauium (vulgo S. Maries Bay) & deinceps verſus ſeptentrionem per directam lineam introitum ſiue oſtium magnœ illius ſtationis nauium trajicientem quœ excurrit in terrœ orientalem plagam inter Regionis Suriquorum & Etechemmorum (vulgo Surriquois & Etechemines) ad fluuium vulgo nomine Sanctœ Crucis appellatum : Et ad ſcaturiginem remotiſſimam ſiue fontem ex occidentali parte eiuſdem qui ſe primum prædicto fluuio immiſcet, vnde per imaginariam directam lineam quœ pergere per terram ſeu currere verſus ſeptentrionem concipietur ad proximam nauium ſtationem, fluuium vel ſcaturiginem in magno fluuio de Cannada ſeſe exonerantem Et

ab

ab eo pergendo verſus orientem per maris oras littorales eiuſdem fluuij de Cannada ad fluuium ſtationem nauium portum aut littus communiter nomine de Gachepe vel Gaspie notum & appellatum, Et deinceps verſus Euronotum ad inſulas Bacalaos vel Cap Briton vocatas Relinquendo eaſdem Insulas à dextra & voraginem dicti magni fluuij de Cannada ſiue magne ſtationis nauium & terras de Neufound-land, cum inſulis ad eaſdem terras pertinentibus à ſiniſtra. Et deinceps ad Caput ſiue promontorium de Cap. Briton prædictum iacens prope latitudinem quadraginta quinque graduum aut eo circa. Et à dicto promontorio de Cap. Briton verſus meridiem & Occidentem ad prædictum Cap. Sable vbi incipit perambulatio includenda & comprehenda intra dictas maris oras littorales ac earum circumferentias à mari ad [mare] omnes terras continentis cum fluminibus torrentibus, ſinibus, littoribus, inſulis aut maribus iacentibus prope infra ſex leucas ad aliquam earundem partem ex occidentali boreali vel orientali partibus orarum littoralium & præcinctuum earundem. Et ab Euronoto (vbi iacet Cap. Briton) & ex auſtrali parte eiuſdem (vbi eſt Cap. de Sable) omnia maria ac inſulas verſus meridiem intra quadraginta leucas dictarum orarum littoralium earundem magnam inſulam vulgariter appellatam Ile de Sable vel Sablon includen. iacen. verſus Carban vulgo South-South-east, circa triginta leucas à dicto Cap. Britton in mari & existen. in latitudine quadraginta quatuor graduum aut eo circa. Quæ quidem terræ prædictæ omni tempore affuturo nomine NOUÆ SCOTIÆ in America gaudebant. Quas etiam præfatus Dominus Willelmus in partes & portiones ſicut ei viſum fuerit diuidet ijſdemque nomina pro beneplacito imponet. Vna cum omnibus fodinis tum regalibus auri & argenti quam alijs fodinis ferri, plumbi, cupri, ſtanni, æris, &c.

IN cuius rei testimonium huic præſenti Chartæ nostræ magnum Sigillum noſtrum apponi præcepimus Teſtibus prædi[le]ctis noſtris conſanguineis & conſiliarijs Iacobo Marchione de Hamilton Comite Arraniæ & Cambridge Domino Auen & Innerdail, Georgio Marſcallh Comite Domino Keith & alt. regni noſtri Mariscallo, Alexandro Comite de Dunfermling Domino Fyviæ & Vrquhant noſtro Cancellario, Thoma Comite de Melros Domino Byres & Bynning noſtro Secretario,

Proceedings in the Plantation

Secretario, Dilectis nostris familiaribus confiliarys Domino Richardo Kokburne iuniore de Clerkington noftri Secreti Sigilli cuftode, Georgio Hay de Kinfawnis noftrorum Rotulorum Registrorum ac Concilij Clerico, Ioanne Cockburne de Ormestoun noftræ Iufticiariæ Clerico, & Ioanne Scot de Scotistaruet noftræ Cancellariæ Directore, Militibus   Apud Caftellum noftrum de Winfore decimo die menfis Septembris Anno Domini millefimo fexcentefimo vigefimo primo Regnorumque noftrorum annis quinquagefimo quinto & decimo nono [respective.]

Sir *Ferdinando Gorge* being entrufted with the affayres of *New England*, after hee had aduifed with fome of the Company ; confidering the largeneffe of the bounds intended to bee planted by his Maiefties fubiects in *America*, and the flow progreffe of Plantations in thefe parts, that the *Scottish* Nation may be perfwaded to embarke themfelues in their foraine enterprife, hee was content that Sir *William Alexander* Knight,[1] one of his Maiefties moft Honorable Priuy Councel of that Kingdome, fhould procure a Patent of fuch a bounds as his Maieftie fhould appoint to bee called *New Scotland*, and to bee held of the Crowne of *Scotland*, and gouerned by the Lawes of that Kingdome, as his faid Patent containing all the bounds, that doth lie to the Eaft of Saint *Croix*, compaffed with the great Riuer of *Canada* on the North, and the Maine Ocean on the South doth more particularly beare.   Whereupon the faid Sir *William* did fet out a Shippe with a Colony of purpofe to plant, which being too late in fetting forth were forced to ftay all the Winter (*Anno* 1622) at *New-found-Land*, and though they had a Shippe with new prouifions the next Spring from the
fayde

---

[1] For the Defcription and Encouragements to this defigne, and for better knowledge of *New Scotland*, befides a Book purpofely publifhed by the Honourable and learned Author (who at other weapons hath plaied his Mufes prizes, and giuen the World ample teftimony of his learning) you may read our Eigth Booke from the fixt Chapter forwards, the laft two Chapiters of the Ninth Booke, and that Defcription of the Country of *Mawooshen*, which I haue added hereto

fayde Sir *William*, yet by reafon of fome vnexpected occafions, the chiefe of the Company refolued not to plant at the firft, but onely to difcouer and to take poffeffion, which a number made choyce of for that purpofe did happily performe

The three and twentieth of Iune (*Anno* 1623), they loofed from Saint *Iohns* Harbour in *New-found-Land*, and fayled towardes *New Scotland*, where for the fpace of fourteene dayes they were by Fogges and contrarie Windes kept backe from fpying Land till the eight of Iuly : thereafter that they faw the Weft part of Cape *Breton*, and fo till the thirteenth day, they fayled to and fro alongft the Coaft till they came the length of *Port de Muton*, where they difcouered three very pleafant Harbours, and went a fhoare in one of them, which they called *Lukes* Bay, where they found a great way vp to a very pleafant Riuer being three fathoms deepe at low water ; at the entry thereof, and on euery fide of the fame they did fee very delicate Meadowes, hauing Rofes white and red growing thereon, with a kind of wild Lilly, which had a very daintie fmell

The next day they refolued to coaft alongft to difcouer the next Harbour, which was but two leagues diftant from the other, where they found a more pleafant Riuer, being foure fathom water at a low water, with Meadowes on both fides thereof, hauing Rofes and Lillies growing thereon as the other had   They found within this Riuer a very fit place for a Plantation, both in regard that it was naturally apt to bee fortified, and that all the ground betweene the two Riuers was without Wood, and was good fat earth hauing feuerall forts of Berries growing thereon, as Goofeberry, Strawberry, Hyndberry, Rasberry, and a kinde of Red-wineberry : As alfo fome forts of Graine, as Peafe, fome eares of Wheat, Barley, and Rye, growing there wild ; the Peafe grow euery where in abundance, very big and good to eate, but tafte of the Fitch This Riuer is called Port *Iolly*, from whence they coafted alongft to Port *Negro*, being 12. leagues diftant, where all the way as they failed alongft they found a very pleafant Countrey hauing growing euery where fuch things as they did fee in the two Harbours where they had beene.   They found likewife in euery Riuer

abundance

abundance of Lobſters, and Cockles, and other ſmall fiſhes; and
alſo they found not only in the Riuers, but all the Coaſt alongſt,
numbers of ſeuerall ſorts of Wild-fowle, as Wild-gooſe, Black-
Duck, Woodcock, Heron, Pigeon, and many other ſorts of Fowle
which they knew not. They found likewiſe, as they ſailed alongſt
the Coaſt abundance of great Cod, with ſeuerall other ſorts of
great fiſhes. The Countrey is full of Woods, not very thick, and
the moſt part Oake, the reſt Fir-tree, Spruce, Birch, and many
other ſorts of wood which they had not ſeene before.

Hauing diſcouered this part of the Countrey in regard of the
Voyage, their Ship was to make to the Straits with fiſhes, they
reſolued to coaſt alongſt from *Lukes* Bay to Port *de Muton*, being
foure leagues to the Eaſt thereof, where they encountered with a
Frenchman, that in a very ſhort time had a great voyage, hauing
furniſhed one Ship away with fiſhes, and had neere ſo many ready
as to load his owne Ship and others. And hauing taken a view
of this Port, which to their judgement they found no wayes inferiour to the reſt they had ſeene before, they reſolued to retire
backe to *New-found-land,* where their Ship was to receive her
loading of fiſhes, the twentieth of Iuly they looſed from thence,
and the ſeuen and twentieth thereof they arriued at Saint *Iohns*
Harbour in *New-found-land*; and from thence ſailed alongſt the
Bay of *Conception,* where they left the Ship, and diſpatched themſelues home in ſeuerall Ships that belonged to the Weſt part of
England, and doe intend this next Spring to ſet forth a Colony
to plant there.

AN EXTRACT FROM

" A Briefe Relation of the Discovery and Plantation of New
England: &c. London, printed by Iohn Haviland, and are to
be sold by William Bladen. M.DC.XXII." 4to. This Relation,
published by the President and Councell of New-England, is
dedicated

of New Scotland in America.

dedicated " To the Prince [Charles] his Highnesse."   An ab-
breviated copy of it is included in Purchase's Pilgrimes, the
Fourth Part, Book x. chap. i. page 1827, &c.]

HEN this designe [the Plantation of New England]
was first attempted, some of the present Company were
therein chiefly interested ; who being carefull to haue
the same accomplished, did send to the discouery of
those Northerne parts a braue Gentleman, Captaine
Henry Challons, with two of the Natiues of that Terri-
tory, the one called *Maneday*, the other *Assecomet*.   But his misfortunes
did expose him to the power of certaine Strangers, enemies to his proceedings, so that by them, his company were seized, the ships and goods
confiscated, and that Voyage wholly ouerthrowne.

This losse, and vnfortunate beginning, did much abate the rising courage
of the first Aduenturers; but immediately vpon his departure, it pleased
the noble *Lord Chiefe Iustice*, Sir *Iohn Popham* knight, to send out another ship, wherein Captain *Thomas Haman* went Commander, and
Martine Prinne of *Bristow* Master, with all necessarie supplies, for the
seconding of Captaine *Challons* and his people ; who arriuing at the place
appointed, and not finding that Captaine there, after they had made some
discouery, and found the Coasts, Hauens, and Harbors answerable to our
desires, they returned.   Vpon whose relation the *Lord Chiefe Iustice*, and
wee all waxed so confident of the businesse, that the yeere following euerie
man of any worth, formerly interessed in it, was willing to ioyne in the
charge for the sending ouer a competent number of people to lay the
ground of a hopefull plantation.

Hereupon Captaine *Popham*, Captaine *Rawley Gilbert*, and others were
sent away with two Ships, and an hundred Landmen, Ordnance, and other
prouisions necessarie for their sustentation and defence ; vntill other supply might bee sent.   In the meane while, before they could returne, it
pleased God to take from vs this worthy member, the *Lord Chiefe Iustice*,
whose sudden death did so astonish the hearts of the most part of the
Aduenturers, as some grew cold, and some did wholly abandon the businesse.   Yet Sir *Francis Popham* his sonne, certaine of his priuate friends,
and other of vs, omitted not the next yeare (holding on our first resolution)
to ioyne in sending forth a new supply, which was accordingly performed.

But the Ships arriuing there, did not only bring vncomfortable newes
of the death of the *Lord Chiefe Iustice*, together with the death of Sir
Iohn Gilbert, the elder brother vnto Captaine *Rawley Gilbert*, who at that
time

Plantation of New Scotland, in America.

time was President of that *Councell* · But found that the old Captaine *Popham* was also dead; who was the onely man (indeed) that died there that Winter, wherein they indured the greater extremities, for that, in the depth thereof, their lodgings and stores were burnt, and they thereby wondrously distressed.

This calamitie and euill newes, together with the resolution that Captaine *Gilbert* was forced to take for his owne returne, (in that hee was to succeede his brother, in the inheritance of his lands in *England*) made the whole company to resolue vpon nothing but their returne with the Ships; and for that present to leaue the Countrey againe, hauing in the time of their abode there (notwithstanding the coldnesse of the season, and the small helpe they had, built a prettie Barke of their owne, which serued them to good purpose, as easing them in their returning

The arriuall of these people heere in *England*, was a wonderfull discouragement to all the first Vndertakers, in so much as there was no more speech of settling any other plantation in those parts for a long time after only Sir *Francis Popham* hauing the Ships and prouision, which remained of the company, and supplying what was necessary for his purpose, sent diuers times to the coasts for trade and fishing, of whose losse or gaines himselfe is best able to giue account

Our people abandoning the Plantation in this sort as you haue heard, the *Frenchmen* immediately tooke the opportunitie to settle themselues within our limits, which being heard of by those of *Virginia*, that discreetly tooke to their consideration the inconueniences that might arise, by suffering them to harbour there, they dispatched Sir *Samuel Argall*, with commission to displace them, which hee performed with much discretion, iudgement, valour, and dexteritie For hauing seized their Forts, which they had built at Mount *Mansell*, Saint *Croix*, and *Port Reall*, he carryed away their Ordnance; he also surprised their Ship, Cattle, and other prouisions, which hee transported to the Coilonie in *Virginia*, to their great benefit And hereby he hath made a way for the present hopefull Plantation to bee made in *Noua-Scotia*, which we heare his Maiestie hath lately granted to Sir *William Alexander* Knight, one of his Maiesties most honourable Councell of the Kingdome of *Scotland*, to bee held of the said Crowne, and that not without some of our priuities, as by approbation vnder writing may and doth appeare. Whereby it is manifest that wee are so farre from making a Monopoly of all those lands belonging to that coast (as hath beene scandalously by some obiected) *That we wish that many would vndertake the like*

An Encouragement TO COLONIES.

By
Sir WILLIAM ALEXANDER,
KNIGHT.

Alter erit tum Tiphis, & altera quæ vehat Argo
delectos Heroas————

LONDON
Printed by *William Stansby.*
1624.

TO THE MOST
EXCELLENT
PRINCE.

Hough you have graced
the Labours of some (as
much admired for your
courtesie as they for their
indiscretion) who might
haue beene condemned for
presuming to importune
you for their Patron; yet
it would seem a prophanation of greatnesse
to place your name vpon the Frontispice of
euery vulgar Paper, but as no Worke hath
more need of your countenance, then the Encouraging of Colonies; So it would appeare
to me (I know not suspecting my own partiali-
tie, whither seduced by Desire, or warranted by
Reason) that there is no ground whereupon your

coun-

*countenance may shine with a more publike ap-
plause. This is the way (making the Gospell of
Iesus Christ knowne in vnknowne parts) by supplying the necessities of many, with a lawfull increase of necessary commerce, to procure glorie
vnto God, honour to your selfe, and benefit to the
World; By this meanes, you that are borne to
rule Nations, may bee the beginner of Nations.
enlarging this Monarchie without bloud, and making a Conquest without wronging of others.
whereof in regard of your youth any good beginning in this (like your vertue vpon which it doth
depend) boding a speedie Progresse Time in your
own time, doth promise a great perfection. The glory of greatness (that it may haue a harmonie with
goodnesse) consisting more in raysing then in ruining of others, it is a farre better course to purchase fame by the Plantation of a new World,
nor as many Princes haue done by the desolation
of this. And since your Royall Father during
whose happie raigne, these seeds of Scepters haue
beene first from hence sowne in America, by his
gracious fauour farre aboue any merit of mine,
hath emboldened mee the meanest of many thou-
sands of his subiects to attempt so great an Enterprize, as to lay the foundation of a Worke that
may so much import the good of that ancient
King-*

DEDICATORIE.

Kingdome, where so many of your Ancestors were buried, and where your selues were borne. I haue both by reading what doth rest vpon Record, and by conferring with sundry that haue beene imbarked in such a businesse, beene curious to remarke the managing thereof, that the experience of times past might with the lesse danger at the charges of others, improue them that are to practize at this present. And the fruits of my Labours I doe humbly offer heere vnto your Highnesse, hoping by the commendable endeuours, therein remembred (though it selfe be but a triuiall Treatise, not worthy your sight) to conciliate your good opinion towards them that are to aduenture in this kind. Amongst whom (if euer my fortunes haue any conformitie with my mind) I purpose to contribute as much as my weake abilities can be able to affoord for accomplishing this braue Designe, wherein my greatest Ambition shall be that both this Age and the Posteritie may know how much I desire by some obseruable effect to be remembred for being

Your Highnesse most humble
and affectionate Seruant,

W. A.

THE

MAPP AND

DESCRIPTION OF

NEW-England;

Together with

A Difcourfe of Plantation, and

COLLONIES:

ALSO

A relation of the nature of the *Climate,*
and how it agrees with our owne *Country*
ENGLAND.

How neere it lyes to *New-found-Land, Virginia,*
Noua Francia, Canada, and other Parts of
the West-Indies.

Written by
Sr. WILLIAM ALEXANDER, *Knight.*

LONDON,
Printed for NATHANIEL BVTTER.
An. Dom. 1630.

FRA

NEW

Riuer of Saguenay

Tadousac

The great riuer of Caneda

Anticos

Kebec

Ile of Orleans

NEW
The Prouince of
Alexandria

Forthe

SCOT.

NEW ENGLANDE

Fort Haldernes
L. of Pembroock
The Sheffield
S. Will Aelly
Cap Lowe
D. Buckneham
D. of Warwick
M. Richmond
M. Thomas
D. Sutchiffe
Le Gorges
S. Sam Argall
D. Bar Gooch

L. of Arundl
S. for Gorge
L. of Carlil

Suba

L. Key
Swil Bale
S. Ro. Mansil

Sagadahock

LANDE Cape

Argals Bay
The Prouince of

Luckesburgh

Cape Sandy B. Blacke

P. Rosigno

Cape Cod

This Scale conteineth 150 English Leagues

10 20 30 40 50 60 70 80 90 100 110 120 130 140 150

C E

GOLFE

OF

NADA

NEW

FOVND

LANDE
Alexandria

Briftolls Hope
S.t Geo Caluert
Lord Vic
Faulkland

B.Plazinta

C Ras

S.t Peters Ilands

C.Brittan

Campfeau

Sandy Ile

53
52
51
50
49
48
47
46
45
44
43
42
41
40
39
38

AN

ENCOVRAGEMENT

TO COLONIES.

He fending forth of Colonies
(feeming a nouelty) is efteem-
ed now to bee a ftrange thing,
as not onely being aboue the
courage of common men, but
altogether alienated from their
knowledge, which is no wonder, fince that courfe though
both ancient, and vfuall, hath
beene by the intermiffion of fo
many ages difcontinued, yea was impofsible to be prac-
tifed fo long as there was no vaft ground, howfoeuer
men had beene willing, whereupon Plantations might
haue beene made, yet there is none who will doubt but
that the world in her infancy, and innocency, was firft peopled after this manner.

The next generations fucceeding *Shem* planted in *Asia,*
Chams in *Africke,* and *Iaphets* in *Europe: Abraham* and
Lot were Captaines of Colonies, the Land then being as
free as the Seas are now, fince they parted them in euery
part where they paffed, not taking notice of natiues with-

B out

out impediment.   That memorable troope of *Ieues* which *Moses* led from *Ægypt* to *Canaan* was a kind of Colonie though miraculoufly conducted by God, who intended thereby to aduance his Church and to deftroy the rejected Ethnikes. *Salmanezer* King of *Ashur* was remarked for the firft who did violate the naturall ingenuitie of this commendable kind of policy by too politike an intention; for hauing tranfported the ten Tribes of *Ifrael*, to the end that tranfplanting and difperfing them, hee might either weaken their ftrength, or abolifh their memorie by incorporating of them with his other Subjects; he to preuent the dangers incident amongft remote vaffals did fend a Colonie to inhabite *Samaria* of a purpofe thereby to fecure his late and queftionable conqueft.

Who can imagine by this induftrious courfe of Plantations, what an vnexpected progreffe from a defpifed beginning hath beene fuddenly made to the height of greatneffe! The *Phœnicians* quickly founded *Sidon*, and *Tirus*, fo much renowned both by facred, and humane writers, and a few *Tirians* builded *Carthage*, which had firft no more ground allowed her than could be compaffed by the extended dimenfions of a Bulls hide, which for acquiring of the more ground they diuided in as many fundrie parts as was pofsible, yet in end that Town became the Miftreffe of *Afrike*, and the riuall of *Rome*: and *Rome* it felfe that great Ladie of the World, and terrour to all Nations, ambitioufly clayming for her firft founders a few fcandalized fugitiues that fled from the ruines of *Troy*, did rife from fmall appearances to that exorbitancy of power, which at this day is remembred with admiration; Though the walls of it at that time were very lowe when the one brother did kill the other for jumping ouer them, either jealoufie already preuayling aboue naturall affection, or elfe vnaduifed anger conftructing that which might haue been cafually or carelefly done, in a finiftrous fenfe to the hatefull behauiour of infolency or fcorne; Their number then was not only very fmall, but they wanted women, without

out which they could not encreafe, nor fubfift, till they rauifhed the daughters of the *Sabins,* by a violent match at
firft, portending their future rapins, and what a furious
off-fpring they were likely to engender.   And when that
haughty Citie beganne to fuffer the miferies which fhe had
fo long beene accuftomed to inflict vpon others, the vene-
rable Citie of *Venice* (keeping for fo many ages a fpotleffe
reputation) was firft begunne by a few difcouraged perfons, who fleeing from the furie of the barbarous Nations
that then encroached vpon *Italie,* were diftracted with feare
and (feeking for their fafety) did ftumble vpon a commodious dwelling.

The *Græcians* were the firft, at leaft of all the Gentiles,
(who joyning learning with armes) did both doe, and
write that which was worthie to be remembred, and that
fmall parcel of ground whofe greatneffe was then only valued by the vertue of the inhabitants, did plant *Trapizonde*
in the Eaft, and many other Cities in *Asia* the leffe, the
protecting of whofe liberties was the firft caufe of warre
between them and the *Persian* Monarchs; then befides all
the adjacent Iles they planted *Siracusa* in *Sicile,* moft part
of *Italie,* which made it to be called *Græcia maior,* and
Marseills in *France.* O what a ftrange alteration! that this
part, which did flourifh thus, whileft it was poffeffed by
vigorous fpirits, who were capable of great enterprifes, did
fo many braue things fhould now (the feate of bafe feruile
people) become the moft abject and contemptible part of
all the Territories belonging to the barbarous *Ottomans,*
whofe infolent Ianiffaries (as the Pretorian Guards did
with their Emperours, and Mamalukes of *Egypt* with their
Soldans) prefume at this time to difpofe of the Regall
power, vpbrayding the miferable follie of Chriftians, who
dangeroufly embarqued in inteftine warres, though inuited by an encountring occafion, neglect fo great, fo glorious, and fo eafie a conqueft.

The *Romanes* comming to command a well peopled
World, had no vfe of Colonies, but only thereby to re-

ward fuch old deferuing Souldiers as (age and merit plea-
ding an immunitie from any further conftrained trauell)
had brauely exceeded the ordinary courfe of time appointed for military feruice, which cuftome was vfed in *Germanie, France, Spaine,* and *Brittaine,* and likewife that the
Townes erected in this fort might ferue for Citadels impofed vpon euery conquered Prouince, whereof fome doe
flourifh at this day, and of others nothing doth remaine
but the very name onely, their ruines being fo ruined, that
wee can hardly condefcend vpon what folitary part to be-
ftowe the fame of their former being.

I am loth by difputable opinions to dig vp the Tombes
of them that more extenuated then the duft are buried in
obliuion & will leaue thefe difregarded relicts of greatneffe
to continue as they are, the fcorne of pride, witneffing the
power of time.   Neither will I after the common cuftome
of the world, ouerua(luing things paft difualue the prefent,
but confidering ferioufly of that which is lately done in
Ireland, doe finde a Plantation there inferiour to none that
hath beene heretofore.   The *Babylonians* hauing conquered the *Israelites* did tranfplant them as expofed to ruine
in a remote Countrey, fending others of their owne Nation (that they might be vtterly extirpated) to inhabite *Sa-
ria* in their places.   And our King hath onely diuided the
moft feditious families of the *Irish* by difperfing them in
fundry parts within the Countrey, not to extinguifh, but
to difsipate their power, who now neither haue, nor giue
caufe of feare.   The *Romanes* did build fome Townes
which they did plant with their owne people by all rigour
to curbe the Natiues next adjacent thereunto, And our
King hath incorporated fome of his beft *Brittaines* with
the *Irish,* planted in fundry places without power to oppreffe, but onely to ciuilize them by their example.   Thus
Ireland which heretofore was fcarcely difcouered, and only irritated by others, prouing to the *English* as the *Lowe-
Countries* did to *Spaine,* a meanes whereby to wafte their
men, and their money, is now really conquered, becom-
                                                          ming

ming a ftrength to the State, and a glorie to his Majefties gouernment, who hath in the fetling thereof excelled all that was commended in any ancient Colonie.

As all firft were encouraged to Plantations by the largeneffe of the conquefts that were propofed vnto them, fearing onely want of people, and not of land, fo in after ages when all knowne parts became peopled, they were quickly entangled with the other extremitie, grudging to be bounded within their profpect, and jarring with their neighbours for fmall parcels of ground, a ftrife for limits limiting the liues of many who entring firft in controuerfie vpon a point of profit though with the loffe of ten times more, valuing their honour by the opinion of others behooued to proceed as engaged for the fafety of their reputation. Then richeffe being acquired by induftrie, and glorie by employments, thefe two did beget auarice, and ambition, which lodging in fome fubtile heads vpon a politike confideration to vnite inteftine diuifions did transferre their fplene to forraine parts, not feeking to rectifie the affections, but to bufie them abroad where leaft harme was feared, and moft benefit expected, fo that where they had firft in a peaceable fort fought for Lands onely wherewith to furnifh their necefsity, which conueniency, or fufficiency, did eafily accommodate, now ayming at greatneffe the defires of men growne infinite, made them ftrangers to contentment, and enemies to reft.

Some Nations feeking to exchange for better feates, others to command their neighbours, there was for many ages no fpeach but of wrongs and reuenges, conquefts and reuolts, razings and ruining of States, a continuall reuolution determining the periods of Time by the miferies of mankind, and in regard of the populouffneffe of thefe ages during the Monarchies of the *Affirians, Perfians, Græcians,* and *Romanes,* the world could not haue fubfifted if it had not beene purged of turbulent humours by letting out the bloud of many thoufands, fo that warre was the vniuerfall Chirurgeon of thefe diftempered times: And thereafter

O what monftrous multitudes of people were flaine by huge deluges of barbarous armies that ouerflowed *Italie, France* and *Spaine!* and the Chriftians haue long beene fubject to the like calamities wanting a commoditie how they might (not wronging others) in a Chriftian manner employ the people that were more chargeable then neceffary at home, which was the caufe of much mif-chiefe among themfelues, till at that time when *Spaine* was ftriuing with *France* how to part *Italie*, as *Italie* had formerly done with *Carthage* how to part *Spaine* Then it pleafed God hauing pitie of the Chriftians who for pur-pofes of fmall importance did prodigally proftitute the liues of them whom hee had purchafed with fo pretious a ranfome, as it were for diuerting that violent kind of vani-tie, to difcouer a new world, which it would feeme in all reafon fhould haue tranfported them with defignes of more moment, whereby glory and profit with a guiltleffe labour was to bee attayned with leffe danger whereunto they are as it were inuited, and prouoked with fo many e-minent aduantages palpably expofed to any cleare judge-ment that I thinke (this obuious facilitie vilifying that which a further difficulty might the more endeare) the eafineffe of the prey hath blunted the appetite.

When *Chriftopher Columbus* had in vaine propounded this enterprife to diuers Chriftian Princes, *Ifabella* of *Ca-ftile* againft the opinion of her husband (though fo much renowned for wit, yet not reaching this myfterie) did firft furnifh him for a Voyage, as if it were fatall that that Na-tion fhould owe the greateft part of their greatneffe to the female Sexe, And if the *Spaniards* would fincerely, and gratefully haue beftowed the benefits whereby God did al-lure them to poffeffe this Land for the planting of it with Chriftians enclined to ciuilitie, and religion, it had at this day confidering the excellency of the foyle, for all the per-fections that nature could affoord ; beene the moft fingu-larly accomplifhed place of the world, but it hath infortu-nately fallen out farre otherwife, that the treafures that are

drawne

drawne from thence (mynes to blow vp mindes and rockes to ruine faith) doe proue the feed of diffention, the finewes of the warre, and nurcerie of all the troubles a-mongft Chriftians.

The *Spaniards* that were fo happie as to chance firft vp-on this new World, were of all others (hauing but a vaft mountainous Countrey) in regard of their fcarcity of peo-ple, moft vnfit for planting thereof, and could not but foone haue abandoned the fame, if they had not fo quick-ly encountred with the rich Mynes of *Mexico, New Spaine* and *Peru,* which were once likely to haue beene loft for lacke of wood, till the way was inuented of refining Sil-uer by quickfiluer, which may bee eafily done out of any oare that is free from Lead, and (all the *Spaniards* difday-ning woike as a ferule thing belowe their abilities) their greateft trouble is the want of workmen: for the Natiues that are extant, furuiuing many vexations, if they become ciuile out of an indulgency to libertie, and eafe, whereun-to all the *Americans* (liking better of a penurious life thus then to haue plenty with taking paines) are naturally encli-ned, that they may haue a fecure eafe warranted by an or-der, doe betake themfelues to Cloifters, fo that they haue no meanes to profecute thefe workes but by drawing yeer-ly a gieat number of *Negroes* from *Angola,* and other parts, which being but an vnnaturall merchandife, are bought at a deare rate, and maintayned with danger, for they once of late, as I haue heard from one that was there at that time defigned to murther their Mafters, by a plot which fhould haue beene put in execution vpon a Good-friday, when all being exercifed at their deuotion were leaft apt to apprehend fuch a wicked courfe, and it is alwaies feared that to reuenge what of necefsitie they muft fuffer, and to procure their libertie hating moft what they feele for the prefent, and hoping for better by a change, they will joyne with any ftrong enemy that landing there dare attempt the conqueft of that Countrey.

I will not here infift in fetting downe the manner how
the

the *Spaniards* made themfelues Mafters of fo many rich
and pleafant Countries, but doe leaue that to their owne
Hiftories, though I confeffe (like wifemen) they are very
fparing to report the eftate of thefe parts, and doe barre all
ftrangers from hauing acceffe thereunto, wifhing to enjoy
that which they loue in priuate, and not inconfiderately
vanting by the vanitie of praifes to procure vnto themfelues the vexation that they might fuffer by the earneft
purfuit of emulating riuals, but as they did brauely begin,
and refolutely profecute their Difcoueries in *America*, fo
hath it juftly recompenced their courage, prouing the
ground of all that greatneffe which at this time (not without caufe) doth make them (as able, or willing, to conquer
others if not both) fo much fufpected by euery jealous
State.　And *Henry* the Seuenth the *Salomon* of *England*
had his judgement onely condemned for neglecting that
good occafion which was firft offered vnto him by *Columbus,* yet did he prefently feeke to repaire his errour by fending forth *Sebaftian Chabot* a *Venetian* who did difcouer
the Ile of *Neu found-land,* and this part of the Continent
of *America* now intended to bee planted by his Majefties
Subjects vnder the name of New *England,* and New *Scotland,* fo that the fruits of his happie raigne ftill growing to
a greater perfection and now ripe to bee gathered by this
age, as he made way by the marriage of his eldeft daughter for vniting thefe two Nations at home, fo did hee the
fame likewife by this difcouerie abroad, but the accom-
plifhment of both was referued for his Majeftie now raigning, and no Prince in the world may more eafily effectuate
fuch a purpofe fince his Dominions affoord abundance of
braue men fingularly valued for able bodies and actiue fpirits whereof the *English* haue already giuen good proofe
of their fufficiency in forraine Plantations ; but before I muft
proceed further in that which doth concerne them I muft
obferue what the *French* haue done in this kind.

All fuch aduentrous defignes out of ignorance, or enuie
(either contemned, or doubtfully cenfured) are neuer appro-
　　　　　　　　　　　　　　　　　　　　　　　ued,

\

ued, nor imitated, til they be juftified by the fuccelfe & then many who had firft been too diftruftfull falling in the other extremitie of an implicite confidence, to redeeme their former neglects, do precipitate themfelues in needleffe dangers. After that the *Spaniards* were knowne to pro- fper, and that it was conceiued by the Voyage of *Chabot* what a large vaftneffe this new Continent was likely to proue, *Francis* the firft did furnifh forth *Iohn Verrizzon* a *Florentine,* who did difcouer that part of *America* which was firft (and moft juftly) called *New France,* and now *Ter- ra Florida.* And vpon his returne he affirming it to be (as it is indeed for all the excellencies of nature) one of the moft pleafant parts of the world, This was the caufe that after a long delay (during the fpace of two Princes whole raignes) fome new Difcoueries reuiuing the memory of this, in the yeere of God 1562. *Charles* the ninth (hauing a haughty mind, and being fo rauifhed with a defire of glorie, that he was fometimes tempted by finiftrous fuggeftions in fee- king after it to goe vpon wrong grounds) was quickly en- amoured with the eminency of fuch a fingular defigne, wherein hee did employ *Iohn Ribaut,* who comming to *Florida,* was kindly receiued by the Natiues there, and ha- uing made choice of a place where to build a Fort, after hee had ftayed a time giuing direction for fuch things as were neceffarie to be done, he left forty men therein when hee came away with one Captaine *Albert* to command them, who after that hee had with difficulty beene freed from the danger of famine, and of fire (vnfeafonably affe- cting the difufed aufteritie of the Ancients) did for a fmall offence hang one of his companie with his owne hands, fo lofing both the dignitie of his place, and the hearts of his people at one time, which hee fhould haue beene extremely ftudious to preferue, efteeming them as fellowes of his fufferings, and coheires of his hopes, at leaft the qualitie of the offence and necefsitie of his death fhould haue beene made fo cleare, that as im- porting a common good, all (if not vrging it) fhould at

C   leaft

leaft haue condifcended thereunto, but this errour of his was acquited in as rude a manner : for his companie putting him to death did make choice of another Captaine, and defpairing of a new fupplie though wanting skilfull workmen for fuch a purpofe (necefsitie fharpning their wits) they builded a little Barque which they calfatted and made fit for the Seas with the Gummes of trees which they found there in ftead of Pitch, and in place of Sayles they furnifhed her with fuch linnens as they had vpon their beds, and being thus fet forth (couragioufly ouercomming a number of admirable difficulties) did return to *France* after a defperate manner.

The dangerleffe returne, and plaufible hopes of *Ribaut*, afsifted by the ferious perfwafions of the Admirall, (the receiued opinion of whofe not queftioned wifedome was enough to warrant any thing that had his approbation) did moue the *French* King to fend out a great number of men with a competent prouifion of all things requifite vnder the charge of Monfieur *Laudonier*, who had a profperous Voyage, and a congratulated arriuall at the *French* Fort by the Sauages in *Florida*, but immediately thereafter hee was extremely perplexed with the vnexpeɛted mutinies and faɛtious oflers of fome whom he had carried with him, who had not gone thither intending what they pretended, out of a cleare refolution to inhabite that bounds, but did onely flee from fome inconueniencies that had vexed them at home, fuch men as hating labour they could not induftrioufly ferue by their endeauours in a mechanike trade, fo were they not capable of generous infpirations that prouoke magnanimitie, but habitually bred to vice were naturally enemies to vertue, which made thirtie of them taking away a Barke that belonged to the Plantation betake themfelues to the Seas in hope (continuing as they had beene accuftomed in naughty courfes) to feize vpon a prize whereby they might incontinent bee made rich ; and their defigne in fome meafure had the projeɛted iffue, but in place of raifing their fortunes (the Lord neuer blefsing
them

them that abandon fuch a worthie worke, much leffe with a minde to doe mifchiefe) it proued in end a way to worke their confufion, And *Laudoniere* being happie to haue his companie purged of fuch peftiferous fellowes did carrie himfelfe brauely as became a commander, aduifedly enquiring concerning the Sauages, what their force was, what relation they had one to another, where they were friends or foes, how their pleafures were placed, and by what accounts they reckoned their gaines or loffes, fo that hee was alwaies ready as might ftand beft with the good of his affaires to afsift, or oppofe, to diuide, or agree any partie, thus by fhewing power purchafing authoritie, til he drew the ballance of all bufineffe to bee fwayed where hee would as being Mafter of the Countrey. Hereupon (the vmbragious afperfions of enuie fo darkening reafon that it could not difcerne merite at leaft out of a depraued opinion with a derogatory cenfure cancelling all naturall ingenuitie, could not or would not acknowledge what was due thereunto) a report was fpread in *France* by fome that *Laudoniere* liued like a Prince difdayning the condition of a Subject, and the *French* out of a prepofterous policie fearing what they fhould haue wifhed that one of their owne Nation could be too great abroad, they fent backe *Ribaut* with a new commifsion to fucceed him in his chaige, (fhaking thereby the firft foundation of a growing greatneffe) who feeking to fteale priuately vpon him to preuent aduertifements that hee might take him at vnawares did hardly efcape to haue beene funke at his firft entrie.

Immediatly after that *Ribaut* was admitted Gouernour (*Laudoniere* hauing fhewed himfelfe as dutifull to obey as he had beene skilfull in commanding) intelligence was giuen them that fixe *Spanish* Ships were riding at an anchor not farre from thence, and he ambitioufly afpiring to grace his beginning with fome great matter, againft the aduice of all the reft, with an obftinate refolution would needs goe and purfue them taking the beft of the companie with him, and fo left the Fort weakley guarded, which made it

to proue an eafie prey for the *Spaniards* of whom the moft
part leauing their Ships (a minde tranfported with hope
not thinking of paine) did march thorow the woods
whence no perill was expected, and in a maruellous ftormy
night, as if the very Heauens (acceffarily culpable) had
confpired with the malice of men for the working of mif-
chief. When the *Frenchmen* (too much affecting their owne
eafe) had neglected their watch, furprizing their Fort did
put them all to the fword ; which extreme crueltie of theirs
was brauely reuenged by one Captaine *Gorques* a Gentleman of *Burdeaux,* who out of a generous difpofition being
fenfible of this publike injurie whereby all his Nation was
interefted, as if it had only in particular imported the ruine
of his owne fortunes, went of purpofe to this part, and fe-
cretly before his comming was knowne contracting a great
friendfhip with the Sauages who did hate the auftere countenance, and rigorous gouernment of the *Spaniards,* when
it came to be compared with the infinuating formes of the
French, he found the meanes by a ftratagem that he vfed to
entrap the *Spaniards,* by the death of them all expiating
that which they had made his Countreymen formerly to
fuffer, yet after the manner of many being more apt to acquire then to preferue (acting greater things when carried
with the impetuofitie of a prefent fury then hee could
confirme with the conftant progreffe of a well fetled refolution) he made no more vfe of his victorie, but returned
back to *France,* flattering himfelf with the hope of a trium-
phall welcome, in place whereof by fome meanes made [at]
Court he was proclaimed a Rebell, as a facrifice appointed
to appeafe *Spaine.* This was the laft thing that the *French*
did in *Florida.*

The next forraine aduenture was likewife procured by
the Admirall, a worthie man, who would gladly haue diuerted the vindictiue difpofitions of his Countrymen from
the bloudy ciuile warres wherewith they were then entangled, to profecute fome braue enterprife abroad whereby
they might not be made guilty, and yet haue glory.   The
                                                      man

man that did offer himfelfe for Condu&tor of the Voyage
was one *Villegagnon* a Knight of *Malta* who then preteded
to be of the reformed religion (as all doe who affe&t to appeare what they are not indeed) making fhew of extraordinary remorfe, and zeale, and that hee had a defire to retire
himfelfe from the vanitie, corruption, and vexation of their
parts to fome remote place in *America,* where profefsing
himfelfe fuch as he was, he might (free from all kind of im-
pediments) begin a new life, and where he hoped to found
fuch a Colony as fhould ferue for a retreat to all thofe of the
reformed Religion who (weary of the perfecutiōs at home)
would goe where they might liue with fafety, and enjoy
the libertie of their confcience, by this meanes hee got a
great number to accōpany him, amongft whom was *Iohn de
Lerie* their Minifter, a learned man who wrote a difcourfe
of all that paffed in this Voyage, and there were fundry
others that came from the Towne of *Geneua,* fo that hauing
a reafonable number and well prouided, hee embarqued
and fayled towards *Brafile,* making choice of a place fit for
a Plantation, where they found (the foile excellent, the Natiues well inclined towards them, and a fupplie comming
in due time) all things fo concurring for their contentment
that they might haue begunne a greate worke happie and
hopefull for their pofteritie, if *Villagagnon* had beene the
man that he made them beleeue he was, but he apparantly
neuer louing them of the Religion in his heart had coun-
terfeited to doe fo for a time, onely (angling their affe-
&tions) by this meanes to draw a fupply from them, for as
foone as hee was fettled in his gouernment, that hee found
himfelfe ftrong enough by Catholikes, and others of his
friends, that he had with him to doe (as hee thought) what
he would, ftraight remouing the maske that hypocrifie
had put vpon him, he difcharged all exercife of the reformed religion which no man with more feruency had profeffed then himfelfe, commanding all to conforme themfelues to the orders that he had fet downe, but (in place of
feare which he purpofed to giue, receiuing but contempt)

C 3   this

this bafe kind of carriage did quite ouerthrowe his authoritie, and they making a partie amongft themfelues did
remoue with their Minifter *Iohn de Lerie*, which diuifion
of their Colonie in two was the caufe that neither could
fubfift, fo that *Villagagnon* abandoning that Countrey, all
after many feuerall defignes returned vnto *France*, hauing found no impediment to fo good a purpofe but
the peruerfeneffe of fuch mindes as they had carried with
them

Monfieur *De Larauerdier* a very worthie Gentleman
did of late enterprife the like courfe in the fame bounds,
and was croffed in the fame manner by the difference of
Religion (difputations quickning them to contrauert who
will not be conuerted) that diftracted his companie with
feuerall opinions, yet at this time a long continuance making that leffe ftrange amongft the *French* then it was wont
to be, the Gentleman did command with fuch judgement,
and difcretion, that what euer priuate diflike was, it neuer
burfted forth in any open infurrection. And for the fpace
of foure or fiue yeeres being befriended by the Natiues,
though continually oppofed both by the *Spaniards*, and by
the *Portugals*, yet he alwaies preuayled, liuing (as himfelfe
told me) with more contentment then euer he had done in
his time either before or fince , hee could neuer difcerne
any Winter there by the effects, feeing no ftormy weather
at all, and finding a continuall greenneffe to beautifie the
fields, which did affoord fuch abundance, and variety of
all things neceffary for the maintaynance, that they were
neuer in any danger of famine, but in end finding no more
people comming from *France*, and fearing that time fhould
weare away them that were with him ; then being flatte-
red with the loue of his natiue foyle, longing to fee his
friends, and tempted by the hope of a prefent gaine, which
as he imagined might the better enable him for fome fuch
purpofe in an other part, he capitulated with the *Spaniards*
to furreder the place hauing affuräce giuen him for a great
fumme of money which fhould haue beene deliuered in
                                                    Spaine,

Spaine, but comming to receiue the fame (it being more easie to pay debt by reuenging a pretended injurie then with money which fome would rather keepe then their Faith) he was caft in prifon, where hee remayned long, till at laft he was deliuered by the mediation of our Kings Ambaffadour, and came here where I fpake with him of purpofe to giue his Majeftie thankes. I heare that for the prefent he is now at *Rochell* (with a hope to repaire his error) ready to embarque for fome fuch like enterprife. This is all that the *Frenchmen* haue done in the South parts of *America,* and now I will make mention of their proceedings in thefe parts that are next vnto vs.

Francis the firft of *France,* a braue Prince, and naturally giuen to great things, after the Voyage made by *Iohn Verrizan* (*Chabot* hauing difcouered the Continent for *Henry* the feuenth) did fend forth *Iames Quartier* one of Saint *Malo,* who by two feuerall Voyages did difcouer the Riuer of *Cannada,* and by his relation doth commend it exceedingly as being fertile in variety of Fifhes, and bordered with many pleafant meadowes, and ftately woods, hauing in fundry parts abundance of Vines growing wilde, chiefly in one Ile which he hath called by the name of the Ile of *Orleans.* This man neuer made any Plantation at all, but onely difcouered and traffiqued with the Sauages, neither was there any further done by *Roberuall,* who did liue one Winter at Cape *Breton.*

The Marqueffe *De la Roche* by a Commifsion from *Henry* the fourth, intending a Voyage for *Cannada,* happened by the way vpon the Ile of *Sablon* (which is now comprehended with the Patent of *New Scotland*) and there (trufting to the ftrength of the place where there are no Sauages at all) landed fome of his men till hee fhould haue found a conuenient place within the maine Land fit for habitation, promifing then to returne for them; but it was his fortune by reafon of contrary winds neuer to finde the maine Land, being blowne backe to *France* without feeing of them, where he was in the time of the ciuile

warres

warres (fuch is the vncertainty of worldly things producing vnexpected effects) taken prifoner by the Duke of
Mercœur, and fhortly after died, fo that his people whom
hee had left at *Sablon* furnifhed but for a fhort time had
quickly fpent their prouifions, and tooke for their maintaynance onely fuch things as the place it felfe did without
labour freely affoord, which hath a race of Kowes (as is
thought) firft tranfported thither by the *Portugals* that
haue long continued there, and fundry roots fit to be eaten,
with abundance of Fifhes, Fowle and Venifon.   And (ha-
. uing no meanes to liue but by fport) as for their apparell
they clothed themfelues with the skinnes of fuch creatures as they could kill by Land, or Sea, fo that huing
there for the fpace of twelue yeeres when they were prefented to *Henry* the fourth who had hired a Fifherman to
bring them home, as I haue heard from them that did fee
them at firft before the King, they were in very good
health, and looked as well, as if they had liued all that time
in *France* ∙ But hauing beene abufed by the Fifherman
who (cunningly concealing that he had beene directed by
the King) did bargaine with them to haue all their skinnes
for tranfporting them home, which were of great value,
fome of them being of black Foxes, which were fold at
fiftie pounds fterling a piece, and aboue, for the recouerie
thereof they intended a proceffe againft him before the
Court of Parliament at *Paris*, wherein by the equitie of
their caufe, or by the compafsion of the Iudges, they preuayled, gayning by that meanes a ftocke wherewith to traffique in thefe parts againe.

Monfieur *De Montes* procuring a Patent from *Henry* the
fourth of *Cannada* from the 40. degree Eaftward compre-
hending all the bounds that is now both within *New England* and *New Scotland* (after that Queene *Elizabeth* had
formerly giuen one thereof as belonging to this Crowne
by *Chabots* Difcouerie) did fet forth with a hundred perfons fitted for a Plantation, carried in two fhips of fmall
burthen, which parting from *France* on feuerall dayes did
                                                    appoint

appoint their meeting at the Port of *Campſeau,* but the ſhip wherein Monſieur *De Montes* had placed himſelfe going firſt, and fearing the huge Mountaines of Ice that diſſoluing from the farre Northerne parts come alongſt the coaſt of *Newfound-land* during the Spring time, did take her courſe more to the South, and arriued at Port *De Muton* a Bay now in the fore-land of *New Scotland,* from whence one of the Natiues of the Countrey (either out of courteſie, or to gayne a reward) leauing his Wife and Children (as a pledge, or elſe to be nouriſhed with them) went to *Campſeau,* and within a weeke brought them newes from their other Ship that had arriued there, which comming to them, and Monſieur *Champlein* who had gone in a ſhallop to diſcouer the coaſt being returned, they ſayled together Weſtwards to Cape *Sable,* and from thence Northwards to Bay Saint *Maries,* where towards the South ſide thereof they found good meadowes and arable ground fit to be planted vpon, and towards the North a mountainous and minerall bounds, hauing diſcouered one veine of metall that did hold Siluer, and two of Iron ſtone : After this, hauing ſeene Port *Royall,* they went to the Riuer called by them *Sante Croix,* but more fit now to bee called *Tweed,* becauſe it doth diuide *New England* and *New Scotland,* bounding the one of them vpon the Eaſt, and the other vpon the Weſt ſide thereof, here they made choice of an Ile that is within the middle of the ſame where to winter, building houſes ſufficient to lodge their number; There, beſides other ſorts of wood, they had ſtore of Cedar trees, and found the ground very fertile as it did proue afterwards, bringing forth that which they did ſow with an extraordinary encreaſe, yet during the Winter time when they could not conueniently goe to the maine Land, they found it a very incommodious dwelling, ſpecially for want of freſh Springs ; And the ſoyle being of it ſelfe humid, and obnoxious to waters, they had not beene ſo induſtrious as to caſt a ditch wherewith to drie the ground whereupon their houſes ſtood, and in end finding that a little Ile was

D   but

but a kind of large prifon, they refolued to returne vnto
Port *Royall*, whereof I will giue a particular Defei iption,
becaufe it was the place of then refidence, as I intend it to
be for the chiefe Colonie of the *Scottish* Nation, giounding
that which I am to deliuer vpon fuch Difcourfes as the
Frenchmen haue written, and vpon that which I haue
heard reported by fundry others who haue feene the fame.

The entry in Port *Royall* is from the South fide of a great
Bay, which doth make the South part of *New Scotland* almoft an Ile, and hath the paffage at firft fo narrow, with a
current fo violent, that Ships can hardly enter if they take
not the Tide right, and may eafily be commanded by any
Ordnance that is planted on either fide, where there are
parts fit for that purpofe; As foone as they are within the
Bay, it doth enlarge it felfe to the bredth of feuen or eight
miles, and doth continue fo as if it were fquare for the like
bounds in length; There are within the fame two Iles e-
uery one of them extending it felfe about three miles in
circuit, and both are well gainifhed with trees, and giaffe;
Diuers Riuers and Brookes doe fall within this large bo-
fome on euery fide, of which the chiefe is one that doth
come from the South, being difcouered to be aboue fortie
miles portatiue, and it hath all alongft on euery fide for the
bounds of a mile, or halfe a mile at leaft, very faire meadowes which are fubject to bee ouerflowed at high tides,
and there is Land fit to be laboured lying betweene them
and the woods, which doe compaffe all about with very
faire trees of fundry forts, as Oakes, Afh, Playnes, Maple,
Beech, Birch, Cypreffe, Pine and Firre; The great Riuer
doth abound exceedingly in Salmon and Smelts during
their feafon, and euery little Brooke in Trouts.   One Lake
within this Bay hath yeerely a great quantitie of Herrings,
which by reafon of a ftrict way which they paffe are eafie
to be taken, and all the yeere ouer they neuer want fhell-
fifh, fuch as Lobfters, Crabs, Cockles and Muffels.   The
chiefe beafts that inhabite the Woods there, are Ellans,
Hart, Hind, and fallow Deere, with ftore of other wilde
beafts,

beafts, fuch as Wolues, Beares, Foxes, and Otters, but the moft vfefull of all is the Beauer, both for his flefh that is efteemed to be very delicate for eating, and for the skinne that is of good value; as for wild foule, there is great varietie and ftore, of Partridges, Plouers, Woodcockes, Larkes, Wild Geefe, Wild Duckes, Heron and Crane, with many other forts peculiar to that part of the World, and not knowne here.

Vpon the Eaft fide of this Port the *French* did entrench themfelues, building fuch houfes as might ferue to accommodate their number, and a little from thence *Monfieur Champlein* did cut a walke through the Woods, where they delighted to repaire in Summer to fhroud themfelues from the heate, and the rather that they had a fweet Melodie which was made by the varietie of voyces, of finging Birds which without any affectation did affoord them naturall Muficke.

Some fixe miles further vp that fide of the Riuer, they built a Barne, and laboured ground for Wheat, ouer againft which they made a Water-mill vpon a Riuer, that doth fall in on the Weft fide, the Damme of it beeing there where the Herrings haunt moft, and they did likewife try fome ground neere by for Wheate, whereas their owne Writers make mention, they reaped aboue fortie for one, but what they did was rather trying the nature of the foile to fatisfie their curiofitie then to haue a quantitie fit for their maintenance, which they trufted to bee fent vnto them by two Merchants from the *Rochell,* and were that way well furnifhed fo long as they keeped their skinnes to giue them in exchange (but the Merchants either by fome priuate conueyances) or by the comming in of fome *Flemmings* to traffique, being difappointed by the Planters as foone as they miffed their prefent Commoditie did likewife fruftrate them of the prouifions that they expected. Whereupon *Monfieur de Montes* betaking himfelfe to trade for Furres, *Monfieur Poutrincourt* refolued to profecute the Plantation at that place, and fent for his Son

D 2

Bien-

Biencourt to *France*, to bargaine with fome that would fend them a fupply, fuch as was requifite for eftablifhing of that Colony.

The firft that embraced his Propofitions were the Iefuites who as they haue ordinarly good wits which made them the rather capable of fo aduantagious a proiect, fo they were the more animated thereunto (by vpbrayding the lazineffe of our Clergie) to fhew with what feruencie they trauell to propagate the Gofpell in doing whereof (whither it be ambition or deuotion that prouokes them fparing no paines) they haue trauelled both to the Eaft and Weft *Indies*, and to that admired Kingdome of *China;* their Societie in *France* preuayling with all that had any inclination either to religion, or to vertue did eafily gather a voluntary contribution for the furthering of fo commendable a purpofe, thereafter they fent away two Fathers of their company with a new fupply of all things neceffarie to the Plantation at Port *Royall*, but fhortly after their arriuall (their predominant difpofition hardly yeelding to any Superiour, fpecially if it be a Secular power) they beganne to contradict *Poutrincourt*, in the execution of thefe Decrees which had beene giuen forth by him as Ciuil Magiftrate of that place. Whereupon the Gentleman extreamely difcontented, and wearie of contefting with them, hauing faid that it was his part to rule them vpon earth, and theirs onely to guide him the way to Heauen, he returned back to *France*, leauing his Sonne *Biencourt* in his place, who being a youth at that time of more courage then circumfpectneffe, difdayning to be controlled by them whom he had inuited thither, and fcorning their infupportable prefumption, and imperious kinde of carriage, vfing Spirituall Armes for Temporall ends, whofe fpleene had excommunicated and branded him with a Spirituall cenfure, hee threatned them by his Temporall power with a more palpable punifhment, fo that after much controuerfie, refoluing to feparate themfelues, the two Iefuites taking a part of the company with them, went from thence to to a place in *New England,* called by them Mount *Defert,* where they feated themfelues, and hauing a fupply from the Queene Mother, did plant fundry fruit trees of the moft delicate kinds in *France,* fuch as Apricockes, and Peaches neuer intending to remoue from thence.

At this time Sir *Samuell Argall,* who hath beene Gouernour of *Virginia,* coafting alongft *New England,* to traffique, difcouer, or to acquire things neceffary for the Southerne Colonie in thefe parts, where the Lands are reputed to be more fertile, and the Seas more frequented, did conceiue by a defcription made vnto him by the Sauages, that there were fome come from this part of the World to inhabit there, and being iealous of any thing that might derogate from the honour, or prooue preiudiciall to the benefit of his Nation, whereof their intereft in this was eafie to be apprehended, hee went whereas hee was informed that they were, and his vnexpected arriuall, as it would feeme, not onely amazing the mindes of the *French,* but likewife preuenting their preparation, and refolution, he approched fo neere to a fhip that lay before their Fort, that hee beate them all that were within, with Musket fhot, from making any vfe of their Ordnance, and killed one of the two Iefuites, who was giuing fire to a Peece; hauing taken the fhip he landed and went before the Fort, fummoning them that were within to yeeld themfelues, who at the firft made fome difficultie, asking a time to aduife, but that being refufed, they priuately abandoned the Fort, ftealing out by fome back way into the Woods, where they ftayed one night, and the next day comming backe rendred themfelues, giuing vp the Patent they had from the *French* King to bee cancelled, hee vfed them courteoufly, as their owne Writers doe make mention, fuffering fuch as had a minde to goe for *France,* to feeke out fifhers fhips wherein they might bee tranfported, the reft that were willing to goe for *Virginia,* went thither alongft with him, no man hauing loft his life, but onely that one Iefuite who was killed whileft they made refiftance during the time of the

con-

conflict, thereafter Father *Biard* the other of the Iefuites comming backe from *Virginia*, with Sir *Samuell Argall*, out of the indigeftable malice that he had conceiued againft *Biencourt*, did informe him where he had planted himfelfe offering (as hee did) to conduct him thither. As foone as they were entred within the Port, neere the vppermoft of the Ilands, Sir *Samuell* directing the Ship to ride at a reafonable diftance to attend occafions before the Fort, did land himfelfe with fortie of the beft of his men vpon a Medow, where immediatly they heard a Peece of Ordnance from tho Fort, and he conceiuing fince it was fhot whilft it could do no harme that it was done either but to giue terrour to them, or to warne fome that might happen to bee abroad, Did make the greater hafte towardes the Fort, where hee prefently entred, finding it abandoned without any men at all, left for the defence thereof, hee went vp the Riuer fide five or fixe miles, where hee faw their Barnes and the ground where a great quantitie of Wheate had growne, which he carried with him to ferue for Seed in *Virginia*, he faw likewife their Corn Mill very conueniently placed, which together with the Barnes hee left ftanding vntouched. As for the Fort it felfe he deftroyed it downe to the ground, razing the *French* Armes, and leauing no monument remayning, that might witneffe their being there.

After this *Biencourt* who had beene fome where abroad trauelling through the Countrey, comming home defired to conferre with Sir *Samuell Argall*, who did meete with him apart from the Company vpon a Medow, and after they had expoftulated a fpace for what had paft controuerting concerning the *French* and *English* Title to thefe bounds, at laft *Biencourt* offered (if hee might haue a protection) to depend vpon our King, and to draw the whole Furres of that Countrey to one Port, where he would diuide them with him, As likewife he would fhew him good Metalls, whereof hee gaue him pieces, but the other refufed to ioyne in any focietie with him, protefting that his Commiffion was onely to difplant him, and that if hee

found

found him there, after that time hee would vfe him as an
enemy, *Biencourt* labouring earneftly to haue had the Iefuit
(as he confeffed)with a purpofe to hang him. Whilft they
were difcourfing together, one of the Sauages came fuddenly forth fiom the Woods, and licentiated to come neere,
did after this manner earneftly mediate a peace, wondring
why they that feemed to bee of one Countrey fhould vfe
others with fuch hoftilitie, and that with fuch a forme of
habit and gefture as made them both to laugh.

After this *Biencourt* remoouing from thence to fome o-
ther part, *Monfieur Champlein* who had liued long here, did
carrie a company with him from *France*, of fome fortie
perfons or thereabouts vp the Riuer of *Canada*, whom hee
planted on the North fide thereof, with a purpofe to ferue
for a Factorie, drawing all the Trade of that farre running
Riuer (which a Plantation would haue difperfed in many
parts) within the hands of a few whom he doth command
otherwife if his defires had beene bended that way, hee
might haue planted many people there ere now, the place
is called *Kebeck*, where the *French* doe profper well, hauing Corne by their owne labour, which may furnifh
themfelues for food, and likewife for a ftocke to tiaffique
with the Sauages, with fundry Fruits, Roots, Vine, Grapes
and Turkie Wheate. *Champlein* hath difcouered the Riuer
of *Canada*, from the Gulf vpwards aboue twelue hundred
miles, finding in it fometimes fuch falles, as to fcape the
fame, he muft carrie his Boate a little way by Land, and
then hee did many times come to great Lakes at the end
whereof hee did alwayes find a Riuer againe, and the laft
Lake where hee came was a very huge one, iudged to bee
three hundred miles in length, by the report of fome Sauages, who did affirme vnto him, that at the further end
thereof they did find Salt-water, and that they had feene
great Veffels which made *Champlein* beleeue that a paffage
might be there to the Bay of *California*, or to fome part of
the South Sea, which would prooue an ineftimable benefit
for the Inhabitants of thofe parts, opening a neere way to
China,

China, which hath beene fo many fundry wayes with fo great charges fo long fought for, howfoeuer in regard of the feafon, and for want of neceffary prouifions, *Champlein* did returne backe at that time with a purpofe to goe againe another yeere, which if he hath done is not yet knowne, but this is moft certaine, that the Riuer of *Canada* hath a long courfe and through many goodly Countreyes, fome of thefe great Lakes by fending forth, or by receiuing great Riuers, do affoord meanes of commerce as farre as to fome parts of *Terra Florida,* as may bee gathered by *Champleins* Difcouerie. And now hauing giuen a breuiarie of all that is done by the *French* in *America,* I will next report of that which hath beene done by fome others.

I will not here make mention of the many and braue Voyages that at the Sea haue happily beene performed by the *English,* which fame by eternall records hath recommended to be applauded by the beft judgements of euery age, but I will only fhortly touch that which they haue attempted by way of Plantation, beginning with the *New-found Land* which was firft difcouered, and doth lie neereft to this Countrey. Sir *Humphrey Gilbert* hauing a commiffion from Queene *Elizabeth* did take poffefsion of it in her name at Saint *Iohns* Harbour, and thereafter purpofed to haue feene *Canada,* but encountring with fome vnexpe- included croffes as hee was returning from thence, feeking to condemne an opinion (malice or enuie ordinarily taxing all afpiring fpirits whofe vertue by way of reflection doth vpbraide the bafeneffe of others) that had beene conceiued of him as wanting courage, he precipitated himfelfe vpon an other extremitie, not to feeme fearefull, prouing defperate ; for in the time of a ftorme, out of a needleffe brauerie, to fhew a contempt of danger, being in a little fmall Pinnace, and refufing to come to his beft Shippe that was of a large burden, hee was fuddenly fwallowed vp by the waues neere to the Ile of *Sablon,* and his death did ouerthrowe great hopes of a Plantation that by the generouf-neffe of his minde might juftly haue beene expected from him;

hım; but long before hıs tıme and euer fınce the *English* had vfed to fıfh vpon the Banke, and within the Bayes of *Newfound Land,* and the fweetneffe of the benefit arrifıng from thence, did perfwade a companie compofed of *Londoners* and Weft-country men to ȷoyne together for fendıng fome to inhabite there, where before howfoeuer the Summer was large as hote as here, the Winter was thought vnfufferable.

The fırft houfes for a habitation were buılt ın *Cupıds* Coue within the Bay of *Conceptıon,* where people did dwell for fundry yeeres together, and fome well fatisfied both for pleafure, and profit, are dwelling there ftill, finding fmall difference betweene the feafons of the yeere ın that Climate, and here. There is another Plantation begunne at Harbour *à Grace* withın the fame Bay by the Cıtıe of *Brıftoll,* called *Brıftols Hope,* whereas by the fowing and reaping of fome Cornes of fundry forts doth appeare what further may pofsıbly be expected; And withın thefe three yeeres Maſter Secretary *Caluert* hath planted a companie at *Ferriland,* who both for building and making trıall of the ground haue done more than euer was performed before by any in fo fhort a time, hauıng already there a brood of Horfes, Kowes, and other beaſtıal, and by the induftry of hıs people he ıs begınning to draw back yeerly fome benefit from thence already: which courfe howfoeuer at fırft ıt proue good, or bad for hıs particular, ıs by example beneficıall for the publike.

Laſt, I heare that my Lord Vıcount *Falkland* now Lord Deputie of *Ireland,* hath this laſt yeere fent a companıe to ınhabite at *Renouze* a place lyıng South-weft from *Ferrıland,* where the foyle is efteemed to be the beſt whereupon any hath fetled there as yet, and hee hath the fhorteſt way, and beft opportunitıe of any within his Majefties Domını-ons for tranſportıng of people and cattell to that part from *Ireland,* which if his courfe bee rıghtly directed, as all haue reafon to wıfh, may promife him a good fucceffe.

The fırft Patentees for *Newfound-land* haue gıuen mee

E   a

a grant of that part thereof which doth lie North-weft from the Bay of *Placentia* to the great Gulfe of *Canada* ouer-againft *New Scotland*, where I had made a Plantation ere now, if I had not beene diuerted by my defignes for *New Scotland*, but I purpofe to doe it as foone as conueniently I may. The moft part of the bounds whereupon any hath planted as yet in *Newfound Land* is found to be rockie and not fit to be manured : it may be thefe that made choice thereof (negle&ing the Land) had onely a regard to dwell commodiouſly for making vfe of the Sea, the prefent profits whereof doth recompence the loffe of that which might be expe&ed by the other, but there can be no hope of any conftant dwelling where the people that inhabite doe not take a courfe to maintaine themfelues by their owne Cornes, and pafture, as all there might doe, if they would refpe& their pofteritie more then the prefent time

Before I come to the Continent I muft remember the Iles of the *Bermudas*, whofe Difcouerie and Plantation was procured by fo ftrange a meanes, for a Ship happening to perifh vpon their Coaft, her pafsingers feeking the next Land for a refuge, they were compelled to doe that out of necefsitie whereunto in good reafon, both for honour and profit, they might more warrantably haue beene inuited ; Thus doth benefit flowe from loffe, fafety from ruine, and the Plantation of a Land from the defolation of a Shippe. they found at the firft ftore of Hogs, which in all appearance had their beginning from fome fuch an accident as theirs was, and the Fowles were there in abundance fo eafie to be taken that they could fcarcely be frighted away, thefe firft people by repairing of their Ship which was caft away vpon the Land, or by building fome other Veffel out of her ruines, comming backe to *England*, and reporting what was paft, fome joyned together in a companie after they had taken a Patent thereof from the King, and did fend people of purpofe to inhabite there, who trufting too much to the goodneffe of the foyle, and negle&ing their owne induftrie, or not gouerning that well which was carried

ried

ried with them, were reduced to a great diftreffe for want of victuals, fo that, if they had not beene confined within an Iland (more fenfible of a prefent fuffering then capable of future hopes) they would willingly haue retired from thence, but a great quantitie of Ambergreece hauing been found by one by chance, and fent backe in a Ship that was going for *London,* their Merchants finding it to bee of a great value, were fo encouraged by fuch a fubftantiall argument, that they prefently difpatched away a new fupply of perfons and all prouifions neceffary, who arriuing there, and hauing confidered what a gulfe of famine was likely to haue fwallowed their fellowes, they improuing their judgement by the others experience, by betaking themfelues to labour in time did preuent the like inconuenience; there is no land where man can liue without labour, nor none fo barren whence induftrie cannot draw fome benefit. All *Adams* pofteritie were appointed to worke for their food, and none muft dreame of an abfolute eafe, which can no where fubfift pofitiuely, but onely comparatiuely, according to the occafions more or leffe

This Plantation of the *Bermudas,* a place not knowne when the King came to *England,* hath profpered fo in a fhort time, that at this prefent, befides their ordinary (and too extraordinarily valued) commoditie of Tobacco, they haue growing there Oranges, Figs, and all kind of fruits that they pleafe to plant, and doe now intend to haue a Sugar worke. Thefe Iles being about twentie miles in bredth can onely be entred but by one paffage, which is fortified and eafily commanded by Ordnance, fo that, hauing no Sauages within, and fearing no forces without, it is efteemed to be impregnable; and the number of the Inhabitants there, being neere three thoufand perfons, are fufficient for the ground that they poffeffe. This part may proue exceedingly fteadable to this State, if euer it happen to haue (as it hath heretofore had) any defignes for feruice in thefe Seas.

The firft Plantation that euer the *Englifh* intended abroad

broad was in *Virginia*, which was firſt diſcouered and named ſo by Sir *Walter Raleigh*, who in the time of Queene
Elizabeth did place ſome perſons to inhabite there, who
not being ſupplied in time, or out of ignorance, or lazineſſe, not vſing the ordinary means (the vſual fault of all be-
ginners) were brought by famine to a great extremity. And
Sir *Francis Drakes* comming by chance that way did tranfport them backe with him to *England*, whileſt at the ſame
time there was another companie furniſhed forth by Sir
Walter Raleigh, who miſsing them whom they expected to
haue found there, did remaine ſtill themſelues; but what
did become of them, if they did remoue to ſome other
part, periſh, diſperſe, or incorporate with the Sauages (no
monument of them remayning) is altogether vnknowne.
This noble worke hauing ſo hard a beginning after a long
diſcontinuance was reuiued againe in the Kings time by a
companie compoſed of Noblemen, Gentlemen, and Merchants, who (joyning priuate purſes with publike ſupplies)
did ſend thither a ſufficient Colonie, well furniſhed with all
things neceſſary, who after their firſt comming had a continuall warre with the Natiues, till it was reconciled by a
Marriage of their Kings ſiſter with one of the Colonie,
who hauing come to *England*, as ſhee was returning backe,
died, and was buried at *Graueſend*.　This euen amongſt
theſe Sauages (libertie being valued aboue life) as they
were induced to conteſt in time, before that power which
they ſuſpected, could come to ſuch a height, that it might
haue a poſsibilitie of depreſsing them, ſo was their malice
with their feares, quickly calmed by the meanes of a marriage; Lawfull allyances thus by admitting equalitie remoue contempt, and giue a promiſcuous off-ſpring extin-
guiſhing the diſtinction of perſons, which if that People
become Chriſtians, were in ſome ſort tolerable, for it is the
onely courſe that vniting minds, free from jealouſies, can
firſt make ſtrangers confide in a new friendſhip, which by
communicating their bloud with mutuall aſſurance is left
hereditary to their poſteritie.

　　　　　　　　　　　　　　　　　　　　　　This

This longed for peace, though it bred a great content-ment for the time, was attended by wrapping them that apprehended no further danger (too common an inconue-nient) vp in the lazie remiffeneffe of improuident fecuritie. For a number leauing the feate of the mayne Colonie, did difperfe themfelues to liue apart, as if they had bin into a well inhabited Countrey, which (as perchance) it had em-boldened the Sauages to imbrace the firft occafion of a quarrell, fo did it giue them an eafie way for executing the mifchiefe that they intended, by killing two or three hun-dred perfons before they could aduertize one another, farre leffe, ioyne to oppofe them in a company together, which courfe might not onely then haue made them able to refift, but preuenting the others refolution had kept them from being purfued : yet I heare of late, that they haue reuen-ged this iniury (though (as fome report) not after a com-mendable manner) by killing their King, with a great number of the chiefe of them whom they fufpected moft.

This plantation of *Virginia,* if it had not beene croffed by the Incurfion of the Sauages abroad, and by the diuifion of their Owners at home, had attayned to a great perfecti-on ere now, hauing had Inhabitants from hence to the number of neere three thoufand perfons, and if fome of them who are there, being Lords of reafonable proporti-ons of ground, and hauing people of their owne, owing no-thing but due obedience to a Superiour Power, and the lea-ding of a life conforme to the Lawes, had no care but (ma-king their Lands to maintayne themfelues) how to build, plant, and plenifh in fuch fort as might beft eftablifh a for-tune for their Pofteritie, they might quickly make vp a new Nation, but it is a great difcouragement vnto them who dwell there, that they muft labour like the Seruants of a Family purchafing their food and rayment from *England,* in exchange of Tobacco, as they are directed by their Ma-fters, many whereof are ftrangers to the eftate of that bounds, and intending to fettle none of their Race there,

haue

haue no care but how the beft benefit may prefently bee
drawne backe from thence, the number of voyces at their
affemblies preuayling more then the foundneffe of iudgement, otherwife that Countrey before this time for
Wine, Oyle, Wheate, and other things neceffary for the
life of man might haue equalled for the like quantitie any
bounds within *Europe,* to which the foile of it felfe lac-
king nothing but the like induftry is no way inferiour
And it is to be exceedingly wifhed by all his Maiefties fubiects that the Plantation of *Virginia* may profper well,
which lying neereft to the part from whence danger might
come, may proue a Bulwarke for the fafetie of all the reft.

That which is now called *New England* was firft comprehended within the Patent of *Virginia,* being the North-
eaft part thereof, it was vndertaken in a Patent by a company of Gentlemen in the Weft of *England,* one of whom
was Sir *Iohn Popham* then Lord Chiefe Iuftice, who fent
the firft company that went of purpofe to inhabite there
neer to *Segadahock,* but thofe that went thither, being preffed to that enterprize, as endangered by the Law, or by
their owne neceffities (no enforced thing prouing pleafant,
difcontented perfons fuffering, while as they act can feldome haue good fucceffe, and neuer fatisfaction) they after
a Winter ftay dreaming to themfelues of new hopes at
home returned backe with the firft occafion, and to iuftifie
the fuddenneffe of their returne, they did coyne many ex-
cufes, burdening the bounds where they had beene with
all the afperfions that poffibly they could deuife, feeking
by that meanes to difcourage all others, whofe prouident
forwardnes importuning a good fucceffe, might make their
bafe fluggifhneffe for abandoning the beginning of a good
worke, to be the more condemned.

About a foure yeeres fince, a fhippe going for *Virginia,*
comming by chance to harbour in the South-weft part of
New England, neere Cape *Cod,* the company whom fhee
carried for Plantation, being weary of the Sea, and enamo-
red with the beautie of the bounds that firft offered it felfe
vnto them gorgeoufly garnifhed with all wherewith
                                                        preg-

pregnant nature rauifhing the fight with variety) can grace a fertile field, did refolue to ftay, and feated themfelues in that place which is now called *New Plimmouth,* where they haue builded good houfes, and by their owne induftry haue prouided themfelues in fuch fort as they are likely to fubfift, keeping a good correfpondencie with the Captaines of the Sauages, who haue done nothing hitherto that might offend them (and after this) though they would dare attempt nothing to their preiudice, who are now aboue two hundred perfons, and doe increafe their number yeerely. They find both the Land and the Seas there abounding in all things needfull for the vfe of man, and doe gouerne themfelues after a very ciuill and prouident manner.

Sir *Ferdinando Gorge* hath beene a chiefe man for the furtherance of all things that might tend to the aduancement of *New England,* hauing beene at great charges thefe many yeeres paft for the Difcouerie thereof, in doing which (a good intention bent for other ends, cafually bringing forth this effect) the fifhing there (not fought for) was found, which doth prooue now fo profitable, as fortie or fiftie Sayle are imployed there from *England* yeerely, and all that haue gone thither, haue made aduantagious Voyages

This laft yeere, he fent his Sonne Captaine *Robert Gorge* with a Colonie to be planted in *Meffafuats* bonds, and as I heare out of a generous defire by his example to encourage others for the aduancement of fo braue an Enterprize he is refolued fhortly to goe himfelfe in perfon, and to carrie with him a great number well fitted for fuch a purpofe, and many Noblemen in *England,* (whofe names and proportions as they were marfhalled by lot, may appeare vpon the Map) hauing intereffed themfelues in that bounds, are to fend feuerall Colonies, who may quickly make this to exceed all the other Plantations.

Hauing fundry times exactly weighed that which I haue alreadie deliuered, and beeing fo exceedingly enflamed to doe fome good in that kinde, that I would rather bewray
the

the weakneſſe of my power, then concealo the greatneſſe of my defire, being much encouraged hereunto by Sir *Ferdinando Gorge*, and fome vthers of the vndertakers for *New England*, I ſhew them that my Countrimen would neuer aduenture in fuch an Enterprize, vnleſſe it were as there was a *New France*, a *New Spaine*, and a *New England*, that they might likewife haue a *New Scotland*, and that for that effect they might haue bounds with a correfpondencie in proportion (as others had) with the Countrey whereof it fhould beare the name, which they might hold of their owne Crowne, and where they might bee gouerned by their owne Lawes, they wifely confideiing that either *Virginia*, or *Neu England*, hath more bounds then all his Maiefties fubiects are able to plant, and that this purpofe of mine by breeding a vertuous emulation amongſt vs, would tend much to the aduancement of fo braue a worke, did yeeld to my defire, defigning the bounds for mee in that part, which hath beene queftioned by the *French*, and leauing the limits thereof to bee appointed by his Maiefties pleafure, which are expreffed in the Patēt granted vnto me, vnder his great Seale of his Kingdome of *Scotland*, marching vpon the Weft towardes the Riuer of Saint *Croix* now *Tu eed* (wheie the *Frenchmen* did defigne their firft Habitation) with *New England*, and on all other parts it is compaffed by the great Ocean, and the great Riuer of *Canada*, fo that though fundry other preceding Patentes are vnaginarily limited by the degrees of the Heauen, I thinke that mine be the firft National Patent that euer was cleerly bounded within *America* by particular limits vpon the Earth.

As foon as my Patent was paffed, refoluing to take poffeffion of the Lands, that were granted vnto me, I prouided my felfe of a ſhip at *London*, in the moneth of March, in *Anno* 1622, but that the bufineſſe might beginne from that Kingdome, which it doth concerne, whereby fome of my Countrimen might be perfwaded to goe, and others by concerning a good opinion thereof, to depend by expectation
tion

tion vpon the reports of fuch of their acquaintance, as were to aduenture in that Voyage, I directed her to go about by S. *Georges* Channell, to *Kircubright*, where fhe arriued in the end of May ; Some Gentlemen of that country, vpon whofe friendfhip I repofed moft, happening at that time to bee out of the Kingdome, I encountred with fundry vnexpe-cted difficulties : the prizes of victuals beeing within the fpace of three monethes, fince I had parted before from *Scotland*, fuddenly tripled, and yet fo fcarce as I could hard-ly in hafte bee well furnifhed, yet fince I was fo far aduan-ced, left I fhould loofe that which was done, if I did not the reft, I vfed the beft diligence I could to prouide the fhippe with all things neceffary. Then the very people fpecially Artizens, of whom I ftood in need, were at firft loth to im-barke for fo remote a part, as they imagined this to bee, fome fcarce beleeuing that there could be any fuch bounds at all, and no wonder, fince neuer any in that part had euer trauelled thither, and all nouelties beeing diftrufted, or difualued, few of good fort would goe, and ordinarie perfons were not capeable of fuch a purpofe.

At laft, in the end of Iune, they parted from thence to the Ile of *Man*, and after fome ftay there, in the beginning of Auguft, leauing the fight of his Maiefties Dominions, did betake themfelues to the Sea. Though by reafon of the lateneffe of their fetting forth, they had the windes very contrary about the middeft of September, they difcouered Saint *Peters* Ilands, and were neere to Cape *Bretton*, but yet were beaten backe againe by a great ftorme to *New-found-land*. And as they paffed by the Bay of *Placentia*, neglecting the occafion to place themfelues in fome part of my bounds, there as they might haue done, they went in-to Saint *Iohns* Harbour, where they concluded to ftay that Winter, and fent the fhip home for a new fupply of fuch things as were needfull.

Though it might haue difcouraged mee much, that they had retired to *Neu-found-land*, forefeeing that what they had with them might be wafted, and that it would bee as

F   charge-

chargeable and difficult to furnifh them forth from thence, as if they were to goe of new from *Scotland*, yet rather then they fhould bee in danger for want of prouifion, making me any way guiltie of their loffe, that had aduentured their liues, trufting to my care, I fraughted a fhippe of purpofe furnifhed with fuch things as were required in a Note, which they fent home with their Meflenger. This fhippe was difpatched by mee from *London* in the end of March 1623, but fhee happened to ftay fo long at *Plimmouth*, firft, vpon fome neceffary occafions, and laft by contrary winds, it being the eight and twentieth of April, before fhee parted from thence, hauing no good windes at all, that they arriued not at Saint *Iohns* Harbour, till the fift of Iune. At their comming they found the company not fit for a Plantation which had firft by an vnexpected caufe been deuided in two during the Winter, and in May fome doubting of a fupply, had engaged themfelues to ferue Fifhermen, by which meanes they gained their maintenance, and fome meanes befide, fo that they could hardly be gathered together againe, and their Minifter and Smith (both for Spirituall and Temporall refpects, the two moft neceffary members) were both dead, fo that feeing no hope to plant themfelues in any good fafhion that yeere, ten of the principall perfons concluded to go alongft with the fhip to *New Scotland*, to difcouer the Countrey, and to make choice of a fit place for a Habitation againft the next yeere, confidering very well, that they could not doe fo much good by ftaying there with fo few a number, as they might doe at their returne, by reporting the truth to their friends, of that which they had feene, whereby a new Colonie might be encouraged to fet forth well furnifhed, and inftructed according to that which might bee learned by their experience.

The three and twentieth of Iune, they loofed from Saint *Iohns* Harbour, and fayled towards *New Scotland*, where for the fpace of fourteene dayes, they were by fogges and contrary winds kept backe from fpying Land till the eight of Iuly, that they faw the Weft part of Cape *Bretton*, and till

till the thirteenth day, they fayled alongft the Coaft, till
they ranne the length of Port *de Mutton*, where they difcouered three very pleafant Harbours, and went afhore
in one of them, which after the fhippes name, they called
Lukes Bay, where they found a great way vp a very pleafant River, being three fathom deep at a low water at the
entry thereof, & on euery fide of the fame they did fee very
delicate Medowes, hauing Rofes white and red, growing
thereon with a kind of wilde Lilly, which had a daintie
fmel, the next day they refolued (coafting alongft the land)
to difcouer the next Harbour, which was but two leagues
diftant from the other, where they found a more pleafant
River then the firft, being foure fathome deepe at a low
water with Medowes on both fides thereof, hauing Rofes
and Lillies growing thereon as the other had, they found
within this River, a very fit place for a Plantation, both
in regard that it was naturally apt to be fortified, and that
all the ground betweene the two Riuers, was without
wood, and very good fat Earth, hauing feuerall forts of
beries growing thereon, as Goofe-beries, Straw-beries,
Hind-beries, Rasberies, and a kind of red Wine berie, as
alfo fome forts of graine, as Peafe, fome Eares of Wheate,
Barly and Rie growing there wilde ; the Peafe grow in a-
bundance alongft the Coaft, very bigge and good to eate,
but did tafte of the fitch : this River is called Port *Iolly*,
from whence they coafted alongft to Port *Negro*, beeing
twelue leagues diftant, where all the way as they fayled a-
longft, they fpied a very pleafant Countrey, hauing growing euery where fuch things as were obferued in the two
Harbours where they had beene before. They found likewife in euery River abundance of Lobfters, Cockles, and o-
ther fhel-fifhes, and alfo not onely in the Riuers, but all the
Coaft alongft, numbers of feuerall forts of Wild-foule, as
Wild-goofe, blacke Ducke, Woodcocke, Crane, Heron,
Pidgeon, and many other forts of Fowle which they knew
not   They did kill as they fayled alongft the Coaft great
ftore of Cod, with feuerall other forts of great fifhes.

F 2   The

The Countrie is full of Woods not very thicke, and the moſt part Oake, the reſt are Firre, Spruce, Birch, with ſome Sicamores, and Aſhes, and many other ſorts of Wood which they had not ſeene before. Hauing diſcouered this part of the Countrie, in regard of the Voyage their ſhip was to make to the Straits with fiſhes, they reſolued to coaſt a-longſt from _Lukes_ Bay to Port _de Mutton_, being foure leagues to the Eaſt thereof, where they encountred with a _Frenchman_, that in a very ſhort time had made a great Voyage, for though he had furniſhed one ſhip away with a great number of fiſhes, there were neere ſo many readie as to load himſelfe & others. After they had taken a view of this Port, which to their iudgement they found no waies inferiour to the reſt they had ſeene before, they reſolued to retire backe to _New-found-land_, where their ſhip was to receiue her loading of fiſhes. The 20 of Iuly they looſed from thence, and the ſeuen and twentieth thereof they arriued at Saint _Iohns_ Harbour, and from thence ſailed alongſt to the Bay of _Conception_, where they left the ſhip, and diſpatched themſelues home in ſeuerall ſhips that belonged to the Weſt part of _England_.

This is no wonder, that the _French_ beeing ſo ſlightly planted, did take no deeper roote in _America_, for they as onely deſirous to know the nature and qualitie of the ſoile, and of things that were likely to grow there, did neuer ſeeke to haue them in ſuch quantitie as was requiſite for their maintenance, affecting more by making a needleſſe oſtentation, that the World ſhould know they had beene there, then that they did continue ſtill to inhabit there, like them, that were more in loue with glorie then with vertue: then being alwaies ſubiect to diuiſions amongſt themſelues, it was impoſsible that they could ſubſiſt, which proceeded ſometime from emulation or enuie, and at other times from the lazineſſe of the diſpoſition of ſome, who (lothing labor) could bee commanded by none, who would impoſe more vpon them then was agreeable with the indifferencie of their affections and ſuperficiall endeuours.

The

The *English* were free from thefe mutinies, and wanted not induftry enough, but either out of a cuftome they haue to trauell more for the benefit that doth flow from graffe, then by manuring of the ground for Corne, or otherwife if they were forced fo to doe by their Owners at *London*, who enforcing a fpeedie returne by their labour, would needs be trufted with furnifhing of them victuals, they applying themfelues to Tobacco, and fuch things as might import a prefent commoditie, neglecting the time that might haue beene employed for building, planting and husbandrie, did liue but like hired Seruants, labouring for their Mafters, and not like Fathers prouiding for their Family and Pofteritie, which can neuer be auoided till the ground be inhabited by them, that being Owners thereof, will truft it with their maintenance, and doe content themfelues with the delight of that which may giue glorie to them, and profit to their heires.

The Plantations in *America* doe approch neereft to the puritie of thefe that (by an induftrious diligence) in the infancie of the firft age did extend the multiplying generations of Mankind, to people the then Defert Earth, for here they may poffeffe themfelues without difpoffefsing of others, the Land either wanting Inhabitants, or hauing none that doe appropriate to themfelues any peculiar ground, but (in a ftraggling company) runne like beafts after beafts, feeking no foile, but onely after their prey. And where of old the *Danes, Gaules, Gothes, Hunnes, Vandals, Longobards,* and thereafter *Sarazens, Turkes* and *Tartarians,* did (with an inundation of people) encroach vpon thefe places of *Europe,* which were moft ciuill, and where the Gofpel was beft planted, out of an ambitious enuie to draw vnto themfelues the glory that any Nation had formerly gained, or out of an exorbitant auarice to fwallow vp their fubftance, and to vfurpe (if they had power challenging right) any Lands that were better then their own, as the moft part did in *Greece, Hungary, Spaine, Italy,* and *France.* We here goe to caufe preach the Gofpel where it was neuer heard,

and

and not to fubdue but to ciuillize the Sauages, for their ruine could giue to vs neither glory nor benefit, fince in place of fame it would breed infamie, and would defraud vs of many able bodies, that hereafter (befides the Chriftian dutie in fauing their foules) by themfelues or by their Pofteritie may ferue to many good vfes, when by our meanes they fhall learne lawfull Trades, and induftries, the Authors whereof (though preuenting the like Superftition) may acquire no leffe reuerence from them, nor in like cafe of old *Saturne, Bacchus, Ceres,* and *Pallas,* by teaching to plant Corne, Wine, and Oyle, did get from the credulous ignorance of them with whom they communicated their knowledge.

When I doe confider with myfelfe what things are neceffarie for a Plantation, I cannot but be confident that my owne Countreymen are as fit for fuch a purpofe as any men in the world, hauing daring mindes that vpon any probable appearances doe defpife danger, and bodies able to indure as much as the height of their minds can vndertake, naturally louing to make vfe of their owne ground, and not trufting to traffique. Then *Scotland* by reafon of her populoufneffe being conftrained to disburden her felfe (like the painfull Bees) did euery yeere fend forth fwarmes whereof great numbers did haunt *Pole* with the moft extreme kinde of drudgerie (if not dying vnder the burden) fcraping a few crummes together, till now of late that they were compelled, abandoning their ordinary calling, to betake themfelues to the warres againft the *Russians, Turks,* or *Swedens,* as the *Polonians* were pleafed to employ thē, others of the better fort being bred in *France,* in regard of the ancient league, did finde the meanes to force out fome fmall fortunes there, till of late that the *French* though not altogether violating, yet not valuing (as heretofore) that friendfhip which was fo religioufly obferued by their predeceffours, and with fo much danger and loffe deferued by ours, haue altered the eftate of the Guards, and doe derogate frō our former liberties, which this King now raigning, we
hope,

hope, will reftore to the firft integritie. The necefsities of *Ireland* are neere fupplied, and that great current which did tranfport fo many of our people is worne drie. The *Lowe Countries* haue fpent many of our men, but haue enriched few, and (though raifing their flight with fuch borrowed feathers, till they were checked by a prefent danger) did too much vilipend thefe fauourable Springs by which their weakneffe was chiefly refrefhed: But howfoeuer fome particular men might profper vnder a forraine Prince, all that aduenture fo, doe either perifh by the way, or if they attaine vnto any fortune, doe lofe the fame by fome colour that ftrict lawes vrged againft a ftranger can eafily affoord, or elfe naturalizing themfelues where they are, they muft difclaime their King and Countrey, to which by time (the obiect of their affections altered) being bound to haue a care of that part where there pofteritie muft liue, they turne euery way ftrangers, which necefsitie impofed vpon them to take this courfe, and inconueniences following thereupon may be preuented by this new Plantation. And where the *Scottish* Merchants before had no trade but by tranfporting Commodities that might haue beene imployed at home, and oftentimes monie, to bring backe Wine from *France*, and Pitch, Tarre, and Timber from the Eafter Seas Now only by exporting of men, Corne, and Cattle, they may within a little time be able to furnifh back in exchange thefe things before named. As likewife a great benefit of fifhes, Furres, Timber, and Metals, drawing forth our people to forreine Traffique, wherewith they neuer haue bin accuftomed before, and that to the great increafe of the Cuftomes, helping hereby to enrich that ancient Kingdome, which of all the reft hath onely loft by his Maiefties greatneffe, being hereby not onely defrauded of his owne prefence, and of the comfort that his countenance did continually affoord, but likewife of many Commodities arifing to any Countrie where a Court is Refident, as the vniuerfall pouertie thereof (hauing few rich vnleffe it bee fome

Iudges

Iudges and their Clerkes) by a common complaint doth too fenfibly teftifie.

I haue neuer remembred any thing with more admiration then *America*, confidering how it hath pleafed the Lord to locke it vp fo long amidft the depths, concealing it from the curiofitie of the Ancients, that it might be difcouered in a fit time for their pofteritie, they were fo farre of old from apprehending it by any reach of reafon, that the moft learned men (as they thought) by infallible grounds, in regard of the degrees of the Heauen, did hold that thefe Zones could not be inhabited, which now are knowne to include the moft pleafant parts in the World.   This neuer came to the knowledge of any Hebrew, Greeke, or Roman, who had the moft able mindes to haue found out fuch a myfterry. and howfoeuer fome would glofe vpon that Fable of *Platoes* Atlantick Iland, I haue neuer obferued any thing amongft the Ancient Writers tending to fuch a purpofe, if it bo not thefe lines of *Seneca* the Tragedian, whereby hee might (if not with a prophetick, yet with a poetick rapture) deliuer that which he had a mind to make the pofteritie expect, and was in poffibilitie to happen.

> *Venient annis*
> *Secula feris, quibus Occanus*
> *Vincula rerum laxet, & ingens*
> *Pateat tellus, Tiphisque nouos*
> *Detegat orbes; nec fit terris*
> *Vltima Thule*

And it is a thing not yet comprehended by the courfe of naturall reafon, how thefe parts of the World came firft to be peopled · We muft grant (according to the grounds of Diuinitie) their people to be defcended from *Noah*, and it is not long fince that (the Load ftone being found out) the beft Saylers (fcorning as in former times to be only coafters) haue brought the Art of Nauigation to that perfection, that they durft refolutely aduenture to fearch the moft remote

parts

parts in the Ocean, and if any had gone thither of purpofe to inhabite, they would haue carried with them the moft vfefull kindes of tame Cattle, fuch as Horfes, Cowes, and Sheepe, whereof neuer any was found in thefe parts, till they were tranfported thither of late yeeres ; but onely fuch wild beafts as of themfelues might haue wandred any where through vaft Forrefts, and Deferts : fo that I doe thinke there muft bee fome narrow paffage vpon the Eaft, towards *Terra Auftralis Incognita,* not yet difcouered, from whence people by time might haue come (croffing the Straits of *Magelane*) to inhabite *Brafile, Chile,* and *Peru,* or rather I fhould thinke that there were fome Continent, or Narrow Sea towardes the North, about the Straits of *Anien,* from whence the firft Inhabitants in *America* might haue come ; becaufe the wild beafts that are there are creatures moft peculiar to the North, fuch as Elkes, Bears, and Beauers, which are knowne to bee ordinary with the *Russians,* and *Tartarians ;* and I am the more confirmed in this opinion, when I remember of the Mountains of Ice that come floting euery Spring alongft the Coaft of *New-found-Land,* which (as it is likely) may diffolue from fome Sea that hath beene frozen during the Winter time, ouer which people, and wild beafts might haue commoditie to paffe , but this is a matter that can hardly bee determined by demonftration or reafon, therefore (all men forming that which they know not, according to the fquare of their owne conceits:) Wee muft leaue this to the vnlimited libertie of the imagination of man

But the thing moft wonderfull of all is this, though now it bee cleerely difcouered, that fo few are willing to make vfe thereof ; This doth chiefly proceed from want of knowledge, few being willing to aduenture vpon that wherewith they are not acquainted by their owne experience, and yet thofe who haue not made triall themfelues, if they will truft others, may bee abundantly fatisfied by the reports of a number, who to Plant and Traffique doe yeerely

G haunt

haunt thefe parts. If the true eftate of that which might bee done at this time by the ioyning of fome reafonable company together were rightly vnderftood, then fo many would not liue at home as they do, lofing their time, where they can make no benefit, and burdenable to them to whom they are not vfefull, rather admitted, then welcommed, the one thinking that their feruice fhould deferue a reward, and the other that their maintenance is an vnneceffary charge, neither gaining, and both difcontented : then would not fo many aduenture their liues for the defence of ftrangers, whereby they fcarce can acquire that which doth defray their owne charges, and howfoeuer the hope of Honour may flatter a generous fpirit, there is no great appearance by this meanes to prouide for a Family, or for a Pofteritie And if we rightly confider the benefit that may arife by this enterprife abroad, it is not onely able to afford a fufficient meanes for their maintenance, who cannot conueniently liue at home, by disburdening the Countrey of them, but it is able to enable them to deferue of their Countrey, by bringing vnto it both Honour and Profit.

Where was euer Ambition baited with greater hopes then here, or where euer had Vertue fo large a field to reape the fruites of Glory, fince any man, who doth goe thither of good qualitie, able at firft to tranfport a hundred perfons with him furnifhed with things neceffary, fhall haue as much Bounds as may ferue for a great Man, wherevpon hee may build a Towne of his owne, giuing it what forme or name hee will, and being the firft Founder of a new eftate, which a pleafing induftry may quickly bring to a perfection, may leaue a faire inheritance to his pofteritie, who fhall claime vnto him as the Author of their Nobilitie there, rather then to any of his Anceftours that had preceded him, though neuer fo nobly borne elfwhere, and if the vafteneffe of their hopes cannot bee bounded within their firft limits, as foone as they haue ftrengthned
them-

themfelues for fuch a defigne, either by Sea or by Land, (in regard of the large Countries next adiacent hereunto) there doth alwaies reft a faire poffibilitie of a further encreafe, either for them, or for their fucceffours ; and fo euery one of inferiour fort may expect proportionably according to his aduenture : The Merchants that are giuen to trade, where can they haue a fairer ground for gaine then here ; and that befides that which may bee expected from fo fertile a Land by induftry or husbandry hereafter, in prefent commodities, fuch as Cod fifhes and Herring in the Seas, Salmouds in the Riuers, Furres, Pype-ftaues, Pot-afhes, and all that may arife from the plentie of good Wood, Mineralls, and other things though not knowne to ftrangers that onely coaft alongft the Lands, that may bee difcouered hereafter by them that are to inhabite the Bounds.

Here thofe that are fo difpofed, without making a Monafticall retreate (free from a multitude of troubles) may inioy the pleafures of contemplation, being folitary when they will, and yet accompanied when they pleafe, and that not with fuch company as (preffed by importunitie) they muft difcontentedly admit, but onely by them of whom they haue made choice, and whom they haue carried with them, with whom (as partners of their trauells) by mutuall difcourfes they may remember their former dangers, and communicate their prefent ioyes . heere are all forts of obiects to fatisfie the varietie of defires. I might fpeake of the fport that may bee had by Hunting, Hawking, Fifhing, and Fowling, where all thefe creatures haue had fo long a time for increafe, without being deftroyed or frighted, as likewife of the great contentment that muft come by daily difcoueries of new Fieldes and Riuers, with the diuerfitie of things not feene before that may happen to bee found in them · but I would rather haue all at firft to thinke of the paines they muft indure, in bringing of fo notable a Worke to perfection, fince no good thing can be had with eafe ; and all the fonnes of men are borne to la-

bour.

bour. But leauing thefe wordly refpects, the greateft incouragement of all for any true Chriftian is this, that heere is a large way for aduancing the Gofpel of Iefus Chrift, to whom Churches may bee builded in places where his Name was neuer knowne ; and if the Saints of Heauen reioyce at the conuerfion of a Sinner, what exceeding ioy would it bee to them to fee many thoufands of Sauage people (who doe now liue like brute beafts) conuerted vnto God, and I wifh leauing thefe dreames of Honour and Profit, which doe intoxicate the braines, and impoyfon the minde with tranfitory pleafures) that this might bee our chiefe end to begin a new life, feruing God more fincerely then before, to whom we may draw more neere, by retyring our felues further from hence.

As I would haue no man that hath a mind for this courfe, to abufe his iudgement, by trufting too much to the fertilitie of the bounds where he is to goe, and too little to his owne prouidence, and induftrie, whereby he may be made to neglect the preparing himfelfe for this Voyage after fuch a manner as is requifite, So I altogether diflike them that poffeffed with the prepofterous apprehenfions of feare (like the lazie man of whome *Salomon* fpeaketh, that pretending difficulties to preuent trauell, would fay there was a Lion in the way) will needs imagine the worft that is in poffibilitie to happen : for fuch a man (too ingenioufly fubtill in coniecturing danger) doth both by preiudicated opinions difable himfelfe, and difcourage them, who not being duely informed, are confirmed by the confidence of other vndertakers, that profeffe to haue knowledge, there is no man at home where he was borne, fo free from the accidents of fortune who may not quickly by a publike, or by a priuate calamitie be brought in fome meafure to fuffer, and much rather fhould wee arme our felues with a high refolution againft all inconuemiences that can occurre in fuch a forraine enterprife (being circumfpectly pro-

prouident, but not cōfounded with a deiecting fear) where the greatneffe of fo well grounded hopes for vs and for our Pofteritie fhould make vs (hoping for pleafure) to difgeft any prefent paine, with a courage greater then can bee braued by any apprehended trouble. And becaufe the Lord in fuch eminent Exploits doth commonly glorifie himfelfe by a few number, I wifh that all fuch whofe hearts doe mifgiue them portending any difafter (like them of *Gideons* troupes that bowed downe like beafts to the water) fhould retire in time, ere the contagioufneffe of their infirmitie come to infect them that are more foundly difpofed. There is no iuft caufe for a reafonable man to feare any worldly thing, but onely difgrace and want of neceffary mayntenance. A man can hardly fall in the firft here, fince an honourable intention what euer the fucceffe prooue muft acquire prayfe, and the other by ordinary meanes, is eafie to be auoyded, but I am fo farre from painting out a fuppofed facilitie to fnare weake minds, that I would haue none (with whom it is not fit to communicate more then they be capeable) to imbarke in this bufines, but onely fuch as do refolue againft the worft, for I poffeffe as *Cato* did, when he was to enter the Deferts of *Arabia*.

> ———*Neque enim mihi fallere quenquam*
> *Eft animus, tectoque metu perducere vulgus.*
> *Hi mihi fint comites, quos ipfa pericula ducent,*
> *Qui me tefte, pati, vel quæ triftiſſima, pulchrum,*
> *Romanumque putant; at qui fponfore falutis*
> *Miles eget, capiturque animæ dulcedine, vadat*
> *Ad Dominum meliore via.———*

And laft fhould not thefe memorable Exploits of late performed in the Eaft and Weft *Indies* by the *Flemmings*, enflame vs with a generous ardour to equall, or rather to exceede them, whofe penuritie of people (euen at home) muft bee fupplyed by the fuperfluitie of ours: They haue
not

not onely in the Eaſt *Indies* by ſeuerall Habitations appropriated large Territories to themſelues, but likewiſe to the
great preiudice of their Neighbours, improouing their
owne profit, haue engroſſed the generall Commerce by
conſequence depending thereupon. And if they ſeate
themſelues (as it is likely they will doe) in *Braſill,* pro-
uidently proſecuting the good beginning that they haue
gotten by ſparing people of their owne, or by intere-
ſting Strangers whom they dare truſt for founding of a ſufficient Colonie, that being ſtrong enough to defend and
command the Inhabitants (Securely exacting a due obedience) may enable them for greater matters; then con-
fining with the very Springs whence the ſtreames flow that
entertayne the power of their enemies (exhauſting their
ſubſtance both by Sea and Land) they haue a maruellous
faire occaſion offered to aduance them ſelues by depreſ-
ſing of the oppoſed partie whoſe proſperous and deſired
ſucceſſe (whileſt the adding to one doth derogate from
another) if not emulated in time, will be enuied hereafter.

I know that many of my Nation if they had beene as
willing as they are able had beene more fit then I am for
this purpoſe, but yet it hath oftentimes pleaſed God to doe
the greateſt matters by the meaneſt Inſtruments And as
no one man could accompliſh ſuch a Worke by his owne
priuate fortunes, ſo if it ſhall pleaſe his Maieſtie (as he hath
euer beene diſpoſed for the furthering of all good Works
more for the benefit of his Subiects, then for his owne particular) to giue his helpe accuſtomed for matters of leſſe
moment hereunto, making it appeare to be a Worke of his
own, that others of his ſubiects may be induced to concurre
in ſuch a common cauſe, no man could haue had my charge
that with more affection and ſinceritie ſhould haue vſed his
endeuours for diſcharging of the ſame, but I muſt truſt to be
ſupplyed by ſome publike helps, ſuch as hath beene had in
other parts, for the like cauſe whereunto, as I doubt not, but
many

many will be willing out of the nobleneffe of their difpofition, for the aduancing of fo worthy a Worke, So I hope
will fome others, the rather out of their priuate refpect to
me, who fhall continue as I haue heretofore done, both
to doe and write in fo farre, fo meane an abilitie as
mine may reach, what (I conceiue) may proue
for the credit or benefit of my Nation,
to whom I wifh all hap-
pineffe.

FINIS.

ENCOVRAGEMENTS,

For such as shall have intention

to bee Vnder-takers in the new plantation
of *CAPE BRITON*, now *New Galloway*
in AMERICA,

BY MEE

LOCHINVAR.

*Non nobis nati sumus; aliquid parentes, aliquid
Patria, aliquid cognati postulant.*

EDINBVRGH,
Printed by Iohn Wreittoun. *Anno Dom.* 1625.

TO THE RIGHT
VVORSHIPFVLL
SIR WILLIAM
ALEXANDER
of Menstrie Knight,

Mafter of Requeftes for *Scotland,*
and Lievetenant Generall to his
Majeftie in the Kingdome
of *NEW SCOTLAND.*

AND

TO THE REMNANT THE NOBLE-
MEN, AND KNIGHTS BARO-
nets in *Scotland,* Vnder-takers
in the plantations of New Scot-
land in AMERICA.

TO THE ADVEN-
TVRERS, FAVOV-

rers, and well-willers of
the enterprife for the inhabiting,
and planting in Cape Briton, *now*
New Galloway *in America.*

* * *

* *

*

Entle Reader,
It hath beene the policie vniverfall, from the creation of the World vnto this time, of all civile States, the replenifhing of the World with Colonies of their owne fubjects. Adam *and* Eva *did firft beginne this pleafant worke to plant the Earth to fucceeding pofteritie.* Noah, *and his familie began againe the fecond plantation. And the confufion of tongues at* Babel, *made divifion of States, fcattering as manie Colonies ouer the face of the Earth after the Flood, as there was diverfitie of Languages : and their feede as it ftill increafed, hath ftill planted new Countries, one after another ; and fo the Worlde to that eftate whereinto it is.*

That the planting of Countries, and civilizing barbarous and inhumane Nations, hath ever beene the worke of the greateft Princes of the Earth, their ever-living actions hath teftified ; wherewith are filled both the records of divine Trueth, and the monuments of humane ftate; and whose heroicke actions (wee

B   *muft muſt not thinke) hath beene vndertaken vpon triviall motives, when as by that, they did aſwell inlarge the limites of their Dominions, and enriche the revenues of their eſtates ; as bridle ſedition at home, and ſettle ſecuritie againſt their enemies abroad.*

Theſe precceding praiſe-worthie Fathers, and their memorable of-ſpring were diligent to plant, that yet vnplanted to their after-livers , wherein ſhined thoſe worthie Founders of the great Monarchies and their virtues· the Hebrues, *the* Lacedemonians, Gothes, Græcians, Romanes, *and the reſt from time to time in their ſeverall ages.*

But to leaue theſe remote times, let vs take a view within theſe 60. *yeeres of the diſcoveries, and plantations in* America, *by the* Engliſh, *the* French, *the* Spaniard, *the* Portugale; *by whoſe induſtrious paines are made knowne vnto vs alreadie their, ſo hudge tracts, kingdomes, and territories, peopled and vnpeopled, as vpon the hither ſide for the ſpace of* 5000. *leagues at the leaſt, and for* 3000 *more on the backe ſide in the South Sea.*

Manie diſcourſes of the diſcoueries which hath beene there effected within theſe few yeeres are made of worthie Perſonages: ſuch as Columbus, Cortez, Pitzora, Soto, Magellanes, *and manie others, who to the wonder of all ages hath ſucceſsiuehe ſeconded one another in thoſe partes.*

Whole Decads are filled with diſcoveries there, and volumes with their actions of plantation : There wee ſee the renowned Drake, *and memorable* Candiſch *twiſe about the round circumference of the whole Earth* Virginia *to perpetrat the memorie of her honourable Knight* Sr Walter Ralegh, Amadas, Arthur, Whyte, Grenuile, *and* Lane *her firſt diſcoverers, and worthie Governours in her plantations* Sr Iohn Haukins *in his* Guinea. Iohn de Verrazano *a* Florentine, Iohn Rinault, Rene Landoniere, Dominique Gorgues *in their* Florida. *The noble* Cortez, *and the other* Spainards, *and* Portugalls *in their golden Mynes of the* 15. *Provinces of new* Mexico, Nueua Gallicia, Nueua Hiſpanna, Nueua Biſcaia, Cibola, Quivivra, *and to the Gulfe of* California *on the back ſide of* America. *The famous*

mous Cabot, Frobiſher, Davis, *whoſe memories ſhall never die in the North-weſt parts: and many innumerable moe Worthies, whom all after-ages ſhall eternize for their vertues, whoſe actions I leave to bee ſearched as they are regiſtred in the monuments of their praiſe-worthie proceedings.*

The ſhining brightneſſe of theſe (Gentle Reader) *and ſuch others, hath ſo beamed a path way to all poſteritie for imitation; as that the baſeſt minde that is, may bee induced to follow their foot-ſteppes. And for my ſelfe, hauing from the ſource of that ever and ouer-flowing fountaine, that was ſtill a running to all, from our late Soueraigne of never-dying memorie* King IAMES *obtained a Patent of* Cape Briton, *which now, by his Royall direction is intituled* New Galloway *in* America: *I haue reſolved to follow the troden way of theſe 'others, whoſe happie ſucceſſe are ſo plainlie ſeene in ſuch honorable deſignes.*

And ſince I doe propone to my ſelfe the ſame ends, which are firſt for the glorie of my great and mightie GOD; *next the ſervice of his M. my dread Soueraigne, and my native Countrie; and laſt the particular weale, and vtilitie of my ſelfe, and ſuch as ſhall be generouſlie diſpoſed adventurers with mee: Why ſhall it bee lawfull for others, and not for mee: and not as poſſible and as commodious for mee, as vnto others of my qualitie?*

The chiefe (then) *and the fartheſt poynt that my intention ſhall ſeeke to arrive at; ſhall bee to remove that vnbeliefe, which is ſo grounded in the mindes of men, to diſcredite moſt noble and profitable endeuoures with diſtruſt: and, firſt, to ſhake off their colourable pretences of ignorance, and then, if they will not be perſuaded to make their ſelfe-willes inexcuſable; I ſhall make manifeſt the worthineſſe of the cauſe to the mindes of ſuch as are deſirous to bee ſettled in a certaintie. As for my ſelfe, I doe giue truſt to the relations of ſuch, whoſe wiſdomes (I know) are not ſo ſhallow, as eaſilie bee deceiued of others; nor conſciences ſo wretched, as by pretences to deceive others; and having the perſonall tryall of ſo honourable and ſufficient reporters, our owne Countrie-men, this naked contemplation, and idle knouledge can*

not

not content mee: but knowing that the chiefe commendation of vertue confifteth in action, I haue refolved a practife, and to trace the footfteppes of those heroicke fore-runners, whofe honourable actions fhall ever live vpon Earth; whiles their Soules live in glo-rie in the Heavens, and fhall increafe heere, and multiplie; as their bodies in the grave fhall putrifie

The inducements which hath incouraged mee to this enterprife, and to fpend my time, and beft abilities in thefe adventures, I fhall heere fette brieflie downe without any inlargment of made wordes, but in fingle fpeach, as beft befeeming a fimple meaning; Intreating thee (Courteous Reader) that thou would with an affectioned mind confider thefe my fubfequent motives, where-with I haue beene induced my felfe: ponder aright my endes. and then but weigh my willing and free Offers, which I doe make for the weale and furtherance of fo worthie a Worke. Wee are not borne to our felves. but to help each others, and our abilities and meanes are not much vnlike at the firft houre of our birth, and the laft minute of our death: and it is our deedes good or bad that all of vs haue to carrie vs to Heaven or Hell after this life.

While wee are therefore heere, let vs imitate the vertues, and glo-ries of our Predeceffours, that heercafter worthilie wee may bee remembred as their Succeffours,

FARE-WELL.

THE MOTIVES,

which hath induced mee,

and may happilie encourage fuch as

haue intention to bee Vnder-ta-

kers with Mee in the plantation

of New GALLOWAY in

AMERICA.

MOTIVE I.

S the chiefe and primarie end of mans cre- *The firſt*
ation is the Worſhippe of GOD; ſo ſhall *motiue.*
the firſt, and ſpeciall motive of my proceeding be the advancement of his Glorie, and
that by the propagation of the Goſpell of
IESVS CHRIST amongſt an Heathen
people, where Chriſtianitie hath not beene knowne, nor
the worſhippe of the true GOD. Where can bee ſe-
lected a more excellent ſubject, than to caſt downe the Al-
tars of Devills, and to raiſe vp the Altar of *CHRIST:* to
forbidde the Sacrifice of men, that they may offer vp
the Sacrifices of contrite Spirites.

Is it not a determined Trueth, that the Goſpell of *Ie-
ſus Chriſt* ſhould bee preached to all the Worlde (*Heaven
and Earth ſhall paſſe away, but GODS Worde ſhall not paſſe
away.*) And is it not as certaine a Concluſion amongſt all
the Divines, that theſe are the latter Dayes, wherein we
live, well knowne by the ſignes that were to come before,
ſette downe by God himſelfe in his ſacred Worde, and
for the moſt part alreadie manifeſted? And hath not Gods

B 3

all-

all-feeing Providence begunne as firſt by difcouerie, and next by plantation of fo hudge and fo waſte a tract, more commonlie, than properlie called the New Worlde; vnknowne but within this 60. yeeres, except by a glimpfe, to make appeare the progreſſe of his divine Providence, how hee will haue the feede of his worke to be fowne amongſt them; Then doth it not belonge vnto vs to profecute his worke; and as by merchandizing and trade wee buy at them the pearles of the Earth; wee ought to communicate vnto them the pearles of Heaven.

The time hath never beene fo apparent as now, vnder our moſt gratious and Soveraigne Lord, King *CHARLES*, whofe generous and gratious goodwill by encouragement to the fame, hath manifeſted the fame fince hee receaved the Crowne, to bee the felected inſtrument to atchieue it.

Then ſhould not that Heroicke, and illuſtrious difpofition in Him, whom wee fee fo prompt to bee ſtill in action, both incite, and invite to fo noble defignes all fuch as would ſhunne the imputation of idleneſſe to imitate His foot-ſteppes.

Is it vnlawfull for vs to come to them? No; it is the duetie of Chriſtianitie in vs, to behold the imprinted footſteppes of GODS glorie in everie Region vnder Heaven; and to them, againſt the Law of Nations, to violate a peaceable Stranger, or to deny vs harbour.

Is it vnlawfull for vs to trade with them? No, vnleſſe *Salomon* ſhould bee condemned of fending for Golde to *Ophir; Abraham* for making a league with *Abimelech;* and all Chriſtendome for having commerce with *Turkes,* and mifcreants.

Nor neither is it vnlawfull that wee poſſeſſe part of their Lands, and dwell with them, and defend our felves from them, becaufe there is no other moderate, and mixt courfe, to bring them to converfion, but by daylie converfation, where wee may fee the Life, and learne the Languages

guages each of others : and becaufe there is rowme fufficient in the Land, (as *Sichem* faid) for them, and vs ; the
extent of an 100. myles beeing fcarce peopled with 500
inhabitants : and chieflie becaufe (as *Pharaoh* gaue *Gofhen,*
to *Ifrael,* ere *Ephron* fold his caue to *Abraham*) they have
folde to our people their Lands for copper (which they
more efteme of, than money) to inherite and inhabite : as
Pafpehay and *Powhatan,* two [of] there greateft Kinges to
thefe our Colonies in *Virginia;* and chieflie (as it is written by Captaine *Iohn Smith,* a worthie actour in the bufineffe) when Captaine *Newport* was defired by *Powhatan*
at *Worowacomaco,* to come from *Iames* towne in *Virginia,*
where hee was, as a place vnwholefome, and to take
poffeffion of another whole Kingdome, which hee gave
vnto him

If any fcrupulous confcience will impute, that yet wee
can poffeffe no further limites, than was alloted by com-
pofition, and that fortitude without juftice, is but the
firebrand of iniquitie. Let him know that *Plato* defineth
it to bee no injuftice, to take a fword out of the hand of
a madde man And Saint *Auguftine* hath allowed, for a
lawfull offenfiue warre that revengeth injuries, and wherein the whole Divines in *Europe,* although contraverting
farre in other things, yet in this they all agree, that it is
lawfull. That the Church of *Rome* allowe it. The *Spaniard,* and *Portugalles* large and ample territories and kingdomes in the 15 Provinces of *Mexico, Nueua Hifpanna,
Nueua Gallicia,* &c. beare witneffe. And for the Church
of *England,* their *Bermudos, Virginian* and *New England*
conqueffe and colonies affirme it. And the Church of *Gene-
va* in the yeere 1555. determined in a Synode (where
Calvin was prefident) to send *Peter Rochier,* and *William
Quadrigarius,* vnder a French Captaine to *Brafilia,* althogh
they were fupplanted by the Cardinall of *Loraine,* and
the treacherie of their falfe Captaine.

When

When therefore it is fo fweete a fmelling Sacrifice to propagate the name of *Iefus Chrift*: if wee haue any graine of faith or zeale in Religion, let vs feeke to convert thefe poore Savages to knowe *Chrift*, and humanitie. Let Religion bee the firft aime of our hopes, and other thinges fhall bee caft vnto vs. Our Names fhall bee regiftred to pofteritie with a glorious Title; Thefe are the men whom GOD hath raifed to augment the ftate of their Countrie, and to propagate the Gofpell of *Iefus Chrift*.

The fame GOD that hath ordained three Kingdomes vnder the Scepter of our gratious King *CHARLES*, will not bee wanting to adde a fourth, if wee would diffolve that froftie yeieneffe which chilleth our zeale, and maketh vs cold in the action.

MOTIVE II.

The fecond motive.

AND next to the Worfhippe of my GOD, is the fervice of my Prince, and native Countrie: which is the fecond end that I haue propounded vnto my felfe, by inlarging thefe Dominions whereof I am a Subject: a duetie mofte proper to all the true and loyall Lieges, whenfoever by fo lawfull and eafie meanes it may bee atchieved.

What is fo truelie futable with honour and honeftie, as to gaine to our native Mother-Countrie a Kingdome to attend her? Wherein can the tafte of true vertue, and magnanimitie bee more fweete and pleafant than in planting, and building a foundation for thy pofteritie; gotte from the rude earth by Gods bleffing, and thine owne induftrie, without prejudice to any? What more conducing

cing to that myſticall bodie politicke, whereof thou art a member, than for to finde imployment for thoſe that are idle, becauſe they knowe not what to doe? Poſteritie ſhall remember thee for it, and remembring, ever honour thát remembrance with praiſe.

Conſider what was the beginninges, and endinges of the Monarchies of the *Chaldeans,* the *Perſians,* the *Græcians* and the *Romans,* but this one rule : what was it they would not doe for the Common-wealth or there mother Citie? for example : *Rome,* what made her ſuch a Monarcheſſe, but only the adventures of her youthe, not in ryots at home, but in dangers abroad? and their juſtice, and judgment, out of their own experience when they grewe aged. What was their ruine and hurt, but this : their exceſſe of idleneſſe, want of experience, hypocriticall ſeeming goodneſſe, & growing onlie formall Temporiſts ; ſo that what their Predeceſſours gotte in many yeeres, they loſt in few dayes : theſe by their paines and laboures became Lordes of the Worlde, they by their eaſe and vyces became ſlaves to their ſervants.

Then, who would live at home idle (or think in him ſelfe any worth to live) onlie to eate, drinke, and ſleepe, and ſo to die? or by conſuming that careleſlie, which their predeceſſours hath got worthilie? or by vſing that miſerablie, that maintained vertue honeſtlie? or, for beeing deſcended noblie, pyne with the vaine vaunt of Kinred in penurie? or (to maintaine a ſillie ſhow of braverie) toyle out the heart, foule, and time baſelie, by ſhiftes, trickes, cardes, or dyce? or by relating newes of others actions, ſharke heere or there for a Dinner or Supper? deceiving his friends by faire promiſes and diſſimulation, in borrowing where hee never intendeth to pay? offending the Lawes, ſurfeting with exceſſe, burthening his Countrie, abuſing himſelfe, deſpairing in want, and then couſening his kinred? although it is ſeene what honoures

C   the

the World hath yet, and what affluence of all things; for fuch as will feeke, and worthlie deferue them. Heere were courfes for Gentle-men, (and fuch as would bee fo reputed) more futing their qualities, than begging from their Princes generous difpofition the labours of his other fubjects.

It woulde bee a Hiftorie of a large volume to recite the adventures of the *Spaniards* and *Portugalles,* their conftant refolutions, with fuch incomparable honour, fo farre beyond beliefe in their difcoveries, and plantations, as may well condemne vs of too much imbecillitie, floth, and negligence. And yet the authours of thefe new inventions were helde as ridiculous at that time: as now are others that doe but feeke to imitate their vnparalelled vertues.

And though wee fee daylie their mountaines of wealth (fprung from the plants of their generous indevoures) yet is our incredulitie, and vntowardneffe fuch, and fo gieat, that either ignoranthe wee beleeve nothing; or fo curiouflie conteft, to prevent wee know not what future events; that fo wee either neglect, or oppreffe, or difcourage both our felves, and others, that might both as eafilie and would as willinglie attempt and embrace the like.

Who feeth not, what is the greateft good of the *Spaniard,* but thefe newe conclufions, in fearching thefe vnknowne partes of this vnknowne Worlde: by which meanes hee diveth even into the verie fecreetes of all his Neighboures, and the moft part of the Worlde.

And when the *Portugalles* and *Spaniards* had found the Eaft and Weft *Indies,* how manie did condemne themfelves that did not accept of that honeft offer of noble *Columbus,* who vpon the neglect of *England,* to whom it was firft offered; brought them to it: perfwading themfelves the Worlde had no fuch places, as they had found: and yet ever fince wee finde, they ftill haue found newe

Lands

Lands, newe Nations, new trades, and ftill daylie doe finde, both in *Afia, Africa, Terra incognita,* and *America:* fo that their is neither Souldiour, nor Mechanicke from the Lord, to the begger, but thefe parts affoord them all employment, and difcharge their native Soyle of fo manie thoufands of all forts, that elfe by their floath, pryde and imperfections, woulde longe ere this haue troubled their neighboures, or haue eaten the pryde of *Spaine* it felfe.

And feeing further, for all they have, they ceafe not ftill to fearch for that, which yet they neither haue, nor knowe not: it is ftrange that wee fhoulde bee fo dull, as not maintaine that which wee haue, and purfue that which wee knowe.

I am fure that manie would take it in an evill part to be abridged of the titles and honours of their predeceffours: when if but truelie they would judge themfelves: looke howe inferiour they are to their noble vertues, fo much they are vnworthie of their honours, and livings: which never were ordained for fhowes and fhadowes, to maintaine idleneffe and floath, but to make them more able to abound in honour by heroicall deedes of action, judgement, pietie and vertue

What was it they would not doe both in purfe and perfon for the good of the Common-weale? and may not this bee a motive for vs to fet out fuch as may bee fpared of our kindred in fuch generous defignes. Religion aboue all things fhould move (efpeciallie the Cleargie) if wee were religious, to fhowe our faith by our workes, in converting thefe poore favages to the knowledge of GOD. Honour might move the Gentrie, valiant and induftrious; the hope and affurance of wealth, all: if wee were fuch, as wee would feeme, and defire to bee accompted.

Or bee wee fo farre inferiour to other Nations, or our Spirites fo farre dejected from our ancient Predeceffoures

or

or our minds fo vpon fpoyle, pyracie, or other villanie, as to ferve the *Portugale, Spaniard, Dutch, French,* or *Turk,* (as to the great hurte of *Europe* too manie doe) rather than our GOD, our King, our Countrie, and our felves? excufing our idleneffe, and our bafe complaints by want of imployment? when heere is fuch choyce of all fortes, and for all degrees in this plantation.

So let thefe anfwere fuch queftionleffe queftions, that keepe vs backe from imitating the worthineffe of their brave fpirits, that advanced themfelves from poore Soul-diers, to great Captaines, their pofteritie to great Lords, their King to bee one of the greateft Potentates on Earth, and the fruits of their labours, his greateft glorie, power, riches and renowne.

MOTIVE III.

The third motive. AND as I haue fpoken of two principall caufes that hath induced me; The third of my ends may hap-pilie bee no leffe forcible to encourage all fuch, whofe e-ducation, fpirits and judgments, wants but onlie the purfe to profecute the fame with mee, and that is the private and particulare gaine, that may bee got by fo lawfull and eafie meanes: whereof it is more than admirable, that fuch fhould either bee fo wilfullie ignorant, or fo negligently careleffe as not to be moved to imbrace, and fpeciallie, fuch imployment as may fearch out commodities, to live happilie, plentifullie, and at eafe.

Ought not everie man to regard, afwell to inlarge his patrimonie, as that hee bee not chargeable to others, fo

farre

farre as hee may by his vertue and induftrie, in a lawfull and honeft manner attaine vnto. Is not a lawfull fearch for fuch commodities, to bee preferred to an idle floathfulneffe? and an honorable policie in a lawfull plantation abroad, before vnlawfull monopolies, and wrangling fuites of Law, by neighbour againft neighbour at home, impoverifhing thy felfe, and thy native Countrie, whereof thou oughteft to bee a more profitable member?

May not the fortunate fucceffe of the plantation of *Ireland,* fo frefh and recent to all, whence fo great commodities are brought both to *England* and *Scotland,* and whereby the Countrie it felfe is enriched, and wee fo benefited, bee inticements to induce vs to the like. The venturous, and generous Spirites of refolute Gentlemen, vnder-takers of this plantation, haue raifed their fortunes worthie of honour; and by his Majefties favour, their vertues rewarded with the titles of Earles, Vice-Countes Lords, Barronets, and Knights, according to their qualities, and his Majefties pleafure. The meaner fort, fuch as artifanes, labourers of the ground, the greater part whereof, were knowne to haue fcarce a competent meanes to defraye the charges of their paffage thither, now promoted to bee Gentlemen, and of great meanes. And why may not time produce as great effects to vertue, in others who fhall follow her pathes with refolution: where as good occafions are offered, in a climate more temperate, a Soyle more fertile, and farre exceeding in greater commodities?

And laft, to fhake off the difficulties, and impedimentes that may bee objected: as the dangeroufneffe of Sea, the barrenneffe of the Soyle, and the vnwholefomeneffe of the climate; all which difcouragements might aftonifhe fome with feare, and to thinke our expenffes, and paines vnprofitable; when as our endes fhall bee vn-

C 3   poffible.

poffible. I haue therefore heere taken a view that you may generallie knowe and learne, what the Countrie is, and her commodities: the temperature of the climate: nature of the natives: and the eafineffe of the paffage; all which I fhall briefly runne over; only to remove from before your feete the ftumbling blocks of impoffibilitie that may affright vs.

The Countrie it is called by the name of Cape Briton, now *New Galloway:* new, not in refpect of the difcoverie thereof, which to the judgment of men of knowledge and vnderftanding is not new, but old; for the much hath been written thereof, yet new, not olde, becaufe of our new vn-dertaking of that plantation. It is fituated betwixt the de-grees of 45. and 57. an Yland within the Sea, but vpon the maine, fevered by the diftance of foure leagues in fome parts, of two or three at other parts: and at others, leffe.

The Yland is in length fome 120. myles, and in breadth 80. myles or thereby: ftanding South-caft, and North-weft to *New Scotland;* vvhere the great river *Canada* ingorgeth her felfe in the maine Ocean. Harbours there bee excee-ding good on all fides, in moft part vvhereof are ancorage for fhippes of all burthen. Yles there be about over-grovvn vvith good timber of diverfe forts of vvood; all as yet not difcovered except the Yle *Sablon,* vvhich is full of vvoodes and vvilde beaftes, but vvithout any people. The Land is vvatered by foure maine rivers, full of Salmond, and di-verfe other fortes of fifhes. It hath plentie of fpringes of fvveete vvaters. Tovvards the North-eaft, *Mountanous:* and tovvard the South-weft *Caimpainge:* promifing as rich entralles as anie other Kingdome to whom the Sunne is no nearer neighbour. The ground in it felf fo fertile and good as may equalize any of the Kingdomes that lyeth in the hight of 45. 46. 47. Onlie this advantage I find in nature, that they haue above this: they are bewtified by the long la-bour & diligence of induftrious people & airt: & this is only as God made it, when he created the world, vncultured, plan-ted & manured by men of induftry, judgment & experience.

The commodities which we fhal reape from thence fhall be great, for the Sea fhall fweeten our labours with her benefites, as the Land, and the Land afwell as the Sea. The Sea fhall reach vs vp her Whale, her turbot, her fturgion, cod, haddocke, fmall ling, makkerell, herrmg, mullet, pearch, Eele, crab, lobfter, muskle, wilk, oyfter, and infinite others. Fifh is the maine Staple, from whence is to be extracted, a prefent commoditie to produce the reft: which howfoever it may feeme meane and bafe, yet it is the Myne, and the Sea is the fource of thefe filvered ftreames of all thefe vertues, which hath made the *Hollanders,* the miracle of induftrie, & patterne of perfection for thefe affaires: and the benefite of fifhing, is that *Primum mobile* that turneth all their Spheare to this hight of plentie, ftrength, honour, and admiration.

The ground it will yeeld vs an admired varietie; fome wee fhall haue that are merchantable, which, by the ferving for ordinarie neceffars of the planters & inhabitantes, may yeeld a fuperplus fufficient, by way of traffick and exchange with other nations, to enriche our felves the provyders; fuch as flaxe, hempe, which the Soyle doth yeeld of it felf not planted. For pitch, tarre, rozen and turpentine, there bee thefe kind of trees there, which yeeld them aboundantlie Saffafras, called by the natives, wmauk, a kind of wood of fweet fmell, and of rare vertues in Phyfick. The Vine, it groweth there wild. Oyle there may be there of two fortes: one of walnuts; and another of berries, like the ackornes which the natives vfe. Furres of manie and diverfe kinds; fuch as the marterne, the otter, the blackfoxe, the luzernes, Deere skins, bevers, wildcat, and manie others. Sweet gummes of diverfe kinds, and many other Apothecarie drugges. Dyes of diverfe fortes: fuch as fhoemake, for blacke: the feede of an hearbe called vafebur, and a litle fmall roote called chappacor, for red: & for blew, the herbe woad, a thing of great vent and vfe at home for Dyers, and many other commodities merchantable, which by planting may be raifed.

Other

Other commodities there are, which the ground doth yeeld vs for victuall and fuftenance of mans life, and v-fuallie fedde vpon by the naturall inhabitants: for it is knowne to bee fo fertile, as without queftion capable of producing of any graine, fruite, or roote, or feede you will fowe, or plant, growing in any other region of the fame hight. The graines are maze, which we call Guinie wheat, according to the countrie from whence the like hath beene brought, and this graine is much about the bigneffe of our ordinarie peafe. There is alfo beanes, called of the natives Oknigier: and peafe called by them, Wickonzour. They haue pompions, millons, and gourds, and an herbe called melden, growing foure, or five foote high, of the feede they make a thicke broth, and potage of a good tafte, and of the ftalke, by burning it in afhes they make a kinde of falt earth, wherewith they feafon their brothes, other falt they know not. They haue the hearbe Tobacco, called by the natives Vppowoc, in great plentie. Fruites they haue of fundrie forts: as chef-nuts, walnutes, grapes, medlars, mulberries, goofe-berries, ref-pices, ftraw-berries, plummes, currans, or a fruite like cur-rans. Rootes they haue of diverfe kindes; Openauk, a kinde of roote, of a round forme and bigneffe of walnuts, which beeing boyled or fodden, are verie goode meate: Okeepauke, another roote found in drye ground, which they eate with fifhe or flefh: Tfinaw, a roote like the china-roote, growing together in clufters, of this roote they make bread. Of beafts; they haue Deere red, and fallow, conies, blacke foxes, and others, bevers, beares, wilde-cats, otters, marternes, luzernes, allanes, wolves, fquirells, and a beaft called Moos, bigger than a Stagge. For fowle they haue the turkie, the goofe, the ducke, the fkeldrake, the cran, the teale, Eagles, Falcons, marlin-hawkes.

And finallie are thofe other commodities, as are behove-full for thofe, which fhall plant and inhabite to know of:

fuch as oakes, afhe, elme, firre, the pine, and afcopo:
which is a kinde of tree like the Laurell, the barke
whereof, is hotte in tafte, and fpycie: hazell, plume-
tree, walnut-tree, chefnut-tree, and manie others, which
I omitt to rehearfe. For to make mention of the feverall beaftes, birdes, fifhes, fruites, flowres, gummes,
rootes, fweete woodes, trees, hearbs, and others commodities, wherewith the ground is fo naturallie, and fo
plentifullie enriched, and ftored withall; I fhould fill vp
Decads: but referring thefe to the relations of fuch as hath
fullie collected the varieties of them, I come to the temperature of the climat.

The nature of the Climate wee maye eafilie conclude
from the light whereinto it is fituated; beeing in the 45.
46. and 47. which is as temperate, and as fruitfull as a-
nie other paralell in the World; and anfwerable to thefe
fruitfull partes in *France*, which are accompted the garden of *Europe*; *Poictou*, and *Anjou*: and where is that famous river of *Loyre*, adorned with fo manie faire, fo ancient, and populous Cities: and manie other notable,
and famous Kingdomes: as you maye looke in the vniverfall Mappe, becaufe I meane not to bee tedious: and
fo having there fuch excellent temperature of the aire at
all feafons, much warmer than heere, and never fo ve-
hementlie hotte as it is vnder, and betwixt the Tropicks,
or neere them, wee neede not thinke of vnwholefomeneffe.

And now for the Paffage: Is not the navigation knowne
to bee fhort, as fufficientlie experimented to have beene
performed with an ordinarie winde in eighteene dayes,
and in as much backe againe? how manie *Dutch*, *Englifh*
and *French* goe yeerelie there for fifhing on the coafte,
and backe againe to their great commodities and profite ·
and by the waye wee neither fhall haue lee fhoare, enemies, coaft, rocke, nor fands, all which in other voyages

D and

and in our coaftings at home wee are fubject vnto.

And now laft, it refteth I fpeake a worde of the nature of the People, in fo farre as you maye knowe, how litle they are to bee feared, in refpect of troubling our inhabiting and planting.

They are a people fo fewe, fo poore, fo bafe, fo incivile, and fo favage, as wanting both multitude, power, or airte to harme vs. They are cloathed with loofe mantles, made of Deere skinnes, caften rounde about their middles, the reft of their bodie all naked, of fuch ftature onelie as wee are heere, having no edge tooles, nor weapons of yron, nor fteele to offende vs, neither knowe they how to make anie, nor howe to vfe them.

Thefe weapons which they have, are onelie Bowes made of Hazell, and arrowes of reedes: flat edged truncheons alfo of vvood, about a yarde long: neither haue they anie thing to defende themfelves, but targes made of barkes, and fome armour made of ftickes vvickered together vvith threed. In number they are verie fewe, in twentie myles, fcarce threefcore people. Townes in the countrie are verie rare, and fmall: containing fewe inhabitants: and hee is a Viroan, or great Lord, that hath the government of one towne. There houfes are litle, made of fmall poles, and faft at the toppes in round forme, in mofte parte covered with barkes. If there fhoulde fall out anie Warres betwixt vs and them, what fight coulde there bee, wee having advantages againft them, fo manie manner of wayes. it maye bee eafilie imagined, by our difcipline, our ftrange weapons, efpecialhe, our Ordinance great, and fmall. And by the experience that others hath had of them there, in places more populous than this of ours: where the taking of them-felves to their heeles, was their beft defence againft them.

So feeing you maye perceive, what the Countrie is, and how fituated: the aire how temperate, and wholefome? the Soyle how fertile, and what affluence it doeth yeelde of commoditie? the natives how both fo fewe, and fo harmeleffe? and the paffage, howe fo eafie, and fo frequentlie experimented? I hope there remaineth no caufe whereby the action fhould bee mifliked.

Thus referring my relation to your favourable conftructions: the fucceffe of the action to Him, who is to bee acknowledged the Author and Governour, not onlie of this, but of all thinges elfe: and thefe my fubfequent Offers, which I have freelie, and willinglie granted, as helpes, and furtherances for your encouragement to fo good a Worke; yee maye pervfe, and onelie imbrace as you fhall thinke your felves difpofed.

THE

DREAD GOD

1625

THE OFFERS

to bee granted to the
Adventurers in the new plantation of
CAPE BRITON, now *called*
by the name of *New Galloway*
in AMERICA,

BY

LOCHINVAR.

ARTICLE I.

For Minifters.

THAT the blefling of GOD may accompanie vs in our indevoures; without whofe gratious, and mercifull affiftance, wee can not have happie, nor profperous fucceffe in our affaires. For the Minifters of the Worde of God; fuch as fhall bee the factours of *CHRIST* for the gaine of Soules: and to propagate his Trueth: and enlighten thofe that are captivate in Ethnicke darkneffe: and for the vfe, and exercife of true Religion amongeft our felves; I doe willinglie, and freelie graunt and offer as followeth,

1. Their paffage from *Scotland* vnto the faid Land of *New Galloway* fhall be free vnto them, without payment of any fraught, either for themfelves,

their

their wiues, and children, if they anie haue, and
their neceſſare houſhold ſtuffe : which all ſhall
bee tranſported thither vnto them, into mine
owne Shippes, and vpon mine owne charges.

2. They ſhall haue their entertainment of mee, then
wiues, and children as ſaide is, in their whole
paſſage on the waye thither.

3. For their maintenance, and their forefaids beeing
there : I ſhall giue them entertainment for the
ſpace of the firſt three yeeres, induring the infancie of our Church there : and howe ſoone it
ſhall pleaſe GOD that our number bee increa-
ſed, that our Companies maye bee diuided in
Paroches, that then a competent meanes ſhall be
alloted vnto each Miniſter in his feuerall charge,
as ſhall bee found expedient for their places.

4. For their affiſtance in ſuch things as belongeth
vnto them in their callings : I ſhall haue a ſpeciall
care to ſee, that ſuch reuerence, and refpeฤt be
had vnto them, as appertaineth vnto their place
and calling : and ſhall fee ſuch goode order, as
by them ſhall bee fette downe for reformation
of life, and manners, duelie obeyed and performed, by cauſing the tranſgreſſours, and contem-
ners of the ſame bee feuerelie puniſhed.

ARTICLE II.

THAT everie one of ſuch as ſhall be vndertakers, ſhall giue his oath of alledgeance : and ſhall
all conforme themſelves in Religion, according to his Ma-
jeſties

jefties Lawes, and manner profeffed within the Kingdome of *Scotland.*

ARTICLE III.

For Gentlemen, and others vndertakers: what I
fhall bee obliged to performe vnto them.

ITEM, for the helpes, and furtherances of fo generous, and well-difpofed vndertakers as fhall willinglie vnder-goe the hazard, and imbrace the enterpryfe: I
fhall performe the particulars in everic point vnto them
as followeth,

1. For their paffages: everie vnder-taker fhall bee
    tranfported, himfelfe, his wife, children, & fer-
    vants, his whole houfhold ftuffe, and their pro-
    vifion of victualles for their intertainment, fuch
    as meale, malt, beefe, &c. and fuch as they fhall
    pleafe to provide to fuftaine them for a whole
    yeere: Together with as much cornes, as they
    fhall bee able to fowe vpon their Lands, the firft
    yeere: and that all, and together paffage free,
    into mine Shippes, from *Scotland* vnto the faid
    countrie of *New Gallouay.*

2. Beeing thither by GODS mercifull affiftance,
    and providence tranfported, to bee eftablifhed
    and placed in the Land: each man according to
    his qualitie, as followeth: The landed Gentle-
    man vndertaker, fhall haue his Landes granted
    vnto him in fee, and heritage to himfelfe, and
    his fucceffours for ever, to bee holden of mee,
    my heires, and fucceffoures in *New Galloway,* in
                                                    manner

manner as they holde their Lands in *Scotland* of
our Soveraigne Lord, the King his Majeftie, either by feaw, wairde, or blanfh, and fhall grant
the fame vnto them in quantitie, according to e-
verie one of their qualities and meanes. And for
tennants, and farmorers, their landes fhall bee
granted vnto them in Lace, everie one of them
to have three Life-rents, and a nyneteene yeere
Tacke thereafter, conforme to their power, and
meanes, and performance of the conditions of
the rent after mentioned

3. And further more that their helpes, and furtherances maye haue a competent time to e-
ftablifhe them-felves in their eftates, and that
their meanes may the better increafe : each vndertaker of the plantation of *New Galloway* fhall
bee free from the payment of any duetie for his
Landes, for all and whole the fpace of the firft
three yeeres.

4. For their affurance of a fecuritie, and peaceable
quietneffe in the poffeffion of their Landes in
New Galloway, whereof they bee vndertakers :
I fhall finde fufficient caution, and furetie vnto
each one of them within the Shyre where hee
dwelleth in *Scotland*, that whatfoever his goods
or geare thither tranfported, and placed vpon
the ground of the faids Landes, fhall bee taken
from him by violence, of the natives, or forraine Nations, that the double thereof fhall bee
payed and refounded againe vnto him in *Scotland*,
or to his heires, executours, or affignayes.

5. And

5. And for artifanes and craftef-men, fuch as Tay-
lors, Shoe-makers, Smyths, Wrights, Webfters,
Wakers, Millers, &c. their paffages fhall bee
made free vnto them without the payment of a-
nie fraught ; and likewife the rents of their lands
fhall bee free vnto them, induring their owne life-
times : and for their fucceffours, they fhall bee
kept in the cafe, and eftate of tenants and farmorers, and fhall haue their Laces of their Lands
granted vnto them, as is fet downe in the Article for Tennants.

ARTICLE IIII.

What the Vnder-takers fhall performe vnto mee.

FOR the whole duetie of my Landes, charges, and
expenffes to [be] beftowed by mee in my fhipping
and other provifion : I fhall bee contented to receive from
everie one of the faid vndertakers, the thirteenth parte
of that increafe, and commoditie, which their Lands fhall
bee made worthie vnto them in the faid plantation : And
that I fhall not require to bee payed vnto mee in moneyes,
but only in fuch commodities, as the Soyle fhall affoord :
fuch as cornes, fifhes, furres, &c.

AND laft, I defire that all fuch, as fhall imbrace the
forefaids offers, may come vnto mee before the firft
day of December next, and giue vp their names, and a
note of fuch things as they defire to bee carried with them,
whereby I may provide for them, conforme to my pre-
ceeding offers, and they received everie one, and placed
according to the order as they firft come : fo that all thinges
may bee duelie provyded, and had in readineffe againft
the due time and feafon of fetting out.

E   And

CONCLVSION.

AND thus (*Right Noble, and worthie Countrie-men*) have I vnfolded the reafons of my refolution to vndertake this enterpryfe, which if I hadde not thought to be both Chriftian, honorable, honeft, eafie, and profitable; I fhould never have attempted. And I have further for the encouragement of all fuch as are well-willers vnto the Worke, made offer of fuch helps, and furtherances as may teftifie my willingneffe to profecute the fame. Defiring yet againe all noble and generouflie well-difpofed Gentlemen, to confider with mee, onelie our eftates in thefe dayes, and how wee ftand in our families, from the greateft, to the fmalleft: and compare them with our Predeceffours, who did keepe great honour, credite, and eftimation; which in fo great a meafure is decayed, and diminifhed in vs. Now let vs compare our felues with Citizens now, whofe credite wee fee doeth furpaffe ours, although wee bee above them, both in qualitie and richeffe. Whence is this woorth of theirs, but from their induftrie, and trueth; which beareth them out both to this credite, and refpect, afwell at home, as abroad?

Were it not (then) better in thefe our dayes for vs to imitate the foot-fteppes of vertue in the *Italians*, that thinketh it neither difhonourable, nor difparagement vnto their greateft Princes, their Dukes, Marqueffes, and Countes, to make themfelves great, and get their patrimonies inlarged by their hazards at Sea? It is their glorie to bee vertuous; and may condemne our diffolutions

and

and idleneffe, that may as eafilie bee great, by fuch honeft and honourable endevoures.

But yet let vs come a litle nearer vnto our felves; and
fee the diftreffes afwell amongft the great, as the fmall,
throughout the whole Kingdome: and what increafe
there is of debts amongft vs in thefe dayes, never heard
of before amongft our Predeceffoures, wee fhall finde,
that if wee followe not fome other induftrious manner
of waye, to relieve them, then by menaging, in what-
fome-evei, and beft forme wee can, our revenues, that
they fhall never bee relieved.

There are three thinges that troubleth our eftates
that wee cannot live as our Predeceffoures did before vs:
Firft, the prodigalitie, both in our felves, our fervants,
and our houfes. Secondlie, wee have not fuch occafions, and vfes at home for the Brethren, and fecond fonnes
of our houfes to get them preferment as of old. Third-
lie, that vniverfall plague of Cautionarie, throughout
the whole Kingdome, whereby their is fuch a generall
intercourfe of diftreffe, each one for another, as all are lin-
ked into it. which all in following out fuch honorable,
and honeft indevoures abroad might bee remedied. I
fpeake not of the favoured Courteour, nor of the fortunate Statef-man, for they have their owne bleffinges from
GOD, and favour of their Mafter in their feverall places. but vnto fuch, my noble friends, and Countrie-gen-
tlemen, fuch as my felfe is, and fo diftreffed as I am;
and fpeaking out of mine owne experience; protefting
that cautionarie hath beene vnto me; vpon mine honour,
and ciedite, the value of an Hundreth thoufand pounds;
which any imployment abroad, either in the fervice of
my King, or my Countrie, might haue fpared vnto me,
and bettered the eftate of mine Houfe. Neither doe I
fpeake fo farre of my felfe, for want of abilitie to doe
mine owne bufineffe, which I praife GOD is knowne

E 2   to to fuch, as knowe my felfe: but to giue euerie man a fenfe, and feeling out of mine owne experience, howe I fee the eftate of the Kingdome.

Then (Worthie Countriemen) let vs lay thefe two things in the ballance, and judge vpon them: whether it is better for vs to goe there, where we may haue to liue in a fruitfull Soyle, and wholefome, in all commodities abounding to our contentments, beeing onlie a litle induftrious and painefull: than to liue heere at home as Runnagates, vnanfwerable to G O D, the King, the Lawes, to all reafon, and confcience: to bee captivate as flaves, and caft in loathfome Prifons, to fatiffie with our perfons, when our goods hath failed vs: and efpeciallie, when wee haue wronged our beft and kindeft friendes, who out of their loves hath engaged themfelves, to be diftreffed, and imprifoned for vs? which fhoulde bee a greater griefe vnto vs, than our owne imprifonments.

And then fhall wee difdaine Plantation: which to enterprife is fo honourable; to profecute fo poffible: to purchafe fo lawfull, and when attained, fo profitable? No, whofoever fhall reafon againft the fame, efpecially fuch as are in diftreffe, may well bee reputed, either the Baftard of generofitie, or the nurfling of fimplicitie, or the abject of frugalitie: and fhall either become for ever, the proftitute of infamie, or confecrated to perpetuall oblivion: and when hee is dead, his actions, his meanes, his name and all, fhall die with himfelfe; and if hee fhall ever happen to bee remembred, that remembrance fhall onelie bee in ignominie, as the Wretch of his Countrie, the Curfe of his Kinred: and an vnthrift for himfelfe.

But I fpeake not to fuch a crew, whofe bafeneffe I knowe cannot climbe to furmount the meaneft imagined difficultie, that may arife. I fpeake to fuch noble Spirites and generous mindes, in whom doeth fhine the light of knowledge to difcerne the differences between a bafe

fecuritie

fecuritie and honourable actions, vice and vertue, ftupi-
ditie, and true worth : and who in end fhall not miffe to re-
joyce in the enjoying the fruits of their labours in themfelves, and their names to bee honoured with a perpetuall remembrance

And if wee would ftudie to bee remembred in our po-
fterities, heere is offered the occafion to infert vs in the
bookes of memorie : for if wee would portion our fecond
children in a plantation, and fuch as in nature wee are
bound to helpe, and advance : both fhall wee bee remembred in their ever-living fucceffions, throughout all
enfueing ages : and they provyded in a competent beeing and meanes for them-felves, and theirs, and to bee
thereafter proffitable for their King and Countrie : which
is better, than either to be kept at home bafelie, & fhort
of that which is befeeming their birth, and qualitie : or
to bee fent to the fervice of the Warres of forraine Princes, and to be cutted away by the fword, and then never more againe remembred : and for fo fmall meanes,
as thereby yee can furnifh themfelves both in rayment,
and foode.

Imbrace then the honours of Plantation. Doe wee
dreame of difficulties? then knowe ; that it is out of the
greateft difficulties, that fpring the greateft honours : &
it is that Knight-hood, which is gotten vnder the banner of a King, and in the Fieldes which is moft honourable , and not that, which wee acquire by our moneyes ;
as the moft part is now a-dayes. And that our actions
may both renowne vs, and beget vs moneyes, wee may
fee in the examples that I haue fette before your eyes,
both of forraine nations, and of our own Countriemen, in
their late plantations of *Ireland*, their eftates now, their
dignities, their honours, their credite, and their riches :
and what they were knowne to haue beene before.

But thefe I leave to your judgments : onche now, to
make

make an end, I muſt entreate thee (*Noble and courteous Reader*) to excufe my freeneſſe in this my homelie diſcourſe, which I perſwade my felfe the generous minde will allowe of: and for the bafe, the ſimple and the vitious; I doe not care for their cenfure, onelie I wiſhe it were a ſpurre to drawe them to more vertue. As for the rudeneſſe of my ſpeach, I hope none will except, wherein I profeſſe no airt, if ſimplie I publiſh my good meaning and earneſt affection to ſo goode a Worke. And wherein their is defect in mee, I hope the purpoſe ſhall bee better inlarged by him, whoſe Pen is more than knowne to bee famous, the principall Actor in the buſineſſe, and to whom I principallie dedicate this my treatiſe : and to bee feconded by the vertues of theſe the Noblemen, and theſe worthilie honoured Gentle-men, the Knights Baronets, Vnder-takers of ſo faire defignes : ſo
that nowe I ceafe with my penne, but never
with my Sword to doe them fervice for
the advancement of ſo good a Worke.

FINIS.

Lightning Source UK Ltd.
Milton Keynes UK
UKHW020639171022
410608UK00009B/583